W9-CEW-968

NO PASSION SPENT

NO PASSION SPENT
Essays 1978–1995

GEORGE STEINER

Yale University Press
New Haven and London

Published in the United States by Yale University Press and in
Great Britain by Faber and Faber Limited.

Yale University Press edition published with assistance from the
Louis Stern Memorial Fund.

Photoset by Parker Typesetting Service, Leicester, England
Printed in the United States of America.

Copyright © George Steiner, 1996.

A catalogue record for this book is available from the British Library.
Library of Congress catalogue card number 95–62289

ISBN 0-300-06630-9

10 9 8 7 6 5 4 3 2 1

For George and Maria Embiricos

Contents

Introduction

The essays and papers in this collection were written during the time when the arts of reading and the status of a text have come under pressure. Movements such as 'critical theory', 'post-structuralism', 'deconstruction' and 'post-modernism', have diversely put in doubt the relations, as these were classically conceived, between words and meaning. They have decomposed not only the notion of an author's intentions in regard to what he seeks to signify, but the ascertainable identity of any such *auctoritas* or creative individuality. 'Deconstruction' in particular negates the possibility of any verifiable 'final sense', however difficult to make out, however much dependent on historical consensus, in written discourse. 'Meaning' is no more than a momentary play of interpretative possibilities, dissolving into self-subversion in the very moment of illusory decipherment. 'Texts' are contingent 'pre-texts' for infinite, ultimately arbitrary appropriations, none of which can aspire to the privilege of truth. In some ways, these strategies of dissemination (which have their source, to a large extent, in the rebellion against the millennial imposition of the written, legislative and inspired word in Judaism) are nihilistic. They tell of an epilogue in our unnerved culture. In another sense, they are, consciously or not, an often seductive, paradoxically 'reconstructive' exercise aimed at restoring to literary studies and hermeneutics a lost passion, a lost intellectual challenge.

The second major pressure is now technical. The revolution in the generation, communication and conservation of semantic material brought on by computers, by planetary electronic exchanges, by 'cyber-space' and (soon) 'virtual reality' is far more radical and comprehensive than was that initiated by Gutenberg. It is today fairly evident that the book as we have known it since the scrolls of the pre-Socratics will survive in only a more or less specialized format and function. Increasingly, printed and bound books will be instruments of scholarship, of local and specific distribution ('home-electronic production' and 'publication' is already available) and of luxury. As were illuminated manuscripts – these were surprisingly numerous – after the invention of printing. Mass culture, the economics of personal space and time, the erosion of privacy, the systematic suppression of silence in technological consumer cultures, the eviction of memory (of learning by heart) from schooling, entail the eclipse of the acts of reading, of the book itself. Nostalgic pathos and lament would be fatuous. Developments on this historical-social scale bring both loss and gain, destruction and opportunity. An immensity of oral and pictorial 'counter-literacy' preceded and has always surrounded the essentially western, Hebraic-Hellenic centrality and prestige of the *Logos*, of the revealed and established word. The western world, after 1914, is in an obvious condition of crisis. Inhumanities, briefly and regionally contained, have reasserted their perennial, instinctual force. Para-doxically, the new agencies of instantaneous, open-ended commu-nication, of 'interface' between text and recipient, may prove more resistant to despotism, obscurantism and the inhuman.

Returning to issues I raised in 'The Retreat from the Word' (1961), the opening essays in this book try to define an act of reading in the classical mould and to elicit the theological-metaphysical presuppo-sitions in such an act (the implicit 'real presences'). With intended banality, this attempt at definition is then brought to bear on three archetypal, foundational language-acts in our civilization: the Hebrew Bible, Homer and Shakespeare. Further examples of 'applied reading' follow: in reference to Kierkegaard and to Kafka and to that most creative mode of reading which is poetic translation.

Of all my work, 'The Archives of Eden' provoked the bitterest rebuke and dismissal. The intuition behind it may indeed prove myopic. If I include it here, it is because it points to the essential differences between a 'classical' and a 'modernist-egalitarian' ideal of quality in the life of the mind. Europe and North America are, in crucial ways, increasingly distant from each other. It may be that this essay retains some use as an instance of 'mistranslation'.

Introduction

To inquire into the status of 'the book' and into the enigma of revelation in language is to touch persistently on Judaism and its tragic destiny. This leitmotif is already apparent in the papers on Péguy, Simone Weil and Husserl. It becomes manifest in the concluding essays. More and more, the question is that of the legacy of Jerusalem and Athens, of Hebraic and Hellenic 'textuality'. The interactions between these two worlds of spirit have given us our western identity and the riches of our moral-intellectual condition. But these interactions also contained seeds of disaster. There are overlaps and reiterations in the concluding essays. Via analogies and contrarieties between Socrates and Christ, between nascent Christianity and its Jewish origins, I attempt to ask certain questions also of the future. It will not, I believe, be possible for European culture to regain its inward energies, its self-respect, so long as Christendom is not made answerable to its own seminal role in the preparation of the Shoah (the Holocaust); so long as it does not hold itself to account for its cant and impotence when European history stood at midnight. In one perspective, such questions are of another dimension than those which pertain to literacy. In another, they are inseparable. It is my hope that this often close-knit collection will make this clear.

A number of these texts first appeared in *Salmagundi*, which seems to me the most scrupulous and trustworthy of 'little magazines'. Much of this book belongs to its editors, Robert and Peggy Boyers. Once again, the verve and acumen of Elda Southern have proved invaluable. If I sense something of the inspiring menace of the imminent age of CD-ROMs and 'internets', this is owing to the cheery rebukes offered to his antediluvian father (I do use a fountain-pen) by my son David.

Those to whom *No Passion Spent* is dedicated would not wish me to say more. Their generosity of heart and mind, their informed joy in so many of the works of language and of art and of music I refer to, have opened worlds for me. Often, they are a reinsurance on hope.

G.S.
Cambridge/Oxford, 1995

[xi]

The Uncommon Reader

Chardin's *Le Philosophe lisant* was completed on 4 December 1734. It is thought to be a portrait of the painter Aved, a friend of Chardin's. The subject and the pose, a man or a woman reading a book open on a table, are frequent. They form almost a sub-genre of domestic interiors. Chardin's composition has antecedents in medieval illuminations where the figure of St Jerome or some other reader is itself illustrative of the text which it illumines. The theme remains popular until well into the nineteenth century (witness Courbet's celebrated study of Baudelaire reading or the various readers depicted by Daumier). But the motif of *le lecteur* or *la lectrice* seemed to have enjoyed particular prevalence during the seventeenth and eighteenth centuries and constitutes a link, of which Chardin's whole output was representative, between the great age of Dutch interiors and the treatment of domestic subjects in the French classical manner. Of itself, therefore, and in its historical context, *Le Philosophe lisant* embodies a common topic conventionally handled (though by a master). Considered in respect of our own time and codes of feeling, however, this 'ordinary' statement points, in almost every detail and principle of meaning, to a revolution of values.

Consider first the reader's garb. It is unmistakably formal, even ceremonious. The furred cloak and hat suggest brocade, a suggestion borne out by the matt but aureate sheen of the coloration. Though clearly at home, the reader is 'coiffed' – an archaic word which does convey the requisite note of almost heraldic ceremony (that the shape and treatment of the furred bonnet most likely derive from Rembrandt is a point of mainly art-historical interest). What matters is the emphatic elegance, the sartorial deliberation of the moment. The reader does not meet the book casually or in disarray. He is dressed for the occasion, a proceeding which directs our attention to the construct of values and sensibility which includes both 'vestment' and 'investment'. The primary quality of the act, of the reader's self-investiture before the act of reading, is one of *cortesia*, a term rendered only imperfectly by 'courtesy'. Reading, here, is no haphazard, unpremeditated motion. It is a courteous, almost a courtly encounter, between a private person and one of those 'high guests' whose entrance into mortal houses is evoked by Hölderlin in his hymn 'As on a festive day' and by Coleridge in one of the most enigmatic glosses he appended to *The Rime of the Ancient Mariner*. The reader meets the book with a courtliness of heart (that is what *cortesia* signifies), with a courtliness, a scruple of welcome and entertainment of which the russet sleeve, possibly of velvet or velveteen, and the furred cloak and bonnet are the external symbols.

The fact that the reader is wearing a hat is of distinct resonance. Ethnographers have yet to tell us what general meanings apply to the distinctions between those religious and ritual practices which demand that the participant be covered, and those in which he is bare-headed. In both the Hebraic and the Graeco-Roman traditions, the worshipper, the consultant of the oracle, the initiate when he approaches the sacred text or augury, is covered. So is Chardin's reader, as if to make evident the numinous character of his access to, of his encounter with, the book. Discreetly – and it is at this point that the echo of Rembrandt may be pertinent – the furred bonnet suggests the headdress of the kabbalist or Talmudic scholar when he seeks the flame of the spirit in the momentary fixity of the letter. Taken together with the furred robe, the reader's bonnet implies precisely those connotations of ceremony of intellect, of the mind's tensed apprehension of meaning, which induce Prospero to put on courtly raiment before he opens his magic books.

Observe next the hourglass beside the reader's right elbow. Again, we are looking at a conventional motif, but one so charged with meaning that an exhaustive commentary would nearly comprise a history of the western sense of invention and of death. As Chardin places it, the hourglass declares the relationship of time and the book. The sand sifts rapidly through the narrow of the hourglass (a sifting whose tranquil finality Hopkins invokes at a key point in the

mortal turbulence of 'The Wreck of the Deutschland'). But at the
same time, the text endures. The reader's life is measured in hours;
that of the book, in millennia. This is the triumphant scandal first
proclaimed by Pindar: 'When the city I celebrate shall have perished,
when the men to whom I sing shall have vanished into oblivion, my
words shall endure'. It is the conceit to which Horace's *exegi
monumentum* gave canonic expression and which culminates in
Mallarmé's hyperbolic supposition that the object of the universe is
le Livre, the final book, the text that transcends time. Marble
crumbles, bronze decays, but written words – seemingly the most
fragile of media – survive. They survive their begetters – Flaubert
cried out against the paradox whereby he lay dying like a dog
whereas that 'whore' Emma Bovary, his creature, sprung of lifeless
letters scratched on a piece of paper, continued alive. So far, only
books have circumvented death and have fulfilled what Paul Éluard
defined as the artist's central compulsion: *le dure désir de durer*
(indeed, books can even survive themselves, leapfrogging out of the
shadow of their own initial being: there are vital translations of
languages long extinct). In Chardin's painting, the hourglass, itself a
twofold form with its iconic suggestion of the torus or figure eight of
infinity, modulates exactly and ironically between the *vita brevis* of
the reader and the *ars longa* of his book. As he reads, his own
existence ebbs. His reading is a link in the chain of performative
continuity which underwrites – a term worth returning to – the
survivance of the read text.

But even as the shape of the hourglass is a binary one, its import
is dialectical. The sand falling through the glass tells both of the
time-defying nature of the written word and of how little time there
is in which to read. Even the most obsessed of bookmen can read
only a minute fraction of the world's totality of texts. He is no true
reader, no *philosophe lisant*, who has not experienced the reproachful fascination of the great shelves of unread books, of the libraries
at night of which Borges is the fabulist. He is no reader who has not
heard, in his inward ear, the call of the hundreds of thousands, of the
millions of volumes which stand in the stacks of the British Library
or of Widener asking to be read. For there is in each book a gamble

against oblivion, a wager against silence, which can be won only when the book is opened again (but in contrast to man, the book can wait centuries for the hazard of resurrection). Every authentic reader, in the sense of Chardin's delineation, carries within him a nagging weight of omission, of the shelves he has hurried past, of the books whose spine his fingers have brushed across in blind haste. I have, a dozen times, slunk by Sarpi's leviathan history of the Council of Trent (one of the pivotal works in the development of western religious-political argument); or the *opera omnia* of Nikolai Hartmann in their stately binding; I shall never manage the sixteen thousand pages of Amiel's (profoundly interesting) journal currently being published. There is so little time in 'the library that is the universe' (Borges's Mallarméen phrase). But the unopened books call to us none the less, in a summoning as noiseless but insistent as is the sift of the sand in the hourglass. That the hourglass is a traditional prop of Death in western art and allegory points up the twofold signification of Chardin's composition: the afterlife of the book, the brevity of the life of man without whom the book lies buried. To repeat: the interactions of meaning between hourglass and book are such as to comprehend much of our inner history.

Note next the three metal discs in front of the book. Almost certainly these are bronze medals or medallions used to weigh down, to keep smooth the page (in folios, pages tend to wrinkle and lift at their corners). It is not, I think, fanciful to think of these medallions as bearing portraits or heraldic devices or mottoes, this being the natural function of the numismatic arts from antiquity to the commemorative coinage or medallions struck today. In the eighteenth century, as in the Renaissance, the sculptor or engraver used these small circumferences to concentrate, to make incisive in the literal sense, a celebration of civic or military renown, to give to a moral-mythological allegory lapidary, enduring pronouncement. Thus we find, in Chardin's painting, the presentment of a second major semantic code. The medallion also is a text. It may date from or recompose words and images of high antiquity. Bronze relief or engraving defies the mordant envy of time. It is stamped with meaning as is the book. It may have returned to the light, as do

[4]

inscriptions, papyri, Dead Sea Scrolls, from a long sojourn in the dark. This lapidary textuality is perfectly rendered in the eleventh of Geoffrey Hill's *Mercian Hymns*:

Coins handsome as Nero's; of good substance and weight. *Offa Rex* resonant in silver, and the names of his moneyers. They struck with accountable tact. They could alter the king's face.

Exactness of design was to deter imitation; mutilation if that failed. Exemplary metal, ripe for commerce. Value from a sparse people, scrapers of salt-pans and byres.

But the 'exemplary metal', whose weight, whose literal gravity, keeps down the crinkling, fragile page, is itself, as Ovid said, ephemeral, of brief durance, as compared with the words on the page. *Exegi monumentum*: 'I have reared a monument more lasting than bronze' says the poet (remember Pushkin's matchless reprise of Horace's tag), and by placing the medals before the book Chardin exactly invokes the antique wonder and paradox of the longevity of the word.

This longevity is affirmed by the book itself, which provides the painting with its compositional centre and light-focus. It is a bound folio, in a garb which subtly counterpoints that of the reader. Its format and physique are those of stateliness (in Chardin's period, it is more than likely that a folio-volume would have been bound *for* its proprietor, that it would have carried his device). It is no object for the pocket or the airport lounge. The posture of the other folio behind the hourglass suggests that the reader is perusing a multi-volume work. Serious work may well run to several tomes (the eight volumes, unread, of Sorel's great diplomatic history of Europe and the French Revolution haunt me). Another folio looms behind the *lecteur*'s right shoulder. The constituent values and habits of sensibility are patent: they entail massiveness of format, a private library, the commissioning and subsequent conservation of binding, the life of the letter in a canonic guise.

Immediately in front of the medals and hourglass, we observe the reader's quill. Verticality and the play of light on the feathers emphasize the compositional and substantive role of the object. The quill crystallizes the primary obligation of response. It defines reading as action. To read well is to answer the text, to be answerable to the text, 'answerability' comprising the crucial elements of response and of responsibility. To read well is to enter into answerable reciprocity with the book being read; it is to embark on total exchange ('ripe for commerce' says Geoffrey Hill). The dual compaction of light on the page and on the reader's cheek enacts Chardin's perception of the primal fact: to read well is to be read by that which we read. It is to be answerable to it. The obsolete word 'responsion', signifying, as it still does at Oxford, the process of examination and reply, may be used to shorthand the several and complex stages of active reading inherent in the quill.

The quill is used to set down marginalia. Marginalia are the immediate indices of the reader's response to the text, of the dialogue between the book and himself. They are the active tracers of the inner speech-current – laudatory, ironic, negative, augmentative – which accompanies the process of reading. Marginalia may, in extent and density of organization, come to rival the text itself, crowding not only the margin proper but the top and bottom of the page and the interlinear spaces. In our great libraries, there are counter libraries constituted by the marginalia and marginalia on marginalia which successive generations of true readers stenographed, coded, scribbled or set down with elaborate flourishes alongside, above, below and between the horizontals of the printed text. Often, marginalia are the hinges of aesthetic doctrine and intellectual history (look at Racine's copy of Euripides). Indeed, they may embody a major act of authorship, as do Coleridge's marginalia, soon to be published.

Annotation may well occur in the margin, but it is of a different cast. Marginalia pursue an impulsive, perhaps querulous discourse or disputation with the text. Annotations, often numbered, will tend to be of a more formal, collaborative character. They will, where possible, be made at the bottom of the page. They will elucidate this or that point in the text; they will cite parallel or subsequent authorities. The writer of marginalia is, incipiently, the rival of his text; the annotator is its servant.

[6]

This service finds its most exacting and necessary expression in the use of the reader's quill to correct and emend. He who passes over printing errors without correcting them is no mere philistine: he is a perjurer of spirit and sense. It may well be that in a secular culture the best way to define a condition of grace is to say that it is one in which one leaves uncorrected neither literal nor substantive errata in the texts one reads and hands on to those who come after us. If God, as Aby Warburg affirmed, 'lies in the detail', faith lies in the correction of misprints. Emendation, the epigraphical, prosodic, stylistic reconstitution of a valid text in the place of a spurious one, is an infinitely more taxing craft. As A. E. Housman professed in his paper on 'The Application of Thought to Textual Criticism' of 1922, 'this science and this art require more in the learner than a simply receptive mind; and indeed the truth is that they cannot be taught at all: *criticus nascitur, non fit*'. The conjunction of learning and sensitivity, of empathy with the original and imaginative scruple which produce a just emendation is, as Housman went on to say, of the rarest order. The stakes are high and ambiguous: Theobald may have won immortality when he suggested that Falstaff died 'babbling of green fields' – but is the emendation correct? The twentieth-century textual editor who has substituted 'brightness fell from her hair' for Thomas Nashe's 'brightness falls from the air' may be correct, but he is, surely, of the damned.

With his quill *le philosophe lisant* will transcribe from the book he is reading. The excerpts he makes can vary from the briefest of quotations to voluminous transcriptions. The multiplication and dissemination of written material after Gutenberg in fact increases the extent and variousness of personal transcription. The sixteenth- and seventeenth-century clerk or gentleman takes down in his hornbook, commonplace book, personal *florilegium* or breviary the maxims, 'taffeta phrases', *sententiae*, exemplary turns of elocution and tropes from classical and contemporary masters. Montaigne's essays are a living weave of echoes and citations. Until late into the nineteenth century – a fact borne witness to by the recollections of men and women as diverse as John Henry Newman, Abraham Lincoln, George Eliot or Carlyle – it is customary for the young and for committed readers throughout their lives to transcribe lengthy political orations, sermons, pages of verse and prose, encyclopaedia articles and chapters of historical narration. Such recopying had manifold purposes: the improvement of one's own style, the deliberate storage in the mind of ready examples of argument or persuasion, the buttressing of exact memory (a cardinal issue). But, above all, transcription comports a full engagement with the text, a dynamic reciprocity between reader and book.

It is this full engagement which is the sum of the varying modes of response: marginalia, annotation, textual correction and emendation, transcription. Together these generate a continuation of the book being read. The reader's active quill sets down 'a book in answer to' (the root-links between 'reply' and 'replication' are pertinent). This response will range from facsimile – which is total acquiescence – and affirmative development all the way to negation and counter-statement (many books are antibodies to other books). But the principal truth is this: latent in every act of complete reading is the compulsion to write a book in reply. The intellectual is, quite simply, a human being who has a pencil in his or her hand when reading a book.

Enveloping Chardin's reader, his folio, his hourglass, his incised medallions, his ready quill, is silence. Like his predecessors and contemporaries in the schools of interior, nocturnal and still-life painting, particularly in northern and eastern France, Chardin is a virtuoso of silence. He makes it present to us, he gives it tactile weight, in the quality of light and fabric. In his particular painting, silence is palpable: in the thick stuff of the table-cloth and curtain, in the lapidary poise of the background wall, in the muffling fur of the reader's gown and bonnet. Genuine reading demands silence (Augustine, in a famous passage, records that his master, Ambrose, was the first man able to read without moving his lips). Reading, as Chardin portrays it, is silent and solitary. It is a vibrant silence and a solitude crowded by the life of the word. But the curtain is drawn between the reader and the world (the key but eroded term is 'mundanity').

[8]

There would be many other elements in the painting to comment on: the alembic or retort, with its implications of scientific inquiry and its obvious compositional thrust; the skull on the shelf, at once a conventional prop in scholars' or philosophers' studies and, perhaps, an additional icon in the articulation of human mortality and textual survival; the possible interplay (I am not at all certain here) between the quill and the sand in the hourglass, sand being used to dry ink on the written page. But even a cursory look at the major components of Chardin's *Le Philosophe lisant* tells us of the classical vision of the act of reading – a vision we can document and detail in western art from medieval representations of St Jerome to the late nineteenth century, from Erasmus at his lectern to Mallarmé's apotheosis of *le Livre*.

What of the act of reading now? How does it relate to the proceedings and values inherent in Chardin's painting of 1734?

The motif of *cortesia*, of ceremonious encounter between reader and book, implicit in the costume worn by Chardin's *philosophe*, is now so remote as to be almost unrecapturable. If we come across it at all, it is in such ritualized, unavoidably archaic functions as the reading of the lesson in church or the solemn access to the Torah, head covered, in the synagogue. Informality is our password – though there is a poignant bite to Mencken's quip that many who think themselves emancipated are merely unbuttoned.

Far more radical and so far-reaching as to inhibit adequate summary are the changes in the values of temporality as these figure in Chardin's placement of hourglass, folio and death's head. The whole relationship between time and word, between mortality and the paradox of literary survivance, crucial to western high culture from Pindar to Mallarmé and self-evidently central to Chardin's painting, has altered. This alteration affects the two essential strands of the classic relation between the author and time on the one hand, and between the reader and the text on the other.

It may well be that contemporary writers continue to harbour the scandalous hope of immortality, that they continue to set down words in the hope that these will last not only beyond their own personal decease but for centuries to come. The conceit – in both its common and its technical sense – echoes still, though with characteristic wryness, in Auden's elegy on Yeats. But if such hopes persist, they are not professed publicly, let alone clarioned to the winds. The Pindaric-Horatian-Ovidian manifesto of literary immortality, with its innumerable repeats in the western syllabus, now grates. The very notion of *fama*, of literary glory achieved in defiance of and as rebuttal to death, embarrasses. There is no greater distance than that between the *exegi monumentum* trope and Kafka's reiterated finding that writing is a leprosy, an opaque and cancerous infirmity which is to be hidden from men of ordinary daylight and good sense. Yet it is Kafka's proposal, ambivalent and strategic as it may have been, which qualifies our apprehension of the unstable, perhaps pathological provenance and status of the modern work of art. When Sartre insists that even the most vital of literary personages is no more than an assemblage of semantic markers, of arbitrary letters of the page, he is seeking to demythologize, once for all, Flaubert's hurt fantasy about the autonomous life, about the life after his death, of Emma Bovary. *Monumentum*: the concept and its connotations ('the monumental') have passed into irony. This passage is marked, with masterly sadness, in Ben Belitt's 'This Scribe, My Hand' – with its reflection on the graves of Keats and Shelley in Rome, by Cestius' Pyramid:

> I write, in the posthumous way,
> on the flat of a headstone
> with a quarrier's ink, like yourself;
>
> an anthologist's date and an asterisk,
> a parenthetical mark in the gas
> of the pyramid-builders,
>
> an obelisk whirling with Vespas
> in a poisonous motorcade.

Note the exactness of 'the posthumous way'; not the *voie sacrée* to Parnassus which the classic poet maps for his works and, by exalted inference, for himself. 'The gas of the pyramid-builders' allows, indeed invites, vulgar interpretation: 'the hot air of the pyramid-builders', their vacant grandiloquence. It is not Plato's bees, carriers of divine rhetoric, that attend the poet, but loud, polluting Vespas ('wasps'), their acid sting decomposing the poet's monument even as the mass-technological values they incarnate decompose the aura of his work. We no longer look to texts, except in mandarin artifice, as negating personal death. 'All is precarious,' says Belitt,

> A maniac
> waits on the streets. Nobody listens. What
> must I do? I am writing on water . . .

The desolate phrase is, of course, Keats's. But it was denied, at once, in Shelley's assurance of immortality in 'Adonais', a denial Keats hoped for and, somehow, anticipated. Today such denials ring hollow ('the gas of the pyramid-builders').

The reader reciprocates this ironic declension. For him, as well, the notion that the book in front of him shall outlast his own life, that it prevails against the hourglass and the *caput mortuum* on the shelf, has lost immediacy. This loss involves the entire theme of *auctoritas*, of the normative, prescriptive status of the written word. It is no oversimplification to identify the classic ideal of culture, of civility, with that of the transmission of a syllabus, with that of the study of sybilline or canonic texts by whose authority successive generations test and validate their conduct of life (Matthew Arnold's 'touchstones'). The Greek *polis* saw itself as the organic medium of the principles, of the felt pressures of heroic-political precedent derived from Homer. At no juncture is the sinew of English culture and history separable from the ubiquity in that culture and history of the King James Bible, of the Book of Common Prayer and of Shakespeare. Collective and individual experience found an ordering mirror in a garland of texts; their self-realization was, in the full sense of the word, 'bookish' (in Chardin's painting the light is drawn to and projected from the open book).

Current literacies are diffuse and irreverent. It is no longer a natural motion to turn to a book for oracular guidance. We distrust *auctoritas* – the commanding script or scripture, the core of the authoritarian in classical authorship – precisely because it aspires to immutability. We did not write the book. Even our most intense, penetrative encounter with it is experience at second hand. This is the crux. The legacy of romanticism is one of strenuous solipsism, of the development of self out of immediacy. A single credo of vitalist spontaneity leads from Wordsworth's assertion that 'one impulse from a vernal wood' outweighs the dusty sum of libraries to the slogan of radical students at the University of Frankfurt in 1968: 'Let there be no more quotations.' In both cases the polemic is that of the 'life of life' against the 'life of the letter', of the primacy of personal experience against the derivativeness of even the most deeply felt of literary emotions. To us, the phrase 'the book of life' is a sophistic antinomy or cliché. To Luther, who used it at a decisive point in his version of Revelation and, one suspects, to Chardin's reader, it was a concrete verity.

As object, the book itself has changed. Except in academic or antiquarian circumstances, few of us will have come across, let alone made use of, the sort of tome being pondered by Chardin's *lecteur*. Who, today, has books privately bound? Implicit in the format and atmosphere of the folio, as we see it in the picture, is the private library, the wall of book-lined shelves, library-steps, lecterns, which is the functional space of the inner lives of Montaigne, of Evelyn, of Montesquieu, of Thomas Jefferson. This space, in turn, entails distinct economic and social relations: as between domestics who dust and oil the books and the master who reads them, as between the sanctified privacy of the scholar and the more vulgar terrain on which the family and outside world conduct their noisy, philistine lives. Few of us know such libraries, fewer still possess them. The entire economy, the architecture of privilege, in which the classic act of reading took place, has become remote (we visit the Morgan Library in New York or one of the great English country houses to view, albeit on a magnified scale, what was once the effective cadre of high bookishness). The modern apartment, notably for the young, simply has no space, no wall-surfaces for rows of books, for the folios, the quartos, the multi-volume *opera omnia* from which Chardin's reader has selected his text. Indeed, it is striking to what extent the cabinet for long-playing records and the record-shelf now occupy spaces formerly reserved for books (the substitution of music for reading is one of the major, most complex factors in the current changes of western feeling). Where there are books, moreover, they will, to a greater or lesser degree, be paperbacks. Now there can be no doubt that the 'paperback revolution' has been a liberating, a creative piece of technology, that it has widened the reach of literature and restored to availability whole areas of material, some of it even esoteric. But there is another side to the coin. The paperback is, physically, ephemeral. To accumulate paperbacks is not to assemble a library. By its very nature, the paperback preselects and anthologizes from the totality of literature and thought. We do not get, or get only very rarely, the complete works of an author. We do not get what current fashion regards as his inferior products. Yet it is only when we know a writer integrally, when we turn with special if querulous solicitude to his 'failures' and thus construe our own vision of his presentness, that the act of reading is authentic. Dog-eared in our pocket, discarded in the airport lounge, lurching between *ad hoc* brick bookends, the paperback is both a marvel of packaging and a denial of the largesse of form and spirit expressly stated in Chardin's scene. 'And I saw in the right hand of him that sat on the throne a book written within and on the back side, sealed with seven seals.' Can a paperback have seven seals?

We underline (particularly if we are students or harried book-reviewers). Sometimes we scribble a note in the margin. But how few of us write marginalia in Erasmus's or Coleridge's sense, how few of us annotate with copious rigour. Today it is only the trained epigrapher or bibliographer or textual scholar who emends, this is to say: who encounters the text as a living presence whose continued vitality, whose quick and radiance of being, depend on collaborative engagement with the reader. How many of us are equipped to correct even the crassest blunder in a classical quotation, to spot and emend even the most puerile error in accent or measure, though such blunders and errata abound in even the most reputed of modern editions? And who among us bothers to transcribe, to set down for personal content and commission to memory, the pages that have spoken to him most directly, that have 'read him' most searchingly?

Memory is, of course, the pivot. 'Answerability to' the text, the understanding and critical response to *auctoritas*, as they inform the classic act of reading and the depiction of this act by Chardin, depend strictly on the 'arts of memory'. *Le Philosophe lisant*, like the cultured men around him in a tradition which runs from classical antiquity to, roughly, the First World War, will know texts *by heart* (an idiom worth thinking about closely). They will know by heart considerable segments of Scripture, of the liturgy, of epic and lyric verse. Macaulay's formidable accomplishments in this respect – even as a schoolboy he had committed to memory a fair measure of Latin and English poetry – were only a heightened instance of a general practice. The ability to cite Scripture, to recite from memory large stretches of Homer, Virgil, Horace or Ovid, to cap on the instant a quotation from Shakespeare, Milton or Pope, generated the shared texture of echoes, of intellectual and emotive recognition and reciprocity, on which the language of British politics, law and letters was founded. Knowledge by heart of the Latin sources, of La Fontaine, of Racine, of the trumpet-calls in Victor Hugo, has given to the entire fabric of French public life its rhetorical stress. The classic reader, Chardin's *lisant*, locates the text he is reading inside a resonant manifold. Echo answers echo, analogy is precise and contiguous, correction and emendation carry the justification of accurately remembered precedent. The reader replies to the text out of the articulate density of his own store of reference and remembrance. It is an ancient, formidable suggestion that the Muses of memory and of invention are one.

The atrophy of memory is the commanding trait in mid and later twentieth-century education and culture. The great majority of us can no longer identify, let alone quote, even the central biblical or classical passages which not only are the underlying script of western literature (from Caxton to Robert Lowell, poetry in English has carried inside it the implicit echo of previous poetry), but have been the alphabet of our laws and public institutions. The most elementary allusions to Greek mythology, to the Old and the New Testament, to the classics, to ancient and to European history, have become hermetic. Short bits of text now lead precarious lives on great stilts of footnotes. The identification of fauna and flora, of the principal constellations, of the liturgical hours and seasons on which, as C. S. Lewis showed, the barest understanding of western poetry, drama and romance from Boccaccio to Tennyson intimately depends, is now specialized knowledge. We no longer learn by heart. The inner spaces are mute or jammed with raucous trivia. (Do not ask even a relatively well-prepared student to respond to the title of 'Lycidas', to tell you what an eclogue is, to recognize even one of the Horatian allusions and echoes from Virgil and Spenser which give to the four opening lines of the poem their meaning, their meaning of meaning. Schooling today, notably in the United States, is planned amnesia.)

The sinews of memory can only be made taut where there is silence, the silence so explicit in Chardin's portrait. To learn by heart, to transcribe faithfully, to read fully is to be silent and within silence. This order of silence is, at this point in western society, tending to become a luxury. It will require future historians of consciousness (*historiens des mentalités*) to gauge the abridgements in our attention span, the dilutions of concentration, brought on by the simple fact that we may be interrupted by the ring of the telephone, by the ancillary fact that most of us will, except under constraints of stoic resolve, answer the telephone, whatever else we may be doing. We need a history of noise-levels, of the diminution in those natural masses of silence, not only nocturnal, which still enfolded the daily lives of Chardin and his reader. Recent studies suggest that some seventy-five per cent of adolescents in the United States read against a background of sound (a radio, a record-player, a television set at one's back or in the next room). More and more young people and adults confess to being unable to read a serious text without a background of organized sound. We know too little about the ways in which the brain processes and integrates competing simultaneous stimuli to be able to say just what this electronic input does to the centres of attention and conceptualization involved in reading. But it is, at the least, plausible to suppose that the capacities for exact comprehension, for retention and for energetic response which knit our being to that of the book are drastically eroded. We tend to be, as Chardin's *philosophe lisant* was not, part-time readers, readers by half.

It would be fatuous to hope for the restoration of the complex of attitudes and disciplines instrumental in what I have called 'the classic act of reading'. The power relations (*auctoritas*), the economics of leisure and domestic service, the architectonics of private space and guarded silence which sustain and surround this act are largely unacceptable to the egalitarian-populist aims of western consumer societies. This, in point of fact, leads to a troubling anomaly. There is a society or social order in which many of the values and habits of sensibility implicit in Chardin's canvas are still operative; in which the classics are read with passionate attention; in which there are few mass media to compete with the primacy of literature; in which secondary education and the blackmail of censorship induce constant memorization and the transmission of texts from remembrance to remembrance. There is a society which is bookish in the root sense, which argues its destiny by perpetual reference to canonic texts, and whose sense of historical record is at once so compulsive and so vulnerable that it employs a veritable industry of exegetic falsification. I am, of course, alluding to the Soviet Union. And this example alone would suffice to keep before our minds perplexities as old as Plato's dialogues about the affinities between great art and centralized power, between high literacy and political absolutism.

But in the democratic-technological west, so far as one can tell, the die is cast. The folio, the private library, at-homeness in classical tongues, the arts of memory, will belong, increasingly, to the specialized few. The price of silence and of solitude will rise. (Part of the ubiquity and prestige of music derives precisely from the fact that one can listen to it while being with others. Serious reading excludes even one's intimates.) Already, the dispositions and techniques symbolized by *Le Philosophe lisant* are, in the proper sense of the term, academic. They occur in university libraries, in archives, in professors' studies.

The dangers are obvious. Not only much of Greek and Latin literature, but substantial portions of European letters, from the *Commedia* to *Sweeney Agonistes* (a poem which, like so many of T. S. Eliot's, is a palimpsest of echoes), have passed out of natural reach. Subject to the scholar's conservation and to occasional, fragmentary visitation by university students, works which were once immediate to literate recall now lead the dreary half-life of those Stradivari fiddles mute behind glass in the Coolidge collection in Washington. Large tracts of once fertile ground are already beyond reclaim. Who but the specialist reads Boiardo, Tasso and Ariosto, that meshed lineage of the Italian epic without which neither the notion of Renaissance nor that of romanticism makes much sense? Is Spenser still a cardinal presence in our repertoire of feeling, as he was to Milton, to Keats, to Tennyson? Voltaire's tragedies are, literally, a closed book; only the scholar may remember that these plays dominated European taste and styles of public utterance for nearly a century, that it is Voltaire, not Shakespeare or Racine, who holds the serious stage from Madrid to St Petersburg, from Naples to Weimar.

But the loss is not only ours. The essence of the full act of reading is, we have seen, one of dynamic reciprocity, of responsion to the life of the text. The text, however inspired, cannot have significant being if it is unread (what quick of life is there in an unplayed Stradivarius?). The relation of the true reader to the book is creative. The book has need of him as he has need of it – a parity of trust exactly rendered in the composition of Chardin's painting. It is in this perfectly concrete sense that every genuine act of reading, that every *lecture bien faite*, is collaborative with the text. *Lecture bien faite* is a term defined by Charles Péguy in his incomparable analysis of true literacy (in the *Dialogue de l'histoire et de l'âme païenne* of 1912–13):

Une lecture bien faite . . . n'est pas moins que le vrai, que le véritable et même et surtout que le réel achèvement du texte, que le réel achèvement de

l'œuvre; comme un couronnement, comme une grâce particulière et
coronale . . . Elle est ainsi littéralement une coopération, une collaboration
intime, intérieure . . . aussi, une haute, une suprême et singulière, une
déconcertante responsabilité. C'est une destinée merveilleuse, et presqu'effrayante, que tant de grandes œuvres, tant d'œuvres de grands hommes et
de si grands hommes puissent recevoir encore un accomplissement, un
achèvement, un couronnement de nous . . . de notre lecture. Quelle
effrayante responsabilité, pour nous.

As Péguy says: 'what a terrifying responsibility', but also what a
measureless privilege; to know that the survival of even the greatest
literature depends on *une lecture bien faite, une lecture honnête*.
And to know that this act of reading cannot be left in the sole
custody of mandarin specialists.

But where are we to find true readers, *des lecteurs qui sachent
lire*? We shall, I expect, have to train them.

I carry with me a vision of 'schools of creative reading' ('schools' is
far too pretentious a word; a quiet room and table will do). We shall
have to begin at the simplest, and therefore most exacting level of
material integrity. We must learn to parse sentences and to analyse
the grammar of our text, for, as Roman Jakobson has taught us,
there is no access to the grammar of poetry, to the nerve and sinew
of the poem, if one is blind to the poetry of grammar. We shall have
to relearn metrics and those rules of scansion familiar to every
literate schoolboy in the Victorian age. We shall have to do so not
out of pedantry, but because of the overwhelming fact that in all
poetry, and in a fair proportion of prose, metre is the controlling
music of thought and of feeling. We shall have to wake the numbed
muscles of memory, to rediscover in our quite ordinary selves the
enormous resources of precise recollection, and the delight that
comes of the texts which have secure lodging within us. We would
seek to acquire those rudiments of mythological and scriptural
recognition, of shared historical remembrance, without which it is
hardly possible, except by constant resort to more and more
laboured footnotes, to read adequately a line of Chaucer, of Milton,
of Goethe, or, to give a deliberately modernist instance, of

Mandelstam (who turns out to be one of the masters of echo).

A class in 'creative reading' would proceed step by step. It would begin with the near-dyslexia of current reading habits. It would hope to attain the level of informed competence prevalent among the well-educated in Europe and the United States at, say, the end of the nineteenth century. It would aspire, ideally, to that *achèvement*, to that fulfilling and crowning involvement in the text of which Péguy speaks and of which such complete acts of reading as Mandelstam on Dante or Heidegger on Sophocles are exemplary.

The alternatives are not reassuring: vulgarization and loud vacancies of intellect on the one hand, and the retreat of literature into museum cabinets on the other. The tawdry 'plot outline' or predigested and trivialized version of the classic on the one hand, and the illegible variorum on the other. Literacy must strive to regain the middle ground. If it fails to do so, if *une lecture bien faite* becomes a dated artifice, a great emptiness will enter our lives, and we shall experience no more the quiet and the light in Chardin's painting.

Real Presences

The turn of the century witnessed a philosophic crisis in the foundation of mathematics. Logicians, philosophers of mathematics and formal semantics, such as Frege and Russell, investigated the axiomatic fabric of mathematical reasoning and proof. Ancient logical and metaphysical disputes as to the true nature of mathematics – is it arbitrarily conventional? Is it 'a natural' construct corresponding to realities in the empirical order of the world? – were revived and given rigorous philosophical and technical expression. Gödel's celebrated proof of the necessity for an 'outside' addition to all self-consistent mathematical systems and operational rules, took on formal and applied significance far beyond the strictly mathematical domain. It is, at the same time, fair to say that certain of the questions raised in the late nineteenth and early twentieth centuries as to the logical foundations, internal coherence and psychological or existential sources of mathematical reasoning and proof, remain open.

A comparable crisis is occurring in the concept and understanding of language. Again, the far sources of questioning and disputation are those of Platonic, Aristotelian and Stoic thought. Grammatology, semantics, the study of the interpretation of meaning and actual interpretative practice (hermeneutics), models of the possible origins of human speech, the formal and pragmatic analysis and description of linguistic acts and performance – have their precedent in Plato's *Cratylus* and *Theatetes*, in Aristotelian logic, in the classical and post-classical arts and anatomies of rhetoric. None the less, the current 'language turn', as it affects not only linguistics, the logical investigations of grammar, theories of semantics and semiology, but also philosophy at large, poetics and literary studies, psychology and political theory, is a radical break with traditional sensibility and assumptions. The historical sources of the 'crisis of

The Leslie Stephen Memorial Lecture, University of Cambridge, 1985.

sense', are themselves complicated and fascinating. I can, here, allude to them only summarily.

Though in many respects conservative, the Kantian revolution carried within it the seeds of a fundamental re-examination and critique of the relations between word and world. The logical and psychological location by Kant of fundamental perceptions within human reason, Kant's conviction that the 'thing in itself', the ultimate reality-substance 'out there' could not be analytically defined or demonstrated, let alone articulated, laid the ground for solipsism and doubt. A dissociation of language from reality, of designation from perception, is alien to Kant's idealism of common sense; but it is an implicit potential. This potential will be seized upon, at first, not by linguistics or philosophic logic, but by poetry and poetics. Our current debates on transformational generative grammars, on speech-acts, on structuralist and deconstructive modes of textual reading, our present-day focus, in short, on 'the meaning of meaning' – derive from the poetics and experimental practice of Mallarmé and of Rimbaud. It is the period from the 1870s to the mid-1890s which generates our present agenda for debate, which situates the problem of the nature of language at the very centre of the philosophic and applied *sciences de l'homme*. Coming after Mallarmé and Rimbaud we know that a serious anthropology has at its formal and substantive core a theory or pragmatics of the *Logos*.

It is from Mallarmé that stems the programmatic attempt to dissociate poetic language from external reference, to fix the otherwise undefinable, unrecapturable texture and odour of the rose in the word 'rose' and not in some fiction of external correspondence and validation. Poetic discourse, which is, in fact, discourse made essential and maximally *meaning-ful*, constitutes an internally coherent, infinitely connotative and innovative, structure or set. It is richer than that of largely indeterminate and illusory sensory experience. Its logic and dynamics are internalized: words refer to other words; the 'naming of the world' – that Adamic conceit which is the primal myth and metaphor of all western theories of language – is not a descriptive or analytic mapping of the world 'out there', but a literal construction, animation, unfolding of conceptual possibilities. (Poetic) speech is creation. Rimbaud's *Je est un autre* lies at the base of all subsequent histories and theories of the dispersal of individuality, of the historical and epistemological eclipse of the *ego*. When Foucault heralds the end of the classical or Judaeo-Christian 'self', when deconstructionists refuse the notion of personal *auctoritas*, when Heidegger bids 'language speak' from an ontological well-spring prior to man, who is only the medium, the more or less opaque instrument of autonomous meaning – they are, each in their own framework of tactical intent, developing and systematizing Rimbaud's anarchic manifesto, his ecstatic *dérèglement* of tradition and innocent realism.

This scattering, this dissemination of the self, this subversion of naïve correspondence between the word and the empirical world, between public enunciation and what is actually being said, is accentuated by psychoanalysis. The Freudian view and use of human speech, of written texts (with its unmistakable analogues to Talmudic and to kabbalistic techniques of decipherment in depths, of revelatory descent into hidden levels of etymology and verbal association), radically dislocates and undermines the old stabilities of language. The common sense – observe that phrase – of our spoken or written words, the visible orderings and values of our syntax, are shown to be a masking surface. Beneath each stratum of conscious, lexical meaning, lie further strata of more or less realized, avowed, intended meanings. The impulses of intentionality, of declared and covert significance, extend from the brittle surface to the unfathomable nocturnal deep structures or prestructures of the unconscious. No ascription of meaning is ever final, no associative sequence or field of possible resonance ever end-stopped (Wittgenstein's dissent from Freud seizes upon this very point). Meanings and the psychic energies which enunciate or, more exactly, which encode them, are in perpetual motion. 'Must we mean what we say?' asks the epistemologist: 'can we mean what we say?' asks the psychoanalyst. And what, after Rimbaud, is that fiction of stable identity we label 'I' or 'we'?

Logical positivism and linguistic philosophy, as they arise in central Europe at the turn of the century and are institutionalized in

Anglo-American practice, are exercises in demarcation: between sense and nonsense, between what can be said reasonably and what cannot, between truth-functions and metaphor. The endeavour to 'purge language' of its metaphysical impurities, of its facile fantasms of unexamined inference, is undertaken in the name of logic, of transparent formalization and systematic scepticism. But the *kathartic*-therapeutic image, the ideal of cleansing and restoration to ascetic clarity so vivid in the Vienna Circle, in Frege, in Wittgenstein and their inheritors, relates obviously to Mallarmé's famous imperative: let us 'cleanse the words of the tribe', let language be made translucent to itself.

 The fourth principal area of the language-critique and deconstructions of classical innocence as to word and world, is historical and cultural. Here also, and with few exceptions, the source is central European and Judaic. (One need hardly stress the Judaic character of the entire movement, philosophic, psychological, literary, cultural-political which I am addressing, or the tensed overlap between this movement and the tragic destiny of European Judaism. From Roman Jakobson, Freud, Wittgenstein, Karl Kraus, Kafka or Walter Benjamin to Lévi-Strauss, Jacques Derrida and Saul Kripke, the dramatis personae of our inquiry declare a larger logic.) This fourth area is that of the critique of language as an inadequate instrument and as an instrument not merely of political-social falsehood but of potential barbarism. Hofmannsthal's 'Letter of Lord Chandos', the parables of Franz Kafka, the reflections on language of Mauthner (a cardinal, hence unavowed source of Wittgenstein's *Tractatus*), tell of man's incapacity to express in words his innermost truths, his sensory experiences, his moral and transcendent intuitions. This despair before the limitations of language will climax in the final cry in Schoenberg's *Moses und Aron*: 'O Word, Word, Word, that I lack!' Or in Kafka's inexhaustible parable on the mortal silence of the Sirens. The political-aesthetic assault on language is that of Karl Kraus, of his auditor, Canetti, or George Orwell (a more pallid but rationally usable version of Kraus). Political rhetoric, the tidal mendacity of journalism and the mass media, the trivializing cant of public and socially approved modes of discourse, have made of almost every-thing modern urban men and women say or hear or read an empty jargon, a cancerous loquacity (Heidegger's term is *Gerede*). Language has lost the very capacity for truth, for political or personal honesty. It has marketed and mass-marketed its mysteries of prophetic intuition, its answerabilities to accurate remembrance. In Kafka's prose, in the poetry of Paul Celan or of Mandelstam, in the messianic linguistics of Benjamin and in the aesthetics and political sociology of Adorno, language operates, self-doubtingly, on the sharp edge of silence. We know now that if the Word 'was in the beginning', it can also be in at the end: that there is a vocabulary and a grammar of the death-camps, that thermo-nuclear detona-tions can be designated as 'Operation sunshine'. It were as if the quintessential, the identifying attribute of man – the *Logos*, the organon of language – had broken in our mouths.

The consequences and correlatives of these great philosophical-psychological underminings and of the western experience of uttermost political inhumanity, are ubiquitous. They are too numerous and various to designate accurately. Much of classical literacy, of *litterae humaniores* as understood, taught and practised from the Hellenistic age to the two world wars, is eroded. The retreat from the word is drastic in the special and increasingly numerate or symbolic codes of not only the exact and applied sciences, but in philosophy and logic, in the social sciences. The picture and the caption dominate ever expanding spheres of information and communication. The values implicit in rhetoric, in citation, in the canonic body of texts, are under severe pressure. It is more than likely that the performance and personal reception of music are now moving to that cultural pivot once occupied by the cultivation of discourse and of letters. The methodical devaluation of speech in political propaganda and in the Esperanto of the mass-market is too powerful and diffuse to be readily defined. At decisive points, ours is today a civilization 'after the word'.

What I want to look at is a more specific ground of crisis and debate.

*

The act and art of serious reading comport two principal motions of spirit: that of interpretation (hermeneutics) and that of valuation (criticism, aesthetic judgement). The two are strictly inseparable. To interpret is to judge. No decipherment, however philological, however textual in the most technical sense, is value-free. Correspondingly, no critical assessment, no aesthetic commentary is not, at the same time, interpretative. The very word 'interpretation', encompassing as it does concepts of explication, of translation and of enactment (as in the interpretation of a dramatic part or musical score), tells us of this manifold interplay.

The relativity, the arbitrariness of *all* aesthetic propositions, of *all* value-judgements is inherent in human consciousness and in human speech. *Anything can be said about anything.* The assertion that Shakespeare's *King Lear* 'is beneath serious criticism' (Tolstoy), the finding that Mozart composes mere trivia, are *totally irrefutable*. They can be falsified neither on formal (logical) grounds, nor in existential substance. Aesthetic philosophies, critical theories, constructs of the 'classic' or the 'canonic' can never be anything but more or less persuasive, more or less comprehensive, more or less consequent descriptions of this or that process of preference. A critical theory, an aesthetic, is a *politics of taste*. It seeks to systematize, to make visibly applicable and pedagogic an intuitive 'set', a bent of sensibility, the conservative or radical bias of a master perceiver or alliance of opinions. There can be neither proof nor disproof. Aristotle's readings and Pope's, Coleridge's and Sainte-Beuve's, T. S. Eliot's and Croce's, do not constitute a science of judgement and disproof, of experimental advance and confirmation or falsification. They constitute the metamorphic play and counterplay of individual response, of (to borrow Quine's teasing phrase) 'blameless intuition'. The difference between the judgement of a great critic and that of a semi-literate or censorious fool lies in its range of inferred or cited reference, in the lucidity and rhetorical strength of articulation (the critic's style) or in the accidental addendum which is that of the critic who is also a creator in his own right. But it is not a scientifically or logically demonstrable difference. No aesthetic proposition can be termed either 'right' or 'wrong'. The sole appropriate response is personal assent or dissent.

How, in actual practice, do we handle the anarchic nature of value-judgements, the formal and pragmatic equality of all critical findings? We count heads and, in particular, what we take to be qualified and laurelled heads. We observe that, over the centuries, a great majority of writers, critics, professors and honourable men have judged Shakespeare to be a poet and dramatist of genius and have found Mozart's music to be both emotionally enriching and technically inspired. Reciprocally, we observe that those who judge otherwise are in a tiny, literally eccentric minority, that their critiques carry little weight and that the motives we make out behind their dissent are psychologically suspect (Jeffrey on Wordsworth, Hanslick on Wagner, Tolstoy on Shakespeare). After which perfectly valid observations we get on with the business of literate commentary and appreciation.

Now and again, as out of an irritant twilight, we sense the partial circularity and the contingency of the whole argument. We realize that there can be no ballot on aesthetic values, that a majority vote, however constant and massive, can never refute, can never disprove the refusal, the abstention, the counter-statement of the solitary or denier. We realize, more or less clearly, the degree to which 'literate common sense', the acceptable limits of debate, the transmission of the generally agreed syllabus of major texts and works of art and of music, is an ideological process, a reflection of power-relations within a culture and society. The literate person is one who concurs with the reflexes of approval and aesthetic enjoyment which have been suggested and exemplified to him by the dominant legacy. But we dismiss such worries. We accept as inevitable and as adequate the merely statistical weight of 'institutional consensus', of common-sense authority. How else could we marshal our cultural choices and be at home in our pleasures?

It is at this precise juncture that a distinction has, traditionally, been drawn between aesthetic criticism on the one hand and interpretation or analysis strictly considered on the other. The ontological indeterminacy of all value-judgements, the impossibility of any probative, logically consistent 'decision procedure' as between conflicting aesthetic views, have been conceded. *De gustibus non disputandum.* The determination of a true or most probable meaning in a text has, in contrast, been held to be the reasonable aim and merit of informed reading or philology.

Linguistic, formal, historical factors may impede such determination and documented analysis. The context in which the poem or fable was composed may elude us. The stylistic conventions may have become esoteric. We may, simply, not have the requisite critical density of information, of controlling comparisons, needed to arrive at a secure choice between variant readings, between differing glosses and *explications du texte*. But these are accidental, empirical problems. In the case of ancient writings, new lexical, grammatical or contextual material may come to light. Where the inhibitions to understanding are more modern, further biographical or referential data may turn up and help elucidate the author's intentions and field of assumed echo. Unlike criticism and aesthetic valuation, which are always synchronic (Aristotle's 'Oedipus' is not negated or made obsolete by Hölderlin's, Hölderlin's is neither improved nor cancelled out by Freud's), the process of textual interpretation is cumulative. Our readings become better informed, evidence progresses, substantiation grows. Ideally – though not, to be sure, in actual practice – the corpus of lexical knowledge, of grammatical analysis, of semantic and contextual matter, of historical and biographical fact, will finally suffice to arrive at a demonstrable determination of what the passage means. This determination need not claim exhaustiveness; it will know itself to be susceptible to amendment, to revision, even to rejection as fresh knowledge becomes available, as linguistic or stylistic insights are sharpened. But at any given point in the long history of disciplined understanding, a decision as to the better reading, as to the more plausible paraphrase, as to the more reasonable grasp of the author's purpose, will be a rational and demonstrable one. At the end of the philological road, now or tomorrow, there *is* a best reading, there is a meaning or constellation of meanings to be perceived, analysed and chosen over others. In its authentic sense, philology is, indeed, the working passage, via the arts of scrupulous observance and trust (*philein*) from the uncertainties of the word to the stability of the *Logos*.

It is the rational credibility and practice of this passage, of this cumulative advance towards textual understanding, which is today in sharp doubt. It is the hermeneutic possibility itself which the 'crises of sense', as I sketched them at the outset, have put in question.

Let me contract, and thus radicalize, the claims of the new semantics. The post-structuralist, the deconstructionist remind us (justly) that there is no difference in substance between primary text and commentary, between the poem and the explication or critique. All propositions and enunciations, be they primary, secondary or tertiary (the commentary on the commentary, the interpretation of previous interpretations, the criticism of criticism, so familiar to our current Byzantine culture), are part of an encompassing *intertextuality*. They are equivalent as *écriture*. It follows in a profoundly challenging play on words (and is not all discourse and writing a play on words?) that a primary text and each and every text it gives rise or occasion to is no more and no less than a *pre-text*. It happens to come before, temporally, by accident of chronology. It is the occasion, more or less contingent, more or less random, of the commentary, critique, variant on, pastiche, parody, citation of itself. It has no privilege of canonic originality – if only because language always precedes its user and always imposes on his usage rules, conventions, opacities for which he is not responsible and over which his control is minimal. No sentence spoken or composed in any intelligible language is, in the rigorous sense of the concept, original. It is merely one among the formally unbounded set of transformational possibilities within a rule-bound grammar. The poem or play or novel is strictly considered, anonymous. It belongs to the topological space of the underlying grammatical and lexical structures and availabilities. We do not need to know the name of the poet to read the poem. That very name, moreover, is a naïve and obtrusive ascription of identity where, in the philosophic and logical sense, there is no demonstrable identity. The 'ego', the *moi*, after Freud, Foucault or Lacan, is not only, as in Rimbaud, *un autre*, but a kind of Magellanic cloud of interactive and changing energies, partial introspections, moments of compacted consciousness, mobile, unstable, as it were, around an even more indeterminate central region or black hole of the subconscious, of the unconscious or the preconscious. The notion that we can grasp an author's intentionality, that we should attend to what he would tell us of his own purpose in or understanding of his text, is utterly naïve. What does he know of the meanings hidden by or projected from the interplay of semantic potentialities which he has momentarily circumscribed and formalized? Why should we trust in his own self-delusions, in the suppressions of the psychic impulses, which most likely have impelled him to produce a 'textuality' in the first place? The adage had it: 'do not trust the teller but the tale'. Deconstruction asks: why trust either? Confidence is not the relevant hermeneutic note.

Invoking the commonplace but cardinal verity that in all interpretation, in all statements of understanding, language is simply being used about language in an infinitely self-multiplying series (the mirror arcade), the deconstructive reader defines the act of reading as follows. The ascription of sense, the preference of one possible reading over another, the choice of this explication and paraphrase and not that, is no more than the playful, unstable, undemonstrable option or fiction of a subjective scanner who constructs and deconstructs purely semiotic markers as his own momentary pleasures, politics, psychic needs or self-deceptions bid him do. There are no rational or falsifiable decision-procedures as between a multitude of differing interpretations or 'constructs of proposals'. At best, we will select (for a time, at least) the one which strikes us as the more ingenious, the richer in surprise, the more powerfully decompositional and re-creative of the original or *pre-text*. Derrida on Rousseau is richer *fun* than, say, an old literalist and historicist such as Lanson. Why labour through philological-historical exegeses of the Lurianic Kabbala when one can read the constructs of the semioticians at Yale? No *auctoritas* external to the game can legislate between these alternatives. *Gaudeamus igitur*.

Let me say at once that I do not perceive any adequate logical or epistemological refutation of deconstructive semiotics. It is evident that the playful abolition of the stable subject contains a logical circularity, for it is an ego which observes or intends its own dissolution. And there is an infinite regress of intentionality in the mere denial of intent. But these formal fallacies or petitions of principle do not really cripple the deconstructive language-game or the fundamental claim that there are no valid procedures of decision as between competing and even antithetical ascriptions of meaning.

The common-sense (but what, challenges the deconstructionist, is 'a common sense'?) and liberal move is one of more or less unworried circumvention. The carnival and saturnalia of post-structuralism, of Barthes's *jouissance*, or Lacan's and Derrida's endless punning and wilful etymologizing, will pass as have so many other rhetorics of reading. 'Fashion,' as Leopardi reassures us, 'is the mother of death.' The 'common reader', Virginia Woolf's positive rubric, the serious scholar, editor and critic will get on, as they always have, with the work in hand, with the elucidation of what is taken to be an authentic, though often polysemic and even ambiguous sense, and will enunciate what are taken to be informed, rationally arguable, though always provisional and self-questioning preferences and value-judgements. Across the millennia, a decisive majority of informed receivers have not only arrived at a manifold but broadly coherent view of what the *Iliad*, or *King Lear* or *The Marriage of Figaro* are about (the meanings of their meaning), but have concurred in judging Homer, Shakespeare, Mozart to be supreme artists in a hierarchy of recognitions which extends from the classical summits to the trivial and the mendacious. This broad concordance, with its undeniable residue of dissent, or hermeneutic and critical disputes, with its margins of uncertainty and altering 'placement' (F. R. Leavis's word), constitutes an 'institutional consensus', a syllabus of agreed reference and exemplariness, across the ages. This general concurrence provides culture with its energies of remembrance, and furnishes the 'touchstones' (Matthew Arnold) whereby to test new literature, new art, new music.

So robust and fertile a pragmatism is seductive. It allows one, indeed it authorizes one, to 'get on with the job'. It bids one acknowledge, as out of the corner of a clear eye, that all determinations of textual meaning are probabilistic, that all critical assessments are ultimately uncertain; but to draw confident reinsurance from the cumulative – that is to say statistical – weight of historical agreement and practical persuasion. The bark and ironies of deconstruction resound in the night but the caravan of 'good sense' passes on.

I know that this praxis of liberal consensus satisfies most readers. I know that it is the general guarantor of our literacies and common pursuits of understanding. Nevertheless, the current 'crisis of sense', the current equation of text and pre-text, the abolitions of *auctoritas*, seem to me so radical as to challenge a response other than pragmatic, statistical or professional (as in the protectionism of the academy). If counter-moves are worth exploring, they will be of an order no less radical than are some of the anarchic and even 'terrorist' grammatologists and masters of mirrors. The summons of nihilism demand answer.

The initial move is one away from the autistic echo-chambers of deconstruction, from a theory and practice of games which – this is the very point and *ingenium* of the thing – subvert and alter their own rules in the course of play. It is a move palpably indebted to the Kierkegaardian triad of the aesthetic, the ethical and the religious. But the resort to certain ethical postulates or categories in respect of our interpretations and valuations of literature and the arts is older than Kierkegaard. The belief that the moral imagination relates to the analytic and the critical imaginations is at least as ancient as the poetics of Aristotle. These are, themselves, an attempt to refute Plato's dissociation between aesthetics and morality. A move towards the ethical rejoins the hermeneutics of Aquinas and Dante and the aesthetics of disinterestedness in Kant (himself an obligatory and representative target of recent deconstruction). It is, I think, the abandonment of this high and rigorous ground, in the name of nineteenth-century positivism and twentieth-century secular psychology, which has brought on much of the (intensely stimulating) anarchy in which we now find ourselves.

If we wish to transcend the merely pragmatic, if we wish to meet the challenge of autistic textuality or, more accurately, 'anti-textuality' on grounds as radical as its own, we must bring to bear on the act of meaning, on the understanding of meaning, the full force of moral intuition. The vitally concentrated agencies are those of tact, of courtesy of heart, of good taste, in a sense not decorous or civil, but inward and ethical. Such focus and agencies cannot be logically formalized. They are existential modes. Their underwriting is, as we shall be compelled to propose, of a transcendent kind. This makes them utterly vulnerable. But also 'of the essence', this is to say, essential.

I take the ethical inference to entail the following, to make the following *morally*, not logically, not empirically, self-evident.

The poem comes before the commentary. The primary text is first not only temporally. It is not a pre-text, an occasion for subsequent exegetic or metamorphic treatment. Its priority is one of essence, of ontological need and self-sufficiency. Even the greatest critique or commentary, be it that of a writer or painter or composer on his own work, is *accidental* (the cardinal Aristotelian distinction). It is dependent, secondary, contingent. The poem embodies and bodies forth through a singular enactment its own *raison d'être*. The secondary text does not contain an imperative of being. Again the Aristotelian and Thomist differentiations between essence and accident are clarifying. The poem *is*; the commentary *signifies*. Meaning is an attribute of being. Both phenomenologies are, in the nature of the case, 'textual'. But to equate and confound their respective textualities is to confound *poiesis*, the act of creation, of bringing into autonomous being, with the derivative, secondary ratio of interpretation or adaptation. (We know that the violinist, however gifted and penetrating, 'interprets' the Beethoven sonata; he does not compose it. To keep our knowledge of this difference at risk, we do remind ourselves that the existential status of an unperformed work, an unread text, an unseen painting *is* philosophically and psychologically problematic.)

It follows from these intuitive and ethical postulates that the present-day inflation of commentary and criticism, that the equalities of weight and force which deconstruction assigns to the primary and the secondary texts, are spurious. They represent that reversal in the natural order of values and interest which characterize an Alexandrine or Byzantine period in the history of the arts and of thought. It follows also that the statement propounded by an academic leader of the new semantics – 'It is more interesting to read Derrida on Rousseau than to read Rousseau' – is a perversion not only of the calling of the teacher, but of common sense where common sense is a lucid, concentrated expression of moral imagining. Such a perversion of values and receptive practice, however playful, is not only wasteful and confusing *per se*: it is potentially corrosive of the strengths of creation, of true invention in literature and the arts. The current crisis of meaning does appear to coincide with a spell of enervation and profound self-doubt in art and letters. Where cats are sovereign, tigers do not burn.

But liberating as I believe it to be, the ethical inference does not engage finality. It does not confront in immediacy the nihilistic supposition. It is formally conceivable and arguable that every discourse and text is idiolectic, this is to say that it is a 'one-time' cryptogram whose rules of usage and decipherment are non-repeatable. If Saul Kripke is right, this would be the strong version of Wittgenstein's view of rules and language. 'There can be no such thing as meaning anything by the word. Each new application we make is a leap in the dark; any present criterion could be interpreted so as to accord with anything we may choose to do. So there can be neither accord nor conflict.'

Equally, it is conceivable and arguable that every assignment and experience of value is not only undemonstrable, is not only susceptible of statistical derision (on a free vote, mankind will choose bingo over Aeschylus), but is empty, is meaningless in the logical positivist use of the concept.

We know of Descartes's axiomatic solution to such possibility. He postulates the *sine qua non* that God will not systematically confuse or falsify our perception and understanding of the world, that He will not arbitrarily alter the rules of reality (as these govern nature and as these are accessible to rational deduction and application).

Without some such fundamental presupposition in regard to the existence of sense and of value, there can be no responsible response, no answering answerability to either the act of speech or to that ordering of and selections from this act which we call the text. Without some axiomatic leap towards a postulate of *meaningfulness*, there can be no striving towards intelligibility or value-judgement however provisional (and note the part of 'vision' in the provisional). Where it elides the 'radical' – the etymological and conceptual root – of the *Logos*, logic is indeed vacant play.

We must read *as if*.

We must read as if the text before us had meaning. This will not be a single meaning if the text is a serious one, if it makes us answerable to its force of life. It will not be a meaning or *figura* (structure, complex) of meanings isolated from the transformative and reinterpretative pressures of historical and cultural change. It will not be a meaning arrived at by any determinant or automatic process of cumulation and consensus. The true understanding(s) of the text or music or painting may, during a briefer or longer time-spell, be in the custody of a few, indeed of one witness and respondent. Above all, the meaning striven towards will never be one which exegesis, commentary, translation, paraphrase, psychoanalytic or sociological decoding, can ever exhaust, can ever define as total. Only weak poems can be exhaustively interpreted or understood. Only in trivial or opportunistic texts is the sum of significance that of the parts.

We must read as if the temporal and executive setting of a text does matter. The historical surroundings, the cultural and formal circumstances, the biological stratum, what we can construe or conjecture of an author's intentions, constitute vulnerable aids. We know that they ought to be stringently ironized and examined for what there is in them of subjective hazard. They matter none the less. They enrich the levels of awareness and enjoyment; they generate constraints on the complacencies and licence of interpretative anarchy.

This 'as if', this axiomatic conditionality, is our Cartesian-Kantian wager, our leap into sense. Without it, literacy becomes transient Narcissism. But this wager is itself in need of a clear foundation. Let me spell out summarily the risks of finality, the assumptions of transcendence which, at the first and at the last, underlie the reading of the word as I conceive it.

Where we read truly, where the experience is to be that of meaning, we do so as if the text (the piece of music, the work of art) *incarnates* (the notion is grounded in the sacramental) *a real presence of significant being*. This real presence, as in an icon, as in the enacted metaphor of the sacramental bread and wine, is, finally, irreducible to any other formal articulation, to any analytic deconstruction or paraphrase. It is a singularity in which concept and form constitute a tautology, coincide point to point, energy to energy, in that excess of significance over all discrete elements and codes of meaning which we call the symbol or the agency of transparence.

These are not occult notions. They are of the immensity of the commonplace. They are perfectly pragmatic, experiential, repetitive, each and every time a melody comes to inhabit us, to possess us even unbidden, each and every time a poem, a passage of prose seizes upon our thought and feelings, enters into the sinews of our remembrance and sense of the future, each and every time a painting transmutes the landscapes of our previous perceptions (poplars are on fire after Van Gogh, viaducts walk after Klee). To be 'indwelt' by music, art, literature, to be made responsible, answerable to such habitation as a host is to a guest – perhaps unknown, unexpected – at evening, is to experience the *commonplace mystery of a real presence*. Not many of us feel compelled to, have the expressive means to, register the mastering quality of this experience – as does Proust when he crystallizes the sense of the world and of the word in the little yellow spot which is the real presence of a riverside door in Vermeer's *View of Delft*, or as does Thomas Mann when he enacts in word and metaphor the coming over us, the 'overcoming of us', in Beethoven's Opus 111. No matter. The experience itself is one we are thoroughly *at home* with – an informing idiom – each and every time we live a text, a sonata, a painting.

Moreover, though we have largely forgotten it, this experience of, the underwriting by, a real presence is the source of the history, methods and practice of hermeneutics and criticism, of interpretation and value-judgement in the western inheritance.

The disciplines of reading, the very idea of close commentary and interpretation, textual criticism as we know it, derive from the study of Holy Scripture or, more accurately, from the incorporation and development in that study of older practices of Hellenistic grammar, recension and rhetoric. Our grammars, our explications, our criticisms of texts, our endeavours to pass from letter to spirit, are the immediate heirs to the textualities of western Judaeo-Christian theology and biblical-patristic exegetics. What we have done since the masked scepticism of Spinoza, since the critiques of the rationalist Enlightenment and since the positivism of the nineteenth century, is to borrow vital currency, vital investments and contracts of trust from the bank or treasure-house of theology. It is from there that we have borrowed our theories of the symbol, our use of the iconic, our idiom of poetic creation and aura. It is loans of terminology and reference from the reserves of theology which provide the master readers in our time (such as Walter Benjamin and Martin Heidegger) with their licence to practise. We have borrowed, traded upon, made small change of the reserves of transcendent authority. Very few of us have made any return deposit. At its key points of discourse and inference, hermeneutics and aesthetics in our secular, agnostic civilization are a more or less conscious, a more or less embarrassed act of larceny (it is just this embarrassment which makes resonant and tensely illuminating Benjamin on Kafka or Heidegger on Trakl and on Sophocles).

What would it mean to acknowledge, indeed to repay these massive loans?

For Plato the rhapsode is one possessed by the god. Inspiration is literal; the *daimon* enters into the artist, mastering and overreaching the bounds of his natural person. Seeking a reinsurance for the imperious obscurity, for the great burst into the inordinate of his poems, Gerard Manley Hopkins reckoned neither on the perception of a few elect spirits nor on the pedagogic authority of time. He did not know whether his language and prosody would *ever* be understood by other men and women. But such understanding was not of the essence. Reception and validation, said Hopkins, lay with Christ, 'the only true critic'. As set out in *Clio*, Péguy's analysis and description of the complete act of reading, of the *lecture bien faite*, remains the most incisive, the most indispensable we have. Here is the classic statement of the symbiosis between writer and reader, of the collaborative and organic generation of textual meaning, of the dynamics of necessity and hope which knit discourse to the life-giving response of the reader and 'remembrancer'. In Péguy, the pre-emptions and logic of the argument are explicitly religious; the mystery of poetic, artistic creation and that of vital reception are never wholly secular. A dread sense of blasphemy in regard to the primal act of creation, of illegitimacy in the face of God, inhabits every motion of spirit and of composition in Kafka's work. The breath of inspiration, against which the true artist would seek to close his terrified lips, is that of those paradoxically animate winds which blow from 'the nether regions of death' in the final sentence of Kafka's *The Hunter Gracchus*. They too are not of secular, rational provenance.

In the main, western art, music and literature have, from the time of Homer and Pindar to that of Eliot's *Four Quartets*, of Pasternak's *Doctor Zhivago* or the poetry of Paul Celan, spoken immediately either to the presence or absence of the god. Often, that address has been agonistic and polemic. The great artist has had Jacob for his patron, wrestling with the terrible precedent and power of original creation. The poem, the symphony, the Sistine ceiling are acts of counter-creation. 'I am God,' said Matisse when he completed painting the chapel at Vence. 'God, the other craftsman,' said Picasso, in open rivalry. Indeed it may well be that modernism can best be defined as that form of music, literature and art which no longer experiences God as a competitor, a predecessor, an antagonist in the long night (that of St John of the Cross which is every true poet's). There may well be in atonal or aleatory music, in non-representational art, in certain modes of surrealist, automatic or concrete writing, a sort of shadow-boxing. The adversary is now the form itself. Shadow-boxing can be technically dazzling and formative. But like so much of modern art it remains solipsistic. The sovereign challenger is gone. And much of the audience.

I do not imagine that He can be summoned back to our agnostic and positivist condition. I do not suppose that a theory of hermeneutics and of criticism whose underwriting is theological, or a practice of poetry and the arts which implies, which implicates the real presence of the transcendent or its 'substantive absence' from a new solitude of man, can command general assent. What I have wanted to make clear is the spiritual and existential duplicity in so much of our current models of meaning and of aesthetic value. Consciously or not, with embarrassment or indifference, these models draw upon, they metaphorize crucially, the abandoned, the unpaid-for idiom, imaginings and guarantees of a theology or, at the least, of a transcendent metaphysics. The astute trivializations, the playful nihilism of deconstruction do have the merits of their honesty. They instruct us that 'nothing shall come of nothing'.

Personally, I do not see how a secular, statistically based theory of meaning and of value can, over time, withstand either the deconstructionist challenge or its own fragmentation into liberal eclecticism. I cannot arrive at any rigorous conception of a possible determination of either sense or stature which does not wager on a transcendence, on a real presence, in the act and product of serious art, be it verbal, musical, or that of material forms.

Such a conviction leads to logical suppositions which are exceedingly difficult to express clearly, let alone to demonstrate. But the possible confusion and, in our present climate of approved sentiment, the inevitable embarrassment which must accompany any public avowal of mystery, seems to me preferable to the slippery evasions and conceptual deficits in contemporary hermeneutics and criticism. It is these which strike me as false to common experience, as incapable of bearing witness to such manifest phenomena as the creation of a literary persona who will endure far beyond the life of the creator (Flaubert's dying cry against 'that whore' Emma Bovary), as incapable of insight into the invention of melody or the evident transmutations of our experiences of space, of light, of the planes and volumes of our own being, brought about by a Mantegna, a Turner or a Cézanne.

It may be the case that nothing more is available to us than the absence of God. Wholly felt and lived, that absence is an agency and *mysterium tremendum* (without which a Racine, a Dostoevsky, a Kafka are, indeed, nonsense or food for deconstruction). To infer such terms of reference, to apprehend something of the cost one must be prepared to pay in declaring them, is to be left naked to unknowing. I believe that one must take the risk if one is to have the right to strive towards the perennial, never fully to be realized ideal of all interpretation and valuation: which is that, one day, Orpheus will not turn around, and that the truth of the poem will return to the light of understanding, whole, inviolate, life-giving, even out of the dark of omission and of death.

A Preface to the Hebrew Bible

What you have in hand is not *a* book. It is *the* book. That, of course, is what 'Bible' means. It is the book which, not only in western humanity, defines the concept of a text. All our other books, however different in matter or method, relate, be it indirectly, to this book of books. They relate to the facts of articulate address, text to reader, to the trust in lexical, grammatical and semantic means, which the Bible originates and deploys at a level and prodigality unsurpassed since. All other books, be they histories, narrations of the imaginary, codes of law, moral treatises, lyric poems, dramatic dialogues, theological-philosophic meditations, are like sparks, often, to be sure, distant, tossed by an incessant breath from a central fire. In the western condition, but also in other parts of the planet to which the 'Good Book' has been taken, the Bible largely informs our historical and social identity. It gives to consciousness the instruments, often implicit, of remembrance and quotation. Until modern times, these instruments were so deeply incised in our mentalities, even, especially perhaps, among the non- and the pre-literate, that biblical reference acted as self-reference, as a passport on the journey to one's inward being. The Scriptures were (for many they still are) a presence in action both universal and singular, commonly shared and of utmost privacy. No other book is like it; all other books are inhabited by the murmur of that distant source (today, astrophysicists tell of the 'background noise' of creation).

At the latest count, the Old and the New Testament have, either entirely or in substantial selections, been translated into 2,010 different languages. The process of translation and retranslation has been continuous for more than two millennia. Biblical texts have been communicated in every conceivable medium and notation: from papyrus scrolls to compact discs, from monumental folios to the miniaturization of psalms or prayers on pin-heads. The

From the Everyman Library edition, 1996.

understanding, interpretation and translation. The Old Testament is as far-flung as the stars; it is also as earthbound, as localized as an Ordnance Survey. Carry it in hand and it will guide you, cubit as it were by cubit, to the field of Gilboa, to the well at Shiloh, to that hillock under the unmoving sun at Ajalon. Drive a spade into the parched ground, be it in the seeming emptiness of the Negev or the busy hills of Galilee, and the biblical past crowds at you. The archaeology of Jericho takes us back six millennia or more; the 'cities of the plain' on which God vented his displeasure have now been given a 'local habitation and a name'; the siege-ramps whereby the armies of Sennacherib conquered Judaea are being laid bare. Dramatically, the discovery of the Qumran scrolls or of the library of inscribed tablets at Ebla, have led to a reconsideration of biblical languages, chronology and imagery.

The weight of knowledge is immense (and growing). The analytic and interpretative resources at our disposal – carbon dating, X-ray and infrared photography – are formidable. The ordering and restoration of minute textual fragments, at times of a single consonantal cluster or torn verse, have attained virtuosity. The philological-semantic grasp of the archaic Middle Eastern languages and alphabets evolves constantly. Above all, modern theories of religion and of its historical-social matrix allow an unprecedented interaction of psychological and material elements, of the combined study of economics and social institutions, of physical geography and the history of medicine, of political science and poetics. A biblical scholar or textual editor of the time of Erasmus and Luther, let alone of the medieval period, would look with perplexed envy on our means.

Yet the plain fact remains: what we know of the Bible and of the intentions of those who composed it, is fractional. The questions we are able to answer with any assurance are nearly trivial when compared to those we cannot. Fundamental unknowns characterize such crucial areas as chronology, lexical meanings, geography, the cardinal relations between historical factuality and myth, record and fable, the literal and the allegorical. Was there, in fact, an exodus out of Egypt? When did monotheism prevail – if prevail it did – in Israel? Can any historical evidence attach to the persona of Abraham or of Moses? How many levels of authorship are at work in 'Isaiah'? What meanings, what purpose, what informing context can we ascribe to Job or Ecclesiastes, to the Lord Jahve's physical onslaught on Moses, to the genocidal chastisement visited on Israel when its ruler had committed the transgression (to us seemingly venal) of instituting a census? Quite simply: what *is* this assemblage of disparate voices, of texts wholly distinct in register and provenance, of Law (*Torah*), Prophets (*Nebi'im*) and Writings (*Kethubim*)? What is this *Tenakh*, the Hebrew name made up of the initial letters of these sections? What range of implication, of faith and of terror, can we attribute to those human beings, in every time and place since, who profess to hear, to harvest from this book the voice of God?

In the rudimentary introduction which follows, there is scarcely an affirmation, an ascription of textual sense or surrounding circumstance, which does not require a question mark. This is the best known and least known of all human (?) products. It is, perhaps, the strangest. An immense light, but seen as 'through a glass darkly'.

I

How did the words in this Everyman edition of an English translation of the Hebrew Bible come down to us?

Received wisdom and common sense have it that a millennial legacy of oral material must precede the earliest vestiges of any biblical text. Certain tales, myths, parables, pieces of folklore and remembered local history must pre-date any written versions, however ancient. In the case of the Homeric epics, we seem to be dealing with formulaic recitations by more or less professional bards and rhapsodes (such as Plato ironizes in his *Ion*). We know something of guilds of 'Homeric singers', the *Homeridae*, whose oral recitations of the Troy story and of the homecomings of the Greek heroes were gathered into a more or less unified whole, edited and committed to writing at the end of the seventh or during the sixth centuries BC. Our sense of the 'pre-biblical' is much dimmer.

The ancient Mediterranean world was, quite certainly, one of folk-song and court bards, of records of dynastic history, notably in Sumeria and Egypt. The telling of tales, often elaborate, and ambiguous, seems characteristic of the people whom we call 'Jews'. A suggestive Hasidic tradition argues that God made man so that he might tell stories, notably to God Himself. The figure of the minstrel – David singing to unquiet Saul – is known to the Old Testament. But these are shadowy generalities. Several thousand years of decisive orality speak to us, but just out of earshot. Resolute endeavours by scholars and textual commentators to trace either elements of language or actual narratives back to the third millennium fire the imagination. Archaeologists conjecture that some episodes in Genesis could reflect Early Bronze Age features of *c.* 2250–2000 BC. As I have mentioned, the five towns in Genesis 14 have been identified with five sites by the shore of the Dead Sea. But all such proposals remain hypothetical. In the current state of knowledge, the oldest shard of language preserved for us in the Bible would be the so-called Song of Deborah in Judges 5:

Lord, when thou wentest out of Seir, when thou marchedst out of the field of Edom, the earth trembled, and the heavens dropped, the clouds also dropped water.

The mountains melted [where the Hebrew has *flowed*] from before the Lord, even that Sinai from before the Lord God of Israel.

It may be that this jubilation, and the vocabulary and syntax in which it is voiced, do go back to the eleventh or even the twelfth centuries BC.

Bedrock surfaces again in the (to us) rebarbative genealogies which punctuate biblical narratives: the lineages of Abraham, of Noah, the descendants of Shem. Very ancient material probably attaches to episodes of nomination, to stories which account for the naming of human beings and localities, the renaming of Jacob at Peniel in Genesis 32 being both the most representative and overwhelming instance. Genealogy and nomination are of the essence. They knit the kaleidoscopic variousness of Old Testament sources and presentational techniques into a signifying continuity. One way of defining the Torah and the historical books of the Hebrew Bible would be to consider them as a vehement labour of self-identification, as the act of discourse and willed memoration whereby Israel claims a destined legitimacy out of the night of time. Whereby it strives to anchor its nomadic, anonymous past in the place-names of the promised land. Names can picture: Deborah is the bee or hornet; Huldah, the weasel. They can bestow kingship, as when Mattaniah is renamed Zedekiah. When compounded to include the syllable 'El', they declare that 'family-relation' to the Almighty which is the seal of Israel. Even more deeply, genealogies and nominations echo the primal Adamic deed of naming in Eden. They enact an instinctual but also ontological impulse to make language at home in the turbulence and mystery of a world which man has not created and will never wholly master.

But whatever the spoors of truly archaic passages and motions of designation in our texts, these texts themselves enter verifiable history only during the late seventh or sixth centuries BC. It is only at some such date that the notion of scrolls written in Hebrew can be realistically adduced. Fragments of papyrus or parchment have come down to us from the second and third centuries BC. The Dead Sea Scrolls may include older bits. But scholars are in general accord that the actual composition of the Old Testament as we know it does not predate 850 BC and that late inclusions, such as parts of Zechariah or the Book of Daniel, could only have been written in *c.* 168–150 BC. It was during the first nine centuries AD, and under more or less tangible pressure of Christian practices, that Jewish scribes and scholars edited and transmitted the consonantal text of the Hebrew Bible (the ancient texts had, in conformity with the Hebrew language, lacked vowel markers). The Masorah or 'tradition' of vowel signs, accentuation and marginal notes, as Jews of today know it, is the product of this collective medieval recension. It established the Masoretic text (of which thirty-one manuscripts from the late ninth century to *c.* 1100 survive). Today's standard *Biblia Hebraica* is based largely on the so-called St Petersburg codex which can be dated AD 1009. The *Biblia Hebraica Stuttgartensia* of

1977 notes the variants to the canonic version found at Qumran.

With the dispersal of Jewish communities throughout the Hellenistic world, translation into Greek became imperative. Fable has it that, at the behest of Ptolemy II, seventy-two elders of Israel translated the Scriptures into Greek in Alexandria in seventy-two days. And it does seem certain that the Septuagint – the name mirrors the legend – was composed in the third century BC for the Greek-speaking Jewish communities of Egypt. This is the Old Testament on which almost all early Christian retranslation and theological commentary is founded. When the New Testament quotes from the Old, it is almost invariably in the wordings of the Septuagint. Such illustrious manuscripts of the Septuagint as the Vaticanus, the Sinaiticus or the Alexandrinus, allow us to hold in hand, as it were, the literal bridge between Judaism and Christianity.

Origen (*c.* 185–*c.* 254) produced a six-column edition of the Bible (the *Hexapla*) which includes the Hebrew translated by the Septuagint together with a transcription of this Hebrew into Greek characters. A so-called Old Latin version of the third century survives only in fragments. In *c.* 393, Jerome turned directly to the original Hebrew – a theologically and psychologically audacious move. He was a translator of somewhat brutal genius, bringing home to imperial Latin the words 'made captive' by his understanding. Jerome's *Vulgata* replaced the Septuagint in the Christian tradition and *ecclesia*. We possess only a modified manuscript version of Jerome's first Vulgate. Current editions, crucial to Roman Catholicism and its liturgy, look back mainly to the complete Bible as it is set down in the early eighth-century Codex Amiatinus. It is Jerome whom Gutenberg will print in 1456 and whose interpretations Erasmus will amend in his edition of the Greek New Testament in 1516. It is the Vulgate that Ximenes reproduces in his great Complutensian Polyglot Bible of 1522, with its superbly printed parallel texts in Hebrew, Greek and Latin. It is both with and against Jerome that Luther produces his German version of the New Testament in that same year, 1522. With Jerome's readings of Hebrew and their implicit theory of translation, we stand, in a sense, at the doors to modernity.

The love affair between the English language and Holy Writ dates back to the late seventh century. When, according to Bede, Caedmon 'the cowherd' retold biblical stories in Anglo-Saxon alliterative verse: 'He sang of the world's creation, the origin of the human race, and all the story of Genesis; he sang of Israel's Exodus from Egypt and entry into the promised land . . . ' It is thought that the Venerable Bede himself (he died in 735) rendered the Fourth Gospel into Anglo-Saxon. Tradition has it that Alfred the Great composed a translation of the Decalogue and of other passages from Exodus 21–3. The ornate Lindisfarne Gospels, written in Northumbrian dialect in *c.* 950, are interlinear glosses inscribed on a Latin manuscript of the seventh century. We find in the tenth-century Wessex Gospels the oldest extant rendering into Old English. A prose translation by Abbot Aelfric follows in *c.* 1020.

It is the struggle for reformation, the resolve to make the divine word accessible 'according to its simplicity' which generates the seminal interaction between the English tongue and Scripture. The first complete translation of the Bible into English appears in 1382. It is ascribed to John Wycliffe and a group of collaborators, Nicholas of Hereford and John Purvey foremost among them. Wycliffe and his colleagues follow the Vulgate almost word for word. In what is known as the Early Version of Wycliffe, the inception of Psalm 23 reads: 'the lord governeth me, and no thing to me shall lack; in the place of leswe [pasture] where he me full set. Over waters of fulfilling he nursed me; my soul he converted.' Scholars point to the indebtedness of such a passage to the earlier fourteenth-century Psalter of Richard Rolle. But the 'waters of fulfilling' were now rising. Before it was condemned and burned, in 1415, the Wycliffe Bible had made its way (107 manuscript copies have come down to us). Although strenuously faithful to the Latin of Jerome, the second or Late Version of Wycliffe exhibits a crucial movement towards the idiomatic, towards the native sinew of English.

This movement unfolds, matchlessly, in the genius of William Tyndale. His rejoinder to an orthodox cleric and proponent of Canon Law remains famous: 'If God spare my life, ere many yeares,

I wyl cause a boye that dryveth the plough shall know more of the scripture than thou doest!' The history of the composition of this sovereign version is complex, because it is that of persecution, exile, clandestinity and, finally, martyrdom (Tyndale was strangled and burned at the stake on 6 October 1536). Founded on the original Hebrew, on the Septuagint, on the *Vulgata* and Luther for the Old Testament, on the original Greek for the New, Tyndale's translations appeared between 1526 and 1535. Printed in Cologne, the 1526 New Testament, followed by revised versions in 1534 and 1535, was smuggled into England. So effective was episcopal suppression and burning, that only two copies now survive out of a printing of *circa* eighteen thousand. It was in Antwerp that Tyndale laboured on the Hebrew Bible. The Pentateuch was issued in 1530, Jonah the year following. Thus the Tyndale Old Testament remained incomplete.

Persuaded that 'the Greek tongue agreeth more with the English than with the Latin. And the properties of the Hebrew tongue agreeth a thousand times more with the English than with the Latin', Tyndale forged an idiom consonant with the glory of God. Beyond Shakespeare, it is William Tyndale who is begetter of the English language as we know it. The nerve and pith of his biblical renditions have become proverbial in both senses of that word. They inwove the Books of Moses and New Testament with the roots of English so that text and idiom have become inseparable. It is Tyndale's cadences, sonorities, amplitudes and concisions (he is a master of both) which, via his commanding effect on the Authorized Version, characterize global English as it is spoken and written today. No translation-act, save Luther's, has been as generative of a whole language:

Though some of the branches be broken off, and thou being a wild olive tree, are graft in among them, and made partaker of the root and fatness of the olive tree, boast not thyself against the branches. For if thou boast thyself, remember that thou bearest not the root, but the root beareth thee. Thou wilt say then: because of unbelief they are broken off, and thou standest steadfast in faith. Be not high-minded, but fear seeing that God spared not the natural branches, lest haply he also spare not thee.

Or this:

> And he said unto them, be not afraid: ye seek Jesus of Nazareth which was crucified. He is risen, but he is not here. Behold the place where they put him. But go your way, and tell the disciples, and namely Peter: he will go before you into Galilee: there shall ye see him, as he said unto you. And they went out quickly and fled from the sepulchre. For they trembled and were amazed. Neither said they any thing to any man, for they were afraid.

'Let there be light, and there was light'; 'Ask, and it shall be given you; seek, and ye shall find; knock and it shall be opened unto you'; 'the salt of the earth'; 'The powers that be'; 'filthy lucre'. All Tyndale's. Luke 2, Colossians, Revelation 21 in the Authorized Version are Tyndale almost to the word. It is his name that passes under silence. But English bears its immemorial stamp.

The first complete English Bible, dedicated to Henry VIII, was that edited and published (still on the Continent) by Miles Coverdale. Portions from Tyndale were used for the OT, and the NT is simply Tyndale revised. Two years after Coverdale, in 1537, appeared the first authorized English version, edited by John Rogers, an associate of Tyndale. The Torah and New Testament are Tyndale's. Rogers, moreover, made extensive use of the unpublished Tyndale manuscripts for the books from Joshua through 2 Chronicles. In 1539, a revision of this so-called 'Matthew Bible' was printed in England. In this same year, in Paris, Coverdale published what is known, due to its format, as the 'Great Bible'. Its text is an amendment of the 'Matthew Bible' and thus essentially founded on Tyndale. The brief reign of Queen Mary stopped all printing and publication of English-language Bibles in the realm. Once more, only Continental presses could serve. William Whittingham's 'Geneva Bible', in small octavo size, and therefore relatively easy to smuggle into England, was published in 1557–60. It was the first to include verse numbers. The 'Geneva Bible' reached some 150 editions. It is that of Shakespeare, of Cromwell, of Bunyan and the Puritans of New England. Piety and erudition were in joint harness: 'Yet lest either the simple should be discouraged, or the malicious have any occasion of just cavillation, seeing some translations read after one sort and some after another, whereas all may serve to good purpose and edification, we have in the margin noted the diversity of speech or reading which may also seem agreeable to the mind of the Holy Ghost and proper for our language.' The Roman Catholic riposte was that of the 'Rheims–Douai Bible', published between 1582 and 1610. Much influenced by Augustine's interpretations, this translation aims to 'discover the corruptions' insinuated into the English Bibles by heretical translators. A revision of the 'Great Bible', purged of unacceptable Protestant glosses, was placed in all cathedrals. Twenty editions were issued before 1606. But the 'Geneva Bible' continued to be that of the common reader. It is precisely the rivalry between these two Bibles which sets the stage for the 'King James Version'.

Scholarship has elucidated a good many aspects of the origins and production of this most famous and formative monument in our language. There is all but unanimous consensus about its prodigal magnificence. Yet, surprisingly enough, much remains unclear as to the actual processes of translation, interpretative options and, above all, as to the tactics of unison in the final text.

Proposals for a new translation of Holy Scripture were put forward at a conference of theologians and divines at Hampton Court in January of 1604. Fifty-four scholars and churchmen were divided into six panels: three for the Old Testament, two for the New and one for the Apocrypha. They began work in 1606 and convened more or less regularly at Westminster Abbey, Oxford and Cambridge. The 'Bishops' Bible', which is to say the amended 'Great Bible', was to be followed wherever fidelity to the original would permit. But the translators were further authorized to consult the Tyndale, Coverdale, 'Great Bible' and Geneva precedents.

Some 'work in progress' has survived. There is, in the Bodleian, a copy of the 1602 edition of the 'Bishops' Bible' with annotations by the new translators. One of the Westminster panels prepared a manuscript meant to solicit further scholarly revisions. One of the translators, John Bois, has left notes at once fascinating and difficult to interpret. They allow a look at some of the opinions of particular scholar-divines and of the discussions to which they gave rise in their final revisions of the Pauline Epistles and Revelation. A close analysis of the Greek text underlies a word-for-word rendition. This, in turn, is set beside a more English, colloquial rendering. Synonyms are listed and alternative translations compared. The dominant impulse is that towards establishing the verity of the word of God. It is He alone who is the author; the 'enditer' is the Holy Spirit. But it is just this certainty which allows, indeed compels the Jacobean translators to examine critically earlier versions, including the Septuagint. Being wrought by infirm and mortal hands, these call for improvement. 'For is the kingdom of God become words or syllables? why should we be in bondage to them, if we may be free? use one precisely when we may use another no less fit as commodiously?'

But despite this programmatic preface and the surviving documents, we know little of the textual criticism and debates that led to the choices made in the Authorized Version as it appeared in 1611. Principally we can only conjecture as to the 'commonwealth' of sensibility, of shared presumption in respect of the Hebrew, Greek and Latin originals that underwrote the tonal coherence, the harmonic interplay of this vast enterprise. One is tempted to image a master-redactor, a mind of eminent scholarship and stylistic powers putting together, 'key-noting' the final version so as to attenuate what *must* have been differences of register between collaborators and panels. There are those who point to Francis Bacon as arbiter and unifier. But there is, so far, no evidence to prove this.

At the turn of the seventeenth century, English stood at high noon. Wherever we meet with it, in political and diplomatic papers, in theology, in the writing of history, in every branch of literature, the language deploys a strength of acquisition – new words taken from European tongues and the new worlds of discovery – a variousness of lexical and grammatical organization, a music of meanings unequalled since. This is the instrument of Spenser, of Shakespeare, of Bacon, of Donne and the young Milton. It encompasses the organ-blasts of the Queen's rhetoric, Sidney's intimacies of desire, the 'lapidary lightness' of Ben Jonson and the compaction of the early Metaphysical poets. It can command, seduce, enchant and think aloud as never before or after. Its two organic components, the Anglo-Saxon and the Latin, are set in contrast or fusion. Sublimity and the colloquial, even the argotic, work to shared purposes of articulate thrust. Chapman's Homer, Golding's Ovid, Florio's Montaigne, North's Plutarch, Urquhart's Rabelais testify to a sovereign spell of metamorphic translations, of 'ingestions' into English (the term is Ben Jonson's) which make of the Greek, Latin, Italian or French original a seminal presence in the national trove. There could not have been a moment, a climate of feeling and general discourse more apt to engender the two foremost constructs in the language: Shakespeare and the Authorized Version.

Solemnities incomparable: 'and darkness was upon the face of the deep' (Genesis 1:2); 'Hast thou entered into the springs of the sea? or hast thou walked in the search of the depth?' (Job 38:16); 'Lift up your heads, O ye gates; and be ye lift up, ye everlasting doors; and the King of glory shall come in' (Psalm 24:7); 'And it shall come to pass, that he who fleeth from the noise of the fear shall fall into the pit; and he that cometh up out of the midst of the pit shall be taken in the snare: for the windows from on high are open, and the foundations of the earth do shake' (Isaiah 24:18); 'And the likeness of the firmament upon the heads of the living creature was as the colour of the terrible crystal, stretched forth over their heads above' (Ezekiel 1:22); 'For wheresoever the carcase is, there will the eagles be gathered together' (St Matthew 24:28); 'Heaven is my throne, and earth is my footstool: what house will ye build me? saith the Lord: or what is the place of my rest?' (The Acts 7:49); 'For I am persuaded that neither death, nor life, nor angels, nor principalities, nor powers, nor things present, nor things to come, nor height, nor depth, nor any other creature, shall be able to separate us from the love of God, which is in Christ Jesus our Lord' (Romans 8:38–9); 'And the angel thrust in his sickle into the earth, and gathered the vine of the earth, and cast it into the great winepress of the wrath of God. And the winepress was trodden without the city, and blood came out of the winepress, even unto the horse bridles, by the space of a thousand and six hundred furlongs' (Revelation 14:19–20).

Observe the exact touches of mensuration: that horse's bridle and those furlongs. If this 'King James Bible' overwhelms by its grandeur, by its evocations of majestic immensity, it is no less inspired in its renditions of the minute particular, of the intimate and small-scale. 'And behold, he formed grasshoppers in the beginning of the shooting up of the latter growth' (Amos 7:1); 'and the grasshopper shall be a burden' (Ecclesiastes 12:5); 'Yet a little sleep, a little slumber, a little folding of the hands to sleep' (Proverbs 6:10); or that epithet, one of the most haunting in world literature, 'And Agag came unto him delicately' in 1 Samuel 15:32. There is no finer erotic poetry than that in the Old Testament. 'I have perfumed my bed with myrrh, aloes, and cinnamon. Come, let us take our fill of love until the morning: let us solace ourselves with loves' (Proverbs 7:17–18). Famously in the Song of Solomon: 'Thy lips, O my spouse, drop as the honeycomb: honey and milk are under thy tongue; and the smell of thy garments is like the smell of Lebanon. A garden inclosed is my sister, my spouse; a spring shut up, a fountain sealed' (4:11–12); 'Thy navel is like a round goblet, which wanteth not liquor: thy belly is like an heap of wheat set about with lilies. Thy two breasts are like two young roes that are twins' (7:2–3). Observe the mysteriously suggestive detail in Amos 6:4: God threatens to vent his fury on those uncaring rich who 'eat the calves out of the midst of the stall'. Or that single forgotten sheaf which, at the harvest, must not be retrieved but left 'for the stranger, for the fatherless, and for the widow' (Deuteronomy 24:19). Throughout the 'legislative' parts of the Books of Moses, but also in the fiery deeps of prophecy, God inhabits the detail.

It is almost fatuous to cite the genius for narrative of these texts, their arts of story-telling (which will, together with Homer, beget our literatures). In terror of futurity, Saul has had the soothsayers, the wizards, the magi with their 'familiar spirits' massacred. But now black fears possess him. Disguised, accompanied by only two men, he comes at night upon the witch at Endor. She fears a deadly trap: 'wherefore then layest thou a snare for my life, to cause me to die?' When her caller bids her summon the ghost of Samuel, she cries out: 'Why hast though deceived me? For thou art Saul.' Samuel's prophecy is one of inescapable doom. Saul collapses on the ground 'for he had eaten no bread all the day, nor all the night' (one of those masterly touches of plain-spoken realism, of naturalism at the persuasive core of the supernatural). Now it is the dark woman of Endor who takes compassion on her ominous guest. She kills her calf, bakes unleavened bread and bids Saul and his companions eat thereof. And 'they did eat. Then they rose up, and went away that night.' The whole story takes up only eighteen verses in 1 Samuel 28. Yet the finesse and wealth of psychological nuances – the woman's fear, her recognition of the king, the unforgiving bitterness of Samuel's reply, Saul's physical and mental exhaustion – are on a level with a comparable episode in *Macbeth*. The biblical economy challenges and, it may be, surpasses the prodigality of Shakespeare. Commentary remains numb before the technical authority, the narrative stroke of the final phrase: the departure into that same night of men hastening towards a murderous dawn.

The Elizabethan-Jacobean period was adherent to traditional faith in prognostication, prophecy, soothsaying of every kind. Astrology and necromantic practices abounded in both everyday life and matters of state. At the same time, 'the new philosophy' of the mathematical and natural sciences put 'all in doubt'. Sensibility hovered, as it were, between Nostradamus and Galileo. It may be this apprehensive ambivalence which endows the Authorized Version's enactment of the prophetic books of the Hebrew Bible with their towering immediacy. Menace reaches an inhuman pitch in Jeremiah 19–21:

And I will make this city desolate, and an hissing; every one that passeth thereby shall be astonished and hiss because of all the plagues thereof. And I will cause them to eat the flesh of their sons and the flesh of their daughters, and they shall eat every one the flesh of his friend in the siege and straitness, wherewith their enemies, and they that seek their lives, shall straiten them . . . Cursed be the man who brought tidings to my father, saying, A man child is born unto thee; making him very glad. And let that man be as the cities which the Lord overthrew, and repented not; and let him hear the cry in the morning, and the shouting at noontide; Because he slew me not from the womb; or that my mother might have been my grave, and her womb to be always great with me. Wherefore came I forth out of the womb to see labour and sorrow, that my days should be consumed with shame?

The facts of Auschwitz and of Rwanda are there.

But if the gamut of imprecation, of annihilating anathema, is characteristic of the Prophets, if their prevision hammers us into dust, the radiance of promise is no less valid. It counterpoints the grimness of Amos:

> Behold, the days come, saith the Lord, that the plowman shall overtake the reaper, and the treader of grapes him that soweth seed; and the mountains shall drop sweet wine, and all the hills shall melt.
>
> And I will bring again the captivity of my people of Israel, and they shall build the waste cities, and inhabit them; and they shall plant vineyards, and drink the wine thereof; they shall also make gardens, and eat the fruit of them.
>
> And I will plant them upon their land, and they shall no more be pulled up out of their land which I have given them, saith the Lord thy God.
>
> (Amos 9:13–15)

Nor is the message only one of messianic Zionism. It is from the Prophets that the western imagination has drunk the hope that there is hope: that the lion shall lie down with the lamb, that swords shall be beaten into ploughshares. The 'King James' vibrates to that hope.

The reception of the 1611 Bible was muted. Other versions, notably the 'Geneva', continued in the field. Only gradually, and with the multiplication of editions – already that of 1614 contains some four hundred amendments – did the Authorized Version establish its dominance. Taken to the corners of the earth by English-speaking colonizers and missionaries, made available in innumerable formats and more and more inexpensively, it had become, by the time of a comprehensive revision in 1769, the text of texts. To be read at home and in church, to be memorized, to be quoted in every conceivable context of private and public life, to be sung (via the Psalms), to be translated, in its turn, into the tongues of Baffin Island and the Kalahari.

Numerous alternative versions followed. Among them: Moffatt's *New Testament* of 1913, Goodspeed's *Complete Bible: an American Translation* in 1938, Phillips's influential *Modern English New*

Testament, 1958–1972, the interdenominational and collective *New English Bible* of 1970 and the *New American Standard Bible* a year later. Roman Catholicism contributed Ronald Knox's translation from the Vulgate in 1955 and a *New Jerusalem Bible* thirty years thereafter. But it is fair to say that none of these endeavours has displaced the AV from its centrality in the English languages and in the multitudinous societies in which, today, planetary Anglo-American is spoken. Indeed, cultural historians incline to see a close correlation between England's current loss of confidence and the relative decline from general awareness of the 'King James' and the Book of Common Prayer directly knit to it. The words now before you in this edition are the very tongue 'that England spake' or speaks when it was, when it is, most itself.

2

What then of the language, of the texts which this resplendent Jacobean tongue purports to convey to us?

Hebrew belongs to the Canaanite branch of the North-West Semitic family of languages. It is written from right to left and consisted, originally, of twenty-two letters indicating only consonants. The designation of vowels by the addition of points to these consonants came very much later. It evolved only gradually between the fifth and tenth centuries AD. Current conventions of vocalization therefore represent modes of pronunciation which date to roughly a thousand years after the end of the biblical age. Outside the Bible itself, ancient classical Hebrew survives in a number of inscriptions, none of which predates the tenth century BC. The consonantal foundation of all Hebrew writing – numerous words grow out of a radical of three consonants – is crucial. It allows, indeed makes unavoidable, a polysemic plurality and richness of possible readings probably unmatched by any other written tongue. The same consonantal cluster can, with different vocalizations, be interpreted in wholly different senses. The omission of vowel markers generates an inherent manifold of putative meanings, of implicit puns and word-play within the identical consonantal unit. A biblical word pulses, so to speak, within an aura of concentric significations and echoes.

Hebrew possesses only two 'tenses' of the verb (where 'tenses' is itself a misleading designation). Actions are either finished ('perfect') or unfinished ('imperfect'). Simple, passive, reflexive, intensive and causative modes are rendered by different forms of the verb. Again, this syntactical particularity entails major hermeneutic consequences. The 'time-world', the notations of temporality in Old Testament narrative, do not translate readily into the past-present-future paradigm of English or other modern European languages. This simple fact makes nearly inaccessible the inward dynamics of Hebrew prophecy and remembrance. Prophecy does not bear in any obvious sense on futurity, as it does, say, in Greek oracles or Christian-Hellenic prediction. The timeliness of God's utterance via His prophets is timeless. In one sense, the foretold has already been accomplished, as it is made 'perfect' in the divine dictum. In another, it is eternally present. It is the 'now' which blazes with God's wrath or benediction. In a third and quite untranslatable sense, the prophecy touches also on the 'imperfect', on the as yet unaccomplished and therefore revocable (Jonah turns on the grammatological paradox of an 'imperfection' housed, as it were, in the eternal absolute of God's initial resolve and pronouncement).

There are, to be sure, linguistic affinities between ancient Hebrew and such neighbouring tongues as Phoenician and, certainly, Ugaritic. Elements of Ugaritic, Canaanite and Aramaic can be made out in the biblical texts. Every tongue spoken by men and women has its singularity. None the less, it is fair to say that the traditional concept of biblical Hebrew as the Adamic tongue, as first among human languages, as marked uniquely by the semantics of God's usage, does reflect, albeit in mythical-anthropomorphic guise, an understandable intuition of 'apartness'. The Hebrew of the Old Testament is like no other verbal-grammatical-semantic construct of which we have direct knowledge. The Law at its heart is, in many respects, a 'law unto itself'. To a degree demonstrably greater, more damaging, than that of any other corpus of language, including the most remote and difficult poetry or philosophy, translations from biblical Hebrew are misreadings. Even in the hands of listeners and wordsmiths of genius such as Tyndale or Luther.

This can be shown almost at random. I am no Hebraist; the examples I will cite are among the more familiar.

Davar can signify 'thing', 'fact', 'object', 'event', as well as the speech-acts of 'saying', 'commandment' and 'revelation'. The word appears for the first time in Genesis 11:1 (where it is often translated, with entirely misleading connotations, by *logos* or *verbum*). This first appearance led Midrashic commentators to suppose that the initial ten chapters of Genesis transpire in some pre-discursive context. Speech goes unfulfilled, as in the 'monologues' of Adam and Eve. *Vayyomer qayin el hevel ahiv*: 'Cain said to his brother Abel.' But we are *not* told what he said. Noah has no dialogue with God. *Davar*, in its full speech-sense, evolves around and is aborted at Babel. Henceforth mankind chatters in a host of 'closed', mutually incomprehensible tongues: *devarim*. More generally, the synthesis between word and act – pronouncement is quintessentially enactment – underlies much of Old Testament theology before achieving its Hellenistic-mystical mode in the Fourth Gospel.

Take the term *toldot*. It designates the constellation of particular semantic values which attach to the OT conception and representation of history. Etymologically, *toldot* points to 'generation', 'begetting' and 'sallying forth'. One of the few gentile readers to have captured the pertinent connotations is the great German medieval mystic, Meister Eckhart. He tells of the 'launching into *exodus*', of the 'begetting into destined motion' of the history of Israel. In that *toldot*, Abraham goes 'before God' (Genesis 17:1) as if Israel in some mystery of anticipation preceded God, clearing His way into the chronicles of man.

The consonant *beth* in *bereshit* – the opening word of Genesis, the word that begins all beginning – also means 'house' when it is vocalized. Creation builds a house for man. And how is translation to cope with the episode of Babel? *Migdal* is not, primarily, a 'tower'. It is a 'great' or 'exceeding' object with 'its head in the heavens'. Most likely, the original inference is that of a giant idol.

The edge of blasphemy throughout the narrative, moreover, turns on the synonymy between the verb 'to make', used for the building of the Tower, and the term of 'divine creation'. The puns are the crux, and untranslatable: the Hebrew root *balal* signifies 'to mix', 'to confound', 'to disperse'. But it can also be read as another echo of 'Babel': as *nebelah*, meaning destruction! And of the great translators of 'Babel', only Luther sees that *safah* is not only 'language' or 'speech', but the actual tongue (*einerlei Zunge und Sprache*).

Let us look, for a moment, at one of the most charged episodes in the Pentateuch, Exodus 32–4, as it is then taken up more concisely in Numbers 14–15. The dialogue between God and Moses attains a truly uncanny pitch of pathos and ruse. The Lord has vowed to destroy his sinful, recalcitrant people. Moses prays to Him so long and insistently that God seems to grow weary. Speaking 'face to face, as a man speaketh unto his friend', Moses resorts to advocative moves of sophistic brilliance: how can God wipe out the seed of Abraham after the promises made? How can He comfort the heathen who will now regard His creation, His election of Israel as an error? Yet God cannot, as He ripostes, cancel His stated resolve. Moses prays and prays: *wajechal*. But this very same verb can also be read as meaning 'to release from'. Moses releases God from His vow of chastisement! *Wajechal*. Now God says *hechaitani bidevarim*: and again, the density of connotations and possible denotations mocks translation. 'Through words you have animated (?) and "revitalized" (?) me.' In Exodus 32:14, on the other hand, the AV gets it absolutely, which is to say scandalously, right: 'And the Lord repented of the evil which he thought to do unto his people.' A penitent God! Which means that the door to dialogue, to persuasion remains open even when, as in Kafka's parable on the Law, we are unable to perceive that this is so.

In the 'King James', Job's lament cursing the day of his birth runs to twenty-two words. Eight words suffice in the Hebrew text. The English misses the cardinal word-play on the Hebrew roots for 'let it perish' and 'I was born', or the cruel parody of Psalm 8 whereby God as benevolent 'watcher over man' now becomes the indifferent voyeur or 'man-watcher'. Rabbinic commentators insinuated their own play on words in order to gentle the unendurable narration. They could not bear *lo achayel*: 'I have no hope.' *Lo*, spelt *lamed aleph*, is corrected to *lo*, spelt *lamed vav*: 'I will trust in him.' Job's rebellious appeal pivots on *sahed*. This term can define a 'witness', an 'advocate', a 'guarantor', a 'spokesman for'. It reaches far back into Hebrew legal praxis. And when Job invokes his *goel*, he pictures for us the 'vindicator' in a blood-feud. God will come to be known as *goel Ysrael*, the 'avenger of/for Israel'. How distant is all this from the Christianized neon: 'I know that my redeemer liveth.' *Shadday* is 'the God not-there', the *deus absconditus* as he will be recognized by the principal Old Testament thinkers in Christianity: Pascal, Kierkegaard and Karl Barth. In the Hebrew, the outcome of a quarrel, of the act of attainder is again 'linguistic'. It is made articulate by the gamut of values in *saddiq*, 'the just man', 'he that testifies justly', and *rasa*, 'the culpable', the 'transgressor', 'the guilty party' (i.e. God). It is the silence of the Comforters which affirms the verdict.

As in no other exegetic tradition, the Judaic perception of the Bible, via recitation, explication and commentary, via Talmud and Midrash, presses not only on the sentence or single word. It excavates the syllable, the consonantal root and the individual letter. The Hebrew alphabet, set down, according to kabbala, in characters of white fire on a dark surface, has been held to contain within itself the most hidden name of the name of God as well as human destiny to the end of time. A dread parable has it that the erroneous transcription, under the Lord's dictation, of a single consonant opened the rift in the universe through which all evil, suffering and injustice has made its way. If it contains any erratum, a Torah scroll must be destroyed. It is Neo-Platonized Christianity which discriminates between the 'word' and the 'spirit', which exalts the latter and accords it a certain detachment from any actual text. Biblical Judaism knows no such separation. The word *is* the spirit. The letter *is* the meaning (every *aleph* has in it something of the breath of God). As Proverbs 18:21 proclaims: 'Death and life are in the power of the tongue.'

But the misprision is global. The notion of an 'Old Testament' is purely Christian. It does not exist for Jews. In the Hebrew Bible, sacredness attaches to the Torah or Books of Moses. The rest of the canon evolved more or less contingently and was arrived at, in an order of books different from that in the Christian Bible, only after AD 100 (the references to a Council at Jamnia determining the Jewish canon are most probably mythical). The *Biblia Hebraica* stands as it is. The New Testament exists in close dependence on it. But this is in no way a Jewish concern.

It is Pauline and Johannine Christianity which labour to make of Hebrew scriptures prefigurations of the coming and kerygma of Jesus. The crucial motifs and thematic structures in the Hebrew Bible are interpreted as annunciations and previsions of the Gospels and Acts. The fatal tree of Adam and Eve will reappear as the wood of the Cross. When Israel crosses Jordan, this move foreshadows the baptism of the Nazarene. Jonah's sojourn in the belly of the whale is a 'trailer' for that of Jesus in the tomb. The Suffering Servant in Isaiah is an inspired intuition of the humiliation and martyrdom of Christ. Point to point, detail to detail, Christian doctrine and exegetics strove to anchor the New Testament in the anticipatory authority of the Old. This concatenation was absolutely vital if Christianity was to present itself as the divinely purposed, clearly proclaimed fulfilment of God's will, of the mission of His son out of Bethlehem and the house of David. (The Koran is far more scrupulous in its invocations of Abraham and of Moses.)

That inspired second-century heretic, Marcion, saw the paradoxical untruths in the whole appropriation of the Hebrew material to Christian beliefs. How could, he asked, the vengeful, often unforgiving Jehovah of the Pentateuch and the Prophets be identified with the Father, with the deity of boundless love and compassion in Christianity? How could the basic mystery of the Trinity, of the man-god Christ, be reconciled with Judaic monotheism? The Marcionite case called for a total rejection by Christians of the Hebrew Bible. With Jesus of Nazareth history and the condition of the human soul had begun anew. The old dispensation could now be seen to have satanic traits. The Church of Rome suppressed the

Marcionite heresy. But its sharp questions stand, and we can only speculate as to how different western history would have been if Christianity had broken loose from what it claimed to be its Jewish validation and the wicked failure of the Jews to accept its preordained message. Out of this claim and ambiguous 'elective affinity' grew interminable suffering and the 'counter-Golgotha' of the Holocaust.

The immediate point, however, is that of translation. Even where linguistic erudition and honesty abound, the 'King James' translators and redactors are, consciously or not, following the presumption of prefiguration. They view the Old Testament as integral to the New. They inflect the Hebrew and the Greek towards a 'meaning in the future'. The consequences can be utterly misleading as in that most famous instance of a 'virgin' bearing a messianic child where the Hebrew word simply means 'a young woman'! Thus it has become almost impossible for the general reader of the Authorized Version (or, for that matter, of any Christian 'Old and New Testament') to grasp the nature of the original text. To see the *Biblia Hebraica* in its overwhelming autonomy and strangeness. To hear in it not the prelude to the promise of salvation in and via the Son of God – a concept incomprehensible to Judaism – but the often opaque promise of a messianic eschatology neither 'gentile nor Greek'. So much in this misnomered Old Testament is as different from the uses to which Christian culture and translations have put it as is the desert of Judaea from the baroque squares of Rome or the spires of Canterbury. Let us, for a moment, read by the blinding, silent light of that desert.

3

In our western alphabets of recognition, in our grammars of time, Genesis is the beginning of beginnings. We know of its analogies with other Middle Eastern creation myths, some of which may well be older. But it is the first book of the Hebrew Bible which has, very largely, determined the religious, metaphysical, moral and literary-artistic coming into being of the west. This fact is, in some sense, paradoxical. There is hardly a more hybrid and, at key points, enigmatic text. Modern scholarship – which actually dates back to Spinoza's questions as to how Moses could have composed an account of his own death – has deconstructed Genesis and the books following into four or five levels of authorship. These comprise a redactor 'J' who uses the name 'Jehovah', who inclines to an anthropomorphic monotheism, who draws richly on etymologies and place-names. 'E' refers to God as 'Elohim' and seems to favour 'Jacob' over 'Israel' when writing of the Patriarch. Scholars consider both 'J' and 'E' to be the most ancient of the several 'authors' of the Pentateuch. The so-called 'Deuteronomist' or 'D' is generally dated as between c. 722 and 621 BC. He revises archaic material so as to eliminate anthropomorphic representations of God. He would scour the ancient texts of their polytheistic and henotheistic spoors (this is to say of the references to competing deities or to deities inferior only in one or another quality to the God of Israel). 'D' appears to have purged thoroughly: none the less, distinct traces of a hybrid pantheon survive, notably in certain Psalms. The 'Priestly Redactor' or 'P' probably operates during the crucial time of historical-legal revision after the Babylonian Exile of 586–536. 'D' had emphasized the absolute centrality to Judaism of the Temple in Jerusalem and of the rites of purification that attach to it. In a city which must, as it were, be reconsecrated, 'P' is a scrupulous constitutionalist and searcher after precedent. He seeks to assemble and make coherent the history, the legitimacy of the reborn community and of its inherited, partially opaque ritual practices. What is rare in Judaism, 'P' is something of a theologian. It is he, one believes, who finds specific terms for the transcendent theophanic and theological attributes of the act of divine creation. The opening strata of Genesis, as we now know them, may be his handiwork. More recently, some exegetes have added a fifth authorship, that of 'H'.

The results of this complex stratigraphy, expounded by German 'Higher Criticism' of the nineteenth century, are visible. The identical narrative material appears two or three times over. There are manifest contradictions: Exodus 24, for instance, states both that Moses alone will be granted access to God and that all the leaders of the people are invited into the divine presence. Genesis 2:4 initiates an alternative account of the process of creation in which formulaic phrases, recurrent throughout the first telling, are wholly absent. The story of Joseph, the appearance of Melchizedek signal abrupt changes of language and style. An obvious extraneous recital of the sins of Judah breaks the continuity of the Joseph saga. Genesis 5 is one of numerous chapters in which different layers are imperfectly conjoined. At certain 'symptomatic' junctures, we can make out phrases which are fairly certainly a later gloss and attempt at 'inserted' explanation (e.g. 'the same is Hebron' in Genesis 23:2).

But it is not these duplications, contradictions, breaks or super-positions which render the Torah, and Genesis in particular, so inexhaustibly perplexing. It is the theological and ethical issues raised, and raised at a depth and imaginative density never surpassed. It is, one conjectures, precisely this insoluble pressure of questioning which ensured the survival and transmission of these '*Ur*-stories' from the late third millennium (?) to their initial redaction in the united kingdom of David and of Solomon. These narrative summons and provocations have never relinquished their grip on the human mind and conscience.

No amount or ingenuity of textual criticism can answer satisfac-torily the question of God's preference of Abel over Cain, of His lack of 'respect' (the troubling AV rendering) for Cain's offering to Him of the fruit of the ground – surely a gentler, less destructive sacrifice than Abel's 'firstlings of the flock'! What possible abyss of motiveless preference, of the injustice of divine love, generates that first act of homicide and of fratricide in which all of the dark of future history is figured? Interpreters, allegorists, religious-moral exegetes, have pondered the Tower of Babel. As so often, the concision of the biblical account is inversely proportional to the teeming prodigality of secondary opinions. What, precisely, is the nature of the transgression embodied in the edification of the Tower? In what ways does monolingualism comport some offence or threat to Jahve (common sense suggests the very opposite)? And why should the polyglot condition, to which human historical and intellectual experience owes its creative wealth, be regarded as chastisement? What ambiguities or mysteries in God's intent towards mankind underlie the scandalous fate of Esau and the fruitful, almost Odysseus-like cunning and knaveries of Jacob? As to Genesis 22, how is moral understanding, on a human scale, be it that of Maimonides, of Kant or of Kierkegaard, formidably penetrating as these are, to cope with the *Aquedah*, the story of the sacrifice of Isaac? None but an evil demon can ask of a father to sacrifice his only son (so Kant); solely the true, omnipotent God can ask of a father to sacrifice his only son (replies Kierkegaard). How could Abraham 'forgive' God for the unspeakable suffering inflicted upon him during the three days of the journey to Mount Moriah? How could Isaac endure his father after the aborted offering? Since the Holocaust, Jewish thought has more than ever before circled around this one chapter in Genesis as around an unendurable but ardent emptiness.

Exodus empowers Israel. The tortuous 'long march' of an enslaved people towards a promised land of freedom and national identity has provided western history and political doctrines with their archetype. The journey out of Egypt, through the desert and into a land of 'milk and honey' yet to be mastered, is as paradigmatic to the Pilgrim Fathers on their way to the New World as it is to the Marxist programme of proletarian emancipation; it is as central to the dreams and idiom of the black slave as it is to that of utopian politics from the time of the medieval millennarians to that of Zionism. Where it knows hope, our history is still on that arduous traverse to Canaan. Moses, moreover, incarnates Judaism at its summit (as Freud, somewhat jealously, noted). His genius for enraged vision, his direct dialogues with God, the mutinies which he must endure from his own people, the momentary trangressions which forbid his entry into the promised land, crystallize the whole historical, psychological and moral condition of the Jew to this day. It is in the life of Moses that Judaism finds its reproachful mirror and the far light of an overwhelming finality. It is in Moses that the dizzying paradox of God's choice of this people, of this people alone, for His especial and terrifying attention, takes on its dialectic of proud suffering.

[66]

The historical evidence, if any, remains very nearly impalpable. Nothing reliable is known of the ethnic origins of the people who were to emerge as 'Israelites'. Their appearance in the Negev, in Transjordan or in the central hills of Judaea seems to have occurred in the late thirteenth and early twelfth centuries BC. The Egyptian monarch involved in their emigration from Egypt may or may not have been Rameses II. The route narrated in the Books of Moses is altogether implausible. Scholars disagree sharply over the possible location of Mount Sinai. Some would deny the 'Exodus' any historical status. This, in turn, is implausible. The core of remembrance at the heart of the narrative is, as it were, 'radioactive' with an inextinguishable energy. It pulses to the touch. As does the persona of Moses, human more than human, psychologically complex, eloquent in its stuttering tongue, such as no tellers of tales or subsequent redactors could have completely invented. It took a Michelangelo to come anywhere near a credible imaging.

What bewilders the modern reader of Exodus, Leviticus, Numbers and Deuteronomy is the disparity of material. The cauldron bubbles with myth, legend, folk-tales, remote wisps of historical recall and a veritable mass of ritual and legislative prescriptions. The Torah contains some of the most primitive, anthropomorphic episodes in any sacred literature. That, for example, of Jahve's murderous assault on Moses in Exodus 4:24–6 (queasy scholarship intimates some obscure lineaments of the origins of circumcision), or that, impenetrable in its archaic resonance, of God's permission to Moses to see what the 'King James' translators render as His 'back parts' in Exodus 33:21–3. Some of the decisive, boundlessly consequential narratives in world literature – the crossing of the Red Sea, the worship of the Golden Calf, the contravening of Balaam's will and mission – alternate with chapters that are grimly 'pedestrian' (that endless march through stone and sand). Even more unsettling are the juxtapositions of archaic savagery, such as the retribution and massacre visited on the mutinous, notably in Numbers 25, with ethical pronouncements and expositions of strictly unmatched abstraction and exigence. (The Sermon on the Mount will, in substantial part, be a set of citations from the message of the Ten Commandments and of Mosaic Law.) For the non-Jewish reader, for the non- or only selectively observant modern Jew, the interminable minutiae of vestimentary, dietary and liturgical ordinance in Leviticus and Deuteronomy verge on the illegible. As do the prolix blueprints for the construction and décor of the tabernacle (Ruskin seems to have known by heart those cubits and that terebinth!). Yet it is just these long and fiercely punctilious codes of conduct, of sexuality, of land tenure, of prayer, which have ensured the miraculous survival of the Jew and of Judaism. Even where theological belief falters or remains conventionally indistinct, the observance of these ritual, dietary and familial practices, so very often in midst of mockery, forced peregrination and massacre, has guarded and transmitted from hunted generation to generation an identity, a contract with survival. With crazed, yet life-dignifying passion, rabbinic scholars on the edge of the gas ovens and fire-pits were heard to debate the manifold meanings – literal, allegoric, topological – of the sacrificial injunctions as to 'the caul that is above the liver' in Exodus 29.

However, despite its hybrid texture and fractures of voice, the Pentateuch deploys a single immensity. It is that of Exodus 3:14: I AM THAT I AM. The tautology, perfectly untranslatable (I AM WHAT I AM or, perhaps, simply I AM/I AM), out of the Burning Bush. It is in these words that the monotheism of Israel and of Islam takes root and validation. As Meister Eckhart noted, the numbing singularity of this statement, our inability to translate, let alone grasp it fully, point to an 'exile of and in language itself'. The divine self-identification, the commandments that flow from it compel the flight from Egypt and that tortuous journey. Language also is in a condition of 'transit'. Word and meaning will not be made one, as they were in Eden, till the messianic hour.

Joshua and Judges contract a series of historical events now undecipherable. As we have them, these epilogues to the Books of Moses are probably put together by redactors intent to prove the triumph of Jahveism and Israel's divinely sanctioned claims to the promised land. Joshua is, I venture, the least attractive text in the canon. It records tribal arrogance and cruelty with undoubted relish. It is brimful of malediction and triumphalism (the stoning of Achan, the taking of Ai, the enslavement of the Gibeonites and other conquered folk). Judges contains two of the most arresting narratives in the Old Testament. That of Jephthah's daughter – she does not even have the privilege of a proper name! – indicates that human sacrifice may have lasted, in some fitful way, long past the rescue of Isaac. The *figura* of the young woman's lament upon the mountains has never relinquished its spell. Nor has the tale, a brilliantly concise novel in its own right, of Samson and Delilah. How much thinner would western poetry, painting and music have been without them. What grounds for inclusion can we argue for that exquisite miniature, the Book of Ruth? To provide a genealogy for David? To illustrate the sanctity of marriage with a member of an alien race? Is this poignant tale intended to illustrate the commandment whereby a man is to take in marriage the widow of a male relative if she is as yet childless?

1 and 2 Samuel, 1 and 2 Kings, the two books of Chronicles, followed by Ezra and Nehemiah are 'historical' in some proper if often unverifiable sense. They aim to tell the history of the people of Judah from Adam to Nehemiah's second visit to Jerusalem in 432 BC. Earlier or variant material is reiterated (much of Chronicles is a variation on Samuel and Kings). If there is, across the entirety of these historical writings, a leitmotif, it is that of warning: time and again, the compositors and redactors organize their material so that it will exemplify and enforce the inevitable symmetries between Israel's return to idolatry and foreign gods and the ensuing chastisement by Jahve. A related theme is that of the primacy of the Temple in Jerusalem, of the establishment of Jerusalem as the royal and ritual centre of the Jewish faith.

The narrative of Samuel and of Saul, the tragic inweaving of their destinies, the figure of Saul himself, are among the master-texts of all dramatic psychology. It is a cliché to say that the 'biography' of David, from the moment of Goliath and the lament over Jonathan (unsurpassed in any poetry), to that of the slaying of Absalom and the king's own death, is like no other 'life-study' out of antiquity or, it may be, since. Is there, prior to the riddle of William Rufus's death in the New Forest, a royal extinction as lapidary as that of Absalom in 2 Samuel 18? Or a better instance of taut translation: 'Then said Joab, I may not tarry thus with thee. And he took three darts in his hand, and thrust them through the heart of Absalom, while he was yet alive in the midst of the oak.' Is there a record of erotic infatuation, of injustice and of retribution more incisive than that of David and Bathsheba in 2 Samuel? No novelist's technique has made obsolete the calm fatality of its beginning in chapter 11: 'And it came to pass in an eveningtide, that David rose from off his bed, and walked upon the roof of the king's house: and from the roof he saw a woman washing herself; and the woman was very beautiful to look upon.' The pressures of suggestion are as vivid as they are economical. We sense the heat of the day, and the king's siesta. There is a magical coolness at eventide on those Jerusalem roofs and patios. Bathsheba's bath is one of ritual purification. She is now ready to conceive. Every touch has its intent.

As it does in the history of Ahab in 1 Kings. Again, we are involved in a process of dramatic foreshortening and psychological implications of evident literary genius. It is difficult to imagine Macbeth and Lady Macbeth had there not been Ahab and Jezebel before them. 'And Jezebel his wife said unto him, Dost thou now govern the kingdom of Israel? arise, and eat bread, and let thine heart be merry; I will give thee the vineyard of Naboth . . . ' But blood cries for blood. Ahab dies in battle 'at even: and the blood ran out of the wound into the midst of the chariot' (where Hebrew, more expressively, tells of 'the bosom' of the chariot). And dogs will lap up the blood of Jezebel. Solomon, Elijah, Sennacherib: the protagonists loom larger than life. But no less memorable are the minor, sometimes seemingly ephemeral agents: the old sorceress at Endor, Amnon and the wretched Tamar or the children who mock Elijah.

One of the latest books in the Hebrew Bible, Esther, only enters the canon at the Council of Carthage in AD 397. It may, originally, have been composed in order to explain the annual feast of Purim. Whatever its source, Esther is among the somewhat rare fairy tales with a happy outcome in Jewish scriptures. But could there be a happier end than that of the Book of Job? Does God not replace Job's slain children with seven new sons and three new daughters? Is Job's 'latter end' not blessed and made prosperous far beyond 'his beginning'?

Asked (absurdly?) to choose the one document or 'speech-act' in which the human imagination, the human questioning of its own condition, the human uses of moral intellectual discourse and metaphor are taken to their highest pitch, one would cite Job. It has no real equal in world literature. It towers above language as it does above the 'commonwealth' (in the root and composite sense) of our understanding. Yet the dimensions of Job are inversely proportionate to our knowledge of the origins, date or philological elements of the work. Scholars now assign its composition to some point between the seventh and the second centuries BC. The earliest reference to Job, in Ezekiel, may advert not to our text but to the heroic person of Job in what was, almost certainly, a very ancient folk-tale of tribulation and recompense. It would seem that Job's homeland, as depicted in the Bible, is northern Arabia or Edom. It is by no means clear whether Job is an Israelite (he does not know the name Jahweh). The actual idiom of Job is characterized by a number of north-Semitic rather than Hebraic features. Exegetes do not agree as to whether or not the framing prologue and epilogue, with their comforting reparations, are a later addendum to a 'primeval' tale of suffering, of eschatological inhumanity. The present sequence of speeches in chapters 21–31 is in dispute. Elihu is referred to neither at the outset nor at the close. Did he figure in the original or initial versions? None of which learned perplexities seem to matter a jot once we enter, to the best of our limited capacities, into the tidal waves of the book, once we make ourselves naked, in spirit, in inmost terror, to the hammering mastery of these voices.

There are three cycles of dialogue between Job and his would-be Comforters. Dialogues which arise, as they were to do in the death-camps of our century, from degrees of suffering, of irrational humiliation and desolation beyond understanding. As early as the third chapter, there is a sense in which Job seizes the initiative, in which he becomes the meaning of his pain: 'Let the stars of the twilight thereof be dark; let it look for light, but have none; neither let it see the dawning of the day: Because it shut not up the doors of my mother's womb . . . Why died I not from the womb? why did I not give up the ghost when I came out of the belly?' It may be that life, as we experience it, has never fully recovered from the curse Job puts upon it. But in that curse, an unquenchable voice persists. And it is a voice that proclaims both its innocence and the scarcely thinkable intimation that there is some mystery of guilt in the bare fact of existentiality, that man has no licit place in a non- or inhuman order.

Compelled by the truth in Job, the Almighty thunders down to give answer. Famously, He does nothing of the kind. What have the song of the morning stars, the treasures of the snow, the service of the unicorn, leviathan drawn on a hook, to do with Job's unmerited torments, with the motiveless malignity poured on his innocent head? Nothing whatever. To a moral challenge, God replies *aesthetically,* with a rhetorical display of His creative magnificence. Is the author of the Book of Job ironizing, is he suggesting that the simple fact of the existential – why is there the world when there could be nothing? – lies beyond good and evil, that the fathomless wonder of being makes injustice somehow trivial or ephemeral? This seems too Nietzschean a lesson. At every reading, the vehement depths, the unanswerabilities in this text open again into a kind of raging light. Those qualified, instruct us that the Hebrew original transcends all rendition into another tongue. But even if this is so, the Jacobean translators of Job excel their reach. They convey to us unmistakably how unnerving it is to be bullied by infinity.

On a less metaphysical plane, the Psalms continue the dialogue with Jahve set out in Job. Greek *psalmoi* signifies instrumental music and words set to music. But we know nothing of the musical accompaniment, if any, to these 151 'poems'. Nor can we say if there is some historical truth in their ascription to King David (in some instances, this may be a fact). As we know them, the Psalms would seem to have been a compilation from diverse hands and dates of a hymn-book for the Second Temple (*c.* 521 BC). We have comparable Egyptian hymns to Amon-Re, the Sun God, that date back to *c.* 1450 BC. But some of the lyrics in our collection may have been added not long before the end of the second century BC. The variety of material is considerable. Psalm 45 is a song of heroic love; 68 is a processional ode; 104 is nature poetry. Broadly speaking, modern scholarship distinguishes hymns of praise, prayers of thanks after deliverance from affliction or danger, psalms of lamentation or even, in Psalm 88, of despair reminiscent of Job, liturgical psalms possibly attached to certain rites and feast days and, though indistinctly, 'wisdom texts' dealing with more abstract issues (e.g. Psalms 34, 49, 73). Exegetes speak of a unique congruence of theological and anthropological themes. In no other book of the OT are national and highly individual voices as poignantly audible. Exultations and confession, dire introspection and jubilation, awe and intimacy in respect of God, alternate and move in counterpoint, sometimes within the same psalm. Nowhere else are the parallelisms, the admixture of prose and verse, the use of metrical prodigality more accomplished. But what remains crucial is the commerce of the human soul and speech with God, this passionate 'conversation' which defines Judaism and from which the Reformation, and Anglo-American Protestantism in particular, will draw their lifeblood. 'I will sing unto the Lord': this motion of voice and spirit has, in Judaism and Christianity, been that of faith beyond denomination. And again, the Jacobean scholar-translators rose to the singular fusion of 'the most sublime of human compositions' (Gladstone) with utter domesticity: 'Let the saints be joyful in glory: let them sing aloud upon their beds.'

Proverbs is another 'collage'. Made up of didactic, gnomic, 'sentential' pieces, it may represent a sort of phrase-book for post-exilic Judaism. We know of Egyptian and Mesopotamian analogues. Ethical dicta are interleaved with religious reflections and a general praise of wisdom. Though probably assembled in the fifth century BC, if not later, Proverbs includes much earlier material, some of it perhaps older than the monarchy. Recent scholarship argues for the 'obvious' oral origins and provenance of some of these sayings. Though seemingly heterogeneous, this book came to take on a coherence of impact. Its implicit and explicit ideal is one of religious humanism, of the moral and intellectual wholeness of men and women in their search for a knowledge of the one God. Mankind strays in error and pride, but divine guidance is never too far away. 'In the light of the king's countenance is life; and his favour is as a cloud of the latter rain' (there may be an echo of Job in this haunting phrase). The critique of wealth, which will blaze high in the Prophets, is already drastic. Gold is dirt when compared to wisdom and right-dealing. 'The rich ruleth over the poor, and the borrower is servant to the lender.' 'The poor useth intreaties; but the rich answereth roughly.' Most fascinating is the emphasis on the ambiguous potency of words. I have already cited the proposition that 'Death and life are in the power of the tongue.' This insight is urgent throughout Proverbs. Language can bind and destroy, curse and bless, speak truth and falsehood. To 'answer a fool according to his folly' is to become one. To speak in hatred (with a 'burning heart') is to cover a potsherd 'with silver dross'. Often, silence is best. In the ancient world, only Aeschylus, perhaps, had as trenchant an awareness of the double-edged nature of utterance.

Vulgarly put, Ecclesiastes (the *Qoheleth*) is the joker in our pack. Once again, the pressure of felt presence in this tractate bears no relation to our knowledge of its date or composition. The third century BC seems plausible. Some commentators identify up to four different hands. Others, more receptive to tone and the 'fingerprints' of a unique sensibility, opt for a single begetter (possibly amended by a later, orthodox redactor). The reception of *Qoheleth* into the Hebrew canon remains as problematic as does the text itself. This may be the only case in the OT in which the possibility of contact with Greek philosophic thought, with that of the Sceptics and Cynics, looks reasonable. The external dialectic is clear enough: the 'all is vanity' of mundane existence, ambitions, possessions, criteria of desirability is posited against the moral sanity, the *pietas* of an inward, scrupulously self-contained personal life. But this message of wise *humilitas* is undermined by a pointed apprehension of death and by deconstructive doubts as to the reality of any ultimate justice. Personal existence within limits of ironic prudence, the containment of hope within somewhat sardonic bounds, are the only rational strategy. Elohim is, presumably, omnipotent and benevolent. But He remains essentially out of reach of human understanding. The dialogue at the heart of Judaism is broken off in bleak courtesy. Stylistically, in precision of imagery and psychological nuance, Ecclesiastes is, repeatedly, not far from the summit of Job. The anaphoric construct of chapter 3 – 'A time to be born, and a time to die' – the theme and variations of 'nothing new under the sun', the bringing low of the 'daughters of music', the image of the grasshoppers that 'shall be a burden' when desire fails – these are among the hinges of feeling and expression on which literature and moral argument in the west have turned. (Hemingway and Auden figure among close students of this enigmatic font of sadness.)

To which the so-called Song of Solomon or Song of Songs is a rapturous rebuke. Put together from archaic oral elements, perhaps influenced by Egyptian amorous and erotic lyrics, our version could date from 450–400 BC. Incorporated into the canon after the destruction of the Second Temple in AD 70, this cantata of love and desire (which Goethe regarded as the finest of its kind in world literature), became one of the five *Megilloth* or sacred scrolls read out at high holidays. Its exuberant beauty graces the last days of Passover. 'Make haste, my beloved, and be thou like to a roe or to a young hart upon the mountains of spices.' The sexuality brims over. Exercises in officious allegory are largely fatuous. Yet Rabbi Akiva, the wisest of the wise, declared that 'the whole world is not worth the day on which the Song was given'.

Prognostication, soothsaying, fortune-telling, oracles are endemic in man and society. They inhabit the uses of future tenses. A promise or a threat are figures of prophecy, inferences drawn from suppositions or intuitions of futurity. Hope and fear, expectation and menace are in essence prophetic. The instruments of prevision range from tea-leaves to astrology, from geomancy or the reading of palms to weather forecasting and the statistical programming and projections now fundamental to our social and economic enterprises. It is solely in Dante's *Inferno* that time is end-stopped, that an unbearable present is eternal. But although prophecy is universal, the *Nebi'im* or Prophets in the Hebrew Bible constitute a unique phenomenon.

I have already mentioned the particular 'intemporality' of Hebrew verb tenses, the grammatological status of the future within the present. Whatever their reference to a fulfilment yet to come, the pronouncements of Jahve are already realized, in the instant of their utterance, and have been from eternity. It is not, therefore, the oracular, the clairvoyant strain which matters most (except in certain 'local' examples such as that of Jonah). It is the reiteration through human lips of God's everlasting will and purpose, of His investment in mankind. The Prophetic Books in the OT press to a climax of overwhelming ethical demand and intimacy the dialogue between God and the Jew, between eternity and time as man experiences it in his own life and in history. From Samuel to Malachi, ancient Israel brings forth human spirits immediately informed, coerced by the breath of the Almighty, visionary moralists, watchmen in the night, criers after social justice whose messages wholly transcend Judaism. These intensely local universalists are both Cassandra and Socrates. Inevitably, they enter into conflict – it may end in cruel death – with sinful royalty or the sclerotic legalism and hypocrisies of the priestly establishment. The Prophets are outsiders at the centre, maddened gadflies calling for reasoned compassion, for public integrity, for the verities of a personal answerability to God in a social order perennially corrupt in its politics, in its law courts, in the purely external unction of its religiosity. Together with the Socratic moment, with certain Buddhist prescripts of purity, these prophetic texts, various and historically complex as they are, have provided us with our touchstones of moral possibility. Often detested in their own day, the Prophets out of Israel continue to exasperate the long sleep of the human conscience (which was, as Hitler stated, 'nothing other than a Jewish invention'). It is from the Prophets that derive Judaism's two principal heresies: Christianity and utopian socialism or communism. As it becomes a bureaucratic, politically engaged *ecclesia*, Roman Catholicism will join the party of the kings and the priests; from the millenarian anarchists and free spirits of the

Middle Ages to Cromwell and Marx, the 'protestants' will be on the side of the Prophets and their messianic imperatives.

Isaiah would appear to be a figure from the eighth century BC based in Jerusalem. Today, most scholars take chapters 40–66 to be an anonymous addendum to the original core. This 'Second Isaiah' has frequently been designated as the most powerful, moving voice in western, indeed in global experience. A supreme thinker-poet in or shortly after exile, he aims to restore hope to his shattered people. It is on the 'man of sorrows', on the 'suffering servant' in Deutero-Isaiah – figurations deep-rooted in Jewish destiny – that the composers of the Gospels and of Pauline Christianity will found their faith. It is towards the 'New Jerusalem' of 'Second Isaiah' that Bunyan and Martin Luther King direct their steps. It is the promise of universal peace, of the lion lying beside the lamb, that continues to both justify and mock our worn hopes. It is, with apposite mystery, the hope that 'the sons of strangers shall build up thy walls', for it is the very concept of 'stranger' which will grow pale in the morning light of human concord and universality. So long as mankind endures by the irrational logic of future tenses, by appealing to 'tomorrow', these passages from Isaiah will be its talismans.

That cry for peace, that furious lament at human stupidity and bestiality, fill Jeremiah. Set down by an amanuensis, the prophecies of Jeremiah, the historical narrative included in this work, are assigned to the seventh or sixth centuries BC. Jeremiah himself is considered to be an actual personage from Anathot in the tribal territory of Benjamin. His are the most savage pronouncements on idolatrous Israel recorded in Scripture. Juvenal or Swift are, by comparison, consolers. Through his servant Jeremiah, the Lord proclaims malediction and annihilation. Famine shall yield to cannibalism. Mothers shall come to devour their offspring. Blood shall tide over the ravaged land. Each time that Elohim is ready to hold His chastising hand, to show mercy and bounty to His chosen people, Israel lurches back into abomination, into the worship of Baal and the practice of injustice. Therefore Zedekiah will be delivered into the hands of his murderous foes; therefore will God 'make the cities of Judah a desolation without an inhabitant'. And Jerusalem falls after a terrible siege. Considered a heretic (Socrates) and traitor (Trotsky), Jeremiah is done to death. No society could bear the inquisitorial rage of his foresight. There are lines in the epilogue, in the so-called Lamentations of Jeremiah, which it is almost impossible to read after the Holocaust: 'Our inheritance is turned to strangers, our houses to aliens . . . Our skin was black like an oven because of the terrible famine' (where 'famine' can, in the Hebrew, also be read as 'terrors' or 'storms', thus corresponding precisely to the term Shoah).

Of the 'Major Prophets', Ezekiel is most obviously exilic. He receives his prophetic calling in Babylon in 593 BC. A late tradition has it that he too was murdered by those whose idolatry, whose recalcitrance against Mosaic Law he had denounced. The literary artistry of this book is highly wrought and, at some points, idiosyncratic. Certain exegetes have argued for oriental influences in Ezekiel's ornate, almost 'baroque' cosmology and apocalyptic imagery. The God of Ezekiel is at once inaccessible to human influence and radically committed to the ultimate salvation of Israel. A nagging sense of futility, of being heard but not listened to, colours the prophet's eloquence. He is, at the last, alone with his surreal visions. This illumined isolation is counterpoised by the imperious nearness of Jahve. He bids this 'Son of Man' – an opaque, key term in Ezekiel – eat the roll on which the divine revelations and monitions are inscribed. The word of God enters and fills the prophet's 'bowels'; in his mouth, it turns to honeyed sweetness. Ben Jonson knew this passage when he urged the 'ingestion' of an inspired poem or piece of prose. For Christianity, Ezekiel's vision of the resurrection of the dead, of the gathering of their bones to new life and homecoming, proved seminal. Hence the palpable striving of the 'King James' translators to knit their rendering, wherever possible, to New Testament phraseology and fulfilment.

There is nothing minor about the twelve 'Minor Prophets' except their concision. The range of tone and method is formidable. The genesis of these texts runs from the mid eighth century to the post-Babylonian. The economy of the voices – Obadiah counts twenty-one verses – yields an urgency, an incisiveness of witness, a brusque splendour as persuasive as any in Holy Writ.

In Hosea, which scholars assign to the eighth century BC, the interaction between autobiography and prophetic allegory is unique. The infidelity of Hosea's wife comes to embody that of the people of Israel towards their God. Whoredom after another man, whoredom after strange gods. With supreme artistry, Hosea leaves the dual structure and narrative open-ended. The prophet buys back his errant wife and God *may* forgive His adulterous people. But, perhaps, only after a passage through death. The extreme linguistic difficulty of Hosea's idiom, the bristling density of his style, may indicate the psychological tension under which he laboured. There are Dostoevskian turns in this torn book. 'The prophet is a fool, the spiritual man is mad, for the multitude of thine iniquity, and the great hatred.'

Joel seems to be a late post-exilic author who draws copiously on the much older manner and tone of prophecy. At moments, Joel reads like a pastiche of Amos. Commentaries continue to differ as to the intended target of this short tract. Does Joel foretell Israel's doom or its eventual salvation? Is the locust plague historical fact or allegory? But whatever these uncertainties, it is difficult to forget the stars that 'shall withdraw their shining' or the Lord who 'shall roar out of Zion'.

Amos is the most ancient of the prophetic books and the first that attaches to an individual. Composed in *c.* 750 BC (some place it even earlier), Amos is one of the pinnacles in the OT. A titanic individuality emerges. Epic, lyric, didactic moves interact to produce an unsurpassed fierceness. In Amos, the desert marches on the rotten city, as it will in the peasant revolts of the Middle Ages and Reformation, as it will in the anarchist risings during the Russian Civil War or in the hideous 'cleansing' carried out by the Khmer Rouge. The ascetic *misère* of the famished and the humiliated turns with numbing rage on those that go shod in silk, who consume 'the calves out of the midst of the stable', who have built dwellings 'of hewn stone' in the face of the homeless. The sum of socialist utopia is compacted into that haunting query: 'Can two walk together, except they be agreed?' It is out of the closing chapter of Amos (which I have already quoted) that Zionism took its promissory note, that the State of Israel can cite validation: 'And I will bring again the captivity of my people of Israel, and they shall build the waste cities, and inhabit them; and they shall plant vineyards, and drink the wine thereof; they shall also make gardens, and eat the fruit of them. And I will plant them upon their land, and they shall no more be pulled up out of their land which I have given them, saith the Lord thy God.' Prophecy so exact, so graphically exact across three thousand years, should not leave us unafraid.

What can we make of Jonah other than delight? Delight in its humour – of which there is not, in the Hebrew Bible, superfluity – in its psychological finesse, in the wealth of its 'fabulous' brevity (a monographic study of early medieval interpretations of Jonah extends to two compendious tomes). We are dealing not with prophecy as such, but with the legend of a prophet. Within this legend, there are elements of a Midrash, of a commentary on prior biblical texts out of Exodus, Numbers and Ezekiel. The questions raised are of the gravest: should mercy prevail over justice? Can God, in some sense, repent of an earlier, thus eternal, decision? Does His writ of retribution and forgiveness extend outside Israel, to Nineveh? But these theological-juridical-ethical conundra are set out, teasingly and directly, in terror and in mirthful irony, by a master of narrative and dialogue. Who was he? When did he fashion this jewel of a text? A Jonah is referred to in 2 Kings as a prophet in the reign of Jeroboam II. Some analysts signal Aramaic and Phoenician linguistic touches. This does not, necessarily, situate Jonah in the post-exilic. Did it originate as late as the third century BC? We do not know. But does it matter? The masterly scenario – Jonah's threefold confrontation with Jahve, interrupted by the 'choral' episodes of the mariners and the Ninevites – the Psalm of supplication out of the belly of the fish, and, above all, Jonah's petulant anger towards God when his prophecy is negated, together with the closing parable of the withered gourd, have spellbound the attention of theologians, moralists and writers since. In its vastness,

Melville's *Moby-Dick* is a single meditation on the sea-deep wonders and mutabilities of these four short chapters.

Then comes Micah, an oracular apocalyptic out of the foothills of Judaea, and probably Isaiah's contemporary. Like Amos, Micah knows of the arrogant ostentation of Jerusalem. The recovery of Zion, at the close, is almost certainly a post-exilic addition. Nahum (the name, ironically enough, signifies 'comfort') is a grim miniature. Three relentless chapters that concentrate on the fall of Nineveh in 612 BC. The Almighty is in absolute control of human politics and history. The idolatrous are powerless against Him: 'Thy crowned are as the locusts, and thy captains as the great grass-hoppers, which camp in the hedges in the cold day, but when the sun ariseth they flee away, and their place is not known where they are.' Habakkuk is a God-questioner. He sets down his interrogation during the Babylonian invasion of 609–598 BC. Why does the Lord allow this horror? When will peace be granted to mankind? Jahve's reply is all too predictable: Judah has transgressed and must be chastised. Fair enough, counters the prophet. But are the ravening hosts of Nebuchadnezzar not more sinful than their victims? Standing on his watch-tower, the express icon of prophecy, Habakkuk waits for God's justification. The Lord assures His tormented servant that fulfilment shall come in its season, that the covenant is no lie. Habakkuk climaxes in one of the most resplendent songs of praise in Scripture: 'Thou didst walk through the sea with thine horses, through the heap of great waters' (where Hebrew 'mud' adverts more tellingly to the miracle at the Red Sea in Exodus). The ninth of the 'Minor Prophets', Zephaniah, is also in dialogue with God. Jerusalem's final destruction in 587–586 BC is ineluctably foreshadowed. But this very catastrophe can bring a new start, a religious-moral rebirth for Israel.

It is this rebirth which lies at the visionary heart of the messages of Haggai (whose prophecy is dated 520 BC), of Zechariah, the seer in the exilic night, the adversary of the official clerisy, and in that of Malachi. The name signifies 'my messenger' and these four chapters are like a typological précis of all that had gone before. The 'great and dreadful day of the Lord' draws near. Elijah shall return. But the heart of the fathers shall turn to the children, and that of the children to the fathers. The Hebrew Bible closes on what has always been the crux of Judaism: the family.

In the canon, the Book of Daniel is placed before the twelve Prophets. It is, in fact, the latest of OT texts. It can be dated 164 BC. It addresses its high literary and structural art to Hellenized, cultured Jews, possibly the Hasidim. But it is also being read at Qumran, in the radical or Zealot camps on the Dead Sea. Like Joseph, millennially his predecessor, Daniel can interpret the dreams of kings. He knows what the alphabet of fire portends for Belshazzar. Daniel's book of the future must now be closed and sealed. When it will be opened, the messianic hour shall strike. 'Blessed is he that waiteth.' The Bible that is in the Bible has yet to be read.

4

How naked would be the walls of our museums stripped of the works of art which illustrate, interpret or refer to biblical themes. How much silence there would be in our western music, from Gregorian chant to Bach, from Handel to Stravinsky and Britten, if we excised settings of biblical texts, dramatizations and motifs. The same is true of western literature. Our poetry, drama, fiction would be unrecognizable if we omitted the continuous presence of the Bible. Nor is there any categorical way of delineating that presence. It extends from the immense volume of biblical paraphrase to the most tangential or covert of allusions. It comprises every mode of intertextuality, of incorporation within and between the lines. How is one to circumscribe a constancy of implication which reaches from the translations or paraphrase of biblical texts in medieval mystery plays to the obliquity of the biblical in Faulkner's *Absalom, Absalom!*? What single rubric can account for the uses of Ahab and of Jonah in *Moby-Dick*, for the redeployment of biblical personae and epistles in Dante's *Divine Comedy*, and for the massively augmented retelling of the world of the Patriarchs in Thomas Mann's 'Joseph' tetralogy? If so secondary a figure as Lot's wife appears already in Middle English poetry, she continues to do so in Blake, in Joyce and at the centre of D. H. Lawrence's poem 'She Looks Back'. The matter of Moses and of Samson looms large in French romanticism (Victor Hugo, Vigny). There would be no Proust, as we know him, without *Sodome et Gomorrhe*. No Kafka without the Tables of the Law. No Racine without *Esther* and *Athalie*. Biblical echoes, the play of hidden quotation or parody, is as indispensable to Goethe's *Faust* as it is to the uncanny reflections of Eden and the Fall in Henry James's *The Golden Bowl* (a title out of Ecclesiastes) or to the desolate, sardonic mutations of this primal intrigue in Beckett's *Waiting for Godot*. Enumeration becomes pointless.

The centrality of the biblical is most obvious in English-language literatures. I have pointed to the symbiosis between biblical translation and the maturing of the language itself from Tyndale to the Authorized Version. At innumerable points of the colloquial and the sublime, the proverbial and the refined, to speak English or Anglo-American is 'to speak the Bible'. Not even the compendious *Dictionary of Biblical Tradition in English Literature* (ed. David Lyle Jeffrey, 1992) can hope to be exhaustive. Not when its entry on, say, Methuselah has to range across Spenser, Sir Thomas Browne, Swift, Burns, Browning, Tennyson, *Ulysses* and George Bernard Shaw's *Back to Methuselah* (not to mention American entries such as Thoreau)!

One can attempt certain informative 'cuts' across this bounty. It is enlightening to observe correlations between periods in English or American history and their preference of corresponding biblical themes. Adam and Samson fascinate the English Reformation and Puritanism both in the Old and the New World. Milton is only the pre-eminent exemplar of a constellation that includes Samuel Butler, Spenser and the countless identifications between North America and a New Eden, between Popery and the Philistines. Cain has never ceased to cast his baleful spell on the literary imagination. He is present in Beowulf and the Arthurian cycle. But he comes most fully into his own with English romanticism. Coleridge's *The Wanderings of Cain* (of which *The Ancient Mariner* is, at many points, a variant) inspires Byron's *Cain: A Mystery*. Blake ripostes to both these versions in his *The Ghost of Abel*. Vibrant echoes of Cain's romantic posture are vital in Melville's conception of Ishmael and in Conrad's study of ineradicable guilt, *Lord Jim*. The prodigality of all too human virtues and failings in the saga of King David has drawn to it numerous novelists of the nineteenth and twentieth centuries: Dickens, Hardy, Lawrence, Faulkner and Joseph Heller among them. Feminist criticism and writing is now bringing to literary-critical prominence figures such as Jephthah's daughter, Judith and Deborah. Not only in the English tongues has the Holocaust generated a whole 'Job literature'. Samuel Beckett's *Murphy* and a host of the destitute or outcast are, today, 'on the jobpath'.

To this ubiquity of biblical presence in English literature, there is a paramount and challenging exception. Secondary studies tell of a goodly number of allusions to biblical material in Shakespeare. Quotations from Scripture, mostly muted or indirect, have been identified. There is, however, no central encounter, no engagement of any scope (as there is, in contrast, with Homer or Plutarch). It is as if Shakespeare had deliberately evaded not only the narrative storehouse of the Old and the New Testaments, but the flowering of this great resource as it shaped the language from Wycliffe and Tyndale to his own immediate contemporaries. I would conjecture that some wary instinct of sovereign autonomy inhibited Shakespeare from too close a contact with the only texts, with the only discourse in action, which might dim his own powers.

But in the literatures of English, at home and as a global medium, the kinship with the biblical, as it began with the Anglo-Saxons and with Chaucer, as it informed Donne, Milton, Blake, Melville, T. S. Eliot and so many others, continues. But *is* the Bible literature?

However rudimentary one's preface to a reading of Scripture, this vexing question cannot be avoided. Two antithetical answers have been declared.

To the fundamentalist, in Jewish Orthodoxy, in Islam, in such Christian communities as the Baptists or the Scottish Free Church or the Pentecostal movements, our Holy Bible is exactly that. It is a collection of ancient *witness* in which every word, or, according to the degree of relevant fundamentalism, nearly every word, is directly inspired and/or dictated by the Lord God. Any derogation from the verity of these 'divinely wrought documents', in the name of positivist natural sciences, of political tolerance, of historical criticism, of ethical change, is absurdity and blasphemy. It is to oppose the paltry intellect of (fallen) man to the omniscience and omnipotence of God. It is to cause a fatal break between man and his Maker. To subvert, qualify or amend the message of the Bible, its account of the origins of our world and of our ultimate destiny, is to stumble into a condition of twilit triviality, of senseless hubris and unconstrained licence. Prise loose a single brick, and the edifice will collapse. Compromise, discard a single affirmation as to creation in Genesis, as to sumptuary and dietary prescriptions in the Torah, as to Elijah's ascent into heaven, and you will, irreparably, bring the sanctuary of God's nearness to man tumbling down. Who is Darwin, who is Freud to raise his voice above that out of the Burning Bush?

Diverse tactics of fundamentalism in the understanding of the Bible are, today, far more widespread than 'enlightened' opinion would have it. They are on the march throughout Islam and the south-western United States. They are the daily practice of a confident, multiplying Jewish Orthodoxy.

The opposed answer is equally trenchant. The Old Testament and the New are congeries of myths, fables, legends, legislative codes, moral treatises, erotica, liturgical and ritual scripts, historical chronicles with political intent, typological sagas, tacked together, more or less contingently, over long centuries, in wholly different social-ethnic settings and by a multitude of hands. This montage abounds in absurdities, self-contradictions, archaic ferocities, repetitions, inequalities of spiritual-discursive talent of a kind to make the mere notion of divine authorship or unison perfectly ludicrous. Men and women – some, no doubt, of rare moral vision and literary skills – produced these diverse writings in ways entirely natural and, in consequence, fully comparable with those of other major thinkers, poets, historians, legislators in numerous cultures and epochs. We may be looking at material whose date and provenance remain unresolved. But this material is mundane, in the proper sense of the word. It is wholly of our world, imagining and composition.

There could, conceivably, be an intermediate stance. In his readings of the pre-Socratics, Martin Heidegger posits a moment in the evolution of language, and of thought and perception within speech-acts, prior to that which we have known since rationalism, i.e. Plato and Aristotle. The auroral texts of the pre-Socratics tell of an immediacy of rapport between word and world, between discrete beings and being itself, unrecapturable since. The very first poet-thinkers 'spoke the world' with a truth and unobscured vulnerability to the core of life which only a handful of supreme poets have echoed after them. This is a wonderfully seductive notion. Biologically, historically, there is not a shred of evidence for it. *Homo sapiens sapiens* has had what is, in evolutionary parameters, a very brief time on this earth. There is no evidence whatever that the mental, psychic organization that generates and is generated by human speech has altered in any fundamental way. If we can, with whatever philological-hermeneutic qualifications, understand, argue with Anaximander or Parmenides or Heraclitus, the simple reason is that we apprehend their means of utterance. As we do those of the authors of the Books of Moses or of the Prophets even at the extreme pitch of vision.

The common-sense and positivist designation of the Bible as a book among books, be it of exceptional quality and impact, looks incontrovertible. As Cardinal Newman observed, mysticism on such issues begins in mist and ends in schism.

And yet.

I speak here only for myself.

Time and again, I have sought to imagine, albeit indistinctly, Shakespeare remarking at home or to some intimate on whether or not work on *Hamlet* or *Othello* had, that day, gone well or poorly, as the case might be. I can picture him, *just*, expressing satisfaction over Feste in *Twelfth Night* or the compactions of syntax (still unique) in *Coriolanus*. And then inquiring as to the price of cabbages. Already when it comes to trying to get a naturalistic grasp of Schubert's compositions in his death-year, or when I labour to make any 'common sense' of Einstein's production, over some eight months, of the four short papers that were to change not only our understanding of the universe, but all human affairs (by virtue of their nuclear consequence), I find myself helpless. But still . . .

What I am unable to do is to arrive at any thought-image, however naïve, at any impression of literary technique or rhetorical transport, however masterful, when confronting the author(s) of God's speeches out of the whirlwind in Job, of much of the *Qoheleth*, of certain Psalms or of considerable portions of 'Second Isaiah'. The picture of some man or woman lunching, dining, after he or she had 'invented' and set down these and certain other biblical texts, leaves me, as it were, blinded and off balance. I find myself groping towards some notion of 'a surrealism', of an order of inspiration and dominion over words for which we have no satisfactory analogy elsewhere or any altogether naturalistic explanation. Could there have been degrees of 'audition', of a concentrated inward hearing amid silences no longer available to us so intense as to endow consciousness with an immediacy to metaphor, to imagery, to what I have called 'real presence' or a 'bodying forth' of meaning, inaccessible since? The Judaic belief that Elijah was the last man to look on God directly, the Islamic postulate of a mutation in religious-philosophic perceptions after the passing of the Prophet's direct descendants, are suggestive also in a semantic light.

'Who is it that darkeneth counsel by words without knowledge?' I am unable to account wholly rationally for the ways of the man or woman who put the question and who asks me where I was when 'the morning stars sang together' or whether 'the rain hath a father?'

Perhaps this is as it should be. It is the Hebrew Bible, of all books, which most questions man.

Homer in English

The *Iliad* and the *Odyssey*, notably Book I of the *Iliad*, are the texts most frequently translated into English – where 'English' comprises not only the varieties of the language spoken and written in Britain since the late Middle Ages, but the entire global spectrum. If we include under 'Homer' the so-called *Homeric Hymns*, there is, more particularly during the eighteenth and nineteenth centuries, scarcely a single year in which some English-language poet, scholar, parson, schoolmaster or gentleman of classical attainments did not translate, and more often than not, publish out of Homer. The British Library listing under 'Homerus', not to mention my own personal collection – a passion dating back to my schooldays – are very far from complete.

Starting with the *Siege of Troy* romance and the *Laud Troy Book* (which runs to more than eighteen thousand lines), the history of imitations, adaptations, sequels and translations is never-ending. We move to the alliterative verses of the anonymous *Gest Historiale of the Destruction of Troy* and a Scottish version attributed to John Barbour, to Lydgate's celebrated *Troy Book* and Caxton's *Recuyell of the Historyes of Troye*. Through these two texts, the 'matter of Homer' informs not only the foundations and growth of the arts of English narrative in verse and in prose, but the origins and dissemination of printing itself. Printing comes to England via a 'Troye Booke'.

Since the end of the Second World War, near to a dozen complete English and American-English *Iliads* and *Odysseys* have been published. Hardly has one appeared, when another is announced. Widely read translations, such as E. V. Rieu's, are reissued and revised. English-language 'Homers' thus decisively outnumber English renditions of the Bible. Unless I am mistaken, the 'translation-act' which renders the Trojan war, the homecoming of

Introduction to *Homer in English* (Penguin Books, 1996).

Odysseus or the *Homeric Hymns* into medieval, Tudor, Elizabethan, Jacobean, Augustan, romantic, Victorian or twentieth-century English, into the English of North America or the Caribbean, surpasses in frequency that of any other act of transfer into any other western tongue and literature.

When we take into account the verse and prose romances, the plays (e.g. Shakespeare's *Troilus and Cressida*), the lyric imitations and evocations (as in Tennyson), the fiction derived from the rape of Helen, the wrath of Achilles, the death of Hector, the fall of Troy, the enchantments of Circe, Penelope's web, the vengeance of Odysseus, the sum of Homeric presences, of creative echo, from Caxton to Joyce and Derek Walcott, from Chaucer to Robert Graves and W. H. Auden, becomes almost incommensurable. And this is to omit the 'lives of the Homeric' in English art from medieval illuminations to Caro, or in music to the times of Walton's *Troilus and Cressida*, Britten's music for a radio dramatization of the *Odyssey* or Tippett's *King Priam*.

But it is not only the numerical prodigality which arrests attention. It is the quality and diversity of the long lineage of translators and respondents to Homer. It is the complexity of modulation, the investment of vision which takes us from Lydgate and Caxton to *Ulysses* and *Omeros*. It is not only on Keats that Chapman's Homer exercised its uneven spell. What might Dryden's projected *Iliad* have been had he persisted beyond Book I? I do not see what English epic poem after *Paradise Regained* – and how abundant Homer is in Milton – rivals the authority and narrative sweep of Pope's *Iliad*. There are persuasive 'domesticities', as from a Flemish interior, in Cowper's *Odyssey*, in his treatment of 'that species of the sublime that owes its very existence to simplicity'. Shelley's *Homeric Hymns* exhibit both poetic virtuosity and a close knowledge of Greek lyric texts. What understanding of modern English and American poetry could set aside the translations from, the imitations of the *Iliad* and the *Odyssey* in Ezra Pound – that magical first *Canto*! – in Auden's 'Shield of Achilles', in Graves, in Robert Lowell, in Robert Fitzgerald or in that incandescent reading by Christopher Logue? The sirens that sing of destruction and temporary relief to the fire-watcher on the London roofs in T. S. Eliot's *Four Quartets* are those of the air-raid alarm; but they are also the temptresses of Odysseus, their fatal music recaptured and, as it were, amplified through Dante's use of the myth.

Nor is it only poets, playwrights, novelists who have mirrored Homer into English, into Anglo-Irish, into American, Scottish or West Indian branches of the language. It is philosophers or inquirers into meaning such as Thomas Hobbes and I. A. Richards. It is thinkers on society such as William Morris and Samuel Butler. It is, in the legacy of Caxton and Ogilby, master-publishers such as Rieu. We find prime ministers (the Earl of Derby's *Iliad* appears in 1864 and Gladstone makes repeated attempts at Homer). Ecclesiastics and headmasters are legion. T. E. Lawrence prefaces his *Odyssey* in lofty modesty. He is a man of war and survival. Unlike scholarly rivals or detractors, he has killed his man in combat and undergone extreme peril. These, he opines, are qualifications not altogether impertinent to the task of voicing Homer. Also Graves could make this claim. Before long, moreover, our catalogue will include more women (two are represented in this anthology). Has Nausikaa not been held to be the author of the *Odyssey*, has Simone Weil not written one of the most challenging (though, to my mind, misguided) commentaries on the *Iliad*?

The bare facts compel the question: why? Why, distinctively among other western literatures, should those in the English languages generate a perennial ubiquity of translations from Homer, of Homeric variants, re-creations, pastiches and travesties (these extend from the Renaissance to a two-volume eighteenth-century burlesque-erotic *Iliad* and *Odyssey* and the calypso-lyrics of Lawrence Durrell)? The recent and current multiplicity is striking. Till *Lady Chatterley's Lover* (now, I suspect, beyond it), Rieu's *Odyssey* marks the greatest single 'hit' in Penguin's publishing history. Not long thereafter comes Richmond Lattimore's *Iliad*, hailed as exemplary. Then we have Fitzgerald's inspired *Odyssey*. Lattimore feels obliged to riposte with an *Odyssey* of his own. Fitzgerald, *à contrecœur* one suspects, now adds his *Iliad*. Robert Fagles acclaims Fitzgerald's achievement, only to present, a few years later, his own Homer. Not to mention Graves, Rees, Mandelbaum and many others. Today, the sequence shows no sign of slowing down. Inevitably, the cut-off point in this collection (1994) is arbitrary. This selection will be out of date when it appears. What induces twentieth-century commercial and academic presses to commission, to edit and issue these costly, voluminous addenda to what is already, so richly, available?

The 'natural' national myth ought to have been Arthurian – as Malory, Milton, Tennyson or T. H. White variously supposed. Did, for Britain, the major Christian legends and typologies not lie to hand as they did on the Continent of Europe? What Faustus after Marlowe in English literature is there to set beside Valéry's or Bulgakov's or Thomas Mann's? What Don Juan except Byron's? No, it is to Achilles and Odysseus, to the 'topless towers of Ilium' and the shores of Ithaka, it is to 'deep-browed Homer' that English-language sensibility turns and returns, incessantly, as if striving to appropriate to itself, to the native genius, material already, by some destined or elective affinity, its own. It is a *Ulysses* which Joyce writes when re-creating Dublin. It is an *Omeros* in which Walcott sings his profoundly Afro-Caribbean music of Eros, of masculine rivalries, of the spirit-world and of the sea.

Again, I ask: why?

The etymologically spurious identification with Britons as Roman descendants of Aeneas, which is to say with those who had battled for and emigrated from Homeric Troy, is medieval and, perhaps, even earlier. It is alive in Tudor historiography, iconography and symbolic perceptions of England's noble ascendancy. Logic suggests that this would have made Virgil and the *Aeneid* the talismanic reference rather than Greek Homer and his cruel paladins. And there *is* a significant Virgilian note in English literature, music and art (consider Dryden, Purcell or Turner). But it pales beside the centrality of the Homeric. A first thought might be this: there shines throughout the *Iliad* an idealized yet also unflinching vision of masculinity, of an order of values and mutual recognitions radically virile. In ways too inwoven, too manifold to be readily categorized, this vision matches, underwrites and images certain primary components in English consciousness and social history. The Homeric saga of warfare and masculine intimacies, with its formidable emphasis on competitive sports, seems immediate, as is no other text, to the boys' school, to the all-male college, the regiment and the club (configurations pivotal to British, not to Continental, societies). This lyric masculinity aches in Keats's desire to be in the trench shouting with Achilles, no less than in the self-identification as Homeric heroes, as lovers before death, proclaimed by English subalterns and poets at Ypres or in that Homeric setting at the Dardanelles.

The topic is both insistent and elusive. As so often in the phenomenology of English sentiments, homoeroticism is, as it were, organic and organizing. In its Homeric context, this factor is sanctified by sacrificial bravery, by devotion to friendship and duty even more than in the Platonizing homoeroticism of the Victorian. What public schoolboy (until recently), what young officer in the Western Desert did not thrill, more or less consciously, to the remembrance of Hector's roar at the very edge of the Greek encampment, or to Achilles' lament over Patroclus – a thrill in which athletic prestige, masculine handsomeness, ambitious valour and a more or less diffuse homoeroticism animate, if this expression may be allowed, a singularly British 'puberty of the spirit'? What observation more in the tenor of the *Iliad* than that whereby the most testing and consequential of British victories on land, that at Waterloo, was said to have been won on the playing-fields of Eton? Remember the naked dead, in the Homeric manner, on English war memorials.

Most subtly, moreover, Homer's *Iliad* sustains a divided, even duplicitous focus. The doom of Hector and the desolation of Priam's city weigh as intensely as do the triumph of Achilles and of the Achaean host. This equable pathos, the balance held so justly, would appear to have struck native chords in British reception. The *Iliad* could be the only supreme tale of human valour and suffering in which we *can* have it both ways. Hector remains the archetype of the 'good loser', a pivotal configuration in English self-regard.

Hector and Priam are the patrons of all Dunkirks. The epic appeals, at an inward level, to that now poignant code of 'fair play' which defined British mores to themselves and the world at large. 'What's Hecuba to him?' ruminates Hamlet. A Danish, not an English question.

The perennial spell exercised by the *Odyssey* could have its more obvious source. The Homeric tale is that of the sea and of all who go down to it in their 'dark ships'. It remains incomparable in its salt-savour, in its orchestration of tempests and of calms, in its nuanced articulations of the dialogue between sea and strand, wave and shore. Homer's is that wine-dark sea which Matthew Arnold heard on Dover Beach. Coleridge's Ancient Mariner, Poe's Gordon Pym, Conrad's seamen at the helm are descendants of peregrine Odysseus. As are the souls overboard or clinging to a raft in Melville. An island-civilization, sea-drenched and guarded by stormy waters at every crucial season in its history, will find in Homer's *Odyssey* not only a book of common prayer – 'may I endure this storm, may I reach the harbour' – but of shared adventure and global promise. Du Bellay's famous sonnet on Odysseus' homecoming from his *beau voyage* is magical; but it is lit by the soft streams in the Loire country. The sea is absent from it. It rolls and thunders in Chapman's couplets. Its rages sing in the North Atlantic 'Homers' of Robert Fitzgerald or the West Indies marines of *Omeros*.

But these conjectures as to the unbroken hold of Homer on English tongues and literatures are probably inadequate. The empathies of vision and revision lie deep. The light from Achilles' helmet, from the eyes of the 'cat-like Penelope' (T. E. Lawrence's epithet), 'screams . . . across three thousand years'. That dizzying phrase is out of Christopher Logue's transmutation of the *Patrokleia*. It 'screams' in English as it does in no other language after Greek. From the beginnings of our literature to the present, to tomorrow. Whatever the underlying causes, this crowded resonance and constancy of echo offer a wealth of implications.

To borrow an image from plant genetics: the sequence of transla-tions from Homer provides a unique radioactive tracer. By its luminescent progress, we can follow the development of the language, of its vocabularies, syntax and semantic resources, from root to stem, from its stem to its multiple branches and leaves. Every model of English lexical and grammatical observance is visible in this chain: all the way from the most ornate and experimental, as in Chapman or Joyce, to the 'basic English' purpose in I. A. Richards's narration of the fury of Achilles. The Homeric sequence is an inventory of metrical means: we find in it alliterative verse, rhyme royal, Spenserian stanzas, heroic couplets, iambic pentameter, blank and free verse. It exemplifies trials in quantitative and syllabic measures of every kind. That intricate subject, the evolution of English prose rhythms, of punctuation, also unfolds in the Homeric sequence. As does that of dialect, of regional idioms from the Scottish Lowlands and Lancashire to Trinidad and Boston.

This vivacity of structural illumination, of dynamic legibility, as in a radioactive tracer coursing through organic tissue, springs from the nature of translation itself. For it is in and through the process of translation that a language is made eminently self-aware. Translation constrains it to formal and diachronic introspection, to an explicit investment and enlargement of its historical, colloquial and metaphorical instruments. Simultaneously, translation puts a language under pressure of its limitation. It will solicit modes of perception and designation which that language had left under-developed, or had altogether discarded. An act of translation draws up a balance-sheet, as it were, for the target-language. When such an act engenders a continuity which extends from Anglo-Norman to English in its twentieth-century planetary variousness, linguistic history and forms are writ large. There is, in consequence, a sense in which this collection is a concise chronicle of English.

Which chronicle begins tangentially. It is via Dares and Dictys, whom the Middle Ages took to be witnesses of the events at Troy, and via Benoît de Sainte-Maure's *Roman de Troie* (running to thirty thousand lines), that Ilium and Ulysses enter into Middle English. Chaucer knows of the *Iliad* only through Boccaccio. It is Latin versions of the Homeric material and, more especially, Virgil's complexly inflected view of Homer, which are fitfully available to

Tudor England. We still are uncertain as to just how much Greek George Chapman knew as he addressed the original and the 'Prince of Poets' between 1598 and 1616. But the vital point is this: these are the years in which English is in the highest state of 'excitation', when it has been richened, energized, made musical as never before or since by its encounter with a transcendent source-text in Wycliffe, Tyndale and the Authorized Version. Now, in the *Iliad* and the *Odyssey*, this same language meets with immanence, with the concrete turbulence and blaze of simile in the Homeric world. It strives to match a swiftness of narrative, a strength of internal connections, an economy of impact (Helen passing the old men and casting silence on them) comparable with yet radically different from that of Scripture. In these very years, moreover, the language is called upon to enact a diversity of rhetorical, oratorical, political discourse which will, in analogue with Homeric *exempla*, enter into its own parliamentary practices.

In Chapman's *Whole Works of Homer*, notably in the fourteeners of his *Iliad*, English is spendthrift, inebriate with waste motion, at times precious and as yet uncertain of its coruscating force. It is also that of Elizabethan and Jacobean drama, charged with sensory, corporeal thrust. At moments, it is already exact in that manual, pragmatic vein which is the virtue of English. At others, it comes armed with lyric sorrow. Homer, as Chapman construes and misconstrues him, makes the English language know itself and impels it to cast its lexical-grammatical net over a thronging prodigality of life:

> such a fire from his bright shield extends
> His ominous radiance, and in heav'n impressed his fervent blaze.
> His crested helmet, grave and high, had next triumphant place
> On his curl'd head, and like a star it cast a spurry ray,
> About which a bright thicken'd bush of hair did play,
> Which Vulcan forg'd him for his plume . . .

> The fair scourge then Automedon takes up, and up doth get
> To guide the horse. The fight's seat last, Achilles took behind;
> Who look'd so arm'd as if the sun, there fall'n from heaven had

shined,
And terribly thus charg'd his steeds: 'Xanthus and Bailius,
Seed of the Harpy, in the charge ye undertake of us,
Discharge it not as when Patroclus ye left dead in field . . .'

So much to be said about the uses of Latinity to give 'ominous' coloration to this passage from the coda of *Iliad*, XIX. Note the adjective: we will hear it again in the most brilliant of later twentieth-century renditions. Chapman's astronomy has a theatrical logic. The shield's celestial radiance, the star with its 'spurry' rays (an inspired concatenation), the fallen sun – each is a *figura* of Achilles' destiny. Observe the formidable placement of the adverb: the son of Peleus 'charges' his beloved steeds 'terribly', where that 'charge' signifies 'address', 'instruction', but evokes, inescapably, the 'charge in battle', the war-lunge of the chariot itself as well as the sombre image of the unloading of the fallen Patroclus ('Discharge').

Next, his high Head the Helmet grac'd; behind
The sweepy Crest hung floating in the Wind:
Like the red Star, that from his flaming Hair
Shakes down Diseases, Pestilence and War;
So stream'd the golden Honours from his Head,
Trembled the sparkling Plumes, and the loose Glories shed . . .

Xanthus and Balius! of *Podarges'* Strain,
(Unless ye boast that heav'nly Race in vain)
Be swift, be mindful of the Load ye bear,
And learn to make your Master more your Care:
Thro' falling Squadrons bear my slaught'ring Sword
Nor, as ye left *Patroclus*, leave your Lord.

Alexander Pope, of course; in an idiom which declares itself dismissive, indeed scornful, of Chapman's or Ogilby's. But which is itself under pressure as it seeks to map a linguistic terrain outside the Shakespearean and Miltonic precedents and in rivalry with the genius for narrated action in Dryden's poems and translations. There is a shorthand of learned, authoritative allusion in 'the red Star' signifying Mars. 'Honours' and 'Glories' are very nearly technically heraldic. That speed, which Matthew Arnold will place foremost among the requisites of Homeric translation, gathers pace towards the laconic climax: 'Nor, as ye left *Patroclus*, leave your Lord.'

Most thought-provoking, however, is the ample footnote on the lines immediately following. How, asks Pope, is one to excuse 'the extravagant Fiction of a Horse speaking'? (Shades of Swift.) Pope invokes 'Fable, Tradition, and History', the latter in the person of Livy. He cites the poignant translation of the passage by Mr Fenton (it is intriguing that we find no such text in what we have of Richard Fenton's works). Then comes Pope's trump card: Balaam's eloquent ass. With this biblical validation, the footnote opens on universality: Homer inhabited an 'Age of Wonders' in which good taste and sensibility were receptive of the miraculous. In voice and pedantry, this note is Nabokovian. But the issue is capital. The tensed energies of Pope's Homer result from a constant conflict between the archaic matter of the epic fable and the new criteria of Cartesian-Newtonian rationality, between the semantics of myth and a language whose ideals are those of the logic of the Enlightenment.

Augustan verse will not really resolve the contradiction. But by virtue of its clarity, concision and supple flow, the heroic couplet prepares the ripening of modern prose (this interaction is already manifest in Dryden). In regard to Homeric translations, this development is, throughout the nineteenth century, shadowed, as it were, by nostalgia for a lost poetic rhetoric and for the sonority of the Authorized Version:

And he lifted the stout helmet and set it on his head, and like a star it shone, the horse-hair crested helmet, and around it waved plumes of gold that Hephaistos had set thick about the crest . . . And terribly he called upon the horses of his sire: 'Xanthos and Bailos, famed children of Podarge, in other sort take heed to bring your charioteer safe back to the Danaan host, when we have done with battle, and leave him not as ye left Patroklos to lie there dead.'

So, with its debt to Chapman's distant find, 'terribly', the 1891 Lang, Leaf and Myers, life-preserver to generations of schoolboys eager for a 'trot', and 'Homer' to a wide general readership in the Victorian era and early twentieth century. In recent decades, English and American poet-translators insist on the advantages of verse-forms, particularly under the impact of the scholarly discovery of Homer's oral and formulaic fabric. There is in these modern versions both a repudiation of prose – E. V. Rieu's publishing triumph being implicitly or explicitly the 'target of rejection' – and an attempt at loyalty to the strangeness, to the remoteness of the Greek original:

> Then lifting his rugged helmet
> he set it down on his brows, and the horsehair crest
> shone like a star and the waving golden plumes shook
> that Hephaestus drove in bristling thick along its ridge.
> And brilliant Achilles tested himself in all his gear,
> Achilles spun on his heels to see if it fit tightly . . .
> 'Roan Beauty and Charger, illustrious foals of Lightfoot!
> Try harder, do better this time – bring your charioteer
> back home alive to his waiting Argive comrades
> once we're through with fighting. Don't leave Achilles
> there on the battlefield as you left Patroclus – dead!'

The speech-patterns of informal prose are audible in the relaxed verse (too much so in the clotted line on Hephaistos). Those 'ands', on which the narrative pulse depends, tell of the King James Bible, but also of Hemingway. Elsewhere in this episode, Robert Fagles has Achilles testing whether or not his heroic limbs 'ran free' in his new armour, where 'running free' helps define his method as translator. 'Gear' is American in flavour; 'Roan Beauty and Charger' even more so. The bristling panoply worn in American football and the Kentucky stud-farms lies close to hand. None the less, what lies in back of that 'spun on his heels' and the verb 'cinch' which Fagles uses when he describes Automedon's preparations of the horses for combat, is not only adherence to Homer: it is Logue's brio in this tempestuous finale to Book XIX.

The radioactive tracer which these successive versions allow us to follow lights up not only the history of the English languages and their interrelations. It tells of the reciprocities 'in motion' as between different translators and readers of Homer. Each translator competes more or less openly with the great family of his predecessors and contemporaries. Respectfully, polemically, mimetically or not, he 'takes on' both Homer and the English or American 'Homers' already in the field. He may do so in a spirit of indebtedness: T. E. Lawrence using Palmer. In salutation: Fagles in respect of Fitzgerald. Often the connection is corrective and agonistic: Cowper announces his quarrel with what he takes to be the unjustified ornateness and ponderous archaeology of Pope. Recent American poet-translators articulate their critique of Lattimore's didacticism, of what they judge to be the plodding academicism of his verse. E. V. Rieu provokes the riposte of all those translators who believe that prose, however fluent or robust, betrays the very essence of the *Iliad* and *Odyssey*.

The interactions are always triangular: if the two epics form the apex, the base and internal spaces are those of other translations – even into other languages (Pope looks to the French precedent). These spaces reflect and, in turn, generate not only the image we have of Homer and the Homeric world, but of the climate of culture and taste in which the translations were commissioned, published and read. Thus the Stuart-Caroline Homer – cf. Ogilby's elaborate biography of the blind bard! – is not that of Chapman and, not yet, that of Dryden and Pope. Victorian and Edwardian versions document British sentiments at the time, in reference to warfare, to masculine bonds, to colonialism and the mastered sea. A cluster of translations was 'set in motion' by Schliemann's spectacular excavations at Troy and Mycenae. For a spell, Milman Parry's revolutionary demonstration of the formulaic conventions of oral epics dominated the practice of translation. Now a certain reaction and emphasis on Homer's innovative powers and operative freedom have set in. But current 'Homers' all come after Moses Finley's revaluation of the socio-economic structures of the Homeric, pre-Mycenaean background.

Augustan representations of political, social and psychological experience are, therefore, as crucial to Pope's Homer as the Vietnam War aura is to Robert Lowell's selection from the *Iliad* or late twentieth-century ethnic, populist pluralism is to Walcott's *Omeros*. Compare Pope's Nestor, so evidently construed out of a characteristic eighteenth-century reverence for and satire on old age, with the figure of the gin-sodden sahib and garrulous expatriate in Walcott. Homeric Nestor moves behind both, but his masks are protean.

Such shifts in perspective determine the fascinating pendulum-swing in the relative placement of the two epics in their Anglo-American lives. For Pope and his forerunners, the *Iliad* stands supreme. It remains not only the unmatched font of the western poetic imagination and the enduring model of sublimity. It is also a lasting manual of statecraft, of the arts of persuasion and of war. The *Odyssey* is felt to be an inspired offshoot, a later redaction, tainted with Mediterranean folklore and patches of pathos in which even early exegetes and translators intuit an almost 'feminine' fibre. Viewed through Virgil, the *Odyssey* often figures in neo-classical estimates as the begetter of the *Aeneid*, itself a sovereign text but not of the primal stature of the *Iliad*. As literary modes grow more introspective, as perceptions come to dwell on psychological motivations and the dramas of privacy, it is the *Odyssey* which looks pivotal. Here lie the germs of the novel. Read through Dante, it is Odysseus' fatal unrest which absorbs Tennyson. It is Circe, Calypso, the Sirens and patient Penelope who people Pre-Raphaelite and *fin-de-siècle* images. After *Ulysses*, as Borges proclaims, time is reversed: Homer now comes after Joyce. Yet the experience of the Second World War produces a counter-current. The proud cities set ablaze, the chivalric heroism of the fighter-pilot or commando, restores Hector and Troy to felt immediacy. The sufferings of civilians at the bloody hands of their captors make of Hecuba and Andromache emblems all too familiar. English and American poet-dramatists turn back to 'the Trojan women', as do Hauptmann and Sartre on the Continent. Today, I would guess, the two epics are in active equilibrium of repute, though it may be that late twentieth-century moods are more at home in the subtle variousness and questionings of the *Odyssey*.

I believe our *Iliad* to be the product of an editorial recension of genius, of a wonderfully formative act of combination, selection and editing of the voluminous oral material. This recension would coincide with the new techniques of writing and of the preparation of papyrus or hides in quantities sufficient for so extensive an inscription. I take the editor of genius (or one of the editors, somewhat as in the case of the Authorized Version) to have been the *author* of the *Odyssey*. In older age, perhaps, and at some ironic distance. Though the motif is adumbrated in Achilles' complaint to Thetis in the *Iliad*, the flat declaration by Achilles in the Underworld of the *Odyssey* that he would choose a life even in abject servitude over one of heroic brevity, puts in drastic doubt the entire world-image of the earlier epic. And it seems to me that only some such relationship between our two texts, between compilation or redaction and composition, could have generated the sheer marvel of the moment in Book VIII of the *Odyssey* in which Odysseus, incognito, hears the minstrel Demodokos singing tales of Troy and of Odysseus' role therein.

The craft, the social functions of the several minstrels who appear in the *Iliad* and the *Odyssey* take us back to the beginnings of western literature and, perhaps, music. The montage-effect, the mirroring inward in this Demodokos-episode (as in Don Giovanni's audition of a piece out of *Figaro* during his last supper!) are 'modern' and, indeed, 'post-modern'. The hybrid arc of Walcott's conception spans inception and modernity:

> A hot street led to the beach
> past the small shops and the clubs and a pharmacy
> in whose angling shade, his khaki dog on a leash,
>
> the blind man sat on his crate after the pirogues
> set out, muttering the dark language of the blind,
> gnarled hands on his stick, his ears as sharp as the dog's.
>
> Sometimes he would sing and the scraps blew on the wind
> when her beads rubbed their rosary. Old St Omère.
> He claimed he'd sailed round the world. 'Monsieur Seven Seas'
>
> they christened him, from a cod-liver-oil label
> with its wriggling swordfish. They were Greek to her
> Or old African babble.

Later, in the spirit of Borges's anti-chronology, the blind singer of Homeric songs hails:

> Anna Livia!
> Muse of our age's Omeros, undimmed Master
> and true tenor of the place!

who

> from the Martello brought one-eyed Ulysses
> to the copper-bright strand, watching the mailpacket
> butting past the Head, its wake glittering like keys . . .

where that 'wake' again celebrates Joyce and those 'keys' adduce Joyce-Homer-Omeros' 'tenor' and the sung structure of the epic saga.

Mark the displacements of identity, the 'deconstructive' tactics of ghostliness in the Demodokos encounter. The minstrel in Book VIII is himself blind. (The early ascription of blindness to Homer is, I think, a move by the *Homeridae*, by the guild of the professional singers-reciters of both epics, to conceal from an increasingly sophisticated public the illiteracy of their begetter.) Demodokos cannot see Odysseus who is 'invisible' through disguise. Who, on arrival at the Phaeacian court, has made of himself *outis*, the 'No one' who, by his act of denomination, of un-naming, had escaped from death at the hands of the Cyclops. The minstrel sings of a fierce quarrel between Odysseus and Achilles in the camp before Troy. The *Iliad*, as we have it, recounts no such incident. It might belong to one of the other epics in the Troy cycle. Or, more subtly, this bitter exchange at a banquet, which brings joy to the scheming heart of Agamemnon, might be Demodokos' invention, which is to say, an invention by the author of our *Odyssey*. In which case, the Odysseus of the epic is listening to, is witnessing his own modulation into fiction, into 'non-being', existentiality fading into the glow of timelessness. The mask, the persona in its original sense, is made shadow:

Thus sang the bard, but Ulysses drew his purple mantle over his head and covered his face, for he was ashamed to let the Phaeacians see that he was weeping. When the bard left off singing he wiped the tears from his eyes, uncovered his face, and, taking his cup, made a drink-offering to the gods; but when the Phaeacians pressed Demodocus to sing further, for they delighted in his lays, then Ulysses again drew his mantle over his head and wept bitterly.

(Samuel Butler)

T. E. Lawrence embroiders. His minstrel is 'very famous'. Odysseus 'with two strong hands drew the purple cloak over his head to hide his goodly face. He was ashamed to let the tears well from his deep-set eyes publicly before the Phaeacians.' Demodokos 'pours a libation to the God'. His verses 'are unallowed delight' to the listening 'chiefs'.

Robert Graves was, *in propria persona*, a warrior and singer of tales:

Odysseus

with massive hand drew his rich mantle down
over his brow, cloaking his face with it,
to make the Phaiákians miss the secret tears
that started to his eyes. How skilfully
he dried them when the song came to a pause!
threw back his mantle, spilt his gout of wine!
But soon the minstrel plucked his note once more
to please Phaiákian lords, who loved the song;
then in his cloak Odysseus wept again.
His tears flowed in the mantle unperceived:
only Alkínoös, at his elbow, saw them,
and caught the low groan in the man's breathing.

We have here a vignette out of Ossian and romantic 'bardolatry' which Graves deliberately entitles 'The Song of the Harper'. The tune is that of Weber or Berlioz, rather than of the street-singers plucking at a Balkan, Anatolian or North African stringed instrument, as we meet them in most recent anthropological-ethnographic portrayals of Homer. What one misses – even in Robert Fitzgerald – is the haunting intricacy of Odysseus' depersonalization, that 'ultra-modern' tension (if such an epithet makes any sense) between the survivance and potential immortality of the hero when he becomes the object of a minstrel's art, and the concomitant eradication of this same hero from actual life. This tension vibrates throughout the *Odyssey* as it looks back to, as it selectively incorporates, the *Iliad*. It gives to Odysseus' descent into the Underworld, to his dialogue with the great shades 'burning still' – as Fitzgerald memorably images the ghost of incensed Ajax – their critical ambiguity. I have already referred to Achilles' bitter repudiation of the heroic ideal: 'Do not make light of Death before me, O shining Odysseus. Would that I were on earth a menial, bound to some insubstantial man who must pinch and scrape to keep alive! Life so were better than King of Kings among these dead men who have had their day and died' (T. E. Lawrence). Derek Walcott presses the question even further, to include the poet's own claims and calling:

> There, in her head of ebony,
> there was no real need for the historian's
> remorse, nor for literature's. Why not see Helen
>
> as the sun saw her, with no Homeric shadow,
> swinging her plastic sandals on that beach alone,
> as fresh as the sea-wind? Why make the smoke a door?

Where 'smoke', I take it, signifies sacrifice and shadow, and where that 'door' leads both to Hades and to the West African and voodoo figurations into which, seemingly without strain, Walcott metamorphoses the *Nekya* in the *Odyssey*.

Walcott's teasing query is: why not see the Helen, Hector, Odysseus, Agamemnon, King Priam in our fields of echo and recognition 'with no Homeric shadow'? We cannot, in fact, do so. No break is visible in the continuing history of translations, adaptations and imitations. The *Iliad* and the *Odyssey* are perennially active in the pulse of the English languages, in the texts and contexts of Anglo-Saxon self-definition. Once more, I ask: why? Let me put forward one further conjecture.

The *auctoritas* of Shakespeare over the language, over the repertoire of our private and public perceptions and sense of the literary fact, is at once inspiring and despotic. At different times in the history of the English tongues, Shakespeare, to cite Edmund Gosse, threatens 'to suffocate' all who come after him or reduce them to mere echo. By contrast, the linguistic-cultural distance to the Homeric is both talismanic and liberating. We revert to Homer as, in some ways, an unattainable dawn and model. But we are sufficiently remote and free from him to answer back creatively. We test our own means of narrative, of poetic pathos, of the presentment of the human and natural worlds, against that originating source – but it remains a source whose strangeness, whose indistinct horizons invite our freedom. Twice, in the prodigal course of our theme, the discrimination is drawn between the Homeric touchstone and Shakespearean prepotence. We need to reflect on Pope's 'Homer' in relation to Pope's editing of Shakespeare. We need to listen, even more closely than hitherto, to the play and flicker of analogies and contrasts as between *Ulysses* as a whole and the 'exagminations' of *Hamlet* in the early part of the book.

Moreover, the issue is not one of 'Homeric shadow'. It is, as Christopher Logue instructs us, one of noon-light. Logue does so in a vocabulary which goes back to Chapman – an 'ominous' radiance floods Achilles' heart – and which moves forward to audacities no previous translator had enlisted:

> The chariot's basket dips. The whip
> Fires in between the horses' ears;
> And as in dreams, or at Cape Kennedy, they rise,
> Slowly it seems, their chests like royals, yet
> Behind them in a double plume the sand curls up,
> Is barely dented by their flying hooves,
> And wheels that barely touch the world,
> And the wind slams shut behind them.

Achilles' helmet is 'a welded cortex':

> Though it is noon, the helmet screams against the light;
> Scratches the eye; so violent it can be seen
> Across three thousand years.

[105]

Not only seen, I would say, but *heard*. As can be heard the swallow-cry twang of the great bow as Odysseus strings it for vengeance. Or the sudden silence of the old gaffers on the battlements of Troy, struck dumb by the beauty of passing Helen. Or the enigmatic song of the Sirens, as it hums through western literature from Dante and Milton to Donne, from Donne to Rilke and Kafka. Each translator in turn has his 'eyes scratched' and blood stopped by the violence of that light 'across three thousand years', by that first and unsurpassed noon. But then, was not Homer blind?

This anthology is a modest *selection* from six and one half centuries of material. If it includes such evident summits of translation as the 'Homers' of Chapman, Dryden, Pope, Shelley or Logue, it also presents much that is of mainly historical or experimental value, which tells of the experience of past and present in Anglo-Saxon political, social and literary feeling. The contents range from the word-for-word, line-for-line interlinear technique (in which Walter Benjamin saw the secret ideal of all 'Adamic' translation) to distant evocations and inferences of the Homeric as in Auden's 'Shield of Achilles' or Hugo Manning's hints towards Odysseus 'the sea-fox'. I have given examples of Homeric travesty and burlesque, of the Homeric substance in lyric, prose-fiction and even dramatic genres. Appropriately, this harvest concludes with passages from the *Odyssey* specially translated for this volume by a younger American poet.

So much has been left out. Of the plethora of partial translations which cluster around Pope. Of the veritable 'pride' of Homeric versions after Matthew Arnold's famous challenge and critique. I have, regrettably, been unable to include examples of film-scripts based on adventures or heroes out of the *Iliad* and *Odyssey*. Nor has there been place for recent comic-book adaptations. Flaxman's illustrations to Homer exercised almost as much influence on British and American readings as did the translation by Pope or the Homeric reprises in Tennyson. More space could have been found for the long tradition of 'Homers for the young', of which Charles Lamb's retelling of the *Odyssey* is an enchanting example. I have not (yet) tracked down certain privately printed fragments of Homer translated, imitated by classically schooled officers on their way to the Dardanelles.

As this Penguin book goes to press, new 'Homers' in English and its planetary variants are appearing or have been announced as forthcoming. As in Odysseus' descent into Hades, the bright shades of the Homeric throng towards one, each with its accent, guise and story to tell. Women-translators, who have already turned to Greek lyric poetry and tragedy, may now be at work. One is haunted by Robert Graves's dictum: 'There is one story, and one story only.'

May this selection bring to its readers something of the joy that has gone into its gathering.

A Reading against Shakespeare

It may be that the fraternal polemic between philosophy and literature, specifically between ontology and poetics, has come to an end. It began with Plato's exclusion of the poets from the ideal state, a motion of argument and of spirit made the more internecine by virtue of Plato's own literary-dramatic genius. Aristotle's reclamation of tragic fiction towards therapeutic ends, his incorporation of poetics into the politics of individual and civic sanity, came next. With Martin Heidegger's insistence on the fundamental unity of *denken* and *dichten*, of the intellectually percipient and the poetically creative functions, with Heidegger's claim that the authentic thinker and the true poet are necessarily engaged in the same act and witness of being, the millennial debate, intimate and agonistic, may have come full circle and reached its formal close.

The kinship between the philosophic and the poetic practices of discourse is one of common origin and medium. Both are solicitations of order, seeking to construe intelligible form out of the suggestive anarchy of the phenomenal. Both bring to bear on language a willed pressure of close notice; the philosopher and the poet are artisans of language scrupulous in their apprehension, always simultaneous and potentially conflictual, of the actual instrument they use and of the possible relations of that instrument to the matter of its articulation. Philosophy and literature are speculative constructs of the commerce between word and world. In person, the master-builders have often been the same man or near neighbours. In pre-Socratic Greece, the exposition of cosmological-metaphysical argument and of heroic or didactic narrative were intimately meshed. Our first ontology, that of Parmenides, is a poem. A number of philosophers in the western tradition have been eminent poets or masters of prose; they have given to their armature of consequent argument – ontological, ethical, political – the

The W. P. Ker Lecture, 1986.

exponential force of considered style. There is in Plato, in Nietzsche, an unmistakable music of meaning; the inward narrative and dramatizations in Hegel's *Phenomenology* are strictly analogous to those in the epic novels of the nineteenth century. Reciprocally, there is little serious literature innocent of concerns, of formulations, of questionings of a philosophic sort. Aristotle's famous preference of the concrete universality of the fiction over the evidential singularity of the historical fact, reaches further. It is in literature, in the poem, in the play, in the novel that philosophic models, that trials of abstract metaphysical and moral possibility, have been given the density, the enacted and existential weight (literally: *Dichtung*) of felt life. Hence the interplay, inexhaustible to reflection and to the schooling of our sensibility, between, say, the atomism of Democritus and that of Lucretius, between the logic and epistemology of Thomism and that of the *Divine Comedy*, between the proposals on temporality in Bergson and their metamorphic reprise in Proust. Hence what I take to be the finalities of interchange, of a mirroring so intense yet subtly distortive, between Heidegger's saying and thinking of being and the works of Sophocles and of Hölderlin which, literally, underwrite that saying and thinking.

The compelling affinities between the philosophic and the poetic modes, their twin inceptions in the primal impulse towards meaning, towards the attempt of human consciousness to find a lodging in the given world – an attempt which we call 'myth' – have induced those conflicts of which Plato's *Republic* remains exemplary. The status of the fictive within the 'truth-values' of analytic and systematic intellection, the status of the fictive within the 'veracity-values' of morality, have been a fruitful irritant to epistemology and to ethics. The irresponsibilities or, more exactly, the internalized autonomies of literary invention are perplexing and, in certain cases, repellent to philosophy. The recuperaton of *poiesis* into systematic critiques of cognition and systematic codes of rational conduct (as in Aristotle, as in Kant) often betrays an excess of protest, a strained anxiety to domesticate. Literature is a voracious and anarchic beast. Loosed upon totality it threatens to ingest the provender, sometimes scarce, sometimes fenced in by an aura of solemnity and technical elevation, which metaphysics, epistemology, ethics, political theory and even formal logic (witness *Alice in Wonderland* or the surrealist movements) would reserve for their own. The result can be an exercise in more or less theoretical negation – Plato's banishment of the poet-liars, Rousseau's condemnation of the theatre. It can be an argument for normative hierarchy in which the philosophic stance, notably in its ethical and transcendent categories, is placed well above the aesthetic (so in Kierkegaard). The result can also be one of fruitful misunderstanding, a misreading or counter-statement whose penetrative strength, whose formal and substantive reach, are such as to bring into radical question both the philosophic and the literary case.

It is with a mis- or counter-reading of this order that I want to deal, in a preliminary and tentative way, in this lecture.

'Shakespeare and no end,' remarked Goethe in awe and, one has licence to suppose, a certain rival testiness. So far as the secondary material goes, the tag is all too appropriate. Trivia begets mountainous trivia. The interminable spate of scholarship has added next to nothing to our knowledge of Shakespeare the man, to the shadow-lineaments of the actual person as they have survived in so very few documents. Genuine critical addenda to insights already available are of the rarest. For one Coleridge, for one G. Wilson Knight, what accumulations of turgid, self-serving gossip. Even the best scholarship and criticism, moreover, can do nothing to restore to our informed imagining the reality of William Shakespeare before he became 'Shakespeare'. What we are quite unable to perceive is the daily fact of Shakespeare the actor-playwright, frequently but not invariably successful, of the socially, materially concerned and condignly ambitious country squire, of the poet-dramatist who left a body of work no doubt esteemed but to which the art of his younger associates, Beaumont and Fletcher, was widely preferred. No insistence of historical inquiry, of psychological reconstruction, will yield to us the decisive context of professional normality within which he appeared to his contemporaries and literary-theatrical peers (nor need one have any sympathy with the nonsense propounded by 'Baconians' and the like to register as strange, even as disturbing, the utter paucity of actual traces of Shakespeare's presence at the time; we happen to know far more about other Elizabethans, men of letters included; there *is* a possible enigma there).

If Ben Jonson seems to have been the first to take the grander view –

> Thou art a monument, without a tomb,
> And art alive still, while thy book doth live, –

if Jonson perceives the author of the First Folio as 'not of an age, but for all time!', he also, and notoriously, wished that this same Shakespeare 'had blotted a thousand lines', found him to have invented much that was merely risible and, in characteristic equipoise, concluded that Shakespeare had 'redeemed his vices with his virtues'. Much in the inward relations between Milton and Shakespeare remains to be explored. What is manifest is the considered thrust of Milton's statement in the brief preface to *Samson Agonistes* that the plays of the antique tragedians, of Aeschylus, Sophocles and Euripides, are 'unequalled yet by any'. The force, the implication of this verdict, coming as it does sixty-five years after *King Lear,* must not be underestimated. It entails a fundamental dissent.

Dr Johnson remains our greatest editor-critic of Shakespeare, one whose learned sanity and alert confidence outweigh the limitations of a moralizing bias. To Samuel Johnson, Shakespeare was, among English writers, *primus inter pares*, but he was a natural man, fallible, uneven, possibly confused about the true direction of his genius (Johnson's famous judgement that comedy was more native to Shakespeare than tragedy). Within the plays themselves, Johnson found much to dislike and amend. The canon, as he saw and edited it, had distinct failures within it. Shakespeare's taste faltered, not only in respect of bawdy and of word-play, but in the management of rhetoric, of dramatic episodes, of poetic-philosophical dénouements – Johnson's bristling malaise over the fifth act of *Lear.* The expositions in Shakespearean drama were often laboured; the repetitions wasteful; the hyperboles self-indulgent. Pope's edition of and notes on Shakespeare (unduly neglected) exhibit an analogous poise and calm of admiring response. The translator of Homer (and Pope's Homer is, after *Paradise Lost*, the only major English epic) could test the contrastive stature of Shakespeare. Much in the latter impresses Pope as inspired; much as botched and dispensable. Hence his practice of marking for particular attention the best passages.

The leap towards transcendence occurs in the late eighteenth and early nineteenth centuries. It is between the mid-1780s and 1830 that the stature of Shakespeare and of his works passes out of the realm of normal valuation and becomes what modern physicists call 'a singularity', a law and phenomenalism unto themselves. Much in this fascinating story remains opaque. A cluster of secondary figures seems to have played a crucial role. Among them was the Lord Rector of Glasgow University from 1826 to 1829, Thomas Campbell. It is he who may have invented the word and thus isolated the very concept of 'bardolatry'. Maurice Morgann's 'Essay on the Dramatic Character of Sir John Falstaff' of 1777 may have exercised a far-reaching, if at first almost subterranean influence. In their self-defining critique of neo-classicism, pre-romanticism and romanticism in Britain and on the Continent may have intuited in Shakespeare a twofold talisman: the counter-classicism of his art could authorize the romantic experiment; but because Shakespeare's art was inimitable, such authorization did not weigh upon, did not crush modern sensibility. To invoke, to worship Shakespeare was to benefit immeasurably from a *mimesis* of spirit, of passionate patronage (as we find them lived, noted matchlessly in Keats's letters) without incurring the subservience of *imitatio*.

Whatever its motives, whatever its complex, deep-seated energies of transmutation, the effects of the 'Shakespeare revolution' were themselves dramatic (dare one say, histrionic?). Within little more than a generation, the finding that William Shakespeare was not only the most gifted of all writers but a being whose powers of creation in some distinct sense rivalled those of nature and of the Deity, had become a cliché. To Keats and to Coleridge, the author of *Hamlet* or of *The Tempest* was a literally superhuman agent, a guardian-presence of the human spirit. Victor Hugo perceived in

Shakespeare a cosmic force, an all-encompassing inspiration fully comparable with that at work in the Book of Job and in the Prophets, but greater yet by virtue of dramatic art. The man who could, with seeming dispassion, with an impartiality of total comprehension again suggestive of the Deity's, create both Cordelia and Iago, Falstaff and Ariel, struck Hazlitt, Schlegel, Pushkin and Manzoni as one to whom normal, immanent codes of critical discrimination were inapplicable. Editorial chicanery or personal preference might still quarrel with or qualify this or that local aspect of Shakespeare's achievement and meaning. But as a whole, the poems and plays tower over any responsible conception we might have not only of literature, but of secular wisdom (witness the innumerable nineteenth-century anthologies of 'maxims on life', of pointers to human behaviour, taken from Shakespeare's plays). Indeed, it was precisely the limitation to the secular which came under exalted pressure. Unhesitatingly, Charles Lamb sets a passage from Shakespeare beside one from the Gospel. Any radical critique of Shakespeare now began to take on the aura of blasphemy.

As a result, serious, sustained dissents from Shakespeare have, after the 1830s, been exceedingly rare.

The best known is that of Tolstoy (which George Orwell sought to expound and analyse in his essay on 'Tolstoy, Lear and the Fool'). Himself a supreme creator of animate form and a playwright of considerable power, Tolstoy found much of Shakespearean drama to be puerile in its sentiments, amoral in its fundamental world-view, rhetorically overblown and often insufferable to adult reason. *King Lear*, in particular, was a cruel, childish farrago (that leap off the Dover cliffs!) 'beneath serious criticism'. Much would be worth saying about Tolstoy's ascetic, puritanical realism; about his almost instinctive loathing of 'make-believe': about the secret, subconscious rage he may have felt in the face of Shakespeare's creation of Lear, a creation which so hauntingly 'previsions' Tolstoy's own destiny and tempestuous end. Nevertheless, even after the inference of psychological motive and ideological myopia, there are points in Tolstoy's critique worth careful notice.

Who now remembers Edmund Gosse's outcry, at the turn of the century, that Shakespeare's sheer weight and precedent was crushing the life out of English verse and out of any attempts to renew serious drama in the English language? Closely related to this protest are the attempts of both Walt Whitman and Ezra Pound to liberate the American language from the Shakespearean hold and, more especially, to find and test American verse rhythms in which the Shakespearean iambic would no longer be the implicit metronome (an attempt crucial to both the splendours and the disasters of Pound's *Cantos*). George Bernard Shaw's niggling attacks on Shakespeare's amateurish dramaturgy, Shaw's peremptory rewriting of *Cymbeline* to demonstrate how the thing 'ought to have been done', are giggly in tone and leave all parties mildly embarrassed. Far more searching, but masked and feline in its cautionary tactics, is T. S. Eliot's dissent, not only from *Hamlet*, but from Shakespeare as a whole. It is Dante in whom Eliot locates those finalities of mastered imagining, of responsible enactment, of philosophic-poetic fusion lacking in Shakespeare. Characteristically, Eliot chose not to pursue and make vulnerably plain what seems to have been a deep-seated discrimination. But how much more palpable in his work and thought are the presences of Virgil and of Dante than is that of Shakespeare (the links which need to be traced here are those between the early Eliot and neo-classicism and the politics of order in both their Continental and American vein).

Scarcely charted is the acute critique of Shakespeare dynamic in the recasting of *Othello* by Boito and Verdi. The decision to initiate the action in Cyprus, the attribution to Iago of a manichaean credo, the strengthening, the 'ripening' of Desdemona effected by Verdi's music, constitute an utterly fascinating, instructive debate with Shakespeare. That that Mozartian masterpiece, Verdi's *Falstaff*, is a far greater work than *The Merry Wives of Windsor* ought not to require argument.

But although both Tolstoy's and Eliot's *différend* with Shakespeare (the French word is precisely right) have ethical-philosophical elements, neither is the expression of a major philosophical witness in any strict sense. It is this fact which makes the more arresting the posthumous publication of a set of brief but absolutely central reservations about, dissents from Shakespeare and the place Shakespeare occupies in western and, indeed, world culture. These reservations and dissents are to be found in miscellaneous remarks, aphorisms, observations set down by Ludwig Wittgenstein between 1939 and 1951. Translated, at times unsatisfactorily, by Peter Winch, they are now available to the English-speaking reader in a volume entitled *Culture and Value* (Blackwell, 1980). The pretentious, wholly non-Wittgensteinian English title has no relation to *Vermischte Bemerkungen*, meaning nothing more than 'miscellanea'.

The point to bear in mind as we consider some of these notes is, I feel, this: Wittgenstein was a human being of uncompromising, unforgiving honesty. He was nakedly at home with truth as he saw and as he lived it. If, as he remarks in 1950, he could 'never do anything with Shakespeare' – 'nie etwas mit ihm anfangen' is more graphic – then there was absolutely no use pretending otherwise. The incapacity had to be faced and, so far as was feasible, unravelled. It had to be *begründet* (given firm ground) in the context of Wittgenstein's aesthetics, investigations into meaning, ethics and, above all, personal modes of feeling and existence. The fact that almost everyone else praises Shakespeare to the skies – a unanimity Wittgenstein had experienced both in his native Vienna, with its passionate theatrical cult of Shakespearean drama and dramatic poesy, and in the England of his exile – was immaterial. The truth is not a matter of majority opinion, even of near-unanimity. On the contrary. As Wittgenstein writes in 1946:

When, for instance, I hear the expression of admiration for Shakespeare by distinguished men in the course of several centuries, I can never rid myself of the suspicion that praising him has been the conventional thing to do . . .

Much of this adulation, adds Wittgenstein, has been expended 'without understanding and for the wrong reasons by a thousand professors of literature'. The grievous inference here being that there can hardly be less qualified or more intellectually venal judges. Now comes what may prove to be a key marker: 'It takes the authority of

Milton really to convince me. I take it for granted that he was incorruptible.' Was Wittgenstein at this date (1946) listening to F. R. Leavis, who had chosen Milton rather than Shakespeare as his vade-mecum in the trenches during the First World War, a selection and a circumstance which would elicit vital resonance in Wittgenstein's own temperament and experience? (We would like to know.) What is evident is the suggestion of mendacity as it surrounds the whole Shakespeare cult and, possibly, certain aspects of Shakespeare's inventions.

Wittgenstein's unease, the bewildered honesties of his distaste, have their confused start. It is during 1939–40, that Wittgenstein seeks to characterize Shakespeare's 'objectivity':

Shakespeare displays the dance of human passions, one might say. Hence he had to be objective; otherwise he would not so much display the dance of human passions – as talk about it. But he displays it to us in a dance; not naturalistically.

Wittgenstein ascribes this idea to his friend and correspondent Paul Engelmann. The point is worth noting, for it is precisely Engelmann who will be Wittgenstein's guide to Kierkegaard and the recipient of Wittgenstein's most intimately religious avowals. *Per se* the observation is innocuous. 'Naturalism' is hardly a criterion of the highest art. What may be latent is the hint – it is no more than that – of a certain playful exhibitionism, of a playful licence in Shakespeare's method.

A cluster of entries for 1946 centre on the dark theme of nuclear destruction, a prospect of some ambivalence to Wittgenstein as it would also entail the end of 'our disgusting, soapy-water [*seifen-wässrigen*] science'. This reflection seems to lead directly to a proposition which is further expounded in the *Philosophical Investigations*, II, iv: 'The human being is the best picture of the human soul.' Note the motif of 'picture' and faithful representation. Shakespeare's similes

are, in the ordinary sense, bad. So if they are none the less good – and I don't know whether they are or not – they must be a law to themselves. Perhaps, e.g., their ring gives them plausibility and truth.

[116]

'Ring' is only a partial rendering of *Klang*: resonance, tonality, register, are implicit. It may be, continues Wittgenstein, that one has simply to accept Shakespeare 'in his ease and authority', 'in the way you accept nature, a piece of scenery, for example, just as it is'. Surely, a commonplace of (admiring) response. Shakespeare is a 'given', as present to immediacy as is nature itself.

But Wittgenstein probes further. If the comparison with nature is valid, 'that would mean that the style of his whole work, I mean of all his works taken together, is the essential thing and what provides his justification'. Why, one ventures to ask, should there be any need of 'justification' (*das Rechtfertigende*)? This, however, is not, I think, the key marker. It is the validating centrality of 'style'. Set down here almost neutrally, this rubric will soon take on a negative tenor. 'My *failure* to understand him [Shakespeare] could then be explained by my inability to read him *easily*. In the way in which one perceives a splendid landscape [*eine herrliche Landschaft*].' The passage is somewhat opaque. We know of Wittgenstein's susceptibility to natural scenery. *If* Shakespeare's art is like the 'presentness' of nature, if the ambient immediacy constitutes its style and coherence, *then* our reading of it should be one of spontaneous reflex, of unforced *Leichtigkeit*. This is not, however, Wittgenstein's experience. (How confident was his English in respect of the more demanding lexical and grammatical elements in Shakespeare? Is Wittgenstein resorting, consciously or not, to the masterly Schlegel-Tieck versions so essential to the central European literacy of his upbringing and so sovereignly acted at the Burgtheater in Vienna?)

Three years later, during the course of 1949, Wittgeinstein is pondering the epistemological and psychological status of dreams. We recall his fitful (to me, as it happens, irrefutable) critique of Freud's interpretation of dreams and of the psychoanalytic practices which sprang from it. Now the two themes, Shakespeare and dreams, coalesce:

A dream is all wrong, absurd, composite, and yet at the same time it is completely right: put together in *this* strange way it makes an impression.

Why? I don't know. And if Shakespeare is great, as he is said to be, then it must be possible to say of him: it's all wrong, things *aren't like that* – and yet at the same time it's quite right according to a law of its own.

It could be put like this too: if Shakespeare is great, his greatness is displayed only in the whole corpus of his plays [*in der Masse seiner Dramen*, where *Masse* is underlined], which create their own language and world. In other words, he is completely unrealistic. (Like a dream.)

On a quite jejune level, Wittgenstein's finding can be read as positive. The marvel of internal consistency in Shakespeare's works, the autonomy and internalized poetic logic of the Shakespeare-world, are commonplaces of admiration. If it is eccentric to deny greatness to individual plays (did Wittgenstein ever read the Sonnets?), it is nevertheless a just and commonplace observation that Shakespeare's stature only emerges integrally from the canon as a whole. The notion of 'realism' is hardly a necessary touchstone. On the contrary: it is Shakespeare's power to create totalities of poetic vision as compelling, as creatively informing as are our deepest dreams, which strikes us as incomparable. But it is not, of course, on this plane of intuition and of argument that Wittgenstein is probing. The perplexities and implications in this passage draw on almost the entirety of Wittgenstein's perennial engagement with the nature and functions of language, with truth and logic, with semantic conventions and reference. The confrontations implicit here are nothing less than those between the analyses of the relations between word and world in the *Tractatus* and the *Philosophical Investigations* on the one hand, and the proposition voiced in *Timon of Athens* on the other: 'The world is but a word' – a proposition which I take to be fundamentally unacceptable to Wittgenstein precisely because he experienced and tested its solicitations so intimately.

For Yeats, 'in dreams begin responsibilities'. Wittgenstein, one supposes, would not accept this affirmation unguardedly. The non-realism of the dream-world, its anarchic articulation and creation of a language of its own, trouble Wittgenstein and are a target for his investigative critique exactly in the same way as is the vexed topic of a 'private language'. Just beneath the surface of the tentative concession – 'and yet at the same time it's quite right according to a law of its own' – fundamental differentiations and refusals are gaining clarity. It is these which will be enunciated and tested in the entries for 1950.

Once again, Wittgenstein declares his bafflement: 'I could only stare in wonder at Shakespeare; I could never make anything of, do anything with him'. The distrust of Shakespeare's admirers is now '*deep*' (Wittgenstein underlines). Shakespeare 'stands alone', he is 'a singularity', 'at least in the culture of the west'. But it is precisely his unique status which is a misfortune for it means that 'one can only place him by placing him wrongly'. Such misprision has induced a fundamentally erroneous estimate:

It is *not* as though Shakespeare portrayed human types well and were in that respect *true to life*. He is *not* true to life. But he has such a supple hand and his delineations, his brush stroke are so particular that each of his characters looks to be *significant*, worth looking at [*sehenswert*].

The irritants in Wittgenstein's dissent are evident. Shakespeare's apartness which, surely, Wittgenstein exaggerated in a manner characteristically Germanic and suggestive of the divinization of Shakespeare as it extends from German romanticism to Gundolf, makes authentic 'placement' (the Leavis word) impossible. Wittgenstein takes Shakespeare's works to be extraneous to general categories of evaluative discourse and debate – and it is on this last point, that of unembarrassed debate, of sincere challenge, that he may well be right. There is, in Shakespeare's invention and articulation of 'human types' (itself an oddly betraying rubric), a semantic individuation, a technical adroitness so specific as to yield, indeed enforce a *seeming* significance, a spectacular meaningfulness with the emphasis on 'visibility', on 'spectacle' in the root-sense. This 'spectacularity' extends to the man and his writings as a whole: 'People stare at him in wonderment, almost as at a spectacular natural phenomenon.' Such scenic significance is not '*true to life*'. It is not '*Naturwahr*'. Such a denial of Shakespeare's 'truth to life', of the overwhelmingly convincing *vitality* and psychological-carnal presence of his personae, is very difficult to place, let alone take seriously.

The Tolstoyan polemic, which Wittgenstein was thoroughly familiar with, lies near to hand. Gloucester's stage-leap off the Dover cliffs infuriates Tolstoy. It does so not only by reason of its material implausibility; but because – and this *is* a point worth thinking about in regard to the whole theory and practice of *mimesis* in western art and literature – it forces the actors and the spectators (prior, certainly, to the twentieth-century theatre of minimalism or alienation) to adopt ridiculous postures. The actor's realization of such an episode (and they are numerous in Shakespeare), together with the spectator's forced suspension of disbelief, constitutes a false situation, a puerile mendacity insulting to both. The very nonchalance of Shakespeare's pictorial, histrionic means induces in both Tolstoy and Wittgenstein the intimation of a confidence trick. In Tolstoy's analysis, the illusion produced is, finally, gross and childish. Wittgenstein's indictment is subtler: the manipulative sovereignty and singularity of Shakespeare's spectacular skills generate a merely *phenomenal* significance. And mere phenomenality is *untrue to life*. 'I understand how someone can admire that and call it *supreme* art, but I don't like it' (and here, 'ich mag es nicht' conveys a colloquial intensity of distaste).

That 'truth to life' need not be a simplistic criterion. That its absence from Shakespeare has been registered by others than Tolstoy or Wittgenstein, and from altogether different aesthetic or ethical points of view, is a fact corroborated by an arresting observation in the young Georg Lukács's *Theory of the Novel*: 'Dante's *Paradiso* is more akin to life [*dem Leben wesensverwandter*], more like the essence of life, than is the prepotent plenitude [*die strotzende Fülle*] of Shakespeare'.

This, however, is not the point. We ask: is Wittgenstein's critique even worth arguing? The answer is, I think, Yes; because it is underwritten by a differentiation of the most challenging and far-reaching order.

Was Shakespeare 'vielleicht eher ein Sprachschöpfer [the word is underlined in the original] als ein Dichter'? Was Shakespeare 'perhaps a *creator of language* rather than a poet'? *Sprachschöpfer* can be translated: the archaic but also (if I am not mistaken) Joycean term 'wordsmith' renders the appropriate stem and connotations. But 'poet' does *not* translate *Dichter*. And it is this gap, indeed it is very nearly an abyss, which is the crux of Wittgenstein's entire case.

Any attempt to analyse and circumscribe the semantic field of the term *Dichter* is outside the scope of this lecture. Such an attempt would, strictly envisaged, comport little less than a history of German philosophic aesthetics, of the theories of art and of education as they evolve from Schiller and Kant to the present, together with a critical review of the status of literature, and of poetry in particular, in German social history. The best I can hope to do is to suggest something of the centrality and exigency of Wittgenstein's use of the word by reference to an analogous use in the work and thought of certain of his immediate contemporaries.

Hermann Broch's philosophical fiction, *The Death of Virgil*, turns on the definition and enactment of the concept *Dichter*. Neither formal virtuosity nor imaginative originality is adequate to its true meaning. Writers of talent, even of genius, are fairly numerous. The authentic *Dichter* is of the rarest. Virgil would have his *Aeneid* consigned to destruction because, in the unsparing light of his imminent death, he feels that the great writer in himself, the master of words and of metrics, has replaced the *Dichter*. For the *Dichter* is 'one who knows ethically, who object-knows' (an inadmissible fusion, in English, but imperative to the implicit notion of meaning). The *Dichter*'s knowing is antithetical to 'knowingness', to encyclopaedic myriad-mindedness (as so many have found it in Shakespeare). In the *Dichter*, knowledge, cognition and re-cognition are, in a sense not unlike that of Plato's epistemology of the loving intellect, *moral acts*. The *Dichter*'s knowledge, his 'criticism of life' (Matthew Arnold's touchstone-phrase) are organized, i.e. made organic, by ethical perception, and the communication of this knowledge and criticism of life is, itself, not so much an aesthetic as it is a moral act. True *Dichtung* bears witness. It 'object-knows' in the concrete sense in which Adam's nomination of living forms in Eden corresponded precisely to the truth, the substantive being and signification of these forms. Like Adam, the *Dichter* names that which is, and his naming defines, embodies its veritable being.

For Canetti, the *Dichter*, more perhaps than any other human being, carries a 'responsibility for life'. It is his pre-eminent and constant ministry 'to oppose death'. This opposition is not a question of artistic glory, of formal survival in time. It is a moral act, perhaps *the* moral act *par excellence*, and it alone justifies art and literature. The dynamics of this act are those of life-giving compassion. The *Dichter* repulses 'nobody into nothingness who would like to be there' (Tolstoy gave a personal name to even the humblest, most ephemeral of characters in his teeming novels and tales). Perceiving nothingness, the *Dichter* 'shall endure in order to learn how to save others from it'. Like Kafka, the exemplar of Canetti's code, the *Dichter* knows the enormity of his venture, the neighbourhood to blasphemy inherent in the exercise of fictional invention, of counter-creation to the divine or the unknown. 'Had I been a better *Dichter*, I could have stopped this war or halted this massacre', is, according to Canetti, not a foolish statement, not a piece of deluded megalomania, but a radical reminder of the power, of the obligations of truth-saying, of the *Dichter*'s refusal 'to deliver mankind over to death'.

In Martin Heidegger, Wittgenstein's secret sharer at so many decisive points in the philosophy of hermeneutics and the investigation of language, the term *Dichter* is cardinal. The *Dichter* – Sophocles, Hölderlin above all, Rilke and Paul Celan – 'speaks being'. It is through his openness, his vulnerability to the pressures of being, that the mystery, that the hidden pulse of primordial coming-into-being in the inorganic and organic presences of our world, are made perceptible. It is by the *Dichter* that the root-question of all thought, 'Why should there be, why should there not be nothing?' is asked most insistently. And it is, correspondingly, in supreme art and literature, in Van Gogh's painting of a pair of torn labourer's shoes, in Hölderlin's odes, that what we can experience, what we can undergo in respect of an answer to this question is most palpable. More than any other man, the *Dichter* is, for Heidegger, the 'shepherd of being'; it is in the custody of *Dichter* that man comes nearest to being what he is (what he could be if he is to be man).

The full range of these several uses – the exaltations of the *Dichter*'s calling, the ethical, salvational function of a true *Dichter*, together with the key inference of a prophetic-didactic explicitness – underlies and animates Wittgenstein's diacritical resort to the term in dissent from Shakespeare.

Shakespeare is the incomparable *Sprachschöpfer*, the prodigal wordsmith, the limits of whose language are, in the idiom of the *Tractatus*, the limits of our world. There is scarcely a domain, a constituent of men's works and days which Shakespeare has not harvested in language, over which he has not cast the encompassing net of his matchless lexical and grammatical wealth. Disposer of a vocabulary of almost thirty thousand words (Racine's world is built of one tenth that number), Shakespeare, more than any other human being of whom we have certain record, has made the world at home in the word. This does not, however, make of him a *Dichter*, a truth-sayer, an explicitly moral agent, a visible teacher to and guardian of imperilled, bewildered mankind. An authentic *Dichter*, urges Wittgenstein, 'cannot really say of himself "I sing as the birds sing" – but perhaps Shakespeare could have said this of himself' (Milton's 'warbling wood-notes wild' is fairly obviously present to Wittgenstein when he makes this suggestion). 'I do not think that Shakespeare would have been able to reflect on the *Dichterlos*' – a term again resistant to translation into English and into the entire register of Anglo-Saxon sensibility, but signifying something like the 'calling', 'the destined ordinance' of the poet.

Innumerable scholars and critics have sought to elicit from Shakespeare's works some evidence of the author's religion or refusal of religion, some evidence of a belief or refusal of belief in God. No shred of evidence on the matter exists. Shakespeare abides our question. Strikingly, moreover, the abstention from explicit theological issues and discourse in his plays is almost total. Nothing is further from Shakespeare's spirit than *Doctor Faustus*, than Marlowe's tortured and torturing question as to whether there are limits, coincidental with human freedom and responsibility, to

God's powers and rights of forgiveness. Hamlet's brief pondering on the state of Claudius's soul when the King is at prayer, the biblical quotation 'I go about my father's business' echoed by Cordelia, are rarities in the general immanence and mundanity – using the word in its proper sense – of the canon. The contrast with Dante, with Goethe, with Tolstoy, *die Dichter par excellence*, is glaring. Where is there a Shakespearean philosophy or intelligible ethic? Both Cordelia and Iago, Richard III and Hermione are instinct with the same uncanny trick of life. The shaping imagination which animates their 'spectacular' presence is beyond good and evil. It has the dispassionate neutrality of sunlight or of wind. Can a man or woman conduct their lives by the example or precepts of Shakespeare as they can, say, by those of Tolstoy? Is the 'creation of words', even at a pitch of beauty, musicality, suggestive and metaphoric originality scarcely accessible to our analyses, really enough? Are Shakespeare's characters, at the last, more than Magellanic clouds of verbal energy turning around a void, around an absence of truth and moral substance? 'Ich mag es nicht,' says Wittgenstein. And our immediate riposte that he is, in a vein of lapidary naïvety, far more myopic even than was Dr Johnson, overlooking the key distinction between explicit morality or didacticism and the far subtler *enactment* of moral insights and teachings within Shakespeare's telling of the world, is, in the dimension of common-sense realization both self-evident and conclusive. But is that the only pertinent dimension?

In what are among the last of his private, miscellaneous notes, Wittgenstein makes one further and profound move (inspired by the writings of Otto Weininger). A counter-presence to Shakespeare enters the argument. It is, I admit, a move which I find utterly unsettling:

'Beethoven's great heart' – nobody could speak of 'Shakespeare's great heart'.

Thus, concludes Wittgenstein, our wonderment at Shakespeare does not give us the feeling of being brought into contact 'with a great *human being*. Rather with a phenomenon.' Beethoven and the

Dichter or, more precisely, Beethoven the *Dichter* on the one hand; 'the supple hand that created new natural language-forms [*Naturformen der Sprache*]' on the other. A 'great heart, a great human being' on the one hand, an enigmatic phenomenon on the other.

So much remains to be documented and understood regarding what I take to be the seminal, often decisive role of music in Wittgenstein's life and thought. It may well be that for Ludwig Wittgenstein, as for other masters of abstraction and of aloneness, music came to be a more *trustworthy*, a more intimate companion than even the best of literature. Wittgenstein confided to Norman Malcolm that the slow movement in Brahms's Third Quartet had, twice, reclaimed him from the brink of suicide. Throughout these notebooks, the contrastive reading against Shakespeare runs parallel with a reflection on the brilliant but, to Wittgenstein, ultimately false, merely technical accomplishment of Mahler and the life-giving, transcendental truth of Bruckner. Like Nietzsche before him, it is not in literature but in music that Wittgenstein may have come to recognize and experience the *opus metaphysicum* in essence. As Wittgenstein's involvement with music becomes clearer to us, it may be that the all too famous, all too often misread coda to the *Tractatus*, a text *durchkomponiert* if ever there was one, will take on a more direct meaning. Outside language lie the imperative spheres of the transcendental, of aesthetic, ethical and, perhaps, metaphysical awareness. Outside language, also, lies music, whose expressive, inferential access to these spheres is, precisely, that denied to verbal discourse.

But the invocation of Beethoven is more specific. It tells of the exemplary role of Beethoven in the romantic and post-romantic mythology of the suffering artist, of the creative titan struggling with forces of inspiration and inhibition even more turbulent and volcanic than his own (a mythology embedded in German and central European culture as Wittgenstein had first known it). Almost immediately after Wittgenstein's final note on Shakespeare comes the admonition: 'if you want to stay within the religious sphere, you must *struggle*'. Of just that struggle, the *Missa solemnis* and the late quartets and piano sonatas (cf. the role of Opus 111 in Thomas

Mann's *Doktor Faustus*) were the overwhelming but utterly human incarnation. Beethoven's music is of the heart: it quickens heart and soul. Hearing it, we are indeed in close touch with a fellow-man tormented by doubt, by infirmity, by a Jacob's wrestling with the presence or absence of the rival Creator. We know nothing of any such doubt, of any such infirmity, of any such wrestling in the supremely disinterested presence of Shakespeare. 'Ich mag es nicht.'

Wittgenstein's jottings and musings *contra* Shakespeare do not make up a systematic, cumulative brief. They entail hybrid elements and assumptions. We find an unargued, distinctly Tolstoyan bias towards realism in adult literature, a baffled resistance to the internalized consistency, dream-logic and fictive self-sufficiency of Shakespeare's dramatic art and poetry. At moments, Wittgenstein's malaise reflects a Continental (or, at least, gallic) instinct for orderly, closed forms of vision: 'The reason why I cannot understand Shakespeare is that I want to find symmetry in all this asymmetry.' This is an aesthetic which bridles at the quintessentially open-ended, tragi-comic genius of Shakespeare's dramaturgy.

On a much deeper level lies Wittgenstein's fragmentary, abbreviated attempt to hammer out a distinction between supreme verbal achievement and what one might call the 'truth-functions', the moral paradigm, the philosophic answerability of *Dichtung*. Via Kierkegaard and Tolstoy, this distinction brings to bear on Shakespeare provocations already commanding in Plato and in Aquinas (provocations which, as we have noted, also underlie the more guarded but no less divisive preference of Dante over Shakespeare in T. S. Eliot). The *Dichter* is not only a matchless artificer and imaginer, but the beneficiary, the communicant with and communicator to his fellow-men of a high, articulate religious-moral-philosophical vision and criticism of life. What Wittgenstein asks Shakespeare, in the name of an urgent and tragic moral need, in the name, finally, of music, is simply this: is language enough?

At every juncture of generality and of detail, Wittgenstein's critique and negation can be faulted. Its misreadings of dramatic discourse, of the principles of enacted truth in poetry, are blatant. The denial of natural vitality, of a lifelikeness more vivid than most of life itself in Shakespeare's men and women, will seem to almost all serious minds and sensibilities to be so wilful, so unsubstantiated as to invite embarrassment and even ridicule. The trust put in Milton, in Beethoven, in Tolstoy may well conceal the accidental fact that we know much of the personal lives and torments of these great teachers, and next to nothing about William Shakespeare of Stratford. A great logician and epistemologist can be a blind reader of literature.

All this is the case. The temptation to label Wittgenstein's remarks as an historical curio, as an aberration somewhat like Socrates' marriage, is pressing. Perhaps it ought not to be resisted. The notion of a western literacy in which Shakespeare would have the suspect status consequent on Wittgenstein's views, is hardly plausible, let alone attractive. How impoverished what is now left of our civilization would be (an ascetic puritanism, a didacticism of abstention in the face of literature, inhabits both the later Tolstoy and Wittgenstein who was, in so many respects, his disciple). All this, as well, is true and obvious.

And yet.

In our culture, taboos and prescriptive reverence hedge Shakespeare's work. There are questions which are hardly asked: about the prolixity and repetitiveness in many of the plays: about the intrusion of vulgarity and waste motion into even the major texts (how many of us have ever seen a production of *Othello* which includes the wretched exchanges with the Clown?). How much there is in the comedies which is rancid or verbally witty rather than funny in any real sense. The laughter of thought as we find it in Aristophanes, in Molière, in Chekhov, is not always abundant. What is the proportion of enduring poetic-dramatic substance which only inspired productions can preserve in such plays as *Measure for Measure* or *All's Well that Ends Well*? It is only of late that the challenging dilemma of Shakespeare's grip, possibly inhibiting, on the development of English and of modern English poetry has been seriously posed.

There will always be sensibilities and traditions of understanding more deeply engaged, more persuaded by the economies, by the absolute of classical dramatic modes – the *adieu, Madame* of Racine's Tite and Bérénice, the tranquil immensity of the final dialogue of Yse and Mesa in Claudel's *Partage de midi* – than by the storms, forests in march, spectral apparitions and pursuant bears, which surround, which people with the anarchic and spendthrift prodigality of life, even the most concentrated, the most inward of Shakespearean moments.

But these are aesthetic concerns. The Platonic, the Wittgensteinian inference lies deeper.

Are there dimensions, specific gravities of art and literature, of our experience of and response to art and literature, which arise from the felt, indeed declared pressure on art and literature of the presence or absence (in many cases, such as Dostoevsky's or Kafka's, absence is a more radical possibility of presence) of God? The theological-metaphysical enactment of what is gravest and most constant in human questioning, of that which lies, or may lie, on the other side of language, gives to certain texts an indispensable vulnerability and stature. The anguished patience of such questioning comes to possess us in the *Oresteia*; in Sophocles' *Oedipus, Antigone* and *Oedipus at Colonus*; it presses on us, almost unbearably, in Euripides' *Bacchae*. We hear it in Marco Lombardo's voice out of the purging smoke in *Purgatorio* XVI; in Ivan Karamazov's prosecution of God; in the parables of Kafka. There is a very real sense, awesome to apprehension, in which Shakespeare does know and say everything; does he know and say anything *else*? Or are such knowledge and such expression reserved to the singular commerce which music has with mystery?

Plato was wrong when he banished the poets. Wittgenstein misreads Shakespeare. Surely, this must be so.

And yet.

Absolute Tragedy

(for Alexis Philonenko)

Absolute tragedy is very rare. It is a piece of dramatic literature (or art or music) founded rigorously on the postulate that human life is a fatality. It proclaims axiomatically that it is best not to be born or, failing that, to die young. An absolutely tragic model of the condition of men and women views these men and women as unwanted intruders on creation, as beings destined to undergo unmerited, incomprehensible, arbitrary suffering and defeat. Original sin, be it Adamic or Promethean, is not a tragic category. It is charged with possibilities both of motivation and of eventual redemption. In the absolutely tragic, it is the crime of man that he is, that he exists. His naked presence and identity are transgressions. The absolutely tragic is, therefore, a negative ontology. Our century has given to this abstract paradox a tangible enactment. During the Holocaust, the Gypsy or the Jew had very precisely *committed the crime of being*. That crime attached by definition to the fact of birth. Thus even the unborn had to be hounded to extinction. To come into the world was to come into torture and death.

Absolute 'tragedy' as systematic philosophic vision or as the literature produced by this vision, is very rare because it is scarcely endurable. Pascal bids us stay awake because 'Christ is in agony until the end of time.' But mankind goes mad without sleep. Where consequence is strict, the tragic absolute solicits suicide. It does not admit of the rationale or therapy of discourse, be it philosophic or aesthetic. It does not look to pragmatic amelioration. Why write plays (paint pictures, compose symphonies) if perception entails a stringent nihilism. Only nothingness is acquitted of the fault, of the error of being ('nothingness' is obsessive in the text of *King Lear*; annulment is a pivot in Beckett's parables). Formally considered, we ought to retain no evidence, no manifest of a model of consciousness and sensibility absolutely tragic. The man or woman possessed of the certitude of existential, ontological unwantedness seeks silence and death. Sentences of death, where they are freely chosen, do not need to be written.

Where the postulate of the absolutely tragic, of man unhoused in being, is made articulate, the performative act – that of the play, of the novel, of the metaphysical or psychological pronouncement – will be fragmentary. 'Fragmentary', here, has a particular sense. The actual drama, the Kafka-tale, the nihilistic or suicidal tract, may be formally complete. Nevertheless, it is a fragment. It cannot be of any great length, because the vision which it embodies is indeed unbearable, because the contemplation and acquiescence in the abyss, where these are honest, where these do not parade pathos or self-flattering metaphor, must compel us over the edge. If it is integral, the confrontation of reason and of form with the finality of the absurd or the sadistic (Pascal again, in his image of 'death and the sun') can only last moments. Not only can human imagining and presentation endure only an abridged spell of unequivocal doom; they can dramatize, fictionalize or systematically argue that spell only by means of extreme compaction. The zero-point is just that: a point, gathering all blackness to it. It is (very rarely) across five acts of a drama, in the bounds of a prose fable, of a lyric, of an abbreviated address (as in Swift or Artaud), that the case that knows no remission can be made. Currently the sayer of absolute desolation is an aphorist (Cioran). Only the fragmentary, whose completeness is expressly that of mutilation, of end-stopping, can be immune to light.

On the evidence we have – the bulk of Greek tragic drama has not come down to us – the list of absolute tragedies is short. It contains Sophocles' *Oedipus the King* and *Antigone*; a number of Euripides' plays such as *Medea*, *Hecuba*, *The Trojan Women*, and the *Bacchae*, pre-eminently; the main plot of Marlowe's *Faustus*; Shakespeare's *Timon of Athens*; Racine's *Bérénice* (absolute tragic precisely in its muteness and outward discretion) and Racine's *Phèdre*; Shelley's *The Cenci*, together with Artaud's adaptation; Büchner's *Woyzeck*; the 'black holes' in the *guignol* and monologues of Beckett.

It is only in these plays and a handful of fictions and acts of discourse and depiction – Goya's last paintings, Alban Berg's *Wozzeck* – that the postulate of the absolutely tragic is thought through, is 'staged' unremittingly. It is only in these few texts that we find fully expressed the conception of human life as lawless chastisement, as some hideous practical joke visited upon man or, to cite an emblem used by both Dostoevsky and Nietzsche, the vision of reality as one best shown in the slow torture of a child or of an animal. (I had not, in *The Death of Tragedy*, drawn the definition taut, or seen how limited is the class of the absolute.)

In scenic forms, the natural pulse is that of tragi-comedy. The matter of human existence is imitated, stylized, selected pluralistically. Where there is torment and ruin, there is also pleasure and hope. It is some such pendulum motion and simultaneity which is seen to be the vital truth, the essential commonplace of human survival. At the very instant in which Agamemnon is butchered or Hamlet poisoned, a wedding, the birth of a child, a meal shared in peace or merriment is taking place in some house outside the palace or even in some room of the palace more or less distant from the royal bath or duelling ground. Ordinary human experience affirms this to be the case and dramatic art acts on this knowledge.

Being wholly tragic in plot and presentation, Greek tragic drama seems 'absolute'. But this is an optical illusion. With one paramount exception, we know no complete trilogy, only discrete sections. The *Oresteia* is, in the exact and compendious sense given to that word by Dante, a *commedia*. It leads towards, it ends in, redemptive absolution and personal-political hope. We simply do not know whether Aeschylus' triptych was an exceptional instance or the norm. What we do know is that a Greek trilogy, with its staging of tragic myths, either interconnected or separate, was followed by a satyr-play. As far as we can make out, this farcical epilogue mocked, ironized, held up to caricature and deflation, elements of the preceding tragic material. We know nothing of the counter-effect achieved. But it is improbable that the satyr-play did not qualify radically, did not subvert the tragic view, that it did not advance, in robust contrariety, the claims of laughter. (Anyone who recalls the quick-change dazzle of Olivier's Mr Puff, leaping on to the stage in Sheridan's farce only seconds, or so it seemed, after the howling, blood-stained end of his performance of Oedipus, will intuit something of the beat of exultant fun after tragic catastrophe which may have been the point of the Athenian tetralogy.)

The Shakespearean example is quintessential. If we enlarge 'comedy' in Dante's or Balzac's sense and usage, Dr Johnson's finding that Shakespeare's natural bent was for comedy rather than tragedy offers a central insight. In no shaping imagination has there ever been a stronger apprehension of the hybrid tenor of life, of the perpetual intermeshing of hope and despair, of winter and of spring, of men's midnight and their noon-time. Almost nothing in Shakespearean drama is ever monistic, is ever of only one nature and consequence. There is, to use one of Shakespeare's own images of the constant 'double-plot' within reality, laughter even in the throat of death. Hence the underlying tragi-comic motion of spirit and of plot even in the major tragedies – a motion whose life-giving strength does not exclude extremities of agony and of injustice.

Scotland will be reborn, the legitimate dynasty will be furthered to glory, after the death of Macbeth. It is made plain to us that Cyprus will be governed serenely, efficiently by Cassio as it could never have been by Othello. Fortinbras will make a heavier, a more vulgar monarch than Hamlet would have, the losses are manifold, but times in Denmark will be back in joint and social services provided. *Lear* is the obvious challenge to any such general reading. Cordelia's execution seems to close the book of life and of reason. But the coda of the play is enigmatic in its music of tentative valedictions. The evil are terribly destroyed. The realm is reknit. There is very nearly a liturgical grace-note and *in pacem* not only in Lear's own end, but in the choral summons and summations it elicits. Such horrors shall not come again.

Only that inexhaustibly perplexing, erratic bloc, *Timon of Athens*, seems to me 'black on black'. In this strangely inspired, misshapen text, the cosmos is made the object of virulent anathema. No good deed goes unpunished. No decent impulse but provokes derision and excoriation. Human generation and birth are nothing but idiotic provocations to pain and betrayal. Decisively, in epitaphs cunningly intended for erosion by the sea, Timon bids 'language end'. This is, so far as I know, the one and only time that William Shakespeare would terminate language knowing – his mastery over it being matchless – that it was the axis and defining instrument of our humanity, of our place in the world. Here, and this one time only, we find the nihilism, the zero and closure of absolute tragedy.

We hear it, unambiguously, in Racine. He dwelt on antique myths not only out of neo-classical conventionality. Racine, like his Jansenist teachers and adversaries, held those whom guilt had consigned to despair and damnation before the coming of Christ to be irremediably, peculiarly damned. Hence the graphic despair of Phèdre as she foresees her descent into Hades. In Racine's tragic theodicy, these damned shall know no remission through grace. Athalie dies under the malediction of the Old Law; her blood-stained shade will weep for ever. Racine can crystallize, 'as through a glass darkly', the totality of tragic waste and sorrow in a single, formal gesture or moment. In these instants of noiseless, even decorous apocalypse, the universe, which Racine's high personages invoke, does come to a halt. There is nothing in it but their annihilating grief, no healing whisper, no breath of tomorrow. The universe (and this is inconceivable in Shakespeare, outside *Timon*) has become the frozen totality of the tragic. I take *Bérénice*, precisely because of its surface-tranquillity, precisely because of its abstention from all 'exits and alarms', from woods on the march or 'spouting hurricanoes' to be the touchstone of absolute tragedy in modern western literature. A man and a woman saying adieu. For ever. In which termination all light is momentarily gathered and put out. As in a pearl, flawlessly black.

There is no hint of succour for justice, for compassion as sadistic cynicism triumphs in Shelley's *The Cenci*. There is not even the dignity and consolation of articulacy (invariably dynamic in Shakespeare) for Büchner's Woyzeck. He mumbles his way to empty death. But I repeat: these monistic or monadic proposals and readings of the existential are very rare. Life, we feel, both ordinary and categorical, be it in its biological, social or psychic sense, is 'not like that'. And in the theatre, more probably than in any other representational mode, likeness, credibility, the underlying gravitational force of the reality principle, are persistent. As they are in the Homeric epics, which are the font of drama. Niobe has seen her ten children slain. Her grief makes stones weep. But as it ebbs, she takes nourishment. Homer insists on this. It is an interposition of daylit truth central also to Shakespeare. The organic is tragi-comic in its very essence. The absolutely tragic is, therefore, not only insupportable to human sensibility: it is false to life.

This critique of the tragic enlists both empirical observation and liberal sentiment. Today, for reasons of the most sombre self-evidence, it needs questioning.

This century has witnessed a carnival of bestiality. It is the century of the death-camps and the 'killing fields', of a systematic resort to torture by political regimes and societies of diverse persuasions. Ours is an era of mass-starvation, deportation and the taking of hostages. The feasibility of thermo-nuclear and of biological warfare, the laying waste of the planet, mean that the eventuality of human self-slaughter and of ecological finality are no longer macabre fantastications. The autumn and winter of 1989 have brought unexpected, almost miraculous daylight to parts of central and eastern Europe. The air freshens. But prior to this dawning, and throughout much of the rest of mankind, Kafka's stark finding that 'there is abundance of hope but none for us' may prove to be sober reportage.

If this perception can, must be dwelt on, if it must be 'thought' (in Heidegger's active sense of that word), do there not attach to it the potential, the likelihood of a renascence of tragic drama? Contingencies and the climate of feeling speak against such rebirth. The scale of modern violence and desolation is resistant to aesthetic form. It cannot be seen whole as, presumably, could be the sack of Miletus or the ruin of a royal clan. We are made numb by the routine of shock pre-packaged, sanitized by the mass media and by the false authenticity of the immediate. At the same time, this graphic directness makes tedious or seemingly archaic the patient means of representation, of uncertain argument which are essential to serious drama. Prophetically, the prologue to Goethe's *Faust* asks whether a sensibility, a nervous and cognitive system attuned to the cadence, to the instantaneous enormities and simplifications of the journalistic (the 'daily'), can respond to the symbolic, provisional rhythms of a tragic or philosophic theatre.

On the level of decorum, of tact of spirit and of heart, it can be, indeed it has been, argued that the sheer dimensions of the inhuman as we have in recent history enacted and experienced it, that the anonymous, mechanistic functionality of modern mass-sadism and oppression, impose silence. The point is that even where they originate in humane outrage and in hope of enlightenment, art, eloquence, controlled shape, inevitably adorn. Should art run the risk of gracing barbarism? The inchoate scream out of the blackened mouth in the Beckett parable may be the only sort of response whose patent inadequacy does not trivialize (in contrast to the theatrical scream in Picasso's *Guernica*).

These are valid and psychologically plausible criteria against the tragic. They illuminate the fact that modern tragic invention has been most convincing in the cinema (in the best of Buñuel or of Bergman, for example). This, in turn, suggests that a tragic reading of the state of present being will prove most effective where it adopts but masters to its deeper purpose the surface-economies, the graphic 'instantaneousness' of the dominant media. Where twentieth-century drama has turned to the matter and voice of tragedy in order to answer to our situation, it has been, deliberately, recursive. It was via the *Oresteia* that Hauptmann, T. S. Eliot, O'Neill, Sartre sought to articulate their sense of modern bewilderment and murderousness. It was via the *Trojan Women* that 'living theatres' and Sartre expressed their view of the wars in Algeria and Vietnam. Variously modernized, the *Bacchae* has served a generation seeking to envisage symbolically, to make some sense of, the drug-culture and the flower-child. Oedipus, Elektra, Prometheus have stalked the modern stage from Gide and Cocteau to Robert Lowell. Antigones proliferate in an age which has known live burial and the obscene refusal of sepulchre to enemies and victims. But these reanimations, this quickening of antique presences, compelling, ingenious, enriching as they often are (notably in modern opera), do not, cannot constitute a formulation, an embodiment of the tragic native, natural to our circumstance. Indeed, it is anthropology and Freudian psychoanalysis which have given to a twentieth-century Oedipus, Orestes or Elektra much of their spectral impact. Most of recent tragic theatre is, in Yeats's sense, a fierce mummery, a more or less bewitching *séance*. Where there is so much blood, the ghosts swarm. But they remain ghosts. One intuits, therefore, that our incapacity to 'make it new' has its reasons in the inmost of modernity.

Of western literary genres, and it is singularly western, tragic drama is the least separable from religion. What very little we know of its origins, tells of sacred precincts and ritual. The actual myth-content which underwrites the Greek, the neo-classical and almost the entirety of twentieth-century tragic theatre, is that of mortal encounters with supernatural agencies of fate, with transcendent visitations, with 'other than human' interventions of an ambiguous or destructive order. The agnosticism of Shakespearean drama in respect of the theological and the metaphysical is undeniable. It relates, as we saw, to the tragi-comic pattern. Yet here also the assumption that human destiny suffers constraints and interpositions of an order beyond the empirical and the rational is imperative. There can be no *Hamlet* without the Ghost, no *Macbeth* shorn of the Weird ones. The *Lear*-world is materially thronged by forces and agencies strange to man.

The inweaving of tragic drama with religious categories has grounds which are at once banal and primary. When they are imaged gravely, when serious inquiry is brought to bear and press on them, conjectures about the source of human suffering, about the nature of evil, about inexplicable misfortune or morally repellent success, will be of a religious tenor. As will be any attempt to make sensible the concept of the 'on sufferance' of men and women in a natural creation in which they seem to have no legitimate dwelling (cf. the choral meditation on man's enormity in Sophocles' *Antigone*, the shredding of human hopes at the close of the *Bacchae*, Timon on the beach, Woyzeck seeking to decipher the cry of the mute stones and drowning amid the whispering reeds). In essence, tragedy is a questioning and an enacted testing of theodicy. It ministers to radical doubts and protests in a confrontation with the non- and inhuman, where these designations have two senses, ominously kindred: they mean that which is more potent, more lasting, more ancient than man, and that which does not demonstrably share the ethics, the compassions, the self-examinations, the graces of pardon and of forgetting in humaneness. Exposed to the death-throes of her beloved Hippolytus, Euripides' Artemis turns away lest human suffering pollute the unfeeling radiance of the divine. (What are we meant to make of the Father's descent into or absence from time during Christ's agony?)

To ask whether 'the gods kill us for their sport' is, by definition, to make plausible, to make enforcedly questionable, their existence and that of our possible place in that existence. The correspondent question as to what, if any, is the availability of theological-metaphysical inference to comedy, seems to me one of the most difficult and least explored. Yet works such as *Twelfth Night*, such as the plays of Chekhov and, supremely, Mozart's *Così fan tutte*, do pose it insistently.

Thus a consideration of the status and potential of tragic drama in the light (in the dark) of our current historical-social position, must entail some propositions on the place of religion in contemporary western affairs. In Nietzsche, though this often goes unnoticed, the early theses on the birth of tragedy form a tight knot with the dramatic allegory of 'the death of God'. The circle within which the Attic tragic chorus performed and that of 'the eternal return' are cognate. If we inquire of modern or future tragic drama, as distinct from variations on ancient tragic themes and myths by twentieth-century playwrights, we are asking about the internalization in consciousness and in our culture of the manifold notifications of God's death and of the eclipse of religion.

Talk about this issue is, generally, just that. References, which do have their evidential weight, to the present-day resurgence of religious fundamentalism (millions of frenetic fundamentalists in the south-western United States are not a jot less religiously possessed than are the Shiites of Iran), arguments, and they too have their weight, pointing to the mindless arrogance of so much of modern science and technocracy, or to the vulgar sufficiencies of our psychology and sociology, do not go to the centre. The obvious question remains as to whether or not the existence of God and what that existence would comport for the sense of our being and the very being of sense itself is, today, a live problem. Does the Bush still burn or is it only the object of the psychologist's and historian's curiosity, resuscitated for purposes of metaphor and retrospective pathos? If the latter is indeed the case, if even the problematic possibility of the question of God is now extinguished among, let us say, the creative imaginers, the explorers and voyager 'past' common language who compose our dramas, then it is difficult to conceive of a renovation or metamorphic evolution of the form.

Look at the two modern dramatists whose poetic means, stagecraft and choice of themes make comparison with Greek tragedians and with Shakespeare legitimate. Both Brecht and Claudel are melodramatists. This is to say that their world-view, that the dramatizations of human suffering, injustice, error and even despair, as we find them in *Mother Courage* or *The Satin Slipper*, present to us four tragic acts. The fifth act is one of reparation or redemption. In the practice of Brecht, the machinery of compensation is twofold. Terror and pity are purged by political understanding, by the realisation induced in the 'estranged' audience that the characters have brought upon themselves, through greed or egotism or political blindness, their own victimization. Secondly, the plays hold out the promise of general amendment. Let historical materialism go before you like a pillar of fire in the capitalist night and the tragic happenings mimed on the didactic stage will recede into the museum of unnecessary sorrows. Claudel's commitment to salvation is robustly theological. His overwhelming plays are 'sacramental mysteries' in the medieval and baroque sense. Suffering, waste, the frustration of love are the long prologue to transfiguration. The inspired casuistry of *Le Partage de midi*, itself a meditation on Racine's *Bérénice*, gives even suicide its ticket to transcendence. Melodrama is the genre of the messianic. The *deus ex machina* who descends prior to its final curtain can be the Redeemer or the commissar. He has been ready and waiting in 'the wings' – an appropriately angelic venue.

These two pivotal examples do suggest that we must refine our definitions. Whatever their religious content and postulates of transcendence, neither the Christian promise of salvation nor that of meliorist and utopian socialism – itself a secularization of Judaic messianic eschatology – will generate tragedy. Theirs is the rubric made explicit by the title of the drama of the Soviet revolutionary playwright Vishnievsky: *An Optimistic Tragedy*. Considered theologically and within the framework of historicism religiously underwritten, what I have called 'absolute tragedy' postulates not only the Fall of Man. It does not only depict the human situation as one directly consequent on original and fundamental disgrace, where the obscurity, where the unremembered midnight of that first disaster are, precisely, a part of its unceasing impact. Absolute tragedy makes implicit or explicit the intuition that there can be, neither through a messianic nor a Christological coming, any reparation. There is no *felix culpa*, only the eternity of the fault and the cursed but eminent dignity of man's refusal either to forgive himself or to forgive the pain visited upon him (this is the dual refusal in Marlowe's *Faustus*). Each absolute tragedy (there are, we know, few) re-enacts the searing mystery and outrage of innate evil, of a compulsion towards blindness and self-destruction incised irreparably in man and woman. The exultant, kerygmatic shout which crowns Claudel's world-theatre, 'Deliverance to captive souls', is never to be heard or, if heard, will be no more than derision.

I take such a reading of the human case to be heretical. It presumes either an unforgiving God whose pique breeds everlasting vengeance, or some manichaean dialectic in which, so far as men and women on this plundered, sullied planet are concerned, the negative principle prevails. Neither view can be admissible for a Judaeo-Christian teleology nor, and this is vital, for secular, rationalist meliorism. Strictly defined, absolute tragedy is *the performative mode of despair*. It sins against the Holy Ghost of hope. Its declaratory terms are 'nothing' and 'never' as we hear them howled in *King Lear* and, in a more reticent but no less uncompromising register, in the 'Adieu' (note the theological twist in that conventionally weightless word) which end-stops the universe in Racine's *Bérénice*.

But even the most drastic of heresies requires an orthodox counter-presence. The tragic absolute can address or metaphorize a receding, an exhausted, a lamed deity. These are the categories explored in Euripides and Beckett. They are the dark conceit at the heart of Kafka's fables. Tragedy can be acted before a 'hidden' God, as it is, explicitly, in Racine. The question, today, is this: is the counter-presence meaningfully available? Can the conventions and raw material of the mythical which are axiomatic to tragedy be quickened into life where the problem, the question of God is either that of His absence – whatever that may signify – or is a non-question, an atavism and ghost of unreason?

The topic (*topos*, trope) of God's absence, after his Nietzschean, Darwinian or Freudian burial, is, together with the kabbalistic conceit of His abstention from a flawed creation, one of utmost abstraction. The word 'abstraction' means just that: a withdrawal from, an emptying. Yet the working metaphor of this vacancy weighs strangely. It is almost unbearable in respect of attempts to give to the phenomenology of Auschwitz any place in reach of human imagining and understanding. Only the poet, Paul Celan, has found condign expression for the 'No-oneness' that was God in the time of the ovens. There is contemporary art – and, again, 'abstract' is a telling epithet – which touches on the void, whose figurative blankness strongly suggests the recent departure of a once validating presence. I have already cited the recurrent motif of abdication, of the spectral or farcical spoor which abdication has left behind, in the black *guignol* of Beckett (or of Jarry or of Pinter).

But these forms of afterglow in the darkroom do not, I think, make for the substantive motions, for the rhetoric, in a positive sense, of tragic drama. Indifference, this is to say the more or less systematic, the more or less generalized inattention of human thought and soul, the espousal of distraction – 'dis-traction' flowing from progressive 'ab-straction' – will not long afford even an 'absent' God. It will not allow such absence the specific gravity which it must have in tragic art. Where theology and metaphysics, be they of a Judaic or of a Christian source, aim to be adult in the face of the strident facts and provocations of the inhuman, of the radically damned, as they inform our recent history, they must make themselves freely accessible to the hypothesis of despair. If this hypothesis is a heresy, it is one which now lies at the centre. But where religion itself gives such access, the agonistic, challenging animus of absolute tragedy is left without a worthwhile target.

It is foolish to prophesy (the ontological freedom of art is always that of the unexpected). But one's intuition is that if representative tragic forms are to arise, they will do so from some unsparing humiliation inside theology itself, from some naked acquiescence in defeat. There are motions of spirit of precisely this tenor in Kierkegaard, in Karl Barth's 1919 commentary on *Romans*. The blandness, the indifference now prevalent may be broken. Kafka invoked an ice-axe with which to reach the frozen spirit. But even if this were to happen, the correlative fictions would not, one senses, be those of absolute tragedy or of high melodrama. They would be nearer to some exercise in nocturnal slapstick, as befits an afterword and a time of epilogue.

What is Comparative Literature?

Every act of the reception of significant form, in language, in art, in music, is comparative. Cognition is re-cognition, either in the high Platonic sense of a remembrance of prior truths, or in that of psychology. We seek to understand, to 'place' the object before us – the text, the painting, the sonata – by giving it the intelligible, informing context of previous and related experience. We look, intuitively, to analogy and precedent, to the traits as of a family (thus 'familiar') which relate the work that is new to us to a recognizable context. In the case of radical innovation, of a poetic or representational or musical structure which strikes us as in some ways unprecedented, the process of response is a complex motion towards the incorporation of the new into the known. Even extreme originality begins, as we enter into questioning dialogue with it, to tell of origins. There is in the perception of and response to intelligibility no absolute innocence, no Adamic nakedness. Interpretation and aesthetic judgement, however spontaneous in utterance, however provisional or even misguided, arise from an echo-chamber of historical, social, technical presuppositions and recognizance. (Here, the legal sense of this term is pertinent: a certain contract of eventual decipherment, of informed evaluation underwrites the encounter between our sensibility and the text or work of art.) In this dynamic process, called 'hermeneutic' perhaps after Hermes, god of messages and fictions, comparison is implicit. How does this novel or symphony relate to what we have previously read or heard, to our expectations in respect of executive form? The notion of 'making new' (Ezra Pound's injunction) is comparative in logic and substance. Newer than what? There are, even at the sharpest pitch of the revolutionary, no utter 'singularities'. We soon learn to hear the part of Brahms in Schoenberg, to observe the lit shadows of Manet in Rothko. The barest assertion of preference is

Inaugural Lecture, University of Oxford, 1994.

precisely that: a comparison with. It may well be that the reflexes that put in play similarity and dissimilarity, analogy and contrast are fundamental to the human psyche and to the possibility of the intelligible. French makes this audible: in 'reason', *raison*, 'comparison', *comparaison*, is instrumental.

Given language, it cannot be otherwise. Each word in either an oral or written communication reaches us charged with the potential of its entire history. All previous uses of this word or phrase are implicit or, as the physicists would say, 'implosive' in it. We know strictly nothing of its invention except where it is a neologism or technical term whose first appearance we can more or less confidently document. Who devised, who used for the very first time the words which articulate our consciousness and organize our relations to the world and to each other? Who originated the similes, the metaphors which encode the unfolding of our perceptions, which make the sea 'wine-dark' or set the number of the stars in concordance with that of the grains of sand? Our recursion, upstream, to the sources of saying is, almost always, partial. We are unable to date, to situate geographically, let alone in some individual act of perception and enunciation, the first light in language. For even the most anarchic, innovative of writers, the linguistic and, to a large extent, the grammatical building blocks are already there, crowded with historical, literary and idiomatic resonance.

The classic artist rejoices in this inheritance. He moves into a house richly furnished, its mirrors, as it were, radiant with the presence of preceding tenants. The counter-classic writer finds himself in a veritable prison-house of language. *In extremis*, we know of drastic attempts at escape. The Dada movement, surrealism, Russian futurist verse experiment, quite desperately, with the concoction of new languages, of non-sense discourse or, in the Russian case, 'star-speech'. Not only are these contrivances haunted by the spectral force of the syllables, of the words they seek to discard; but they are unintelligible. If a poet was able to construe a new language and syntax he would, in order to be understood, have to teach it first to himself, then to another. In which 'loquacious' motion the prison-house would begin to be built. When Joyce, in his copy of *Finnegans Wake*, lists some forty tongues from which he has made the collages of his word-play, macaronics or acrostics, he does so in the knowledge that the history of these languages and their literary and public use press on even the most *outré* of his inventions. At best, the major writer adds graffiti to the walls of the already extant house of language. In turn, these graffiti enlarge the walls and further complicate their echoes.

Linguistically, we come to grasp and use words diacritically, which is to say by virtue of what differentiates them from other words. In poetics, as Coleridge argues in the *Biographia Literaria*, both understanding and pleasure derive from the tensed imbalance between the expected and the shock of the new, which is itself, at its finest, a shock of recognition, a *déjà vu*. The poet's language takes us home to that which we did not know. It is in this precise psychological and epistemological sense that the 'Library at Babel' (Borges) and, above all, its dictionaries, do contain the totality of literatures past, present and to come. The semantic process is one of differentiation. To read is to compare.

From their inception, literary studies and the arts of interpretation have been comparative. The pedagogues, the textual commentators, the literary critics and theoreticians of Athens and Alexandria compare diverse aspects within the works of a single writer, such as Homer. They observe the dynamics of analogy and contrast between the treatment of identical mythological themes by different tragedians such as Aeschylus, Sophocles and Euripides. As Latin literature develops, linguistic-critical comparisons between Homer and Virgil, between Roman pastorale and its Greek-Hellenic inspiration, between Herodotus and Roman historians, become the commonplace of the curriculum and of the teaching of rhetoric. Plutarch's 'pairings' of a Greek and a Roman statesman, legislator or man of war are exemplary of a comparative method also used in the study of writers and rhetoricians. Soon centuries of clerics and of schoolboys were to toil over the comparison of Cicero with Demosthenes, of Virgil with Theocritus, of Seneca with Euripides. And it does not escape the polemic notice of early adversaries of

Christianity that the scenario of agonized death and glorious resurrection is comparatively discernible in the myths of Osiris or Adonis.

Aesthetic judgement, hermeneutic exposition by way of comparison – Dryden and Pope, as seen by Dr Johnson; Corneille and Racine as read by Boileau; Shakespeare and Racine in Stendhal's polemic – is a constant in literary study and debate. Techniques of intra- and inter-linguistic confrontation are sharpened during the quarrels between 'Ancients' and 'Moderns' in the seventeenth and eighteenth centuries and by the reprise of this quarrel in the late eighteenth- and nineteenth-century conflicts between romanticism and various modes of neo-classicism. Wordsworth is a comparatist in action when he seeks to dismantle a text by Gray in the preface to the *Lyrical Ballads*; Victor Hugo is a comparatist when he invokes Aeschylus, the Book of Job, and Shakespeare against Racine in the programmatic preface to *Cromwell*.

Weltliteratur ('world literature') is Goethe's coinage. We find it for the first time in a diary entry for 15 January 1827. But it formulates intimations and practices which span Goethe's lifetime. Goethe translates out of eighteen languages including Gaelic, Arabic, Chinese, Hebrew, Persian and Finnish (to be sure the translation is often indirect and at second hand). These translations span seventy-three years, from a fragment from Lipsius's Latin in 1757 to extracts from Carlyle's life of Schiller which he translates in 1830. European awareness owes to Goethe some of its seminal moments of translation: that of Cellini's autobiography, of Voltaire's *Mahomet*, of Diderot's *Neveu de Rameau*. Within Goethe's own poetry, the *West-östlicher Divan*, adapted from the Persian, the version of the Song of Songs from the Hebrew, or the translation and 're-composition' from the Italian of Manzoni's ode *Il cinque maggio*, represent sovereign achievements. The theoretical programme for the translator set out in the introduction to the *Divan* is one of the most demanding and influential in the long history of the craft.

But the study and practice of translation is only a part of the concept of *Weltliteratur*. Behind the word lies *Weltpoesie*, an expression rooted in the conceptions of language and of literature put forward by Herder and Humboldt. The faculty for, the impulse towards verbal invention, towards the organization of words and syntax into formal patterns of measure and musicality, is universal. *Poiesis*, the ordering *ingenium* which gives to the world a narrative guise, which concentrates and dramatizes the raw material of experience, which translates grief and wonder into aesthetic pleasure, is ubiquitous. Man is not only, as the ancient Greeks had it, 'a language-animal'; he is a being in whom greater or lesser degrees of formal imagining and stylized communication are innate. In Goethe's view, all modes of literary enunciation, oral or written, are of cardinal relevance to man's understanding of his history, of his civil condition and, strikingly, of his own language. 'He who does not know foreign languages,' rules Goethe, 'knows nothing of his own.'

The entailments of *Weltliteratur* are also philosophical and political. Goethe was, we know, obsessed by the quest for primordial unities. Tenaciously, he pursued the chimera of the *Urpflanze*, the vegetable form from which all other species would evolve. *Faust II* is, in several respects, the inspiration for subsequent notions of 'archetypes', of original and originating configurations in the final deeps of nascent consciousness (Jung is steeped in Goethe). Like the alchemists, whom he read closely, Goethe believed in the interrelationships, in the hidden harmonies of all matter. The voice of nature was best audible in great chords and unison. *Weltliteratur* and *Weltpoesie* connote a conjecture, though indistinct, as to the universals which underlie and generate all languages and which occasion, between even the most formally remote, subterranean structural and evolutionary affinities. Goethe's ecumenism implies a moral-political stance. By the late 1820s, the ageing and partially isolated Olympian – isolated by his world-fame – had a vivid apprehension of the new forces of nationalism, of militant chauvinism on the march in post-Napoleonic Europe, and especially in Germany. He knew and feared the Teutonic verbiage and archaicizing fervour of the new German philology and historiography. Thus the late coinage, *Weltliteratur*, seeks to articulate ideals, attitudes of sensibility which belong to the universalizing civilities,

[146]

to the international freemasonry of liberal spirits characteristic of the Enlightenment. The study of other languages and literary traditions, the appreciation both of their intrinsic value and of that which interweaves them with the sum of the human condition, 'enriches' that condition. It is integral to 'free trade' in an intellectual and spiritual sense. In the life of the mind, as in that of politics, isolationism and nationalist arrogance are the road to brutal ruin.

It is these persuasions and the poetic-critical realization which Goethe gave them, that lay the express foundation for comparative literature. They are its ideals of responsibility still.

The history of comparative literature as a professional and academic discipline is a complex and, in some measure, a sombre one. It is made up of accidents of personal and social circumstances together with larger currents of a cognitive and historical nature. The interactions between these generative elements are so manifold and, at points, opaque as to rebuke any attempt at a brief or confident summation. A field or manner of study, of reading, of secondary discourse (edition, commentary, critical classification) becomes a visible entity in the modern scholastic-academic edifice when it produces books explicit to itself, when it establishes university chairs, journals and a syllabus. In steps at first tentative and almost unnoticed, comparative literature begins to accede to these criteria around the turn of the century. Its immediate backdrop is that of Franco-German tensions, particularly in Alsatia and the Rhineland, between the end of the Franco-Prussian war and the outbreak of the First World War (which was, as we ought never to forget, a European civil war). Almost every psychological, geographical and topical aspect I have touched upon is crystallized in the fact that one of the very first books of modern comparative literature in any self-conscious vein should have been Fernand Baldensperger's *Goethe en France* of 1904. Nor is it an accident that it was from a German reading of French literature and from an endeavour to re-define the *Latinitas* primary to Europe before divisive nationalism that came such classic work in comparative literature as that of E. R. Curtius and Leo Spitzer. No less crucial is a related but tragic component.

It is no secret that Jewish scholars or scholars of Jewish origin have played an often preponderant role in the development of comparative literature as an academic-critical pursuit. One is indeed tempted to associate the early history of the subject with the crisis of fact and of mood triggered by the Dreyfus Affair. Endowed, it would appear, with an unusual facility for languages, compelled to be a *frontalier* (the grim Swiss word for those who, materially and psychologically, dwell near or astride borders), the twentieth-century Jew would be drawn naturally to a comparative view of the secular literatures which he treasured but in none of which he was natively or 'by right of national inheritance' altogether at home. Driven into exile – the masterpiece of modern comparative literature, Auerbach's *Mimesis* was written in Turkey by a refugee deprived, overnight, of his livelihood, first language and library – the Jews (my own teachers) fortunate enough to reach North America, would find traditional departments of literature, departments of English first and foremost, barred to them. Thus much of what became comparative literature programmes or departments in American academe arose from marginalization, from partial social and ethnic exclusion. (There are fascinating parallels in the case of atomic physics in the United States.) Comparative literature therefore carries within it both the virtuosities and the sadness of a certain exile, of an inward diaspora. I need hardly say that it is this central truth which renders so particularly apt and comely Lord Weidenfeld's generosity in establishing this visiting chair and the honour accorded to me in inviting me to be its first incumbent.

In a characteristically American scenario, the pursuit of comparative literature rapidly became professionalized and organizational. Professorships, journals, specialized library-resources, doctoral dissertations flourished. This *floruit* may already be over. With the natural deaths of the refugee-masters, the polyglot requisites, the Greek-Latin and Hebraic background, the obvious necessity, wherever practicable, of reading texts in the original, have ebbed. In too many universities and colleges, comparative literature today is conducted, if at all, nearly entirely via translation. The amalgamation with threatened departments of modern languages, with 'core-courses' on western civilization and with the new demands for pan-ethnicity, for 'global' studies, lies readily to hand. In more and more curricula 'comparative literature' has come to signify 'a reading of great books which one ought to have read anyway in, preferably, paperback and in the Anglo-American tongue'. Or a resolve, assuredly arguable, to set classics too long prepotent, too long dusty beside, often in the boisterous shadow of, the Afro-American, the Chicano, the Amazonian traditions (a displacement which already tempted that brilliant comparatist, Maurice Bowra).

More traditional teaching of and research into comparative literature flourishes, at present, in the sometime communist sphere. Certain centres in Russia and eastern Europe are among the most productive and convinced. Here again, a natural necessity for the acquisition of languages, a bitter experience of exile, be it internal, an often vexed questioning of historical, linguistic identity, makes of the comparative approach a relevant method. But prophecies are idle. What can be ventured is this: the instauration of this visiting professorship at Oxford, the hope that a full and professorial programme in comparative literature – and not only European – will follow, do coincide with a time of some uncertainty, potentially fruitful, in this subject.

But *is* it a subject? Can it distinguish itself from the practices of comparison, of parallel and contrastive readings and reception which I have briefly mentioned and which are a natural part of all informed literacy? Is the comparatist, in any professional, entitled sense, a man or woman who will (who should) wake up one morning knowing that he or she, just like Molière's Monsieur Jourdain, has, like all his colleagues, been 'speaking prose'?

The brief replies I want to try and give to this insistent question are bound to be tentative. They are inevitably personal. They cannot hope to speak for this hybrid and protean field as a whole. May Goethe be my guide when he avows, in a Yiddish of Frankfurt provenance, that 'every man prophesies out of his own little book'!

In the humanities (proud, sad word), aspirations to systematic definition end, virtually always, in sterile tautology. 'Theory' has its precise meaning and criteria of falsifiability in the sciences. This is not so in the humanities where claims to the 'theoretical' produce, as we know to our current cost, arrogant jargon. In reference to literary and aesthetic experience and judgement, 'theory' is nothing but subjective intuition or descriptive narrative grown impatient. Pascal reminds us: the sphere of finesse is not that of geometry.

I take comparative literature to be, at best, an exact and exacting art of reading, a style of listening to oral and written acts of language which privileges certain components in these acts. Such components are not neglected in any mode of literary study, but they are, in comparative literature, privileged.

Any reading engages the history and tenets of language. Comparative literature, while alert to the contributions of formal and abstract linguistics, is immersed in, delights in, the prodigal diversity of natural languages. Comparative literature listens and reads after Babel. It posits the intuition, the hypothesis that, far from being a disaster, the multiplicity of human tongues, some twenty thousand of which have, at various times, been spoken on this small planet, has been the enabling condition of men and women's freedom to perceive, to articulate, to 'redraft' the existential world in manifold freedom. Each and every language construes the facticity of existential reality, of 'the given' (*les données immédiates*) in its own specific way. Each and every window in the house of languages opens on to a different landscape and temporality, to a different segmentation in the spectrum of perceived and classified experience. No language divides time or space exactly as does any other (consider Hebrew verb tenses, if one can speak of such); no language has identical taboos with any other (hence the profound Don Juanism of making love in different tongues); no language dreams precisely like any other. The extinction of a language, however remote, however immune to historical-material success or diffusion, is the death of a unique world-view, of a genre of remembrance, of present being and of futurity. A truly dead language is irreplaceable. It closes that which Kierkegaard bade us keep open if our humanity was to evolve: 'the wounds of possibility'. Such closure may, for late twentieth-century mass-media and mass-market technocracy, be a triumph. It may facilitate the *imperium* of the fast-food chain and the news-satellite. For the lessening chances of the human spirit, it is destructive.

Jubilant at the intractable diversity of Babel, comparative literature privileges a twofold principle. It aims to elucidate the quiddity, the autonomous core of historical and present 'sense of the world' (Husserl's *Weltsinn*) in the language and to clarify, so far as is possible, the conditions, the strategies, the limits of reciprocal understanding and misunderstanding as between languages. In brief, comparative literature is an art of understanding centred in the eventuality and defeats of translation. I have tried to show elsewhere that this process begins within the same language, that individuals, generations, genders, social classes, professions, ideologies, past and present, 'translate' when they would understand any communicative discourse inside their own tongue. This immensely complex, ontologically enigmatic process – how is it that they do understand and decipher one another, even if always imperfectly? – becomes fully visible and crucial inter-lingually, across language boundaries.

Every facet of translation – its history, its lexical and grammatical means, the differences of approach that extend from the word-by-word interlinear to the freest imitation or metamorphic adaptation – is absolutely pivotal to the comparatist. The commerce between tongues, between texts of different historical periods or literary forms, the complex interactions between a new translation and those that have gone before, the ancient but always vivid contest of ideals as between the 'letter' and the 'spirit', is that of comparative literature itself. To study, say, some of the more than one hundred versions into English of the *Iliad* and the *Odyssey*, is to experience the development of the English language from Caxton to Walcott (one should say 'languages'); it is to gain insight into the successive, constantly altering relations between British sensibility and representations of the ancient world; it is to observe Pope reading Chapman and Dryden as readers of Homer, and Pope himself reading Homer as through the glass brightly of Virgil. To consider Pound's *Cathay* or Christopher Logue's work-in-progress on an *Iliad*, is to meet head-on the outrageous miracle of supreme translation made in ignorance of the relevant language, made by some osmosis of insight which might, if only we knew how it works, take us to the very heart of the mystery of language itself. It is, furthermore a close hearing of the failures or incompletions of even the finest of translations which, more than any other means of access, helps us throw light on the life-giving residue of the untranslatable, on the *genius loci* as it were, in any language. Labour as we may, *bread* will never wholly translate *pain*. What, in English, French or Italian is *Heimat*?

This primacy of the matter of translation in comparative literature relates directly to what I take to be a second focus. It is that of the dissemination and reception of literary works across time and place. The hoary topic of 'influence' is necessarily vague. Writers have heard of, have 'taken from the air' and surrounding climate of notice, books they have not read. But the careful investigation of the history of publication (which may go back to the rolls inscribed or dictated by Heraclites), of the sale and transport of books and periodicals, of library facilities or the absence thereof in any given period and locale, are vitally illuminating. Who read, who could read what and when? What excerpts, reviews, citations and translations of the German idealists were actually available to Coleridge? How much did Dostoevsky actually know of Dickens or Balzac? How long – the question busied Nabokov in his magisterial, querulous edition of *Eugene Onegin* – did it take for French translation-imitations of Byron to reach the Caucasus? Had Shakespeare any acquaintance with the opening books of Chapman's Homer when he composed *Troilus and Cressida*?

The obverse seems to me an equally significant question. Why do certain authors, works, literary movements 'pass' (to use a French idiom) whereas others remain stubbornly native? For all his immeasurable verbal, syntactical complication, Shakespeare 'passes', even at the level of the comic-book, into the world's language. Racine, whom I believe to be wholly comparable in dramatic strength and, at times, more adult by virtue of his matchless economy, does not. Thomas Otway's *Titus and Berenice* of 1676 is just about the only inspired attempt in English to come to 'transferable' terms with the towering fact of Racine. Sir Walter Scott lies at the source of romantic historicism from Madrid to Odessa. The greatest of English novelists, George Eliot, remains an essentially domestic presence. No less instructive are the examples of overestimate, the exaltation of a writer beyond his true and native rank by way of translation or *mimesis*. Poe is a major poet-thinker from Baudelaire and Mallarmé to Valéry. Charles Morgan enters the French Academy. Deconstruction is a fundamentalist faith on the campuses of Nebraska.

There are no ready explanations. Intrinsic linguistic difficulty does not seem in any way causal: look at Urquhart's Rabelais or at German, Italian and French renderings of Joyce's *Ulysses*; consider Pierre Leyris's resplendent French versions of Gerard Manley Hopkins. Sometimes the accident may be one of biography: had Roy Campbell lived to carry out his recurrent intention of translating Camoëns's *Os Lusiadas*, one of the masterpieces of European literature could well be part of the Anglo-American canon of recognition. Too often, we simply do not know a good reason. But the phenomenology of the untranslatable, the untranslated, the 'unreceived' (*le non-recevoir*) is one of the subtlest of challenges in comparative studies.

A banal but imperative footnote attaches to these two privileged interests. No comparative literature scholar or teacher knows enough languages. Roman Jakobson was reputed to know seventeen, but 'all in Russian'. René Etiemble insisted that even a 'Europeanist' must have knowledge of Chinese and Arabic. For the vast majority among us, such requirements are reproachful dreams or reminders of Joseph Needham! But it is just because much of his work will draw on translations, be it only from the Hebrew Bible, that the comparatist must, at every stage, be intensely responsive to those very matters of translation and dissemination which I have pointed to.

Thematic studies form a third 'centre of gravity' in comparative literature. Analysis, notably by Russian formalists and structural anthropologists, has confirmed the remarkable economy of motifs, the recurrent, rule-bound techniques of narrative which prevail in mythologies, folk-tales and the telling of stories in literature the world over. Tales of triadic temptations and choices, as between three roads, three caskets, three sons, three daughters, three possible brides relate Oedipus to King Lear, Lear to the Karamazov family and countless variants of this root-structure to the tale of Cinderella. It has been argued that there is, as Robert Graves pronounced, 'one story, and one story only': that of 'The Quest'. The episode of avenging execution in Micky Spillane's *I, The Jury* may derive its undeniable power from that ritual slaying of the priest-king whose global ramifications Frazer sought to inventory in his *Golden Bough*. In the West, twentieth-century art, music, film, literature have returned incessantly to classical mythology: to Oedipus, to Elektra, to Medea, to Odysseus, to Narcissus, to Hercules, or Helen of Troy. My study of *Antigones* appeared in 1984. It is already out of date. A dozen further scenic, narrative, lyric treatments of this 'sad song' (Chaucer's tag) have appeared since. A recent bibliography of the Faust-motif in drama, poetry, the novel, films and music runs to several volumes and is incomplete.

We touch here on deep, perhaps troubling waters. Why this economy of invention? I have put forward the hazardous conjecture that the primal Greek myths coincide, in some ways, with the origins of Indo-European grammar. Tales of uncertain or disputed identity would echo the gradual, halting determination of the first and second person singular; the legend of Helen's innocent stay in Egypt while only her exact shadow inhabited and doomed Troy, might preserve traces of the development of those truly fantastic grammatical resources known as 'if' clauses and counter-factuals. Whatever the reason, the fact is that only one fundamental story-theme has been added to the classical stock (Goethe himself adverted to the derivation of Faust from Prometheus). It is that of Don Juan, a theme inconceivable before Christian readings of sexuality and damnation. It is, moreover, distinctly possible that the mechanics of theme and variation, essential to music, are incised also in language and representation. It may be that a 'formulaic' way of telling the same story differently – observe our 'Westerns' – is an impulse of quasi-genetic force. When current 'post-modernism' declares that the 'time of the telling of the great stories is now over', it is worth remembering that the invention of these stories has been over for a considerable time. And that, as in the physics of 'strangeness', time in literature is reversible: the *Odyssey* now comes after *Ulysses* (cf. Borges) and the argonauts of Greek and Hellenistic epics follow on *Star-Trek*.

Let me repeat: a persistent engagement with natural languages, an inquiry into the reception and influence of texts, an awareness of thematic analogies and variants, are part of all literary studies. In comparative literature, these concerns and their creative interactions are given particular emphasis. It is in the light of this emphasis that I would want, again on an obviously personal basis, to point to some area of further exploration and development in the field.

European knowledge, European habits of argument and recognition, arise out of the transmission of classical antiquity and Hellenism to the West. This transmission turns on the role of Islamic philosophy and science in Mediterranean Europe. It tells, notably in certain regions of Spain and the Languedoc, of a unique moment of coexistence between Islam, Judaism and Christianity, between Hebrew, Arabic and Latin and its vulgate descendants. (Europe was not to know this armistice of spirit again.) We lack, almost scandalously, scholars, intellectual and literary historians or critics, capable of reading or judging the Islamic material in its penetration of European Latinity. It is my amateurish belief that this lack has caused severe gaps and distortions in our maps of feeling and of thought. It is my guess that far more than medicine, natural sciences and philosophic fragments from the ancient Greek made the crossing. Despite Islamic iconoclasm, so often exaggerated in western accounts, shards, maybe more, of Greek literature, buried perhaps within quotations, reached the medieval ear. (I see no other way of accounting for Chaucer's association of Antigone with 'her sad song' or *threnos*.) Here, so much work lies before us.

This is true, as well, of the whole domain of Neo-Latin. In successive lexical and grammatical guises, Latin continues to be central to European law, politics, philosophy, science and literature from the time of the collapse of the Roman Empire to the later nineteenth century. It is, quite obviously, the idiom of philosophical and scientific proposal, debate and critique from Aquinas to Leibniz, from Roger Bacon to Copernicus, Kepler and Newton. Academic theses are composed and 'defended' in Latin. But so is literature. This ubiquity comprises dramas, lyrics, satires, epic poems composed in Latin from Portugal to Poland. Latin is the medium for Milton's reach outside England. Baudelaire can, does write Latin verse, as does Tennyson or Hopkins. But the effect, the aura is much larger. It is scarcely possible to interpret coherently the rhetoric of European literatures, the key notions of sublimity, of satire, of laughter which they embody and articulate without a just awareness of the Latin 'implication', of the unbroken, often almost subconscious negotiations of intimacy or of distance between the author in the vulgate and the Latin mould. This is as decisive for Dante as it is for Swift or Dryden; it is as crucial to Corneille as it is to Valéry. As it happens, Neo-Latin can be exceedingly difficult. The brute fact that relatively few among us can deal with it adequately has left a hollow near the very pivot of European comparative studies. Here, as well, necessary and fascinating work lies ahead.

A poem, a play, a novel can never be separated altogether with the illustrations or other pieces of art which it inspires, from its settings to music, from the films, radio versions, television treatments which are based on it. Roman Jakobson called this motion of a text across other media 'transmutations'. These seem to me vital to the disciplines of understanding and valuation in comparative literature. Elsewhere, I have sought to show that different musical settings of the same Goethe or Eichendorff lyric by Schubert, Schumann and Hugo Wolf constitute a compelling process of hermeneutic and critical 'placement' (F. R. Leavis's word, so precisely echoed in 'setting'). Verdi's *Otello* and *Falstaff* have a close, as it were exponential relation to the understanding of Shakespeare in late-romantic Europe. The lives of *Hamlet* are also those of the very different operas, films, paintings, even ballets which the play has generated. For generations of Continental readers, Coleridge's 'Ancient Mariner' was the haunting product of

Doré's illustrations. Today, exact technical reproducibility, electronic encoding and transmission and, before long, the graphic-aural technologies of 'virtual reality' will bear, in ways nearly unpredictable, on the reception of language and of language in literature. Comparative studies are certain to proceed from an informing sense of metamorphosis to one of mutation. But was this not already the case when Greek vase-painters imagined Orpheus or Achilles, when Daumier painted Don Quixote or when Liszt composed his purely instrumental 'translations' of Petrarch?

In the weeks to come, I will be lecturing on 'The Song of the Sirens', from archaic Greece to Joyce, Kafka and Magritte. In part, I have chosen this thematic introduction precisely because of the seminal role of music and the arts. Iconography, as practised by Aby Warburg, Panofsky and the Courtauld tradition, the history and philosophy of music, in the modes of Adorno, are an elemental part of comparative literature.

Lastly, I would point to a rubric which is, I admit, a personal passion. Outside formal and mathematical logic, all philosophy, all metaphysics, is a deed of language. No philosophic argument or picture of the world can be divorced from the language, style, rhetoric, means of presentment and illustration in which it is stated. This is self-evident not only when we are seeking to understand and interpret such virtuosos of language and poetic recourse as Plato, St Augustine, Pascal or Nietzsche. It is true of every philosophic-metaphysical-theological text. The political doctrines of a Hobbes or a Rousseau are integral to their 'stylistics', to the *technē*, to the pacing and dramatizations of their discourse. What pressures did his native Spanish, his acquired Dutch and Hebrew exercise on Spinoza's choice and construction of a marmoreally timeless Latin, of a Latin that infers the Greek of Euclid? Can we dissociate the singular voice of Wittgenstein's *Tractatus* from the history of the German aphorism, notably in Lichtenberg? Once more, matters of translation are pivotal. Exactly as in poetry, so in philosophy and metaphysics, terms and turns of phrase are compacted with a density of potential significations, of questions to themselves and to the reader which make of even the most 'literal', unguarded attempts at translation an intricate process of commentary. There is more than hyperbole in Heidegger's contention that inadequate or erroneous translations of the word 'being' or the verb 'to be' in ancient Greek have determined the intellectual and, it may be, political history of the West.

Here is an area in which every resource of the comparatist in reference to languages, to dissemination, to reception, and thematic *ricorso* comes into play. Even the most abstract thought, once it is verbalized (and can there be pre-verbal thought?), exhibits its idiom. It takes on 'a local habitation and a name'. To my mind, there is nothing at once more fascinating and conducive to hermeneutics than an endeavour to observe, to elucidate the 'intertextuality' of philosophy and poetics, to hear the music which inhabits thought.

The present moment in Europe is hardly consoling. The ideals, the pragmatic dreams abroad in 1945 have faded into rancorous bureaucracy. Almost incomprehensibly, after the massacres, after the devastation of 1914 to 1945, crazed nationalism, tribal hatreds, religious and ethnic intolerance blaze again: in the Balkans, in Northern Ireland, in the Basque country, and our inner cities. The notion of a European concord, except on a commercial, fiscal or mercantile basis – and even here there is little accord – seems to recede from realistic expectations. There are ways in which the Channel is today wider than before, in which Britain, during the Renaissance, the Augustan age or the romantic decades, was closer to Continental Europe than it is today. In paradoxical ways the status of English as the planetary tongue, as the only working 'Esperanto' of science, trade and finance, has further isolated England from the post-Latin and German heritage of mainland Europe.

It would be fatuous bombast to suppose that any individual plea or contribution, especially from within the suspect, because still partly sheltered, confines of the academic could make much difference. The vaunt of money and the mass media mocks the voice of the intellectual – a designation which can itself be used only with a considerable measure of irony and of remorse. Who are we to preach to others? What vanity, what treason sadder than that of many a cleric in the face of political seduction or menace?

Nevertheless, the generosity which has established this chair, the collaboration intended between this programme in comparative literature and other branches of European studies, signal a positive resolve. The history of the organic relations between Britain and the Continent, of the relations – now wholly decisive of our future – between western and eastern Europe, the study of the foundations of spirit on which a potential European community could be built, are to have their place at Oxford.

There is in this project a modest but authentic hope. And if there is a chronic infirmity by which every teacher ought to be afflicted, it is, indeed, hope.

Drumming on the Doors – Péguy

'His great shade burning still': Homer on Ajax, unforgiving, in the Underworld. Charles Péguy was slight of person, though formidably hardened to long marches and weaponry. Like Ajax, he had made of his existence a hand-to-hand duel: against compromise, against the oil sheen of political discourse, of fiscal manipulation, against facility in public and private relations, *contra mundum*. To the pitch of seeming derangement and self-destruction (there was, at the close, scarcely an ally, a supporter, a well-wisher whom Péguy had not broken with and consigned to the limbo of mundane dishonour). Like Socrates, another disturber, Ajax and Péguy remained *fantassins*, infantrymen to the core, with an exact sense of the bitter ground under their feet and of the weight of arms on their backs. Both were past masters of rage. A consuming anger possessed them at the scent of condescension, of what they took to be injustice (the false attribution to smooth Odysseus of the armour of Achilles, the politically motivated amnesty for Dreyfus, the repeated refusal of the Sorbonne, of the French Academy, of the public at large, of the Vatican to recognize, to celebrate the genius, the disinterested virtue of Péguy's *Cahiers* and of their only begetter). Ajax, maddened, slaughtered cattle; Péguy, no less incensed, turned the immensities of his fury and stylistic devastation on one Fernand Laudet, a minnow among pseudo-theologians. Enter the unchanged little bookstore yards from the portico of the loved–hated Sorbonne, blow the dust from the narrow shelves, and Péguy's presence is immediate still.

This third, final volume in the Pléiade edition of Péguy's prose covers the writings from June 1909 to August 1914 – in essence those of the eleventh to the fifteenth series of the *Cahiers de la quinzaine*, author (largely), producer, corrector, distributor Charles Péguy – together with a number of texts ready for printing at his death. The *Œuvres poétiques*, including the thousands of lines of

Review of Charles Péguy, *Œuvres en prose complètes*, vol. 3, edited by Robert Burac (Paris: Gallimard, 1992), from the *Times Literary Supplement*, 25 December 1992.

Ève and the 'Quatrains', have appeared previously (1957). The material productivity of the man has few parallels in the history of literature; thousands of pages of verse and prose pouring from that famous steel-nibbed pen, often day and night. And the 'materiality', the bodily stress of this prodigality is key. Péguy regarded himself as a journeyman, a foot-soldier in the incessant battle with words. No minutiae of typography, of binding, of the choice of paper left him indifferent. Each *Cahier*, each ream of epic or epic-dramatic poetry came of a fierce physical struggle, of a craftsman's love for his tools and of the details of technical cunning invisible to the consumer.

Charnel is a talismanic term for Péguy. There has been no great writer more 'carnal' in his encounter with language, with the enactment of the motions and music of meaning via manuscript and typography. There has been none more obsessed with the manual care demanded by rightness of saying as it is by boots, by a rifle and back-pack if these are to be clean for use. An erratum in the typesetting, looseness of definition, both in the visual and the semantic registers, were to Péguy symptoms of malady at the nerve-centre of speech and of feeling, hence of the body politic (there are analogies in this respect with two other angry loners and editors of journals largely devoted to their own works: Kraus in Vienna, Leavis in Cambridge).

There blows through Péguy's early writings – the Pléiade collection begins with 1897 – an energy of morning, an innocence of excess, which disappointment and private griefs eroded in later years. The first 'Jeanne d'Arc' (she remains Péguy's elected saint to the hour of his death) is, particularly in the scenes between Jeannette and Hauviette, and between Jeanne and Maître Jean during the trial, a masterpiece still awaiting discovery (as is Kraus's 'drama' of 'The Third Walpurgisnacht', so strangely analogous with Péguy in its provocative magnitude and hybrid of lyric and philosophical rhetoric). We cannot hope to get Péguy into any right focus without rereading 'De la cité socialiste' and 'Marcel'. It is here, in 1897–8, that the grandson of an illiterate mender of chairs in Orléans, now *Normalien*, hammers out his urgent ideals, his demands on modern society. Already, he has come upon the tactics of verbal reiteration –

biblical, more than biblical – of 'tidal' pressure on ordinary grammar, which will make his life-work at once exemplary and insufferable. Proust writes of a passionate *hommage* turning, be it involuntarily, to exasperation as he reads and seeks to help the *Cahiers*.

But it is the cause which compels more even than the originality of the manner. The 'cité harmonieuse' belongs to those who labour in it. It is from this creative ownership of the means both of production and of justice that art, science, philosophy must derive their legitimacy. The artist, the thinker is a workman among others, though one endowed with an exceptional degree of disciplined freedom and an exceptional sense of responsibility. Serious art is always respondent to human needs. Philosophy is 'the art of science'. To 'justify' signifies to serve social justice and to keep one's text harmoniously shaped, precisely as does a printer when he 'justifies' the margin of even the most autonomous of poems.

These early texts and the vision of the *Cahiers* arise from the crucible of the Dreyfus Affair. I conjecture that the pounding beat, the strategy of stress and over-stress which became Péguy's hallmark, directly echo the situation of the first *Dreyfusards*. It was not the street-battles, the xenophobic crowds, the officious cover-up which were the worst. It was the feeling, literal and bodily, of Dreyfus's defenders that they were hurling themselves at brick walls, at an unyielding weight of blindness or vicious falsehood when the truth was so evident. Péguy ripened and arrived at his idiosyncratic style – where 'style' defines the seamless cohesion between writing and daily life – when wrestling together with an initial handful of pro-Dreyfus intellectuals against the sheer mass of the state. The same question had to be posed publicly over and over; the same slogans proclaimed. Hopelessness in the face of the leviathan had to be overcome even after Zola's thunderous intervention and the deepening pressure of international disquiet. The tug-of-war, heels nailed to treacherous ground, hands skinned as are those of quarrymen, became Péguy's second nature. Be it in respect of capitalism, of pacifism, of Vatican obscurantism, of the academic-journalistic power-brokers, be it – and this, finally, weighed most – in respect of the subversion of the

French language by mendacious educational reforms and the bellowing of the *bourse* and the politicians, Péguy's method remained that of the *Dreyfusard* drumming with his fists, incessantly, stridently, with raw urgency, on the doors of stupidity and moral betrayal. The 'music', though the term is perhaps out of place, of a Péguy sentence, of the long paragraphs on their march, is almost invariably that of a battering-ram.

When that first great bastion fell, Péguy saw no true victory. Captain Dreyfus's acceptance of amnesty and, thereafter, of a pardon, outraged Péguy. How can there be an amnesty, let alone a pardon, for total innocence? Worst was the decision of French socialism, incarnate in Péguy's beloved friend, master and backer, Jaurès, to support this lie. Together with a handful of ethical purists, of logicians of justice – among them Julien Benda, another *fantassin dans le siècle*, whose *Treason of the Clerics* came out of this sombre imbroglio – Péguy remains intransigent. His most loyal patrons and companions in the Dreyfus wars, the actual and potential funders of the *Cahiers*, the socialists and Christian socialists who had been drawn to Péguy's heroic eloquence, seeped away. As did many of those who, already at the École Normale, had sensed in their singular, unbending comrade a future leader. It was at this juncture that Péguy's isolation began and that a perennial anger lodged in his spirit. Correspondingly, it is in the lengthening shadow of the Affair, resolved for Péguy only in part even by Dreyfus's rehabilitation, that he clung to his mode of address: rebarbative, monotone, oratorical, yet generative of a strength, of an incisive poignancy, of a paradoxical intimacy which has very few rivals in western prose.

The five brief years gathered in this last volume witnessed Péguy at his summit. It was in January 1913 that appeared the most sovereign of his poems: 'La Présentation de la Beauce à Notre Dame de Chartres'. In December of that same year, Péguy, in defiance of minimal prudence, published, in the fourth *Cahier* of the fifteenth series, the interminable quatrains of *Ève* – interminable, but charged nevertheless with a tenacity of vision, with an investment in rebirth – consider the doomed date – which tower over lesser things. Often the provocation is awesome:

Ce n'est pas leur courant et leur haute fréquence
Qui nous fera jaillir le sang de nos artères.
Ce n'est past leur bavette et leur grandiloquence
Qui viendra nous chercher dans nos tacites terres.

Here is the most prolix of poets (when *Ève* thumped on their doorstep, a number of the dwindling coven of subscribers told of being driven crazy by its *haute fréquence*!), here the most grandiloquent of publicists attacking prodigality and grandiloquence. Nevertheless, 'tacites terres' is magnificently exact: in its Latinity, Péguy being after Milton and Corneille the most Latin among moderns; in its evocation of that laconic, watchful acre which Péguy had crossed and recrossed with his peasant or soldier's boots and in which he was, so soon, to lie. Or note the epithet *soudains* in

Et ce ne sera pas ces maîtres de dédains
Qui viendront nous chercher sous nos couches d'humus,
Et ce ne sera pas ces professeurs soudains
Qui viendront nous sonner un dernier angelus.

'Professeurs soudains', brusque in impertinent judgement, breathless in punditry and the media, insensible to scruple, to the tranquil reticence demanded by new art and thought, incapable of scratching even the surface of those 'couches d'humus' (again, the warm dark Latinity) beneath which the seed germinates and the dead are in waiting. How immediately Hardy would have understood this stanza.

'Masters of disdain': the tag cannot be bettered. Overnight critics and panders of literary gossip, regius professors who cackle on the radio or in the glossy press at works which they dread in their envious impotence. Mandarin specialists policing their patch of professional ground and mouthing venom at those who seek to see a larger horizon. Piercingly, Péguy labels them the 'December men'. During 1909–14, their chill breath, their efficacious scorn, harried him almost to ruin. Though thoroughly documented in earlier studies, the tale continues to make grim reading. In October 1910, one Alfred Dreyfus cancelled his subscription to the *Cahiers*; despite Barrès's support and unctuous promises on all fronts, Péguy is, at the last turn, denied the 'Grand prix de littérature' of the Académie française which would have given him not only desperately needed money but some immunity (Péguy felt the note of contempt in the attribution to him of a lesser award); exhaustion and sickness during 1911; Romain Rolland, Bergson, writers and philosophers whom Péguy had championed and published, ascend to eminence and public laurels. Péguy fights on 'dans la misère'. 'Je suis pauvre, pauvre,' he writes to Joseph Lotte in the spring of 1912.

Every number of the *Cahiers*, composed, printed, mailed against absurd odds, brings with it further desertions. Soon Péguy, for whom the distribution of free copies to those too poor to subscribe was of the essence, has to limit the print-run to the exact number of his *abonnés*. He sells what he can of his manuscripts to a clairvoyant collector. Already, a certain aura of fame surrounds him. Proust, Claudel, Bergson know of his genius. Gide is characteristically percipient and feline in his tributes. The press speaks of the man and of his quixotic enterprise. *Sorbonnards* and academicians hurry past the exiguous boutique with occasional twinges. 'Something should be done for dear Péguy' (the similitudes with *Scrutiny* and the marginalization of Leavis are sadly obvious). But nothing or very little was. Which makes the more spellbinding the volume and elevation of the *œuvre* produced in these very years.

No account of friendship after Montaigne surpasses *Notre jeunesse*, published in July 1910. Historians of the Dreyfus Affair have long known it to be the classic in their sprawling bibliography. But it is Péguy's memoir of his vehement, flawed intimacy with Henri Bernard Lazare, one of Dreyfus's very first partisans and a Jew numbed by the sudden self-discovery of his own imperilled status, which makes this piece unforgettable. The relationship of the two men is set alight by the 'mystique' of their common cause, by their commitment to an ideal of justice so absolute that it transcends even the moral imperatives – they are acknowledged to be such – of national fraternity and security. It is the *dégradation* of this 'mystique' into 'politics', into the expediences and manoeuvres of parliamentarians and the press which leads to a break between Péguy and Bernard Lazare (as we will see, relations between the Montagne Sainte-Geneviève, the Sorbonne quarter and Israel have, since Peter Abelard, been complex). Now, looking back, Péguy recognizes in Bernard Lazare the witness who, like too many prophets out of Judaism, had been silenced and passed over: 'Et il était mort avant d'être mort.' Whatever, moreover, their tactical differences, he and Péguy had never really parted. The 'mystique', the contract of justice at the core of the Affair, had become that of the relation. The great music of Péguy's prose mounts:

Il avait cet attachement mystique à la fidélité qui est au cœur de l'amitié. Il faisait un exercice mystique de cette fidélité qui est au cœur de l'amitié. Ainsi naquit entre lui et nous cette amitié que nulle mort ne devait rompre, cette amitié parfaitement échangée, parfaitement mutuelle, parfaitement parfaite, nourrie de la désillusion de toutes les autres, du désabusement de toutes les infidélités.
Cette amitié que nulle mort ne rompra.

The marvel is the verbal precision in midst the motion: 'dégradation' always in the background because it is that of Captain Dreyfus; 'exercice mystique', because *exercice*, in its Latin provenance, is a military term, exactly connoting both the Affair and Péguy's own 'soldiering on'; the threefold 'parfait' because, of course, of *perfectum est* with its full implications of terminal suffering and ultimate benediction.

Victor-Marie, comte Hugo appears in that same *annus mirabilis* of 1910. It strikes one as being among the half-dozen pre-eminent acts of literary criticism in our century; 'literary criticism' being, here, a wholly inadequate rubric. It is throughout this radical meditation that Péguy defines and enacts what is, what ought to be *une lecture bien faite*. To 'read well' is to engage the immediacy of felt presence in a text at every level of encounter: spiritual, intellectual, phonetic, even 'carnal' (the text acts on nerve and sinew as does music). The issue is that of a true philology, of a 'love of the *Logos*' that calls on every instrument of understanding – lexical, prosodic, grammatical, semantic – but whose motor is a scruple, a bestowal of trust on the part of the reader when he apprehends (there is terror in understanding) the demands which any serious literature or art makes on him. 'Change your life,' says Rilke's archaic torso of Apollo to those who seek to experience its full presence. Péguy, like perhaps almost no other commentator, generates this bruising mystery of change in himself and in us as he narrates his reading. The parallel (Plutarchian) reading of Corneille and Racine, with its deliberately hyperbolic view of *Polyeucte* and its unjust estimate of Racine's Jansenist 'cruelty' – Péguy lights on that word in *Bérénice* – of Racine's 'perpetually intelligent avarice' (an insight for which I will cheerfully exchange all recent tomes of post-structuralist and deconstructionist verbiage) is a classic in hermeneutics. Yet in this same tract, Péguy surpasses even himself.

His exegesis (the biblical resonance is entirely justified) of Victor Hugo's 'Booz endormi' matches, strength for strength, meaning for meaning, the splendour of its occasion. It has a poetic of close reading, of inward concordance that refuses paraphrase, reminiscent of Coleridge on the Wordsworth of the *Lyrical Ballads*. Péguy's hermeneutic 'conceit' is notorious: Hugo, peer of France, *membre de l'Institut* (a warning shot) invents *Jérimadeth* and must find a rhyme. Out of this obbligato, ostentatiously exhibitionist as it may well be, springs one of the handful of supreme lyrics in French, indeed in any literature. Out of this virtuoso turn, comes the 'plénitude souveraine' and the 'calme horizontal' of the closing line (is there any other like it?):

> Cette faucille d'or dans le champ des étoiles.

Then go back to that suspect *Jérimadeth*:

comme Jérimadeth, ainsi placé (je ne parle pas de *Judith*) est hébraïque, QUAND ON Y PENSE. Non seulement il a le même départ que *Jéricho*. Mais il a ce même grand *J* initial que *Judith*. Rien n'est Juif comme un *J* de grande capitale. Et il rime si merveilleusement avec tous ces beaux noms, juif: (Josabeth), Japhet, (que de *J*; comme j'avais raison . . .

Indeed: how right he was, and how alone he remains.

Had I to introduce a reader to Péguy's mature thought, it would be via *Clio, Dialogue de l'histoire et de l'âme païenne*, composed in

1912–13 and published only posthumously: more than eight hundred manuscript pages produced under extreme personal stress and shadowed by a tranquil intimation of the nearing European catastrophe. Characteristically, the dialogue between Clio, Muse of History, and the reader, who embodies worldliness (*l'âme charnelle*), spirals around a number of general concerns: historicity and truth, conscience and mundanity, the mendacious claims of the study of the humanities to a scientific methodology and status, the illusion of progress in the arts. Underlying and relating these topics, in an intensely personal reticulation, is a meditation on remembrance, on the creative intelligence of memory, as searching as that in Proust (the two 'quests' being so closely contemporary). There are no more inspired pages in Péguy than those in which he tells of the life-giving custodianship of the reader in respect of Homer or of Sophocles. Well before Heidegger, Péguy touches on the talismanic primacy of certain Greek texts, on their unmatched energies of renewal.

But this renewal comes into being in the answerability of the modern reader, in his 'responding responsibility' to the questioning of the text. Here, crucially, the questioning is dialectical. We ask of the text; it asks of us. Péguy pleads for immediacy, for an encounter with the master-singers and thinkers as fresh, as lacking in sclerotic awe as is our encounter with the morning paper. May the reader's soul remain 'pagan' so that the pressures of existential immanence in the classics, the pressures of actuality in the *Iliad* or in *Antigone* can bear on him without mandarin or scholastic interposition. 'Comme si ce fût la dernière *nouveauté*.' Lived remembrance is never archival: it is discovery (whence Péguy's scorn of the new schools of 'scientific-sociological' history). The authentic historian is also a poet of precise imagining. He knows that a single verse of Hesiod may bathe in sudden light a landscape, a complex structure of temporality otherwise unrecapturable. Again, there are luminous pages on Hugo, in whom history and poetry, matter and spirit are so 'immensely' interwoven.

The book closes with two posthumous and fragmentary works: the 'Note' on Bergson and the 'Note conjointe' on Descartes (a shorter version of the 'Bergson' had appeared in the *Cahier* for April 1914). Péguy's final meditation takes Descartes for its almost contingent occasion. What is at stake here is an anti-modernist, highly idiosyncratic reaffirmation of Péguy's Catholicism. Modern civilization would annihilate 'le spirituel sous toutes ses formes' precisely by rationalizing faith, by accommodating revelation to positivism. The truth of Aquinas cannot be that of Herbert Spencer. Mystery cannot be politics. Magnificently, Péguy one last time identifies the arch-daemonic: *l'argent*. Not even Marx has spoken with more prophetic anger of the ubiquity of money in modernity, of its contagious omnipotence. By compromising with capitalism, by becoming itself a fiscal might, the church has forfeited its claims to spirituality. For Péguy, whose socialism remained to the end 'mystical', there can be no tenable divide between charity and justice. Both are dynamic within the privilege of poverty. One last time, with a kind of serene 'impertinence', Péguy celebrates his beloved Corneille and the supremacy of *Polyeucte*. One last time, his high 'patrons', St Louis, Joinville, the Maid of Orléans, come to his aid. Honour against profit; the wonder of language against journalism; patriotism against the unhoused emptiness of internationalism.

Not everything in Péguy's close is admirable. He carries some measure of responsibility for aiming at Jaurès a violence of patriotic hatred which proved homicidal. What remains wholly impressive is the economy inside the prodigality. In the moment in which he left incomplete the last paragraph (as we have it) of his essay on Descartes and faith, Péguy had virtually brought to consummation his vast enterprise. *Bon à tirer*, the password to the publication of the *Cahiers*, of the leviathan poems and dramas, now marked the true and foreseen end. *Nihil obstat*.

The Pléiade has, of late, not always met its own declared standards. Robert Burac's Péguy is editorially admirable. Yet at one point, at least, its grave reticence frustrates. *Œuvres* are not, are not meant to be, a biography. But both the editorial preface and the chronology, often day by day, pass under almost total silence a vital element in Péguy's end. Something is known, more could be said of his love for Blanche Raphaël, of his urgent, ambiguous role in her marriage (a marriage which was intended to guard him from desperate temptation and actions he regarded as inadmissible). Our only reliable account dates back to 1938. The issue is not one of prying gossip. Péguy's profound, both sombre and at moments festive relationship to Judaism, needs to be far better understood than it as yet is. In this context, the matter of his love for Blanche may be of the essence, as was that of the Dreyfus years.

On 2 August 1914, in a hired *fiacre*, Péguy criss-crossed Paris bidding farewell to friends with whom he had quarrelled (Blum, Jean Variot among them). He said adieu to Bergson and to Blanche. It was not at home that he spent the last two nights before joining his regiment at Coulommiers. On 16 August he mailed to Blanche handwritten Latin texts of the *Pater noster*, *Ave Maria* and *Salve regina*. It is believed that Lt Péguy took Holy Communion in the field on the morning of 5 September. As he led his men in an infantry advance that afternoon, he was struck in the head by a German bullet. The exact location of his death near Villeroy has never been fixed. Six weeks later, the Berlin periodical *Die Aktion* paid tribute to the fallen poet. Egon Schiele provided a portrait. They did, in those distant days, order matters differently.

When the opportunistic obscurantism which currently dominates so much of our sense of the life of language and of feeling will have faded, Péguy's implacable integrity will persist. He is, to a growing number of poets (consider Geoffrey Hill), indispensable. In evident ways, this edition, now complete, is a monument. But more important, it is itself like a fragment which burns to the touch.

Sainte Simone – Simone Weil

Reportedly, Plato said of Diogenes the Cynic: 'He is Socrates gone mad.' In which remark there is as much of uneasy homage as there is of scorn. Can one help but recall this description when considering Simone Weil?

With characteristic reserve, her brother, André Weil, the great algebraic topologist, concluded that his sister's 'sensibility had gone beyond the limits of the normal'. More brusquely, de Gaulle, a masterly judge of human beings, declared that 'the woman was mad'. Exalting her largely self-inflicted death in 1943, feminists, to whom Simone Weil has become talismanic, speak of 'mystical anorexia' as it has been attributed to certain female saints. On the humbler level of recorded evidence, what is one to make of a thinker-scholar who ruled with apodictic, magisterial certainty that 'Shakespeare's tragedies are second-class with the exception of *Lear*'? Who states that 'The *Iliad*, the tragedies of Aeschylus and those of Sophocles bear the clearest indication that the poets who produced them were in a state of holiness'? Who repeatedly propounded the notion that the 'Languedoc civilization of the twelfth century' came close to utopia because in it Cathars and Catholics had achieved harmonious equilibrium? How are we to cope with extensive, often painfully forced writings in which Simone Weil labours to discover in Greek lyric poetry and drama, no less than in Platonic philosophy, specific, material prefigurations of and analogues with the Gospels?

But if the pathology (perhaps, indeed, the 'madness') is there – and why are Simone Weil's acolytes so unwilling to countenance the facts? – so is the Socratic. The contributions to our climate of understanding of Simone de Beauvoir, of Hannah Arendt are manifest. Is there until now a philosophic imagination among women to set beside Simone Weil's? At her best, she coerced pain

Review of *Simone Weil's Philosophy of Culture*, edited by Richard H. Bell (Cambridge University Press, 1993), from the *Times Literary Supplement*, 4 June 1993.

and eccentric circumstance into disinterested universality in precisely a Kantian sense. Her observation, at the very moment of the occupation of Paris by German troops, that this was a great day for Indo-China (for all peoples under French colonial rule) has the axiomatic, chilling purity of a Stoic maxim. Modern philosophic theology and metaphysics have produced few more challenging propositions than Simone Weil's 'We have to believe in a God who is like the true God in everything except that he does not exist, for we have not reached the point where God exists.' Is there any social philosopher outside Marx (a constant presence in Weil) who has striven as stringently to grasp the implications – psychological, social, physical, political, but also, in a genuine sense, philosophic – of work in the factory, of the 'laborious' technological condition of modern men and women?

Biographical, analytic, literary treatments of Simone Weil multiply. There are *Cahiers Simone Weil*, study circles and international colloquia. A complete edition is in progress. The heat is evident; the light less so. Uncritical reverence on the one hand, exasperation and distaste on the other, mark the debates around her 'works and days'. Feminism, whose immediate antecedents she seems to have found irrelevant and falsifying, has added a vehement note. In my opinion – it can be no more than that – much in this 'dialogue of the deaf', in the hyperboles both of praise and of dismissal, arises from an unwillingness, conscious or repressed, to explore the central issue of Simone Weil's Judaism and rejection of Judaism. This issue is (as, perhaps, in the case of Wittgenstein) not only immensely complicated, requiring in any approach the most scrupulous delicacy of inquiry, the utmost provisionality and *pudeur* on the part of the inquirer: it is, at many points, highly unpleasant, indeed repellent. It would need the psychological penetration of a Dostoevsky and the *caritas* of a saint to ponder equably a human being who, at the time when her own people were being harried to bestial extinction, refused baptism into the Catholic Church because 'Roman Catholicism was still too Jewish'. Or whose prolix meditations on the crisis in European culture and the programmes needed for its resurrection found (so far as I am aware) nothing whatever to say about the unfolding Holocaust. Has there ever been a philosophic thinker on love, at often compelling and originating depths, more loveless?

The avoidance of this dilemma, at all but two or three points which I will revert to, renders *Simone Weil's Philosophy of Culture*, this collection of 'readings towards a divine humanity', strangely hollow. In only one paper, also the most distinguished in style and reflection, is there any real element of critique. Otherwise, the tone is largely one of hagiography.

To Richard H. Bell, the editor, it is self-evident that Simone Weil is 'a moral philosopher' whose spiritual illuminations and social-political findings accumulate to a coherent 'philosophy of culture'. Even when she was summarizing and setting out Descartes or Marx, 'the stamp of *her* thought was everywhere'. Weil's views on twentieth-century science (often embarrassing in their pastoral facility) are to be taken with *gravitas*. Hers is, above all, 'the world of a radically incarnational Christology without dogma'. In this world, the concept of 'decreation' plays a fundamental role. J. P. Little does her valiant best to make 'decreation' intelligibly arguable. We must, urges Simone Weil, suffer a 'moral death', an extinction of self which entails a total acceptance of everything, independent of the ego and its volitions. The personal self can be redeemed only if we offer it to God for annihilation. This offer, in turn, will allow the recuperation of the created within the perfect oneness of the Creator. The coming into being of creatures other than God enacts a fatal rift, a divine abdication and self-dispersal. Every act of egotism – and there can, by definition, be no human deed which is not tainted to a greater or lesser degree with self-will – aggravates God's withdrawal from Himself. Abnegation, the autistic 'infolding' which Weil exercised existentially, are small but decisive steps towards the 'reunification' of God and, one presumes, the abolition, perhaps temporary or temporal (the argument here is blurred precisely because it lies outside common discourse) of a soiled, corrupted reality. Dr Little locates 'decreation' inside the tradition of mystical negative theology as we find it in Meister Eckhart or St John of the Cross. Weil perceives creation in the sacrificial terms of the Incarnation and the Passion. The Incarnation of the Son would represent the 'separation of God from God'. It is only in the very last pages of this book that we find a passing allusion to the obvious fact that, long before Catholic mysticism, the concept of *Tsimtsum,* of divine creation, rupture and withdrawal, plays a major role in Jewish mystical speculations and throughout the kabbala! 'We need to invoke Isaac Luria,' remarks H. L. Finch. Better late than never.

Rowan Williams's discussion of 'the necessary non-existence of God' in Simone Weil's 'theology' is outstanding. Very nearly alone in this collection, Professor Williams presses closely the logical weakness, the tendencies towards argumentative fiat in Weil's position. He asks, in a taxing but key sentence: 'Is it possible to see Weil's language here as a kind of ethical and spiritual transcription of this canonization of cognitive disinterest?' Gently but incisively, Williams points to the 'enormous problems' Weil has with the actual 'possibilities of self-love or love of the particular'. Which induces, which compels him to raise the crucial issues: 'What, as a woman, is she culturally "allowed" to think about her body? What on earth is going on in her extraordinarily vitriolic and silly comments on Judaism – a real demonization of her own heritage?' – at the exact moment, I repeat, when that heritage was being done to unspeakable death in Christian Europe. Williams's decorous but inescapable questioning comes as a breath of fresh air.

D. Z. Phillips is enlightening on conceptual-linguistic tactics in Weil's uses of the word 'God'. He reminds us of the horror she felt at what she took to be the anthropomorphic 'empowerment' of the divine person in Judaism and in Roman religion. She was acute in her perceptions of the idolatrous as it is, almost necessarily, implicit in the deifications of human power in the ordinary language of paternalistic faiths. No less than Spinoza, Weil distrusted the mimetic impulses of the imagination. In a radically Jewish sense, she loved language supremely – see her on Pindar, on Sophocles, on the Gospels – and utterly distrusted its bias to fantasy, to image. Hence her awesome dictum: 'We must prefer real hell to an imaginary paradise.' Martin Andic takes up this critical theme of 'imagination'. Persuasively, he expounds Weil's lifelong summons to concreteness, her insistence, surely right, that abstractions, spurious ideological absolutes and the rhetorical delusions on which our politics feed, foster man's inhumanity to man. (There are suggestive affinities between Weil's language-critique and that of Orwell, under sometimes comparable circumstances.)

But, as Professor Andic points out, this critique is, in Weil's case, again 'theological'. It relates to the necessary 'decreation' of the collective 'We' – the locus of the political: 'The devil in us is the "We", or rather the "I" with a halo or "We" about it, for it is the imagination that makes us want to be like God without God, like him in his power not his love, and that bestows upon us a fictitious divinity by putting us at the centre of the universe in space and time, values and being.' Perception cleansed of imagination is 'discernment'. Surely, Andic should, at this point, alert us to the noble source of Weil's advocacy, which is the rubric *clair et distinct* in Descartes. Ultimately, 'discernment' of the authentic, of our own motives and the facts of the world, is accessible solely through the 'eyes of love'. Only these will pick up the secret spoors of God's absent presence in a nauseating, self-blinding reality. But even prior to such loving (Platonic?) clairvoyance, 'discernment' can apply to everyday life. Nothing in Weil's work seems to me more moving than her lucid observations of working-class conditions inside and outside the assembly line, where lucidity is achieved at the cost of fierce personal suffering, where disciplined sight proceeds via pain into insight. And though it is concerned more with the neo- or post-Marxism of Agnes Heller, Clare Fischer's chapter, 'Simone Weil and the Civilization of Work', contributes authoritatively to this vital topic. For Weil, 'Passion and bread-getting' are indeed closely concordant.

The later papers in these *acta* address more directly the wider 'cultural' bearings in Weil's enterprise. The editor, followed by Professors Collins and Nirlsen, presents the personal and social tenor of Weil's considerations on law. They underline the discriminations she draws between an excess of 'freedom' and a lack of 'thought' in current social-political arguments and ideals. She pleads for a 'rule of equity' articulated by almost Platonic judges whose function would be that of mediating between mutual, inevitably conflictual obligations. Weil strove, during the last months of her working life, to redefine the notion of social justice, of the very legitimacy of law in the grey light of the European catastrophe and, most especially, of the collapse of moral authority in France. The relevant reflections on tyranny and the ambiguous status of a secular liberty are among the most poignantly lucid in Simone Weil's perfectionism.

Patrick Sherry discusses Weil's religious aesthetics. He urges the Trinitarian matrix of her models of 'perfect harmony'. It is the bond of love between Father and Son which provides Weil (as it did Augustine) with both the underwriting and paradigm of absolute concord and disinterested beauty. This beauty is compacted, as it were, in the infinite light shed by the Holy Ghost. Incisively, Ann Loades takes up the motifs of innocence and of suffering as these are dramatized in Weil's several treatments of the Antigone-myth and of the Sophoclean paradigm. Most courteously, Dr Loades challenges the absence of these treatments from my own *Antigones* of 1984. I was, no doubt, remiss on this point. But nothing in this moving and acute chapter persuades me that Loades is not making bricks out of straw. Weil's sketches of Antigone and of Creon hardly add to what Hegel and Kierkegaard had already postulated. And if there is, today, a reading of Sophocles which goes beyond these great unravellers, it is that of Heidegger.

It is the coda, 'Simone Weil: Harbinger of a New Renaissance?' by Professor Finch, which is the most revealing moment in this whole collection.

Did the editor, Professor Bell, at the last, feel queasy about the evasions and question-begging in what went before? For what we have here is quite obviously an exercise in 'damage limitation'. Finch rides forth to slay what he archly calls 'the four dragons' standing in the path of a just valuation of the beautified lady Simone. The first is that of anorexia as it may be envisaged by vulgar psychology. 'Is it not an understandable response to the manufacture and dropping of bombs on tens of thousands of people for a single woman to die by refusing to eat out of sympathy for these victims?' Delicate ground ill concealed by rhetorical query. Weil's own testimony bore not on air-raid victims but on the meagre rations in occupied France which she proposed to share, more or less melodramatically, in her London exile. The second dragon is the imputation of masochism (cf. J. P. Little's earlier, flat assertion that 'There is no martyr-complex in Simone Weil'). We are to understand her espousals of pain as imperative stations on the way to 'the Good'. Again, this is a most complex topic. But the fact remains that even Weil's intimates were shocked by her confessed envy of the physical agonies of Christ, by her wish to emulate the Passion. However concordant it may be with a mystical tradition of holy maceration, such a sentiment lies at the shadow-line of the pathological.

Dragon three is Weil's alleged *anti-Judaism* (Finch's italics). *Pace* such ill-informed psychologists as Anna Freud, Weil was brought to Christianity by love of Christ and not by Jewish self-hatred. 'Is it a principle that no Jew can be drawn to another religion without it being an expression of Jewish self-hatred?' Did she not have the simple good fortune of seeing the light and ending as 'an orthodox Christian' (Ann Loades)? Jesus is not, 'as he might in Judaism', addressing 'a people-self'. He talks to 'essential individuals, impersonal friends', among whom Weil is eminently attentive.

Words are being juggled here. I have already mentioned the seemingly systematic oversight of the Judaic sources and tenor of Weil's thought which marks this book. But matters are both plainer and uglier. In Weil's detestation of her own ethnic identity, in her strident denunciations of the cruelty and 'imperialism' of the God of Abraham and of Moses, in her very nearly hysterical repugnance in the face of what she termed the excess of Judaism in the Catholicism she, finally, refused to join, the traits of a classical Jewish self-loathing are carried to fever pitch. In that uncomely respect, Weil is of the family of Marx, of Otto Weininger and, at passing moments, of Karl Kraus. Worst of all, to repeat, is her refusal to envisage, in the very midst of her eloquent pathos in respect of suffering and injustice, the horrors, the anathema being enacted on her own people.

The fourth dragon, a somewhat arcane beast, is that of the

example and nature of Weil's acts of prayer. We baulk, says Finch, at her supplications for extinction, for 'paralysis' before God. We ascribe psychologically suspect motives to her reaching out towards the universal obedience represented by 'dumb, insentient matter'. Witness the Sufi doctrine of 'animal unveiling'. Once these dragons of misprision are slain, we can follow Weil's teachings on a shining path towards a renascence of true humanity.

On this plane of apologia, serious discussion is scarcely feasible. What needs careful sifting is the distinction to be drawn – if it can be drawn – between the singularity of the person, with all its pathological markers, and the autonomous weight of the work. It is only very gradually that this distinction is beginning to take on coherence in the case of Nietzsche. Generations will pass before any confident delineation can be proposed in our sense of Martin Heidegger. It may well be that Weil was not of that stature, but the opacities are comparable. If, for example, we can learn to look away from biography and confessional provocation, what in Weil's 'existential negativity' does or does not go beyond key texts on the annihilation of the wilful and tortured ego in Schopenhauer? How, to touch on another set of themes, are we to situate Weil's sociology of labour in relation to Engels, or her recurrent if often covert considerations of suicide in relation to Durkheim? In what ways are her 'Judaeo-Christological' glosses on classical Greek literature a development of Philo and Plotinus? Can her deeply felt but bizarre interpretation of the *Iliad* as a poem of suffering – a reading almost blind to the wild joy and ferocity of archaic warfare which makes the epic blaze – be placed more consistently within the ambience of Alain's teachings on war? There is so much here which awaits scrupulous, non-hagiographic insight.

This, of course, is the point. Simone Weil's is an utterly fascinating presence. There are sentences, even whole pages, in her writings which make one's blood stop: through their impassioned, lacerated humanity (an old Jewish handicap); through their edgy abruptness of philosophical or social sight. A night-vision, as it were, of insomniac conscience. *Gravity and Grace* is no mean heir to the best of Kierkegaard. *The Need for Roots* remains a profoundly suggestive argument with more than a touch of Kant's clarity in regard to politics. There are flashes, and more than flashes, of supreme moral intelligence in Weil's *Notebooks* and letters. Our vexed times would be much poorer without Simone de Beauvoir's lived 'anthropology', without the political-literary diagnoses of Hannah Arendt. But of the great feminine spirits abroad, that of Weil does strike one as the most evidently philosophic, as the most at home in the 'mountain light' (as Nietzsche would have it) of speculative abstraction. In that cold air, incense is out of place.

Trusting in Reason – Husserl

When Adorno (innocent soul) sought a foothold at Oxford during the bitter years 1934–7, he presented his critique of Husserl's theories of perception. This had been the topic of his doctoral dissertation of 1924. Further expanded, the *Metakritik der Erkenntnistheorie*, an inquiry into the internal contradictions (*Antinomien*) in Husserl's phenomenology, appeared as a book in 1956. As late as 1968, Adorno regarded the *Metakritik* as one of his two most important works (together with the *Negative Dialektik*). It is indeed a dense, scrupulously argued text. Adorno engages what he terms the fundamental inconsistencies in Husserl's 'Platonic realism'. He queries Husserl's apodictic trust in the validity, in the timelessness of the exact sciences. Adorno ironizes the *horror intellectualis* which characterizes Husserl's thought in the face of contingent materiality, of the inchoate. He sees something 'brittle' and solipsistic in the entire phenomenological enterprise. Characteristically, Adorno presses the claims of the social context, of historicity in regard to any metaphysical constructs of method and of truth. Husserl, according to Adorno, simply fails to see that the transience of any idealistic phenomenality is as necessary as its origins. The anguish for conservation of bourgeois-liberal sensibility in a time of crisis informs and debilitates Husserl's world-view. Yet it is with more than a touch of awed nostalgia that Adorno quotes the Husserlian credo: 'The realm of truth is no disorderly chaos; unison and law [*Gesetzlichkeit*] prevail in it. Thus the search for and exposition of truths must be systematic; it must mirror the systematic relations of truths.'

Jacques Derrida's *La Voix et le phénomène*, an introduction to the 'problem of the sign' in Husserl's phenomenology, appeared in 1967. This brief monograph, at once profoundly respectful of Husserl's achievement and radically critical of its epistemological

Review of Edmund Husserl, *Briefwechsel*, edited by Karl Schuhmann and Elisabeth Schuhmann (Louvain: Husserl-Archiv/Dordrecht: Kluwer Academic, 1994) from the *Times Literary Supplement*, 24 June 1994.

presuppositions, contains the essence of Derridean deconstruction and of the doctrine of 'difference'. Its examination of the unresolved contradictions in Husserl's 'intuitions of presence', in his semantics of representation, is incisive. So are the analyses of the 'visual constant' – a legacy of the privileges of geometry in Plato – in the Husserlian model of apprehension and communication. This visual constant elides the central problems raised by audition and 'voicing'.

Nothing in Derrida's subsequent work surpasses in seriousness, in subtle patience, his teasing out of the opacities in Husserl's concept of self-address, of the '*Je* dans le discours solitaire', of the ineluctable ambiguities which attach to the process of 'listening to one's inwardly intended discourse'. In their turn, the philosophical-historical essays of Jan Patočka take on a particular strength when in dialogue with Husserl, when the questions are those of the historicity of human consciousness (Husserl's qualified debt to Dilthey) or of the manifest failure of Husserlian phenomenology to find for itself a convincing answer to the dilemma of interpersonal relations, to the 'sociology of monads'.

This incapacity to develop a persuasive model for the sharing of an intuitive consciousness of reality between individuals gravely flaws the whole phenomenological faith. Phenomenology sets out to explain our consciousness of our own ego, of its processes of perception and integration, and of the manifold ways in which these processes build our inhabiting and understanding of the world. Has it, ask even its sympathetic critics, escaped from solipsism, from a narrative of the isolated ego?

Is there some vital clue in the fact that so many modern thinkers are at their finest when writing about, be it *contra*, Edmund Husserl? That phenomenology, as Husserl conceived and argued it, should be most fruitful in deviant modes, in appropriations and deflections some of which the master himself regarded with utter distaste? What other philosophy after Kant and Hegel has created so many imitative but selective or frankly mutinous offshoots? Husserl saw with mounting rebuke Max Scheler's attempts to convert phenomenology into a theory of values and tragic humanism. Adolf Reinach proposed a phenomenological jurisprudence. Faithful, wherever possible, to Husserl's intuitionalism, Roman Ingarden developed an aesthetics and paradigm of the structure of the work of art. Via Jaspers in Europe and Binswanger in North America, Husserl's thought entered theoretical and applied psychology. It generated a kind of philosophic psychopathology directed towards the patient's states of consciousness and psychic existentiality. Also in the United States, Alfred Schütz sought to extend phenomenology to the social sciences. In France, the Husserl-current has been seminal. It sustains Sartre's work on perception and the imaginary; Merleau-Ponty's phenomenology of presence; Paul Ricoeur's theory of volition; and the phenomenology of the 'face to face' of Levinas, now so influential.

But the drama of betrayed inheritance is, of course, that of the relation to Heidegger. Certain aspects of this tragically creative discipleship and rejection may take decades to unravel. Personal factors, most notably Heidegger's feline behaviour towards his teacher and benefactor at the time of the Nazi take-over, further complicate and obscure the problem. Dedicated to Edmund Husserl, *Sein und Zeit* is that rarest of paradoxes: a monument which would destroy. Dry, self-governed as they are, Husserl's marginal notes to Heidegger's leviathan (they have been published and are already translated into French) ache with bewildered pain. Quickly but against, as it were, the grain of his hopes and legitimate expectations, Husserl realizes that Martin Heidegger has, almost totally, subverted the phenomenological quest and criteria of rationality (*Wissenschaft*). Heidegger's ontology and narrative of a primordial 'forgetting of Being' enact a repudiation of life-work the more ruinous as it is unspoken. Husserl is too lucid, too committed a thinker not to perceive the grandeur, the rhetorical spell of Heidegger's enterprise, or to guess that it would command a large following. Heidegger's triumph after 1927 (he succeeds to Husserl's chair at Freiburg in 1928) will determine both Husserl's isolation and the genius of his late, incomplete writings.

It is almost ironic that out of this isolation – Husserl, in 1934, remarks on 'the eerie silence' which surrounds him – should have come the most prodigal, detailed archive of any modern philosophic career except, possibly, Bertrand Russell's. Rescued to Louvain by H. L. von Breda, the Husserl material has long been in the process of the most minute scholarly inventory and publication. (The Heidegger edition now in spasmodic progress is, by contrast, an often irresponsible muddle. *Justice faite.*) Husserl bequeathed forty thousand pages in stenographic script. Key lectures and treatises, notably that masterpiece, *Die Krisis der europäischen Wissenschaften*, were left either incomplete or in an editorially unsatisfactory version. Now, under the aegis of the Husserl-Archiv, massive portions of the iceberg are surfacing. Karl Schuhmann's copious *Husserl-Chronik* (1977) and Hans Rainer Sepp's volume of documents and photographs, *Edmund Husserl und die phänomenologische Bewegung* (second edition, 1988), allow us to follow, often from day to day, the master's writings, teaching, encounters and travels. The arduous academic ascent from Halle (1887–1901) to Göttingen (1901–16), from Göttingen to Freiburg (1916–28) can be traced in every detail. How much less we know of Wittgenstein's personal existence. Edmund Husserl was a voluminous correspondent, though not quite on the scale of Locke or Voltaire. He complained of the incessant pressure on his time, but used letters – also composed, often, in Gabelberger stenography and then transcribed by his wife or assistants – to expound his doctrine, to attempt to shape and hold together an international phenomenological movement, to debate with his peers. Edited by Karl and Elisabeth Schuhmann, these nine volumes of *Briefwechsel*, together with a tenth volume of editorial comment and indices, constitute one of the major acts of scholarly-philosophic publication in this bleak time. They contain 1,314 letters written by Husserl and 704 letters addressed to him and/or his wife, Malvine. References and citations in each letter are footnoted. At the end of every volume, the editors append a *textkritischer Anhang* indicating the location of the original and justifying all doubtful or problematic readings. Soberly but spaciously printed, concordant with the format and binding of the other *Husserliana Dokumente*, this edition of the correspondence honours not only Husserl but his devoted editors and the Dutch publishers who have made it possible.

The correspondence extends from 1893 to the eve of Husserl's death in 1938. It includes letters to and from some 250 correspondents and institutions. The division between successive volumes is chronological in only a partial sense. We begin with letters to and from Brentano and to and from other disciples of Brentano. Thus this opening set comprises the fascinating exchanges with Masaryk and Meinong. Volume two covers the dialogue with such Munich phenomenologists as Alexander Pfänder, who was among the first of the 'rebellious sons', and Scheler. The third and most ample gathering (it alone runs to some 550 pages) is that of the 'Göttingen school'. A dozen different nationalities were present in Husserl's seminars, and the letters to Winthrop Pickard Bell, to William Ernest Hocking, to Roman Ingarden, to Dietrich Mahnke, to Edith Stein (only two letters seem to have survived) reflect this range. The fourth volume, that of the Freiburg years, may, from a strictly philosophic point of view, prove to be the richest. In it are the correspondence with Dorion Cairns, Ludwig Landgrebe, Karl Löwith, Jan Patočka, Alfred Schütz, Herbert Marcuse, Eugen Fink, Aron Gurwitsch, all of whom play their part in the history of phenomenology and twentieth-century philosophic and social argument. Here as well are the twenty-eight letters from Husserl to Martin Heidegger, the two letters from Heidegger and the unctuously correct yet somehow poignant letter of 29 April 1933, in which Elfride Heidegger, an impeccable anti-Semite and acolyte of the new regime, conveys her sympathy to the Husserls, now ostracized and in peril. In a sentence of masterly opaqueness, Frau Heidegger recalls both the sacrificial merits of Husserl's two sons (Wolfgang had fallen on active service in March 1916) and the accord of such sacrifices with the new spirit of the German *Volk*.

Volumes five and six are of a 'professional' cast. They contain the exchanges between Husserl and the Neo-Kantians, most notably Paul Natorp, between 1894 and 1924, Heinrich Rickert, Hans Vaihinger, as well as more general philosophic contacts: four exchanges with Frege, four with Dilthey, letters to or from Gouhier,

Ernst Mach, Jaspers, Bertrand Russell's note of 19 April 1920, informing Husserl that he had with him in prison the *Logische Untersuchungen*, the eight letters to Shestov, a clutch of letters from Simmel to Husserl. Though marked *Wissenschaftlerkorrespondenz*, this is to say of a strictly scientific order, volume seven contains a crucial letter on art and poetics from Husserl to Hofmannsthal (12 January 1907) as well as a brief but telling letter to Albert Schweitzer of July 1923. Volume eight covers academies, journals, learned institutions, publishers, the German academic bureaucracy. Grimly enough, it includes those missives sent by Husserl to the Rector of Freiburg University in which the banished master (we are in 1935) signs 'Mit deutschem Gruss', the new Nazi shibboleth. The ninth and concluding volume of letters assembles the private correspondence within the Husserl family and with intimates such as Gustav Albrecht. Even a first look at this treasure trove shows that it is not only an invaluable history of phenomenology and of Husserl's intellectual and moral existence; it is also, both immediately and by virtue of reference, a chronicle of European consciousness between the turn of the century and the collapse into barbarism.

If there is an *idée fixe* uniting this harvest, it is that of a mission, of a calling in a sacralized vein. In a long letter to Arnold Metzger (4 September 1919), Husserl defined his credo. The years of desperately concentrated philosophical-logical investigation had been 'goal-oriented, pre-destined, "daemonic"' as was no other systematic intellection. It was Edmund Husserl's God-given task to set philosophy in the West on its true and only path: that of an 'exact knowledge', of a foundation even more rigorous than that of the natural sciences which must derive from such a philosophy their legitimacy. A striking phrase (to Pannwitz, in May 1934) characterizes Husserl's sense of his task: he is a 'pure functionary of the absolute'. Only phenomenology, with its elucidation of 'absolute data grasped in pure, immanent intuition by the transcendental ego', can provide an authentic, verifiable model for the relations between acts of consciousness, the self, and the world; between *noesis*, the detailed structure of these acts revealed by the famous 'phenomenological reduction' – the world having been put in 'brackets of total, Cartesian doubt' – and *noema*, the objective entities revealed to us. Guided by 'intentionality', Brentano's key insight that consciousness is always 'consciousness of' and 'directed towards' something, phenomenology will, ultimately, arrive at an understanding of those primary psychic acts through which the logical structures of human understanding are given. The consequence will be that of 'Philosophie als strenge Wissenschaft' (the title of the keynote essay of 1910–11). And here *Wissenschaft* implies, as it would in Plato, the ideal of axiomatic rigour and certitude of proof found in mathematics (it was with the epistemology of numbers and geometric theorems that Husserl began).

But the stakes are higher than those of abstract conception. Even before the catastrophe of 1914–18 and of the postwar period, Husserl was possessed by a vivid intimation of *Krisis*. Only a complete change in western practices of rationality, only a radically innovative 'psycho-logy' or, more precisely, 'psycho-logic' (there are, here, evident debts to British empiricism and Mill), would prevent the breakdown of European civilization. Hence Husserl's declarations of his 'enormous life-task' (*ungeheure Lebensaufgabe*). The mission of phenomenology was nothing less than messianic. This solicits certain arresting analogies with Freud – a name unmentioned in the correspondence. The Mosaic paradigm is common to both. To Helmut Kuhn in February 1937: 'It is the descendants who will settle in the holy land of immeasurably richer discoveries, in which all philosophic problems will, for the first time, achieve their authentic sense.' The founders, the leaders of the exodus out of error, will suffer the rebellions of their disciples and followers; they will be betrayed by those they had chosen as their spiritual sons; they will end in bitter aloneness. But the great cause will prevail. Without the which assurance, philosophic activity would lack its 'Ernst auf Leben und Tod' (the 'matter of life and death' as Husserl defines it in a letter to Albrecht after the Prague colloquium of 1934), and without which there can be no valid 'sense to the world' (*Weltsinn*).

The theological implications lie close to hand. 'Genuine philosophy is *eo ipso* theology' (to D. M. Feuling in the sombre March of 1933). Walter Benjamin would concur. But what kind of theology? The *Briefwechsel* permits unprecedented clarifications of the complex matter of Husserl's Judaism. The letter to Mahnke of 17 November 1921 is of the first importance. Husserl's entire existence has evolved without any real connection to his Jewish origins. It is the reading of the New Testament that has been decisive in the genesis of his ethical and intellectual self (this determinant reading had taken place in Vienna in 1882, at Masaryk's suggestion). When the National Socialist racial laws were promulgated, Husserl felt lacerated in the very 'roots of my existence' (to Adolf Grimme, 9 October 1933). Pathetically, he hoped and believed that his son Gerhart and he himself, together with Malvine, would be allowed to continue more or less normal life in the new Germany. No one felt more German than he did, no one had, since Fichte, woven a tighter bond between the destiny of Germany and that of philosophy. German philosophical idealism, in which the phenomenological enterprise had its Kantian-Fichtean source, was, for Husserl no less than for Heidegger, a triumph of the 'German *Geist*', an irrefutable proof that metaphysical speculation was inherent in the destiny of the German *Volk* as it had been in that of Platonic-Aristotelian Athens. Husserl's 'imperial-nationalism' caused him to regard Germany's defeat in 1918 as a disaster for humanity (again, the parallels with Heidegger are trenchant). Such views, together with an inward identification with Fichte as summoner and educator of the *deutsche Nation*, further estranged Husserl from Judaic sensibility. The closing years of his life were the grimmer. The 'God who has in grace received me and allowed me to die', one of Husserl's last dicta in April 1938, was hardly the God of Sinai. He was the deity of Immanuel Kant, identifiable with 'the supreme, always adjourned task' of philosophic and, more specifically, of phenomenological striving. As Husserl had written to Hans Driesch in July of 1917: 'seit Jahren streben meine Gedanken diesem Reich der Sehnsucht zu' ('for years my thoughts aspire to this realm of *Sehnsucht*' – that untranslatable marker of German romanticism, of the desiderated which is also the platonically recalled).

Has Husserl's phenomenology, have his labours, which he himself qualified as pathological in their 'trance-like' abstraction and focus, reached that land? Any summary answer would be frivolous. I noted at the outset the force and reach of Husserl's presence in contemporary philosophical argument and throughout the *sciences humaines*. The 1930 Sorbonne lectures (the *Méditations carté-siennes*) stand as one of the classic documents of thought-in-progress, of the philosophic method itself, in the history of western questioning. Much in the *Krisis der europäischen Wissenschaften* is yet to be understood and developed. Those who heard the relevant lectures in Vienna and Prague in 1935–6 regarded them thereafter as probably the single most consequential philosophic proposal of the century, even beyond the *Tractatus* or *Sein und Zeit*. Yet it would be misleading to suppose that Husserl's 'orthodox' phenomenology and the programme which he mapped for it have succeeded in any specific, systematic manner. Cardinal difficulties and *aporias* within the Husserlian construct have proved basically damaging. How can states of consciousness be intentional? How does the transcendental ego relate to others in order to arrive at a shared, collaborative *Lebenswelt* – the seductive but unclear concept which emerges from Husserl's late work? How can the all-decisive motion of phenomenological reduction and the 'return to things' be liberated of presuppositions which Husserl never wholly elucidates? Where has Husserlian phenomenology been of tangible aid to the natural sciences? More and more, Husserl's narrative of perception looks to be a chapter in that very history of psychology and of cultural sensibility which he sought to eradicate from a 'scientific philosophy'.

Paradoxically perhaps, it is these doubts which make the correspondence so illuminating. Honesty, in the final connotation of moral nakedness, to oneself first and foremost, is not necessarily a virtue among all philosophers. Their high wire spans and conceals more than one abyss. Edmund Husserl's probity, his high seriousness and perception of possible defeat, shine through these letters. The man emerges as capable of uninterrupted, disinterested, formidably exact and exacting meditation on a scale comparable with that of Spinoza and of Kant (cf. the fascinating critique of Spinoza in the draft of a letter to Carl Stumpf of 1919). The *daimon* who compelled Husserl to his overwhelming labours – Husserl invokes him in a letter to Metzger of September 1919 – was, like Socrates', an imp of truth. Levinas recalls the matchless 'radiance' (*rayonnement*) of one for whom the nearing 'end of the world' was not a rhetorical trope, but who set against it his own prevision and a stoic trust in reason. So magisterially presented, this *Briefwechsel* safeguards the live presence of a human being who not only knew that the unexamined life is not worth living, but who set out to examine the conditions, the possibilities of that examination.

An Exact Art

There is an *a priori* leap which precedes every act of translation; there are assumptions/presumptions, usually unexamined, of 'translatability'. We take it that the text in front of us can be, more or less exhaustively, deciphered and transferred. This axiomatic motion is based on philosophic and formal expectations together with pragmatic evidence. The epistemological premises are at once so thoroughly internalized and so diffuse that we hardly bother to elicit or examine them. Thus translation may be said to proceed from bases of more or less occult conventionality. Mathematicians after Frege and Russell would say the same with regard to certain branches of their own arts; the thing works though its foundations are unstable or elusive. But I want to see whether we can bring to partial light at least the substance, the authority of the a priori foundations of 'semantic trust' which *underwrite* – the analogy with insurance, with validation is here instrumental – the actual business of translation.

In the daily practice of translation, the sum of empirical evidence, of 'pragmatics', is, self-evidently, the most telling. We have sound reasons to suppose that the translation of messages between languages has been a fact of human communication and coexistence since 'Babel'. The self-evidence of this historical finding is so compelling that we elide the question whether the 'Babel postulate' – the ubiquitous myth of the punitive fragmentation of a single primal tongue, the ubiquitous evocation of an Eden prior to translation – was devised in order to give to translation the necessity, the dignity of a cosmic origin, or, on the contrary, whether the myth follows long after the bitter perception of mutual incomprehensibility. We do not pose this categorically unanswerable question but proceed from the manifest immensity of the corpus of interlingual exchanges as we know them since the beginnings of history.

Are there no counter-examples, no cases where attempts at translation, in some roughly practical sense at least, have simply failed?

We cannot, until now, satisfactorily decipher and consequently render into any other language the texts produced by the Easter Island, Indus Valley or Etruscan cultures. But we assume this barrier to be contingent and temporal. If archaeology turns up a larger mass of inscriptions, if it turns up a 'Rosetta stone' for any of the relevant cases, decipherment and translation will follow. Or it may be that a more astute, a luckier linguistic analysis will discover the true relations of these rogue-systems to other, known phonetic and syntactic clusters. We shall then be able to make them out. In short, no failure in the field is considered to be of either formal or general bearing. No actual instance of non-translatability is considered as establishing in any way the inherent possibility, let alone existence, of 'the untranslatable'. Indeed, so forceful is the pragmatic presumption of universal linguistic transfer that it is difficult to imagine that even a large number of specific intractabilities – a hundred 'Etruscans' – would negate the confident induction through which the translator gets on with the job.

Why, moreover, torment ourselves with fictive contrarieties? The cases of failure to translate are, in actual fact, statistically almost insignificant. Closely considered, they arise either from a banal accident of insufficient documentation (the Etruscan problem) or from situations of rank, perhaps arbitrary eccentricity (the so-called Voynich manuscript, a coded text of twenty-nine symbols which turns up in Prague in the late seventeenth century has, so far, resisted every method of decoding). There is nothing in all this to falsify the working hypothesis – it is very nearly a dogma – that translation, that the transference of semantic energies between mutually distinct and reciprocally incomprehending tongues, is always feasible.

Indeed, if we try to construe a counter-instance to this presumption, we run into subtle, instructive trouble. Using W. V. O. Quine's model of the necessary indeterminacy of translation (see *Word and Object*, chapter two), we arrive at the conclusion that no behavioural evidence can account wholly or unequivocally for the totality of speech-acts and speech rules in any given linguistic system. It follows that we can 'specify mutually incompatible translations of countless sentences insusceptible of independent controls'. It would, therefore, be very difficult, most likely impossible, to show that the translation proposed to us by the translator is wholly, or even in substantial measure, false, that the language and text in question have, in actual fact, remained untranslated. We could attempt to resolve the doubt by setting up behavioural tests, by devising an alternative analytical-grammatical hypothesis and decision procedure. But both claims and counter-claims would derive, ultimately, from what Quine calls 'blameless intuition'.

In short, translation *works* in the vast majority, in the near-totality, of known cases. And it turns out to be exceedingly difficult to demonstrate a case in which it has not worked. Even by the most wary standards of induction and empirical doubt, this is a formidably enabling basis on which to go ahead.

Pragmatic, formal and philosophic assumptions behind the act of translation are closely interwoven. It is, in part, arbitrary to classify them separately. But recent developments in the theory of grammar, developments which are themselves rooted in the universalist linguistics of Comenius, of John Wilkins, of Leibniz, have emphasized what they postulate to be the formal, properly axiomatic structures underlying all human speech. Noam Chomsky's *Aspects of the Theory of Syntax* explicitly ascribes translatability to the innateness in man of 'the universal properties of language', the which properties are analysable in terms of 'deep-seated formal linguistic universals'. We are able to translate from *any* language into *any* other, because all languages are 'cut to the same pattern'. I have tried to show in the exchange with Chomsky reprinted in *Extraterritorial* and throughout *After Babel* that the universalist claims put forward by transformational generative grammars fall far short of their promise. So far, there has been little evidence forthcoming as to genuine 'formal universals' and next to none of any 'substantive' ones. The distinction between 'deep' and 'surface' structures involves a manifest *petitio principii*, and I can observe nothing but a drastic retreat or *non sequitur* in Chomsky's remark that the fact that all languages are cut to the same rule-constrained pattern does not imply 'that there must be some reasonable procedure for translating between them'. Surely, this is exactly what it must imply. And whether or not they are also formal linguists or comparative grammarians, working translators – and you and I when communicating across languages – do proceed with some such implication. Thus, even without assenting to a Chomskyan model we are 'universalists' in the rough-and-ready sense of assuming that we can decipher and translate any given language, however remote it may be in its phonetics, its alphabet (if any), or its grammatical conventions, just *because* all languages share certain necessary features and operational means.

Here again, despite the high abstraction and formality of the underlying assumption, the evidence is essentially empirical. And the pertinent empiricism seems to me of the crudest, most questionable kind.

Even to assert that each and every human tongue has syntactical rubrics which correspond to our verb tenses or that it obeys rules which allow, say, of the dependence and relativity of clauses, is to simplify drastically. Wittgenstein's conclusion, echoing Humboldt's, that a particular 'mythology', an uncircumscribed complex of semantic-cultural values and internalized recognitions, inhabits each particular language, is crucial. As is Bakhtin's insistence on the temporal-spatial singularity and core irreducibility of every distinct speech-act. We cannot analyse or enunciate formally the levels at which, the osmotic interface at which, the 'mythology' and the 'singularity' in discourse act upon, organize, are in turn modulated by, the lexical, grammatical, semantic procedures ('rules') of the system. But it is just this opaque interaction, this dialectic of manifold relations which concern the translator. It is they which severely curtail the relevance to understanding and translating language of what may or may not be innate features of the human cortex, of what may or may not be 'universal' prescriptive constants. It may well be that the affirmation that 'all languages are cut to the same pattern', and the descriptive formalities which such an affirmation generates, are, certainly so far as the translator goes, a *trivial* truth. All men breathe oxygen. This verity has its medical consequences. These, however, are neither of the most revealing nor creative force in respect of what Blake called 'the holiness of the particular'.

What, finally, are the broadly philosophic presuppositions of the translator?

He assumes that the utterance, the text in front of him, is *meaning-ful*. He takes it for granted that 'normal' men and women do not emit systematic vocal or graphic signals in order to achieve either gibberish or vacancy. The deductive and inferential moves in the *Discours de la méthode* must start with the assumption that the Deity will not have constructed phenomenal evidence in ways which confound reason. The deed of translation springs from a closely analogous Cartesian wager. Nonsense verse, *poésie concrète*, 'automatic writing', the idiolectics of the deranged are, precisely and instructively, untranslatable. They lie outside the semantic contract with its universal preamble of intentional articulacy. (The special marginality of some of these modes is looked at in my *After Babel*.)

But the presumption of *meaning-fulness* also entails a far more arguable hypothesis. The translator proceeds as if, he *must* proceed as if, meaning was, to a large degree at least, a discrete product of the executive forms of expression. He must proceed as if the *signifié* can, to a greater or lesser extent, be extracted from the particular *signifiant* and 'taken away from it' via diverse operations of analogy, mirroring or parallelism. Whether it will or not, all translation implies a primitive model of 'form and content'. It assumes that 'form' somehow generates 'content' and that the one is always potentially separable from the other. It is the astute allegoric aim of Borges's famous parable of 'Pierre Menard' to show just how primitive this model is even when it is applied to mere transcription, to the recopying of a text with a view to facsimile. How, asks Borges, can meaning ever be separated from singular and specific embodiment when the latter is grounded, inevitably, in the unrepeatable specificity of one time and of one place?

It is exactly at this point that there is ontological conflict – conflict in and of essence – between the ideals of language and those of translation. Even at its most 'rule-bound' (and transformational generative grammars grossly overstate the normative constraints on grammatical innovation), language strives to be necessary, to be singular to itself, to its unique immediacy of enunciatory form. Where it is most meaning-ful, where it is most packed with realized signification, an act of speech will strive to shorten as much as possible, even to annul, the distance between *signifiant* and *signifié*. It will seek to make *every* aspect of form substantive and thus to make content indissolubly formal. Such fusion is total in the symbolic codes of mathematics and in music. It is not merely a Pythagorean or Platonic conceit to regard these two other great semiotic constructs as somehow 'higher' than language. Both are integrally performative: in mathematics and in music (they are kindred), form is content and content is form. Hence there is no possibility of that severance which we call translation.

And although it can never arrive wholly at this seamless unison of being, language will labour towards it. Any poetic, philosophic, rhetorical pronouncement worth taking seriously will compact its executive means and meanings. It will resist, it will frustrate to the greatest possible degree, the dissociative, the deconstructive agencies of paraphrase and translation. A major text exposes pitilessly the *necessary* innocence and arbitrariness of the translator's assumption that meaning is some sort of 'packageable content' and not an energy irreducible to any other medium. Language is, therefore, the adversary of translation. Thus there is more than cautionary allegory in the prohibition which numerous cultures have set against the translation of their sacred texts.

Having, consciously or not, internalized these pragmatic, formal and philosophic presumptions, the translator 'attacks' his target. When analysing this cardinal motion of aggression in *After Babel*, I concentrated on its psychological and its technical aspects. We 'break' a code. We 'extract' meaning from a vocal or graphic message. St Jerome's simile is famous: translators bring home meaning as conquerors bring home captives. I tried to show that this penetrative incursion of the original by the translator causes complex shifts in relative values. Every schoolchild, but every working translator as well, will have experienced the transfer of substantive presence, of authority, which follows on a successful act of translation. The original text has 'thinned', its fibres have loosened. It has been 'mastered' – itself a telling idiom. Ortega y Gasset speaks of the peculiar sadness of the translator. He ascribes this *tristitia* to the translator's perception of the inadequacies and probable transience of his labours. But there is, I conjecture, a deeper source of malaise. The process of mastering comprehension and of 'transportation' (the word carries sombre political-judicial overtones) can leave the original text lessened and inert.

But now, it is not the psychological elements in the imperialism of translation I want to consider. It is the political and social aspects of the current conditions of transfer between tongues.

Today, the phrase *lingua franca* enshrines ironically the spent claims of ecumenical sovereignty of Latin and of French. For even at the height of their dissemination, of their legislative, ecclesiastical or pedagogic primacy, neither Latinity nor Gallicism came anywhere near the status of a true 'world language'. It is this status which English and American English are now rapidly attaining. The most recent estimates, obviously approximate, put at seven hundred million the number of those who now use some form of English in their daily affairs. Of these, over three hundred million are native speakers. These figures are increasing constantly. In both the Soviet Union and China, the acquisition of English as a second language begins at an early stage of schooling. In every continent and region of the planet, types of 'basic English' are being instituted both as the general 'second tongue' in a given community and as the currency of linguistic exchange between communities. More than eighty per cent of the scientific data produced globally is first expressed and then processed for international consumption in English. In technology, commerce and the world's money markets the percentage may be even higher. When speakers of different, mutually incomprehensible tongues meet in Africa, in Asia, in Sino-Japanese parley, in the fiscal, administrative, trading centres of Europe, they communicate in one or another form of English. So far as the underdeveloped nations and peoples are concerned, to learn (American) English is to acquire the one possible password to modernity, to gain access to the escalator of material emancipation and progress. Via the mass media and the new means of electronic information storage, retrieval and diffusion, English and American English have become the sole genuine Esperanto, the jargon of socio-economic hope the world over.

The underlying causes are, in part, evident and, in part, difficult to demonstrate. American economic power, the exemplary promise of the 'American way of life' in the postwar decades were, naturally, magnetic. But it may also be the case, as C. K. Ogden and I. A. Richards argued when formulating Basic English, that there are features intrinsic to the language which make its acquisition easier than that of other major languages, that acquisition of some degree of fluency in English is swifter than it is in any rival idiom. Whatever the deeper causes, the facts are plain. The Adamic ideal of a unifying world-speech, of a homecoming from Babel, is, today, in realistic reach. From England, the language has spread to Australia and New Zealand, to Canada and the United States, to the West Indies and large segments of the African continent, to India, Pakistan and South-East Asia. It serves as the dialect of reality in Amsterdam and Cairo, in Tokyo and Bogotá.

For the nuclear physicist, the banker, the engineer, the diplomat, the statesman, English is the indispensable window on the world. It is fast becoming so for the writer. To be a writer in a 'small language' ('small' in respect of the number of speakers, of the area in which it is spoken), is, to borrow Henry James's phrase, 'a complex fate'. To go untranslated, and, specifically, untranslated into English and/or American English, is to run the risk of oblivion. Novelists, playwrights, but even poets – those elect custodians of the irreducibly autonomous – feel this achingly. They *must* be translated if their works, if their lives, are to have a fair chance of coming into the light.

This need has inspired diverse tactics. Many writers in such countries as Norway, Denmark, Sweden, in Holland, in Israel, throughout Africa, compose their books in the native tongue *and* in 'world-English'. They act either as their own translators or collaborate from the outset of the relevant project with an English-language interpreter. More obliquely – this can be seen fascinatingly in recent Dutch, Scandinavian, Israeli, African, Indian and even Japanese literature – writers have, more or less knowingly, angled their works towards an English-speaking market, thus making the hoped-for translation more important, more expectant of echo than is the original. Sensibility bends towards an Anglo-American resonance. There are arresting instances in which even readers in the writer's own native speech-community find his work more accessible, more worthy of attention once it has appeared in its English garb. Flemish, Finnish, Serbo-Croatian, Israeli writers have had bitter and perplexed things to say on this point.

Not only must the writer in a minority tongue find an escape hatch into 'Anglo-American': he must often struggle against the predominance of English and American imports. It is books, plays, films, periodicals written in English, produced and packaged in the English-speaking *imperium* (*Time*, *Reader's Digest*, *Playboy*), which are hungrily consumed. They pre-empt the market either in (American) English or in translation. The home product competes, usually on economically and technically inferior terms, against the glamorous import. To look at a news-stall or bookstore window in Amsterdam, in Oslo, in Milan or Tel Aviv is to apprehend at once the irony of the situation. For very often the native novelist, dramatist, poet will be represented, if at all, as the translator of the works of his privileged English and American rivals. This somewhat Kafkaesque practice is, increasingly, the rule even in eastern Europe.

In the buyer's market, the English or American publisher, editor, anthologist, critic, literary agent, is patron and impresario. It is he who calls the tune (the annual Frankfurt Book Fair provides an unvarnished picture of the relevant power relations). The selection of authors and of texts to be translated into the dominant world-tongue is, of course, made on very diverse grounds. In the case of hoped-for mass consumption, commercial and technical motives are foremost. Works with a minority readership or arcane appeal, may be favoured on grounds of modish rumour. Often, choices result from entirely haphazard circumstance: a chance meeting between writer and publisher, the monetary bustle of a literary agent, a package deal in which the newest 'blockbuster' can only be acquired if bids are entered also for 'trailers' and deadwood on the same publisher's stall. But whatever the motives, the consequences press upon the life of feeling and of letters across its entire spectrum. There is pressure at the sublime end; it is notorious that the Nobel jury peruses works nominated from 'small' and marginal literatures in English-language versions. There is pressure of the most strident kind at the best-seller end.

Thus it is the roulette of translation into Anglo-American which has very largely mapped the current landscape of literary eminence and response. The presence in the United States of a clutch of talented, productive translators from the Spanish has been decisive in giving to Latin American fiction and verse its recent incandescent elevation. Concomitantly, the relative sparsity of translators from the Portuguese has meant that the Brazilian novel (judged by competent observers to match Colombian, Mexican, Venezuelan or Argentine prodigality) has gone largely unnoticed. It is not only inherent merit but the luck of the translational draw which has secured for a Günter Grass, for a Moravia, for an Isaac Bashevis Singer, much of their repute. The express to Parnassus is an English-language paperback. No harm in that. It is the obverse which is deeply worrying: it is the relegation to mandarin notice or blank silence of work of the first rank which has, either through its specific density of linguistic autonomy, or by mere bad luck, failed to find translators. It is this relegation which distorts, which trivializes the antennae of sensibility and the household of imagining.

It is my conviction that the Hungarian poet Sandor Weöres is one of the master voices of the century. The poetry of Paul Celan can be justly measured only against that of Hölderlin and of Rilke at his summit. I take Carlo Emilio Gadda to be a virtuoso of philosophic fiction fully comparable to Broch and to Musil. If there is today a 'political imaginer' to match Stendhal and Conrad, it is Leonardo

Sciascia. Louis Gilloux towers above a number of French novelists who have won international celebrity and fortune via transfer into English-American. Several of Thomas Bernhard's fictions (only one has been translated into English) are masterpieces, challenging Kafka. Should these convictions sound wilful or hermetic, it is simply because the writers in question have passed only fragmentarily, or not at all, into the world-club of English-language publication and reception.

The whole situation is doubly ironic for it is by no means evident that English and American literatures are themselves, currently, among the major springs of being, that their centrality is not principally a beneficiary of economic-political weight. What English English of decisive vitality has been written after D. H. Lawrence and J. C. Powys? Much of American poetry and fiction is overblown and disconcertingly innocent of the primary moral, philosophic, political concerns of this dark age. Say 'Thomas Mann, Joyce, Proust, Kafka' – and what American name is to be appended? But it is the global success of the language which counts. Currency speaks American English.

The English and American translator is, therefore, peculiarly responsible. *Fata libellorum* lies, very largely, in his hands.

But responsibility or, as I prefer to call it, 'answerability', is the very crux of translation. And it is a concept which wholly transcends those present-day political, economic, technical determinants which I have briefly considered. It is only by attempting to clarify the exact nature of the translator's responsibility – by pressing home the questions 'What sort of answer is he giving to the original text?', 'To whom is he answerable?' – that one may hope to say something useful about the perennially vexed, elusive matter of 'fidelity'.

The translator has 'mastered' the original: he has, to a greater or lesser extent, possessed himself of its meanings and carried home, to his native speech, the spoils of his inroads. This dissociative visitation does not, it cannot, leave unaltered or inviolate the object of translation. The categories of metamorphosis undergone by the original text are varied. There are cases where the translator's ingress has been of so piercing and appropriate a force that the original withers, that it loses something of its autochthonous savour and presentness. This is notably the case when an inspired translator turns to a text in a 'small' or esoteric tongue and implants it in one of the major currencies of world discourse. Biblical translation, especially via the Authorized Version, has interposed great wings of (suspect) splendour between western literacy and the often sparse literality of the original. But this effect can occur also when the original is lamed by the mere fact that the translator is too high a master in his own right, that his version is too sovereign (I have called this paradoxical betrayal 'transfiguration'). Consider Baudelaire's Poe or, more obviously, his translation of Thomas Hood. Compare the grainy, domestic feel of Louise Labé's sonnets to the seraphic brio of Rilke's renditions.

In the great majority of cases, of course, the damage done is that of diminution. What happens is not upward betrayal and magnification but traduction. The translator has, in this or that respect, been inadequate to his chosen task. He has levelled, simplified, abrogated, mistaken, cheapened the original. He has exposed it to the public in a stripped, bent form. One thinks of the long, lamentable history of successive 'translations' into English and American English of Dante or Goethe. Nabokov's jingle is a mordant summation:

> What is translation? On a platter
> A poet's pale and glaring head.
> A parrot's screech, a monkey's chatter,
> And profanation of the dead.

More indirectly, a translator may do violence to the original less by transfiguring or traducing it than by exploiting it for his own ends, by appropriating it for an alien purpose. He may translate mainly so as to argue for, to deploy, to give tactical precedent and support to his own work or to the programme of the literary movement to which he adheres. Though frequently spellbinding, Pound's translations strike one as opportunistic in just this way. The translator may choose and render his target-texts because particular traits – the construction of plot, the governance of narrative, the control of the symbolic – are lacking or feeble in his own equipment. He will then make of the text which he is translating the scaffold, the vehicle of his own, perhaps very different, needs. This seems to be the case with Brecht's piratical takings from Villon, Marlowe or Kipling. It is certainly the case in a number of Lowell's transparently self-regarding 'imitations'. More grossly, there is a large mass of translation which, intentionally or by strategy of instinctive bias, misreads, misrepresents the original towards proselytizing, propagandistic or adversative ends. The industry of Nietzsche translations would be worth reviewing in this murky light.

Conversely, and patently, translation gives new and further lives to the original. It loosens the moorings which, by definition, bind even the greatest of poetic creations to the locale and time of their inception. Translation is the donation of being across space and time, the counter-statement to Babel without which culture, the 'monuments of intellects', the arts of speech would subsist, if at all, in monadic isolation. All this is self-evident.

But even here there is loss. The outward radiance of the translation will draw, subtly but unmistakably, on the primal energies of the source. We have seen that it is no naïve superstition which hedges liturgical, sybilline, prophetic scriptures and language rites against translation. The 'theft of identity', of numinous efficacy, is precisely that which makes many 'primitive' communities shy of the camera. There *is* fragmentation and dispersal when 'content' is elicited and distanced from the nativity of original form.

How, then, is the translator to restore vital equity between original text and translation? How can his 'counter-creation', his metamorphic reiteration be truly answerable to the original and enact, demonstratively, its existential dependence on the original? What disinterestedness on the part of the translator can insure that the original is at all times, is at all times seen and felt to be, the *raison d'être*, the literal source and authority of being, of and within his translation? Alternatively phrased, these are in fact one single question – that of the technique and ethics, the two being strictly inseparable, of fidelity.

Fidelity is not, *pace* Walter Benjamin's kabbalistic speculation, guaranteed by literalism. It is not some ruse of solicitation whereby 'spirit' is weaned from 'letter'. The translator, the interpreter, is faithful to his text, he makes his response to it responsible, only in so far as he endeavours to restore the balance of forces, of integral presence which his appropriative comprehension, 'ingestion', and transfer have disrupted. Implicit in 'answering and answerable' translation is a profound *moral* economy, a transcendent tact. The translator-interpreter aims for a condition of significant exchange. The arrows of meaning, of cultural, psychological benefaction are to move both ways and reciprocally. There is, ideally, exchange of energy without loss. Perfect translation is (or would be) the negation of entropy. Order, coherence, potential energy are preserved at both ends of the cycle: source and receptor. Supreme translation, which is no more frequent than eminent poetry, makes live restitution to the original not only in that it gives to it a new range of spatial and temporal resonance, not only in that it can illuminate the original, compelling it, as it were, into greater clarity and impact. The process of reciprocation goes much deeper. A great translation bestows on the original *that which was already there*. It augments the original by externalizing, by deploying visibly, elements of connotation, of overtone and undertone, latencies of significance, affinities with other texts and cultures or defining contrasts with these – all of which are present, are 'there' in the original from the outset but may not have been fully declared. 'To re-create what has been created,' says Goethe, 'so that it does not take on the armour of rigidity: this is the purpose of eternal, living action.' To re-create what has been created so as to affirm, to enunciate its primacy, its seniority of essence and existence, to re-create it in ways which add presentness to presence, which *ful-fil* that which is already complete: this is the purpose of responsible translation.

'Adding that which is there already' has the air of a paradox. It is, despite current semiotic claims to the contrary, a process which cannot be formalized or construed analytically. An account of the dialectic and ethics of exchange in great translation will be, inevitably, metaphoric (metaphor being itself 'translation' and refusal of entropy). It is in practice that the model takes on verifiable life.

Creusa's spectral valediction to Aeneas out of the fires of Troy (*Aeneid* 2. 776–89), is one of the canonic turns in western literature and sentiment. Creusa knows, such knowledge being the harvest and compulsion of death, that Aeneas will remarry regally in a distant land, that she will not be allowed to plough with him the long salt furrows of the sea – 'vastum maris aequor arandum'. The music of meaning in her adieu is quintessentially Virgilian. The *dignitas* of divinely inspired command – Creusa bids Aeneas flee, she urges him to leave her behind – inflects into an irremediable pathos of human, of secular desolation. Already, we are meant to hear in Creusa's farewell the high note of abandonment, of eternally endangered womanhood, which will unfold in Dido. And this foreshadowing is made even more poignant, more poignantly ominous, by the fact that Aeneas is recounting the episode *to* Dido. Here is the coda of the passage:

> Non ego Myrmidonum sedes Dolopumve superbas
> Aspiciam aut Grais servitum matribus ibo.
> Dardanais et divae Veneris nurus.
> Sed me magna deum genetrix his destinet oris.
> Iamque vale et natis serva communis amorem.

Five lines in Virgil: ten in the Scottish-Chaucerian version by Gavin Douglas, composed *circa* 1500. Creusa shall 'neuir behald' either 'mighty Dardanus' of 'Of Mirmidonis the realme'. This 'neuir', so characteristic of the Anglo-Saxon poetic repertoire of indistinct, lacerating finality, is not formally stated in 'Non . . . Aspiciam' – but it is, to be sure, vehemently there. Creusa shall not live to serve 'Grais . . . matribus'. The Latin term is too richly endowed and compacted for single translation. Both *le donne dei Greci*, the standard modern Italian transfer, and Douglas's 'facsimile', 'matroun Gregioun', are active in Virgil: the wives of the victorious Greeks, the mothers of their fortunate sons. Neither translation is sufficient to the original. But Douglas finely apprehends and answers to the plangent reference to maternity as it is now made universal in Virgil's 'magna deum genitrix'. There is even a sense in which Gavin Douglas goes 'upstream' from the Latin. 'The grate moder of goddis' (*Gran Madre* in our Italian test-version) is the Magna Mater of the Indo-Aryan pantheon, and she is truly 'mother of the gods'. No less, however, is it the Christian 'Mother of God' who stands numinously at the edge of Douglas's idiom and of his reading of the original. And though this marginal presence is, strictly argued, extraneous, it is none the less a dynamic component of that 'echo forward' which, from the Fourth Eclogue onward, made of Virgil a herald to Christian revelation.

E ora addio: 'Adew, faire weile, for ay we man disseuir!' Both phrasings expand on the dread concision of 'Iamque vale'. Yet the commendation of Aeneas to the gods and the benediction which Creusa herself bestows on him, are fully inherent in the Virgilian formula. But it is now that translation comes to a crux: 'et natis serva communis amorem'. The conjunction of imperative bidding and of measureless sorrow for the son whom Creusa will never see again, for the husband now speeding from her, is encoded in the syntax and word order of the Latin. It is realized in the initial placing of *natis* and in the fall of the line on *amorem*. 'E del nostro bambino conserva l'amore' is almost risibly inadequate. It is inadequate in a way Italian often succumbs to when it mimes, when it transposes from a Latin too near at hand. Gavin Douglas expands:

> Thou be guide frend, luif wele, and keip from skaith
> Our a young sone, is common till us baith.

But this 'inflation' and internalized paraphrase is beautifully apposite. Virgil's *serva* entails both 'service' and 'custodianship'. Aeneas is, indeed, to shield Ascanius from harm ('keip from skaith') on the long voyage of ordained perils, warfare and political destiny. There is an infinitely delicate reproach in *communis amorem*, an invocation of that past conjugal love which Aeneas' coming encounter with Dido and royal wedding in Latium will obscure, will banish from remembrance twice over. But parenthood cannot be cancelled, not even by the will of the almighty gods and the glory of Rome. Ascanius remains 'natis . . . communis'. Creusa's part in him, her rights of anguish over him endure. He shall always remain 'common till us baith'.

I take this concise phrase to be a definition of the morality of translation. The original text has begot the translation and must preserve its generating presence within the translation, whatever the latter's brilliance and far-flung good fortune. The text must remain 'common to both' author and translator, even where, perhaps doubly where, the author's autonomous status, his *auctoritas*, is made shadowlike by time and linguistic distance (Virgil's Latin, we are told, is a 'dead language'). Such preservation, *serva*, is the yield of an exact art. Exact in its ideals of precision: 'exacting' in its demand, both moral and technical, that the translator make of his pursuit a paradox of creative echo, of metamorphic mirroring. There is no more necessary trusteeship, no summons worth more scrupulous response, in the life of letters.

The Historicity of Dreams
(two questions to Freud)
(for Vittore Branca)

Anyone who has lived near animals, with his dog or his cat, knows of their dreams. Vivid, often clearly tempestuous, currents of agitation or pleasure will set in unmistakable motion the body of a sleeping dog or cat. In fact, this banal phenomenon is our most direct (our only direct?) behavioural evidence for the frequency and force of dreams. All human reports on dreams come to us via the screen of language.

Animals dream. Am I altogether in error in thinking that the philosophical and historical implications of this platitude are momentous, and that they have received remarkably little attention? For if animals dream, as they manifestly do, such 'dreams' are generated and experienced outside any linguistic matrix. Their content, their sensory dynamics, precede, are external to, any linguistic code. They unfold in a semantic world closed to our perceptions, except in its superficial aspects of bodily tremor or content. We know this world to be temporally far more ancient and 'statistically' far larger and more various than our own (i.e. animals precede man in the history of the planet and vastly outnumber the human species). But only rare artists, a Rilke, a Dürer or a Picasso, have *seemed* to penetrate (this too may be anthropomorphic illusion) into the outward penumbra of the pulsing and manifold consciousness of animals. The tiger does not answer Blake's questions.

What can we say of these dreams before language?

The hermeneutic trap is all too obvious. Our intimations of that which lies prior to and outside verbalization are nothing but translations into further metaphor and analogy. The concept of the pre- or non-linguistic is itself inescapably verbal. We can imagine, in a fiction of abstractive isolation, the deployment of images, sounds, tactile and olfactory data without conceptual paraphrase, without a verbalizable signification. But not only can we have no proof that the dreams of animals occur in some such 'imagistic-sensory' mode, but we cannot ourselves even 'think' any such mode without adulterating it into verbal discourse. Man can almost be defined as a species with only exceedingly limited and falsifying access to the universe (for it is nothing less) of silence.

One speculates, of course – and in its etymology of mirroring the verb at least edges just past speech. Biology, genetics, our rudimentary intuitions do affirm that there are primordial continuities between ourselves and animals. Could it be that the primal *myths* (what current structural anthropology calls *les mythologèmes*), those archetypal configurations of immediate, seemingly remembered recognition, whereby we order and give general echo to our individual and inward existence, are related to, are a modulation from, the unspoken dreams of animals? Did hominid species, in their intimate co-existence not only with primates but with the whole animal kingdom, dream *zoo-logically*? It is, since Vico at least, a commonplace to suppose that the evolution of mythology and of human speech are concomitant and dialectically interactive. But perhaps we can take a step further. The archetypes, the *Ur*-myths which we sense as arising from the no man's land (because everyman's) just outside daylit consciousness and will, are vestigial, atavistic forms of *dreams before language*. Language is, in a sense, an attempt to interpret, to narrate dreams older than itself. But as he narrates his dreams, *homo sapiens* advances into contradiction: the animal no longer understands him, and with each narrative-linguistic act, individuation, the break between the ego and the communication of shared images, deepens. Narrated, interpreted, dreams have passed from truth into history. Two things alone remind us of their organic source: that resonance and meaning beyond conceptualization which inheres in myths, and that mystery of psychosomatic affinity with animals which can be observed in many young children, in the 'untutored' and in the saint. (It is when he meets with the eyes of a beaten horse, that Nietzsche steps from the cruel summit of articulate intelligence into the second childhood, innocence and ascetic sanctity of his *Umnachtung*.)   *

The Historicity of Dreams

The historicity of dreams is twofold.

Dreams are made the matter of history. Dreams of victory or of defeat, dreams annunciatory of personal elevation or disaster, oracular or enigmatic dreams deciphered in the light of subsequent events, all these are recorded by chroniclers, historians and biographers. Indeed, and almost paradoxically, the appeal made to the relevant dream reinforces and underwrites the authenticity of the historical event. The dream is a prime document; it is deposited in the historical archives. This is particularly true of antique 'biographies', bearing in mind the extent to which the concept of the exemplary or illustrious life of the monarch, hero or sage overlaps with the concept of history itself. Pharaonic dreams, the dreams either heartening or ominous of kings and men of war as they are recorded in the Bible, Hamilcar's dream and Scipio's, the innumerable dreams set down in Plutarch's 'Lives' are treated as historical facts. Well into the sixteenth century, sleep is one of the prodigal sources of historical documentation, of which the court astrologer is archivist.

More difficult to circumscribe but also more important in the dynamics of history are those dreams which transcend the consciousness of the individual. History knows of collective dreams of panic or of hope, of refuge or of action (notably if we extend the notion of 'dreams' to comprise also the twilit but coherent constructs of 'reverie', of 'day-dreams', of emblematic fantasies which are active along the whole spectrum between privacy and mass-feeling, between deep sleep and sharp wakefulness). Apocalyptic dreams have been recorded by social historians not only in the decades preceding and surrounding *les grandes paniques de l'an mille*, but around such numerologically portentous dates as 1666 or, right now, in what certain social groups (and not only in the American south-west) sense to be the nuclear 'Revelation' of the year Two Thousand.

The critique of apocalypse is utopia. 'Promised lands', even when they are first dreamt individually, by a Moses or the founder of the Mormon quest, are re-dreamt a thousandfold by the community of the convinced. Revolutions are dreamt before they are made; first by individuals – perhaps *charisma* could be defined as 'anticipatory dreaming' of a force which can be the initiator of homologous dreams in others – then by the social group. If the rhetoric of 1789 and of the utopian impulses of 1792 and 1793 is often a rhetoric of 'feasts', of baptismal celebrations, it is also a rhetoric of dreams, of marvellously 'concrete' dream-visions just before dawn. The great grammar of messianic dream-interpretation argued by Ernst Bloch is based precisely on the potential for collectivity of the 'forward-dreams' of political, economic and social hope. The *Wachtraum* of radical and revolutionary hope, says Bloch, is no less a dream than that of night; perhaps more so, inasmuch as so great a part of night belongs to the *ancien régime* both psychically and historically. To limit the concept of dreams to those of the nocturnal ego, is to negate a primordial mechanism of history:

Diese Nacht hat noch etwas zu sagen, nicht als brütend Urgewesenes, sondern als Ungewordenes, noch nirgends recht Lautgewordenes, das darin streckenweise eingekapselt ist. Doch sie kann nur etwas sagen, sofern sie von Wachphantasie belichtet wird, von einer, die aufs Werdende gerichtet ist; an sich selber ist das Archaische stumm. Lediglich als ein *unabgegolten, unentwickelt, kurz, utopisch* Brütendes hat es die Kraft, in dem Tagtraum aufzugehen, erlangt es die Macht, sich vor ihm nicht verschlossen zu halten; als solches aber, wenn auch nur als solches, kann es umgehen in freier Fahrt, erhaltenbewahrtem Ego, Weltverbesserung, Fahrt ohne Ende.

(*Das Prinzip Hoffnung*, I, 115)

This night has still something to say, brooding not something that has been from the beginning, but something unborn, something not really uttered anywhere but latent in the night at various points. But the night can only say something inasmuch as it is being exposed to the light of waking imagination, that is, directed toward becoming; in itself the archaic is silent. Only as something brooding which is unredeemed, undeveloped, condensed, utopian, does it have the strength to expand into the day-dream and attain the power not to keep itself locked away; as such, however, although only as such, it can circulate without restriction, upholding and preserving the ego, for world reform, a journey without end.

(*The Principle of Hope*)

And it is, teaches Bloch, *ein Ineinander der kollektiven Traumspiele* (an intertwining of the collective dream plays) – of night and of day – which sets history in hopeful motion.

Such motion can be and is, as we know, constantly interrupted and set back by defeat and barbarism. But here also, dreams, both private and public, play their part. They can be the last refuge of freedom and the hearth of resistance. There is a momentously menacing yet ambiguous insight in a boast made by Robert Ley, National Socialist *Reichsorganisationsleiter*, shortly after the regime came to power: 'The only person in Germany who still leads a private life is one who is asleep.' Precisely. Up to a certain point (not for the physically tortured, not for the starving), dreams can remain outside the reach of political totality. Up to a certain point, the 'safe houses' of clandestine resistance to totalitarian despotism are those of dreams.

Here again, I would venture to say, is an historically vital and socially dynamic dream-function outside the psychoanalytic focus.

The second aspect of the historicity of dreams has been virtually ignored. Dreams are a part of history and of historical documentation. But there is also *a history of dreams* or, more precisely, a history of the phenomenology of dreaming.

I have tried to show elsewhere ('The Distribution of Discourse', *On Difficulty*, 1978) that the ways in which we speak to ourselves, that the style, frequency, content and outward effects of unvoiced soliloquies, of the interior monologue which comprises the major part of our linguistic output, are subject to historical change and sociological constraints. I have tried to suggest that men and women (itself a primary distinction) have made different uses of the great and constant current of internal discourse at different times of history, in different social-economic settings, and in diverse cultures.

The same, I believe, is true of the activities – they are manifold – which we associate with the generation, formulation and recollection, whether wholly private or published, of dreams. Sleep, that truly massive psychosomatic activity, about which so little is understood, is both an individual and a social reality. We lack 'histories of sleep' though these would be as essential, if not more so, to our grasp of the evolution of mores and sensibility as are the histories of dress, of eating, of child-care, of mental and physical infirmity, which social historians and the *historiens des mentalités* are at last providing for us. Different climates, different social strata (master and slave, cleric and peasant, soldier and craftsman), different historical epochs, produce different patterns of sleeping and waking. Solitary or merely connubial sleep, the privilege, as it has been for a small social élite throughout history, is a profoundly different phenomenon from the collective sleep in the peasant-hut or urban slum. And both of these 'sleep-structures' are, in their turn, different from the division of the sexes in communal slumber as it is practised not only in the 'long houses' of certain Pacific and Australasian cultures but, nearer home, in the military barrack, the *internat* or the cloister. The invention and dissemination of successive technologies of artificial lighting has altered the psycho-physiology of 'sleep-acts'. A culture of afternoon siestas differs significantly from one whose economy of repose is almost exclusively nocturnal. The history of sanitation, of domestic plumbing or of its absence, is part of the contextual historicity of individual and of group-sleep. We have great poets of the worlds of sleep, such as Shakespeare or Proust (there is scarcely a Shakespearean play without some meditation on the multiple enigmas of sleep; *Macbeth* can be accurately defined as the drama of the exile from sleep). In Goncharov's *Oblomov*, we find the outlines of a satiric sociology of sleep. But we wait still for the true historians of a condition which, at the very least, enfolds a third of the life of the human species.

Exactly these same historicities and bio-social determinants pertain to dreaming. We do not sleep at the same hours, in the same milieu, in the same physiological aura – climatic, nutritive, sexual – as did, say, an ancient Greek, a medieval serf, a Trobriand islander. Our dreams or, to put it very carefully, a good many of our dreams, will differ correspondingly. The dreams recorded by the royal scribes of ancient Egypt or the Bible, by Plutarch or the medieval allegorists differ among themselves as radically as they differ from those set down by anthropologists and ethnographers in the field. They differ strikingly, also, from those cited as typical in the literature of psychoanalysis.

The history, the social psychology of the production, storage and distribution of human dreams, is too vast and, as yet, uncharted, to allow a general view. Let me, therefore, adduce only one transformation, but a *fundamental* transformation, in the received function of dreams and of dreaming, as we can document it in western cultures.

Mediterranean antiquity, be it classical, Semitic or 'barbarian', is unanimous in relating dreams and the act of dreaming to the phenomenology of *foresight*. Dreams, teaches Penelope in *Odyssey*, 19, may be truthful or deceptive. They may be enigmatic, thus making precarious a determination of either their truth or their falsehood (Macrobius, in his commentary on 'Scipio's Dream', designates the enigmatic kind as *oneiros*). They may have the quality of nightmare (*enypnion*) or of promissory delight. But one thing is absolutely clear: dreams arise from some visitation of/by futurity. They are, in essence, truly or falsely oracular (*chrematismos*) and prophetic (*horama*). The art of interpreting dreams is a branch of the general arts of augury. Oracular dicta, prophecies, omens, the decipherment of bird-flights or of the entrails of sacrificial victims, are immediately cognate to the decoding of men's dreams and dream-visions (*phantasma*). Dreams are the momentary runes which the future inscribes on the sleeping soul. The very obscurity of dreams, their hermetic manifold of possible meanings, is warrant of their prophetic tenor: 'If dreams prophesy the future, if visions which present themselves to the mind during sleep afford some indices whereby to divine future things, dreams will be at the same time true and obscure and the truth will reside in their obscurity' (Synesios of Cyrene, *c.* AD 410). Aristotle's scepticism, gently argued in his opuscule *On Prophecy in Sleep* – 'the thing is not incredible but rather reasonable', yet ought to be distrusted – represents an exceptional and deliberately mandarin point of view. To the ancient world at large, witness the famous 'Egyptian Dream Book' (British Museum Papyrus 10683, dated *c.* 2000 BC), witness Homer, Hesiod and the compilers of the Old

Testament, the question is not whether dreams are prophetic – this is taken to be a manifest fact – but whether such prophecy stems from good or evil sources and whether mortal decipherment is capable of unriddling the foresights (*pré-voyances*) of the night.

In psychoanalysis, on the contrary, dreams feed not on prophecy but on remembrance. The semiological vector points not to the future but to the past. The dynamics of opacity are not those of the unknown but of the suppressed. When did this essential reorientation come to pass? And why?

There can be no persuasive dating of so diffuse a change. Every indication is, furthermore, that this reversal of aetiology and temporality is by no means synchronic in different cultures and at different levels of society. Hume's scepticism as to the evidential claims of dreams, the critique of oracular visions as we find it in Bayle, were not shared by the less emancipated but numerically overwhelming plurality of eighteenth-century Europe. Freud's *Interpretation of Dreams* does not banish from mass readership countless traditional 'dream-books' and more or less occult 'keys to the unriddling of the future through dreams'. On the contrary – and this is a phenomenon which calls for subtle evaluation – the therapeutic rationalism and technicity of the psychoanalytic focus on dreams actually *augments* the status and popularity of alternative and inherently 'archaic' decodings. It is a confident guess that despite the Enlightenment and positivism, that despite modern agnosticism and Freud, a great majority of mankind – even in so-called 'advanced' and technological societies – continues to attach prophetic, oracular values to its dreams.

Nevertheless, it *is* possible to say that the great shift from the categories of prophecy to those of remembrance begins to occur, at least so far as the philosophic and the scientific sensibilities are concerned, in the mid and later seventeenth century. It is just this time-frame which gives to the celebrated 'Dream of Descartes', dated November 1619 – and to which I will come back – its 'antique' character and functionality. The *crise de conscience* of the eighteenth century, the vocabulary and the grammar of dreams of romanticism, can be characterized in reference to the 'pastness', to the recollective motion of their dreams. The pilgrimages of sleep lead not to the *terra incognita* of tomorrow; they are homecomings to 'the visionary gleam' of birth and of childhood.

How are we to account for this recycling, for this about-turn?

A number of possible causal factors come to mind. After Copernicus, Kepler and Galileo, the respectable futurologies become those of the celestial and mechanical sciences. The 'forward-dreams' of the western mind are those of Newtonian cosmology, of the statistical and stochastic sciences or of Darwinian evolution. The educated man reads not the stars but articles on astronomy. By a very gradual yet observable process, responsible knowledge is assimilated to daylight (cf. the light-symbolism, the noon-poetics in the iconography and discursive conventions of the Newtonian revolution). Concomitantly, night and its output are assigned to the domain of illusion, of childishness, of pathology. As Goya has it, in that most haunting of his engravings, nightmares are born of the sleep of reason. How could they communicate knowledge of the future? A second factor in the great reversal of the time-axis of dreams may well have been the revaluation of childhood itself, the fascination with beginnings and the genesis of consciousness as we find them throughout every aspect of Rousseauism and romanticism. If dreams do not exhibit the hieroglyphics of futurity, they set forth the night-alphabet of our authentic past. They are the history of our coming into being. Far from being a mark of chaos or irresponsibility, the 'childishness' of dreams is proof of their journey from the lost core of our psyche. The 'seer blest', proclaims Wordsworth, is the very young child, to whose immediacies of perception dreams are, perhaps, our only access. A third factor – it may well include the two I have just cited – is that of the internalizations of experience which come near to defining modernity itself. One need not be a Hegelian to grasp the inward shift of consciousness, of disciplined scrutiny, which distinguishes 'modern' from 'classical' and even 'medieval' man. Our perceptions of 'reality', where they are not scientific, utilitarian or teleological, in the special sense in which technology is teleological, are very largely ego-directed. When Rousseau gives to the *moi* its singularity as against Montaigne, its claims to transcendence as against Pascal, when the late eighteenth century gives to the words *egoism* and *egotism* their new magnetism, when Narcissus begins a triumphant *fuite*, which will carry him from Rousseau to Valéry, dreams too turn inward and relinquish that lunge towards the gods, towards the objective unknown of the future which defined their function in a classical world.

Such conjectures are, I realize, too vague, too portentous, to be of real use. But the overriding fact is undeniable: at some time in the evolution of western sensibility (at different times in different classes and societies in the West) dreams and the activities of the dreamer came to be valued not for their prophetic content but for their freight of remembrance, licit or clandestine.

This is a fundamental transmutation. It underlines the historicity of dreams and dreaming. Can the Freudian model, with its implicit, axiomatic emphasis on the economy and functionality of dream-remembrance, really be a universal key?

This is my first question.

'Haec, etiam si ficta sunt a poeta, non absunt tamen a consuetudine somniorum' (Although they were thought out by a poet, these are nevertheless not far away from the usual matter of dreams), affirms Cicero (*De divinatio*, I, 42). Freud entirely concurs. The dream 'invented' by the poet or playwright or novelist has equal revelatory status with that reported by the patient under analysis. Indeed, throughout the dream-interpretations of Freud and his direct disciples, fictive dreams – as we find them in Homer, in Aeschylus, in Virgil, in Shakespeare, in Goethe, in Dostoevsky or in Jensen's novel, *Gradiva* – have a privileged force of evidence. One may ask whether the Ciceronian-Freudian postulate is at all self-evident. Do the dreams which *ficta sunt a poeta*, such as Klytemnestra's complex dream in Sophocles' *Elektra* or the great dream of drowning narrated by the Duke of Clarence in Shakespeare's *Richard III* or the macabre dream which wakes Alyosha from innocent piety in *The Brothers Karamazov*, really have the same psychosomatic status as the dreams told by the patient to his analyst or mentioned, often casually, to one another by 'common folk' such as you and I? The psychoanalytic argument, of course, is this: even where he is most deliberately and contextually composing a fictional dream, the writer draws upon and inevitably discloses aspects of his own subconscious. Is this a convincing rebuttal? Does it not betray that arbitrary naïvety as to the nature of literary construction, of *poiesis*, which marks so much of Freud's reading of great writers, and which goes so drastically wrong in his paper on *The Poet and Day-dreams*?

But the question is a larger one.

Our knowledge of dreams and of dreaming, the material which constitutes the history of human dreams, *are wholly inseparable from the linguistic medium*. (I leave to one side the epistemologically teasing possibility that a mute or deaf-mute dreamer can somehow provide a pictorial or gestural *mimesis* of his dreams.) Dreams are told, recorded, interpreted in language. The phenomenology of dreaming is imbedded in the evolution and structures of language. A theory of dreams is *also* a linguistics or, at the very least, a poetics. No account of any human dream, whether provided by the dreamer himself, by a secondary source or by the dream-interpreter, is linguistically innocent or value-free. The account of the dream, which is the sum total of our evidence, will be subject to exactly the same constraints and historical determinants in respect of style, narrative convention, idiom, syntax, connotation, as any other speech-act in the relevant language, historical epoch and milieu. Dreams were no less splintered at Babel than were the tongues of men.

Logicians and epistemologists, notably in the wake of Descartes and of Wittgenstein, have wrestled with many aspects of the reporting of dreams:

if one thinks that a man's account of his dream is related to his dream just as my account of yesterday's happenings is related to them, one is in a hopeless difficulty; for then . . . it may be that we are always only under the *illusion* of having had a dream, an illusion that comes to us as we awake . . . In the case of remembering a dream there is no contrast between correctly remembering and seeming to oneself to remember – here they are identical!

(It can even appear surprising that we should speak of 'remembering' a dream.)

I am not competent to consider the logical-epistemological issues raised by Professor Malcolm (*Philosophical Essays on Dreaming*, 1977, p. 121) and his colleagues. But Sigmund Freud *was* a contemporary of Wittgenstein and the total imperception of linguistic philosophy in the psychoanalytic paradigm of human utterance remains disturbing. Can one really consider as philosophically responsible an aetiology and interpretation of dreams which regard the linguistic medium in which all dreams are reported as transparently neutral? When Freud does resort to linguistic factors, notably to etymology, his evidence can, as S. Timpanaro has shown in his devastating study of the *lapsus freudien*, be very slippery. But what I want to look at briefly is a more specific point.

Consider three eminent dreams.

At the start of Book II of the *Iliad*, Zeus summons *oulos Oneire* (a 'baleful dream', *un rêve fatidique*). He bids the Dream, a personified messenger, go to Agamemnon who is lying in his tent, 'in ambrosial sleep'. The Dream is to declare to the son of Atreus that the gods are no longer taking sides in the battle for Troy. Hera has prevailed and the city will fall to the attack of 'the flowing-haired Achaians'. Let Agamemnon assemble his forces for victory. The dream-text is spelt out three times: in Zeus' injunction to *Oneiros*, in the actual message spoken to the sleeping Agamemnon by and in the process of dreaming, and by Agamemnon himself who, at dawn, repeats this communication verbatim to his war council. The modulation is extremely subtle. The dream, exactly scripted by Zeus, traverses Agamemnon's sleep and re-emerges unaltered in the medium of public discourse. Its threefold articulation produces both a sense of inspired authority and precisely that effect of compulsion, of *Zwang*, which we associate with totally remembered dreams.

As we know, the dream is an ambush set by Zeus to avenge outraged Achilles. It comes through the Gates of Ivory bearing falsehood. Nestor's proof of the verity of this dream is a peculiar one: if any man except Agamemnon had reported it, 'we might call it false and dissociate ourselves. But he has seen and dreamt it who knows himself to be the most powerful of the Achaians. Come, then, let us set about arming . . . ' It is as if the high social and military status of the dreamer validated the truth of his dream. There is, I imagine, some archaic touch of social psychology here which is lost to us.

Does Agamemnon's deceptive *oneiros* call for any interpretation 'in depths'? If we so wish, we can argue that a secular-psychological explanation lies to hand. Agamemnon's dream is a typical case of wish-fulfilment. The delivery of Troy into his hands by grace of Hera and without the intervention of detested Achilles, the fall of the city to a final assault – these can reasonably be seen to be Agamemnon's most ardent desires. The dream is so efficacious just because it corresponds so fully to Agamemnon's spoken and unspoken thoughts.

The second dream is one I have already referred to. It is the celebrated *songe de Descartes*, of which, we are told, the philosopher had himself written down a minute account, but which is known to us in Baillet's précis or recollection of this account (observe the semantic-informational complexity and possible degeneration implicit in such a sequence). Descartes's dream is unusual in that it comports three distinct parts interrupted by one or by two – this is not entirely clear – awakenings. In the first 'chapter' of his dream, Descartes is thrust by a whirlwind against the walls of the collegiate church at la Flèche, and is told that an acquaintance has a melon to give him. Awakening, Descartes prays to God for protection against any ill effects of this odd dream. In a second dream-stage, he is woken (?) by a thunderous noise and sees blazing sparks in his chamber. The third section reveals to the dreamer a dictionary and a *Corpus poetarum* open to a passage from the fourth-century AD Gallo-Roman poet Ausonius: *quod vitae sectabor iter?* (Which road of life will I follow?) An unknown man presents the dreamer with a piece of verse, in which the words *Est et Non* spring to view.

Now comes the striking moment: *asleep*, Descartes decides that the dream *is* a dream and proceeds to interpret it. As Maritain points out, in his essay on this event, Baillet's documentation here is too sketchy to be of much help. But the general lines are plain enough: Descartes interprets the two first dream-fragments as warnings concerning the waste of his past life. In dream-chapter three, the Spirit of Truth reveals to him that he must now choose his road in life (*quod vitae iter*). The dictionary represents 'toutes les sciences ramassées ensemble'. *Est et Non* are 'le oui et le non de Pythagore' signifying the diacritical cut between truth and falsehood in human knowledge. Descartes now knows that he must choose the road of self-examination and of method which will lead to universal truth.

All this is complex enough in its emblematic-allegoric code of presentation. But the ultimate complication is this. According to Baillet, Descartes asserted that

le génie qui excitait en lui l'enthousiasme dont il se sentait le cerveau échauffé depuis quelques jours, lui avait prédit ces songes avant que de se mettre au lit, et que l'esprit humain n'y avait aucune part.

the genius that incited in him this enthusiasm which he felt had been inflaming his brain for several days, had foretold these dreams to him before going to bed and intimated that the human spirit had no part in it.

In other words, we have here a dream of precise augury which is *itself* the object of clairvoyant intimation. And we have Descartes's affirmation that this double motion of prediction and foresight is of supernatural provenance. Exactly as is the *oneiros* of Agamemnon.

The third dream, which I can only allude to summarily, is that of Tatiana in *Eugene Onegin* (V, xi–xxi).

Our heroine crosses a snowy plain, finds herself on a frail bridge above a raging torrent, is pursued by a roaring bear. The bear catches up with her, transports her to a forest hut, where he sets her down *gently*. Round the table in the hut, Tatiana perceives a round of monstrous creatures – a horned dog, a skeleton, a dwarf, a crayfish riding on the back of a spider and, of course, Onegin *en personne*. The witches' sabbath dissolves and she finds herself in Onegin's arms. But Olga and Lensky intrude. A terrible wrangle erupts, and Tatiana wakes, a scream echoing out of her torn sleep. 'Who was it that you dreamt about?' asks inquisitive Olga.

The *oneiros* of Agamemnon is a natural part of a 'transcendent psychology', this is to say of a world-view in which human subconsciousness (sleep) is directly accessible to the insinuation of the divine and the daemonic. The epic poet knows of the duplicity of dreams and of their libidinal motivations (wish-fulfilment). He reflects the compulsory impact of Agamemnon's dream in his technique of repetition. What has psychoanalysis to add?

The *songe de Descartes* raises formidable problems as to the *secondary* and *stylized* format of all narrated dreams. Inevitably, one wonders as to the authenticity of either Descartes's own record or of his communication to Baillet and attentive posterity. But no interpretation can even begin to be responsible to the evidence if it does not proceed via the allegoric devices, the *emblemata*, the rhetorical conventions, the multilingualism (French, Latin, Greek) which organize not only this particular dream but baroque sensibility as a whole. Early seventeenth-century dreams, especially when offered to us by educated and eloquent men, are rhetorically dramatic, are choreographic and sententious, as ours are not.

Consulted as to the meaning of Descartes's dream, Freud wisely remarked that any interpretation made without the possibility of questioning the dreamer would be feeble. He proposed what Maritain terms 'une interprétation fort gratuite du melon' and classified the dream as a whole as a *Traum von Oben*, i.e. a dream whose sources lie very near the surface of consciousness and of the dreamer's waking concerns. This is, certainly, a tempting possibility. But what does it tell us of the actual density of the dream's content, of the primordial importance which Descartes attached to it or of the dreamer's insistence on a supernatural provenance?

In Tatiana's dream, Pushkin opens fertile ground to a psycho-analytic reading. The relation of the dreamer to the bear, the surrealistic creatures she encounters in the forest hut, the fragile bridge over the raging torrent, the explicit presence of Onegin – all these make for a symbolic-erotic coherence along Freudian lines. The 'crayfish on the spider's back' could be out of a psychoanalytic primer (yet, even as we say this, the very different iconographic code of Hieronymus Bosch springs to mind). However, unless we treat a

Freudian gloss on Tatiana's nightmare of hope as only one among several hermeneutics, we will gravely impoverish and simplify the text. Equally, if not more significant, are the elements which Nabokov cites in his leviathan commentary; the formal parallels to Pushkin's *Ruslan and Ludmilla*, the analogy between the frail bridge and the small weave of birch withes which were placed under a maiden's pillow as an instrument of divination, the overlap between the bear in the dream and the fur-clad footmen who attended on young ladies of noble station, the possible borrowings which Pushkin made from Kamenev's *Gromval* and Nodier's *Shogar*. In each of these aspects, both the historicity and the linguistics of dreams are manifest. Any technique of dream-interpretation which assumes a synchronic universality of symbolic equivalences is inevitably reductive.

The dream of Agamemnon, the *songe de Descartes* are radically different from the dreams reported to Freud by his middle-class, largely female and predominantly Jewish informants in Vienna at the turn of our century. How could it be otherwise? Tatiana's dream *does* exhibit that shorthand of sexuality of which Freud and psychoanalysis have made us too aware. But it *is* only a shorthand, and we must not reduce to it the specific wealth, the historical-poetic concreteness of Pushkin's text.

Is there not in the application of psychoanalysis to language, and to language under utmost pressure of meaning which we call 'literature', an inescapable risk of deterministic impoverishment? This is my second question.

First published in 1966, *Das Dritte Reich des Traums* is a neglected classic. In it, Charlotte Beradt summarizes her analyses of some three hundred dreams recounted to her in Berlin 1933–4. That the images, symbols, fantasms which crowd these dreams should so obviously mirror the political changes taking place in Berlin at the time, is not surprising. What is of the very first importance, however, is the degree of depth to which external history penetrates into the subconscious and unconscious. It does not take long to discover that patients dreaming of the loss of limbs or of the atrophy of arms or legs are not displaying symptoms of a Freudian castration-complex but, more simply and terribly, revealing the terrors inflicted on them by the new rules demanding the Hitler-salute in public, professional and even familial usage.

Am I mistaken in feeling that this finding, even by itself, presents a fundamental challenge to the psychoanalytic model of dreams and their interpretation?

It is best to let the writers have their say. In his cunning fable, *Il serpente*, Luigi Malerba says:

Tutti i sogni sono sempre un po' misteriosi e questo é il loro bello, ma certi sono misteriosissimi, cioé non si capisce niente, sono come dei rebus. Mentre i rebus hanno una soluzione, loro non ce l'hanno, puoi dargli cento significati diversi e l'uno vale l'altro.

All dreams are always a little mysterious and this is their beauty; but some are very mysterious, that is to say, one does not understand anything; they are like rebuses. But while rebuses have solutions, dreams do not. You can give them one hundred different meanings, and one is as good as another.

This may be a bleak conclusion; but I find it bracing.

Totem or Taboo

Our three cardinal terms of race, nation and religion probably derive their modern valence (if you will allow me to borrow a very exact and beautiful word from chemistry) – their exact weight, density, determinacy of order – from two brief moments, two brief constellations of the thematic, in which all three find a new salience, and a new declaratory force.

The first goes from 15 October 1894 to 19 September 1899. You will have recognized these two dates: they mark the arrest, and the formal amnesty, of Captain Dreyfus. That is the first moment in which nation, race, religion, receive much of the dynamic pulse they now have. The second moment (I will come back to it in detail) extends roughly from March 1933 to, let us say, September 1939: the moment in which the race argument, the church argument and the nation argument are again debated, this time in the context of Hitler.

Two decisive moments. One will lead immediately and directly, as we know, to Zionism, in as much as Herzl, witnessing the public disgrace, the breaking of Dreyfus, conceived the programmatic possibility for the rebirth of Israel. The second, by hideous prolongation, will lead to the actual State of Israel, whose own nascence and fate are profoundly tied to the National Socialist crisis.

In these two thematic constellations, we have the interpenetration of new definitions of religion, of ethnicity or race, of nationhood and nationalism. They are tested, they are expounded, they are made programmatic.

The Dreyfus Case

The Dreyfus conjunction is one of particular and instructive complexity, where almost every problem we would want to touch

From a colloquium held at Skidmore College, Saratoga Springs, New York in 1988.

upon is already being debated. Consider the nuances of possible positions.

There is a Catholic nationalism *against* Dreyfus, a Catholic nationalism which sees a renaissance of the France of Joan of Arc, of St Louis – the identification of the *patrie* not with the Revolutionary vision, but against. We have a long lineage of royalist loyalty: the eldest daughter of the church, as France is known in the official canonic definition in Roman Catholic Doctrine, turning against the outsider, the traitor, the virus of treason, not only of Jewish treason but, as we shall soon see, the virus of agnosticism and of secularism. In the burning ferocity of this affair, the nation again becomes something much greater than itself; it becomes a credo. It re-establishes its relationship to a traditional and territorial presence of God.

There is a Catholic nationalism for Dreyfus. Just as strong. And here the chief figure who should busy us, in whom I think every issue we're discussing finds its most powerful expression is, of course, Charles Péguy – Péguy, whose whole lifelong argument and meditation will be on nation, race and religion, and for whom Catholicism means the City of God, the City of Justice, *La Cité Divine*, the Augustinian vision whereby the innocence of Dreyfus supersedes any militaristic or nationalistic interest, in the name of a conception which identifies a nation with a transcendent purpose. The nation is not a secular accident; the nation is a *forma divina*, an enacted shape of God's will upon earth, and it is the innocence of the victim which it is the very first, signal and talismanic duty of the nation to preserve.

We have an agnostic nationalism *against* Dreyfus, a group of secularists, of those who do not seek to condemn him in the name of any transcendent theology or religious practice, but entirely on pragmatic grounds. They invoke the modern political state's duty to defend itself from treason, its supreme obligation to demand absolute loyalty. And it is this agnostic nationalism which will develop one of the most powerful arguments of all, and an argument that must haunt many discussions – that the condemnation of the individual, though tragic, though in this case possibly unjust, must be countenanced, lest the nation itself be put in peril; that no individual man's life finally counterbalances the preservation of the nation-state in the modern conflictual world.

We have an agnostic nationalism for Dreyfus. This stance is a particularly subtle and fascinating one. We now finally are getting the publication of all the relevant documents, not only those of Péguy during those years, but most signally, of Marcel Proust – documents which have not until recently been widely known (the great edition of Letters, as you know, is only now under way). Proust's sympathy for Dreyfus has nothing to do with Proust's semi-Judaism. And that complicated position has nothing to do, of course, with any mystery or transcendent belief, but on the contrary, is the expression of a patriotism so great, that France among all nations is seen to stand as the example of untrammelled justice. France cannot betray her mission, for which she alone is strong and great enough to risk her own destiny. *Pereat mundus* is Proust's argument as a young man. The very excellence of the *patrie*, the Frenchness, which Proust feels so intensely as a young semi-outsider, makes imperative the rejection of any compromise with injustice.

Finally, we have a very small group, Socratic, anti-nationalist and *for* Dreyfus. This is a group prepared to discard the claims of the nation-state (it is very small), which sees in this conflict the very indictment of the principle of nationalism, which sees nationalism being shown up for the sadistic and infantile force it may become as it turns blind and ruthless against an innocent victim. This group senses in the Dreyfus case the very argument for a kind of abstract universalism. A representative, and he's inexhaustibly fascinating, of this position is Julien Benda who at the very famous dinner at the Revue Blanche at the time of the amnesty, refused to drink the toast, the toast of relief that was drunk by everyone, in hope that Dreyfus, home from Devil's Island, would now be spared further torture or agony. Benda immediately pointed out that an amnesty settled *nothing*, that it was not a proper legal procedure, but an ad hoc, contingent invention of mercy, and that the true issue was not Captain Alfred Dreyfus, but a kind of Socratic, perhaps Platonic, principle of procedure, or right procedure. Just procedure, the rule of law above any national frontier, was at stake, and unless man began to see the supremacy of the rule of law, disaster would follow.

Each of these positions had its own potential mystique, its own strategic gamut or spectrum within which are beginning to be hammered out the issues that still intensely concern us.

The German Case

In the German case, the nuances are again complex. I name two figures only, though there are many more to consider. The remarks I will be making are based on the careers, on the work, of Gerhard Kittel and Immanuel Hirsch, two of the commanding presences in modern German theology and the German Lutheran movement. I add as a footnote, an ambiguous and curiously haunting footnote, that Hirsch is also our greatest Kierkegaard editor and the man who in many ways brings Kierkegaard into the mainstream of European thought and into the background of existentialism.

Kittel and Hirsch, in 1933, espouse the Party, the National Socialist Party, and give the great authority of their senior theological chairs to the Party. Slightly different positions are expressed. For Kittel, the Party is an act of God; its rise, its triumph, the immensity of the support it receives after the humiliation of Weimar Germany, have the nature of a miracle. And Kittel several times points out that no positivistic, socio-economic, cliometric (these are our expressions, but we can easily parallel them in the 1930s) explanation will account for the immense explosion of energy, of support and enthusiasm which has mobilized humanity throughout Germany, man, woman and child – only the charismatic power of the leader, the prophetic power of Hitler can offer an explanation. Kittel says: We are always asked to name miracles. We have far too narrow a view of the miraculous; it is not somebody tapping a stone and producing water. God knows there are deep miracles in history which are collective psychic phenomenologies of recognition, of revelation, of a kind of new dawn in human consciousness. Why do we not recognize these as genuine miracles, not demanding any hocus-pocus or magic? The rise of the Party, its coming to power swiftly, with almost no violence (he's perfectly right: with almost no violence), a national revolution unlike the Bolshevik Revolution, spared civil war and permitted the Party to achieve total power on a wave of almost miraculous accord from the population.

This is what Luther had been calling for, in his waking of the German nation. The cry is there in Fichte's famous letters to the German nation, but this time there is a validation of the Lutheran belief that the state *must* be a religious phenomenon, in a very concrete sense, that is to say, a collectivity transcending individual motives, and giving to individual hopes (this I think is very important) the sanction and structure of a utopian, messianic promise for all.

For Hirsch, there is also a judgement of God upon the Weimar folly, upon its self-destruction, waste, miscegenation. We now speak not of a nation, we speak about *das Volk*. Hirsch argues with great subtlety, great incisiveness, that the precise difference between a nation and a *Volk* can only be formulated in non-immanent, in non-secular ways. A *Volk* is an identity transcending all individual identity; a *Volk* has a common faith; a *Volk* is marching towards a promise. That promise is not only a social or economic promise, it is ultimately a religious promise. The vote for Hitler is an act of faith; it is, for Hirsch, a Kierkegaardian leap into the dark of the unknown, a leap towards the possibility of an inspired, prophetic, messianic leader.

Throughout the great debate with Karl Barth, one of the commanding debates in this century, the issue is precisely this: in what way is the extraterritorial the key to the transcendent nature of the phenomenon of 1933 and the undoubted resurgence of Germany? In what way does the return to hope of millions and millions of people who had been in suicidal despair represent something in the lineage of the Gospel promise? In what way is a *Volk* a religious, rather than a geopolitical or economic ensemble and conception?

The terms become complex and blurred. The *Volk* and the nation, the church and the race. The issue of purity, the issue of endogamous marriage – and I would like to think of it in terms of classical anthropology, of 'not marrying out' – the issue of the coherence of the community around inherited genetic and blood types, is argued in terms which are an insidious imitation of the Old Testament. The question is this: does modern nationalism essentially reiterate the promise to Abraham, the promise to Moses of the invasion of the Holy Land of Canaan?

Here we stand at the heart of our difficulties. What is the nature of God's true inhabiting of history? This debate, which will help provoke Barth's refusal of the link between God and man, will force Karl Barth into the famous position that the distance between man and God is so vast that the insinuation of God into history is a dangerous political lie. The Barth position is itself open to a counter-attack (as it was counter-attacked in 1934 and 1935), which says: either you're serious about the church being a living part of the tissue of history now, or you are preaching a kind of Pascalian, ascetic museum religion. The debate is a real one, and though Barth wins it by his immense moral dignity, by his decision to leave Germany and by the fact that he foresaw the ensuing catastrophe, he does not necessarily win it on theological and dialectical grounds. The polemic remains ardent and open.

In the Dreyfus case there is no doubt that the trial was revised. It was revised against Dreyfus by that phenomenon which we call Vichy: Vichy is the vengeance of the anti-*Dreyfusards*. The Vichy movement is as alive in France today as it has ever been; France is in a constant state of spiritual civil war; and the Dreyfus case is by no means over yet. The movements, the complicated cyclical movements of French politics, have since the Dreyfus Affair set at odds those who want to convict Dreyfus in the larger sense of that term, and those who glory in his acquittal. Both positions have as their basis the problem of the Jew. This of course is no accident. It is the experience of the Jew which most graphically poses the conceptual and pragmatic problems and provocations of racial and ethnic identity, of nationhood and of religious validation.

Both cases, the French and the German, show that we are dealing with what mathematicians have called a 'three-body problem'. In ways I'm not qualified to understand, they tell us that a three-body problem is an insoluble, or an undecidable. These are not vague metaphors. Race (or ethnicity), religion, nationhood – these three terms are in a reticulative interrelationship, certainly since Dreyfus and 1933, which makes the problem formally and substantively undecidable. We can hammer out our disagreements, but there will be no solution.

We have arrived, inevitably, at the formulation by Péguy, 'When we touch upon the relationship of race to nation, and the relationship of both to the concept of a religious faith, we pass from *politique* to *mystique*.' It is a famous formula, evolved during the Dreyfus Affair. We pass from the realm of the political into that of the mystical. And the mystical is not in any way pejorative, it is not a cheap hit or insult. There is a politics of mysticism, of the mystical, which has its own lineaments, its own logic, its own demands, but which moves outside the realm of consensus through debate, through vote, through political education, through the expounding of meliorist solutions.

In consequence of the Shoah – 'Holocaust' has become an almost unavoidable term, but it is a comely Greek word signifying a sacrifice, solemn and festive – deep taboos now hedge most discussion of our theme. The liberal position, the taboos which liberalism imposes, or (if one wants to be dangerously provocative) the cant of liberalism, may well be the necessary idiom of decency. That is my problem.

Perhaps one should not talk of the things we're going to talk about. Maybe decency no longer is an option, but an imperative. Maybe liberalism cannot open the doors on truth in certain issues, because these doors lead into hell. After all, we could argue, one must pay for a period of history. There are events in history after which for a time, perhaps for a long time, certain possibilities of dispassionate or ironic discussion are not available to decent human beings. One shuts up about certain things. And I am acutely conscious of this possibility. What commands against it is precisely the need to avoid the 'treason of the clerics'. To get things clear – this is the cleric's duty, this is the Hippocratic oath we have taken as scholars and teachers.

The thornbush is that of Israel's election into ethnic national destiny. We find no parallel for this in the Hellenic, in the Greek world. There are very complicated local loyalties to the *polis*, but they are not dictates of election-contracts with ethnicity, as in the Burning Bush, as in the pact with Abraham to people the earth. The rootedness of that chosenness in a concrete locale is inescapable.

Originally, it is a chosenness within a time and place. The theological underwriting is there, overwhelming. Earlier today I heard the remark, the moving, poignant remark that oppression is not in the tradition of Judaism, and I wondered whether once again I was witnessing that very frequent privilege of the Old Testament, which is not to be read any more. The Book of Joshua is one of the cruellest books ever written; it is a book of savagery and triumphalism which puts beyond doubt who are to be the hewers of wood and the drawers of water. There are the Malachites and the Hurites, the Ammonities and the Jebusites.

Children used to know such texts by heart in an earlier culture. And one wonders whether such knowing by heart prepared certain events. Or if we wish to shift to a more glowing and metaphoric promise, it is that of the end of Amos, that whatever has been the sin of the people, whatever has been their fall from grace, and the chastisement of the Lord over them, they shall be gathered to march home. They shall be gathered to return to *eretz* Israel, because that is God's solemn promise. The metaphor of the messianic becomes the politics of the *aliyah*, of those who go to the promised national home.

The messianic becomes the politics of return and we are moving from *mystique* back into *politique*. Péguy knew very well that the arrows can move both ways.

First question: how can these politics be justified by the agnostic, by the non-practising, by the atheist Jew? What possible borrowing from illicit metaphor underlies the Zionism of the agnostic or the atheist? How can he have it both ways? How can he say: it is God's promise that has brought him to Israel? He does, but in truth he cannot. He knows he cannot, yet he must. So there is a troubling and lacerating ambiguity in the very position. He can try to do so, in

Justice Holmes's famous phrase, on grounds of 'Clear and present danger': there is no other place to go. This is the law of survival.

Or he can do so on grounds of race. He will not overtly admit these grounds. He can't. Liberalism must espouse the view that the very notion of the racial is wholly suspect, that it has no demonstrable content or meaning. It is a shibboleth of superstition and obscurantism, there is no such thing, there is nothing unmixed, the mixtures are beyond human computation, the melting pots are everywhere.

The question of intermarriage or non-intermarriage, the question of 'is there such a thing as a gene-pool', are already in the grey zone of the forbidden, of the taboo. Anyone who has taught in China, as I recently have, or been in Chinese schools or universities, will be struck by the unashamed racist centrality of the Chinese vision of a culture that does not easily mix with outsiders and which has some five thousand years of testing this proposition. There is far less cant there, on these matters.

I don't think most of us wholly believe the nationalist-agnostic. Let me put it much more carefully: the fiction, with all the darkness it has carried, the fiction of a certain racial inheritance and typology – if it is a fiction – exercises an enormous grip on the human imagination. And I think, again and again, that if one is a Jew, one has quite extraordinary experience, perhaps illusory, perhaps not, of going down a street in a distant land, even where one does not know the language, and the other Jew in the street is a man one recognizes by the way he walks. I know this to be true of my own experience. And I have been in too many countries of the world. But we deny it, we reject it, we say it is a conditioned superstition. Fair enough. Yet if it be that, its grip upon our soul and spirit has got stronger than ever today.

The triangulation is unstable and tragically suspect. The orthodox quarter of Jerusalem has its perfect logic. There is no doubt there that to the orthodox God has given a promise, a messianic promise. That promise has not yet been realized. The State of Israel does not exist, for nationhood without the Messiah is spurious and fake. Mea Shearim knows that those who invoke the messianic promise to justify the new state are lying, lying by the very texts they invoke. Mea Shearim always proclaims, in ways that madden the rest of the Israelis, that they in their ghetto have no quarrel with Arafat, and indeed they do not have any quarrel with Arafat. That is entirely correct. *They* know. And the rest of us cannot join. This is the argument, curious and powerful, in Isaac Bashevis Singer's novel *The Penitent*. For the rest of us, I suspect, that way to peace isn't open.

The Diaspora and assimilation also have their logic, their justifying tiredness. Now in America, in a way that is deeply moving, human beings are saying: not again this ghastly argument about double loyalty, about every Jew having a treasonable sense of his being a Jew before he is an American. But the ghostly keeps at us. It inheres in the very nature of the identity of a people which claims to be a race but not a race, a nation but not a nation, to have its religious call, when this call is meaningless to the secular majority.

When we look back at Voltaire, at Matthew Arnold, at Jefferson, at some of the great voices of humane enlightenment and hope, we find ourselves today in a rather nightmarish position. Nationalism is blazing from one end of the globe to the other. Men are prepared to kill each other for that piece of coloured fabric we call a flag. My father, a man without any means, a student, before 1914, travelled the whole of Europe with a University of Vienna student canteen card, and there was only one bizarre country called the Russian Empire which had something called a visa. This was regarded as comical, as asiatic throughout the rest of Europe. Today bureaucracies of exclusion prevail. Seeking to defend itself against terrorism, enraged at America's immigration procedures, France now makes Americans stand in long and angry queues to get visas.

Nationalism blazes, in the Basque country, in Transylvania and Armenia. Belgium is being kept together by a shoestring. Inside the television and radio station at Brussels, there is a line down the middle of the building: French-speaking on one side, Flemish on the other.

Nationalism is rampant. Ours is not McLuhan's global village, which we now look back on as a utopian, almost Jeffersonian dream. Our world is tribal to an unprecedented extent, and the great universalist dream of the eighteenth and nineteenth centuries, Kant's 'cosmopolis', now strikes us as a distant illusion.

Consider too, race hatreds are as deep and as vivid as they have ever been. Since the Shoah, there have been massacres of a racial, tribal kind. Half a million, a million, in Burundi; no one knows the figures for the destruction of certain tribes in Uganda. Race hatreds: the re-enactment of that classical and more easily surveyable historical horror that is the massacre of the Armenians, which began to give the model for the technology of the total destruction of a hated tribe. All over the earth, they can explode at any moment. The recent events in Kashmir, in Punjab, in Islamabad, in Azerbaijan insist that we must slaughter people who belong to a different tribe, who smell different, whose hair has a different oil, whose eyes are said to have a different slant.

The resurgence of religious wars and religious fundamentalism is now a banality. It is the beginning of every consideration of the situation we are in. We have talked and listened and learned a great deal about Islam; let's look nearer home. Too few of us – here I can include myself – have any competence or any experience of Islamic fundamentalism (except in our nightmares, in our fears, which may be ill-informed). But when we look right at home we see that we have one of the most fundamentalist Catholic Churches since the Hildebrandian Middle Ages (Cardinal Ratzinger would be a distinguished guest at this gathering, to tell us about the nature of heresy and the nature of truth). It is a medieval church; it is a church which is reviving many forms of censorship. We ask: are we back in the world of Galileo? Perhaps. And I need not tell an American audience of other kinds of religious fundamentalism in *this* country. The dislocation of modernity has fuelled atavisms of *enracinement* – Barrès's prophetic word. Rootedness isn't quite right, rootedness has something about it that is passive, rootedness is a state, *enracinement* is an action. It is taking root in a world where the centrifugal forces of modernity, the changes of technology and communication, the breaking up of certain traditional forms (this is a sociological commonplace, though not always easy to prove) have bewildered men and made them wild.

And here I come to the taboo – to that which in decent and cultured communities should not, perhaps, be said. Let us for a moment forget about academic, liberal discourse. Let us dare ask ourselves whether there are certain subjects not 'discoursable', not sayable.

Let us ask whether there may not be constants in our biological and communal make-up which do make it very difficult for us to live with others.

It would be fantastically arrogant to suppose that we *know* that we have evolved into a kind of creature that likes living with those that smell different, look different, sound different. Sit in a railway carriage or bus in a land where you don't speak a single word of the language. Have you ever noticed the panic that starts growing in your civilized soul, the sense that something is hideously wrong, that your very identity may soon be torn apart? It could be that autonomy is the natural form of the social unit, and that those who would thrust others together may be doing so in the name of a transcendent vision of justice, hope, human fairness, but that they may also be hurrying something very complicated. We don't know. Human beings do tend to be with their own. Not all. Not the exceptional. But most human beings.

We're speaking across a statistical mean, but it is a very massive one. Environment *is* heredity, and heredity *is* environment. That which you are born into – the privileges, the luck or the misfortune – is both heredity and environment. They cannot be separated. Cautionary rhetoric occludes this complicated recognition of interaction. The dialectic, the osmotic, which relate the mutations conceivable or feasible in this interaction, are radically beyond our understanding.

Nevertheless, questions have been asked, and it is only our terror, our embarrassment (as, we hope, decent human beings) which make us forget those questions. There is one that does haunt one. It goes back to Herodotus. Herodotus says: 'We Greeks risk our lives on leaky ships and camels and elephants and whatever to go to the most incredible parts of the earth to ask other people about how they live, who they are, what their laws are. Not one of them has ever visited us.' The implicit enigma stands.

I will rephrase it. We have no evidence for the notion that God has made this earth justly or nicely or liberally. The overwhelming suggestion goes the other way: He has made a hellish place of it. A very interesting place, but hellish. It is perfectly conceivable that there is a small strip on the world map (this was Herodotus' view, also Thucydides', also Plato's) where the climate is more or less bearable, temperate, where there is enough protein for people to eat, where there are *slaves* – that is, subject peoples who allow you to get on with the business of thinking, which means that you can spend your day doing something fantastic, like examining the geometry of conic sections (which is what Archimedes dies for), that you can do this quite insane and obsessive thing – to give your life to an abstraction, to a speculation, to pure mathematics. Perhaps there is one part of the earth that produces complex theorems, algebraic theorems, of a very involved and difficult and totally useless nature, that produces not religious faith but that immense luxury we call metaphysical speculative systems, and perhaps this is not a universal possibility. Climatically, foodwise, survival-wise, this folly is not open to everyone.

Those who have produced canonic texts and textualities by which they organize their politics – be they the Koran, the Scriptures, the *Kapital* – are not everywhere. And there are many cultures that have, until now, refused textuality, and which are now paying a bitter price for what may be a perfectly natural condition of their being.

We are here in the realm of questions we don't want to ask or press home, because an awful ugliness attaches to the asking and the consequences may be totally intolerable. I am only trying to underline that one's taboo extends over certain areas of asking and of wondering. This may be essential and this may be the decency by which we must live, but it will exact its price.

Of course, there is another possibility, another direction. Bear with me, for I have said it too often, and said it indeed before this very generous *Salmagundi* audience on other occasions. Somewhere there are people I would like to call 'compelled Trotskyites', using 'Trotskyite' in a rather special and illegitimate sense. They are the migrants, they are what the Nazis declared to be, in a wonderfully complimentary word, the *Luftmenschen* – the human beings of the air. *Luftmenschen* are those who cannot take 'roots', those who, as it were, are always with their feet off the ground. And I alluded to Kant's forging of the word 'cosmopolitics' – the politics of the 'cosmopolite', another term that became charged with literal blood, both in Nazi Germany and in Stalinist Russia. We hear often that even Stalinist Russia wasn't incarnate evil – of course not, of course it wasn't. As it happens, however, there have been millions of human beings in Soviet camps, and there are millions who have been hunted to their death, and there are others in the Soviet Union who are still not being allowed to be *Luftmenschen*. It is one thing to root yourself, it is another thing to be chained to a tree.

To be a guest among other men *is* a possibility. All of us, I firmly believe, are guests of the planet, of its ecology. We did not make our world, we were thrown into it. We are born without knowing why. We haven't planned it. We are trustees of a dwindling space for survival. We had better learn very quickly that we are guests, or there will be not much left to live in.

There is no synagogue, no *ecclesia*, no *polis*, no nation, no ethnic community *which is not not worth leaving*. This is my conviction. A nation is a place always worth leaving, because it will behave in ways that we may or must come to find unacceptable. A synagogue will one day excommunicate Spinoza. It must.

We have all heard moving and very just things about groups, about not being a loner. Personally, I believe that anarchy is one of the ideals and hopes and utopias of anyone who wants to do serious thinking and work. It is when you find yourself agreeing with another person that you should begin to suspect that you are talking nonsense. I repeat: there is no community of love, no family, no interest, caste, profession or social class not worth resigning from.

Socrates knew that. Why did he choose to die instead of leaving the unjust city? That's the question I want to end with. It seems to me absolutely central. He is told he can escape: the jailers have been bought, the doors are open. He is urged to escape. He refuses. One reading would be that not leaving was his supreme pedagogic act, that the city would have to face its own guilt by killing him, that the last piece of teaching he could do (and he was a teacher, obviously, to the roots of his hair) was: I've got one more lesson to give – they've got to kill me so that they know what they have done. The city will have to face its own culpability. It is a decision which remains enigmatic. I turn around it in helplessness and incompetence. Could it be that, and that time only, even Socrates was in error? Because there is always sufficient hemlock elsewhere.

A Note on Kafka's 'Trial'

The thought that there is anything fresh to be said of Franz Kafka's *The Trial* is implausible. For three reasons.

This short novel has passed into far more than classical literary status. It is a part of the immediacy of recognition and of reference throughout our century. Countless are those who have not read it, who may not even have seen stage, film or television versions, but who are familiar with its main outline and situations. Scarcely published at his early death, known to a narrow circle of Prague and Vienna acquaintances, Kafka has become an adjective. In more than one hundred languages, the epithet 'Kafkaesque' attaches to the central images, to the constants of inhumanity and absurdity in our times. The letter K is his as S is not Shakespeare's or D Dante's (it is in analogy with Dante and Shakespeare that W. H. Auden placed Franz Kafka as the shaping mirror of our new dark ages). In this osmosis out of an almost esoteric source, out of one virtually buried alive – the theme of one of his last parables – in this diffusion of the Kafkaesque into so many recesses of our private and public existence, *The Trial* plays a commanding role. The arrest of Joseph K., the opaque tribunals, his literally bestial death, are the alphabet of our totalitarian politics. The lunatic logic of the bureaucracy which the novel sets out is that of our professions, litigations, visas, fiscalities, even in the lighter greys of liberalism.

The secondary literature is cancerous. It multiplies daily in the academy, in *belles-lettres* and literary journalism. It is parasitic on every element (one is tempted to say 'every paragraph') of this inexhaustible text. As do very great works in language, in the arts or in music, Kafka's fiction invites decipherment, and makes of this invitation a trap. However acute the critic, whatever his systematic strengths – be they Marxist, psychoanalytic, structuralist or in some traditional vein – the readings offered fall almost risibly short.

Preface to the Everyman Library edition, 1992.

(There is, we will see, one exception.) Nevertheless, the cumulative volume of interpretation and scholarship makes it unlikely that any substantive aspect or salient detail in *The Trial* has been altogether overlooked. Indeed, it is an unguarded access and the shock of immediacy which are now most difficult to achieve.

The third reason why there may be nothing novel and illuminating to be said of Kafka's fable is of most interest. There is a sense in which works of the imagination of sufficient seriousness and density always enact a reflection on themselves. Almost always, the major text or work of art or musical composition tells critically of its own genesis. Incomparably, our truest analyst of drama is Shakespeare. Cézanne's paintings enforce a persistent consideration, unrivalled in depth and economy, of the nature and modalities of pictorial representation. The case of Kafka is more specific. There has been inspired lyric poetry written by Jews during the millennia of dispersal and prior to the secularization of literature in a figure such as Heine. There had been isolated experiments in drama and fiction from within the walled community. But broadly speaking, the epic, scenic, lyric and narrative impulses manifest in the Bible – the New Testament also was, in greater part, written by Jews – is stifled and goes underground between antiquity and the nineteenth century. The reasons are complicated. They attach to historical circumstance, to social isolation, to linguistic plurality and exile. But they relate also to a central iconoclasm, to a distrust, graven at Sinai, of *mimesis*, of the whole semantics of representation for purposes of aesthetic experience and via means of fiction. More coherently than even the Plato of the *Republic*, or Calvin, Judaism rejects the image. Its elected genre became that of commentary. Each commentary on the revealed Scriptures generated further commentary, in an unbroken chain and exfoliation of secondary, tertiary discourse. The arcane wit, the delicacy of probing, the finesse of Talmudic, of Midrashic and Mishnaic commentaries, the fine-spun inventiveness of the acts of reading by orthodox and kabbalistic masters of textuality are truly accessible only to those schooled in the labyrinth and echo-chamber of the rabbinic legacy. (The force of this legacy persists in parodistic or bastard guise in such current Judaic derivatives as Freudian psychoanalysis or Derridean deconstruction.)

Franz Kafka was heir to this methodology and epistemology of commentary, of 'unending analysis' (Freud's phrase). His parables, fables, tales and always incomplete novels are commentaries in action in a sense both materially and more diffusely Talmudic. The techniques of teasing out the abyss, of circling the unnameable, of weaving meaning on meaning, of labouring to make language wholly transparent to the light which consumes that through which it passes, have their antecedent and validation in the twice-millenary debates of Judaism with itself. Thus *The Trial* is not only self-reflexive as is nearly all mature aesthetic form. It embodies the particular techniques of exegetic commentary, of rabbinic hermeneutics. Self-evidently Franz Kafka meditates on the law. It is the original mystery and subsequent applications of the law, of legalism and judgement, which are the essential concern of Talmudic questioning. If, in the Judaic perception, the language of the Adamic was that of love, the grammars of fallen man are those of the legal code. It is the modulation from one to the other, as commentary and commentary on commentary seek to hammer it out, which is one of the centres of *The Trial* (kabbalistic geometries know of ordered constructs with several centres). Set beside Kafka's readings of Kafka, ours are, unavoidably, feeble.

Kafka's breakthrough to mastery came during the night in September 1912 in which he set down *The Judgement*. This nightmare notation already contains the core of *The Trial*. The ubiquitous theme of guilt in Franz Kafka's life and work has been the object of interminable conjecture. He himself was prodigal of hints and verdicts. In respect both of Jewish ideals and of his father's brutally voiced expectations, Kafka pronounced himself an abject failure, a deserter. He had founded no family. His career in the insurance business was, at best, middling. Literary success on any conventional and public scale eluded him almost entirely. His physique solicited amused sympathy or troubled prognostication. Where his father was coarsely robust, Franz existed shadow-like. His vehemently gnarled relations with women – the lengthy engagement to Felice Bauer, his love for Milena – aborted. At the edge of commitment, K. flinched and took sanctuary in illness. This illness, the tubercular condition, was real enough. It was to cause early death. But Kafka himself and his intimates were too percipient, were too aware of the psychosomatic aetiology of consumption not to observe the contracts between patient and infirmity. Kafka used his sickness as it used him, and this reciprocity deepened his sense of culpability.

Guilt inhabited both his language and his art, the two being inextricable. A Prague Jew assimilated to German language and culture, momentarily drawn to rising Czech nationalism but in essence an outsider, even a traitor to it, stood on condemned ground. Compelling alternatives loomed: significant literary work was being done in Yiddish, the renascence of Hebrew as a modern tongue immemorially rooted in Jewish experience, was palpably imminent. Kafka looked with wary pathos in both these directions. Yet he chose German for his truths. He tells of his estrangement within the very tongue of his genius, of his incapacity to sense meaning in the word 'mother' when it is *Mutter* (a remark the more lacerating in that it points deliberately to the absence of a 'mother tongue'). The translucency of Kafka's German, its stainless quiet, suggests a process of borrowing at high, very nearly intolerable interest. Kafka's vocabulary and syntax are those of utmost abstention from waste: as if every German word and grammatical resource had been drawn from an unforgiving bank. To write in German was to be in debt.

To have done so in Czech, Yiddish or Hebrew might have been more licit, but only partially. I have cited the iconoclasm radical to Judaism, the unease of imaginary contrivance. The precedent of Heine – baptized, rent between languages, a victim of venereal disease – appeared to confirm Jewish sentiment. Scholarship, particularly when in reach of religious studies and exegesis, was one thing. The avocation to *belles-lettres* something altogether different. At many levels and in contrast with his eminent friend Max Brod, Kafka acknowledged the justice of this distinction. To mute his calling by not writing would be to incur guilt. But to write 'made up' stories, in pursuit of seemingly profane fulfilment, was most likely an even worse transgression. The circle closed on Kafka as it does on the man serving a life-sentence in the round of the prison yard.

Yet even those motives for self-condemnation, even these 'crimes', grave as they are, do not define the source. Franz Kafka lived original sin. The theology, the rhetoric of this condition has been pervasive in the West after the Pentateuch, after Pauline and Augustinian readings of human affairs. It has, for example in stringent Calvinism and seasons of apocalyptic, penitential fear, darkened communities. But a mere handful of individuals have ever endured in their daily existence and conviction the consequence of their fallen state. Like Pascal and Søren Kierkegaard (here the analogies are non-trivial), Kafka knew hours, days perhaps, in which he identified personal life itself with ineradicable existential guilt. To be alive, to engender further life, was to sin. Against the enraged father. Against the lost sanctities of a creation made corrupt and sordid by man. It was, at some enigmatic deeps, to sin against oneself to the precise degree that survival entails lies, the failures of love, suffering and the anguish which whispers pitilessly out of 'the great winds from under the earth'. Only a psyche possessed by this interdiction could have written that those voices whose song sounds angelic are in fact in the pit of hell or could have said (though the citation is disputed) that there 'is abundance of hope, but none for us'.

To live is to be sentenced for living. This is the metaphysical but also private dynamic of *The Trial*.

Written during 1914–15, the book was published in 1925, a year after Franz Kafka's death. Its translation into English, by Edwin and Willa Muir, which followed in 1935, itself took on a classic aura. This is in one sense regrettable. Max Brod's recension of Kafka's text had been amateurish and, at certain points, arbitrary. Despite its famous conclusion, *The Trial* remains unfinished and there is argument about the order of various chapters. Additional and cancelled matter has survived (and this can be found in the appendix to the present edition). It is, however, the Muir version, with its stylistic distinction and freshness of encounter, which, so far as the English-language world goes, remains canonic.

But Muir's reading and the translation which it underwrites are distinctly his. Religion was, says Muir, 'the whole world' to Kafka. 'His imagination moves continuously within that world and does not acknowledge that there is anything, no matter how trivial or undignified, which it does not embrace. Accordingly, it is in its unique way a complete world, a true though unexpected reflection of the world we know. And when Kafka deals in it with the antinomies of religion, he is throwing light at the same time on the deepest riddles of human life.' The religious core, claims Edwin Muir, is that of the incommensurabilities between divine and human law which 'Kafka adopted from Kierkegaard'. For such adoption there is hardly any evidence. Muir reads out of a Kierkegaardian Calvinism. He misses almost altogether the immersion of *The Trial* in motifs and concerns of a radically Judaic-Talmudic kind.

If, moreover, one is to grasp the pungent terror of Kafka's fiction, it is vital to test approaches of a non-religious tenor. Marxist glosses have been reductive but enlightening when they insist on the sociology of the black fable. Original as it is, *The Trial* has its antecedents and its material context. The *Comédie humaine* of Balzac, the caricatures of Daumier, are replete with acrid depictions of the law, of judges, advocates and snoring juries. Jarndyce vs Jarndyce in Dickens's *Bleak House* fascinated Kafka and inspired numerous touches in *The Trial*. Specifically, it was the persona, at once self-important and pathetic, of the clerk, and of the bureaucracy which the clerk inhabits or infests, which attracted the satiric, spellbound notice of the nineteenth-century novel. Here indeed was a new fauna bred of the swift growth of administrative, fiscal, statistical services and agencies, both public and private, which made possible the industrial revolution and the parallel instauration of the modern nation-state. Again, Balzac is seminal. But it is in Russian fiction, in the tales of Gogol, in the novels of Dostoevsky – Kafka was steeped in both authors – that the clerk, harried to the point of madness by his contemptuous superiors, by the ashen monotone of his labours and by poverty, yet avenging himself on the unfortunate who require his arcane services, becomes archetypal. He figures crucially in both Dickens and Flaubert. The pressure on Kafka's attention of *L'Education sentimentale* and of *Bouvard et Pécuchet*, in which the barren pomp of the new clerisy is monumentalized, was intense. K. is of that rodent tribe. The maze in which he operates and is entrapped, the instrumental routines, absurdities and pretence which characterize the Tribunal, the Bank, the idiom of lawyers and tellers, point immediately to the structures of the decaying Austro-Hungarian dual monarchy. In *The Trial* and in Robert Musil's *The Man Without Qualities*, the bureaucratic hydropsy of the Habsburg twilight is the very substance of the fiction. Kafka's politics were those of a fitful outrage. His daily practice as an assessor of insurance claims, frequently arising from industrial accidents, put him in raw touch with the *misère* of the exploited and the unctuous cunning of their masters. At the same time, he had few illusions about the mendacities and opportunism with which the humble and offended seek retribution and manoeuvre for survival. The result is, throughout Kafka's writings but most notably in *The Trial* and in *The Castle*, a mordant strain of social satire. Marxist commentators are right when they isolate the transparent analyses of an inefficient, wasteful often self-contradictory 'liberal capitalism' on the edge of catastrophe in *The Trial*. They, but by no means they alone, are justified in emphasizing the intimacies of gesture and of perspective which bind K. the 'bank official' and sycophant in the social hierarchy to the strictly analogous ambience of the judiciary. No less than Micawber in Dickens or the maddened clerk in Gogol's 'Overcoat', Joseph K. is both a product and agent in a very particular matrix of bourgeois mercantilism. The sarcasms, the vengeful allegories which fill *Das Kapital* are more than relevant. They find a nightmare-echo in the mere fact that the torture-chamber in the novel is located in an enlarged broom-closet in K.'s bank and *bureau*.

More oblique are the sexual themes in this book. For a long time, what was known of Franz Kafka's personal asceticism and infirmities inhibited any clear cognizance of the erotic urgencies in his novels and parables. Unendurably, the fiasco of Kafka's engagement to Felice Bauer (the F. B. in *The Trial*) and the aborted relation to Milena, probably the most deeply beloved, bore witness to some central flaw in Kafka's relations to women. Today, the picture is far less clear. The possibility of one or more liaisons of a more or less 'normal' order, even of a child born of one such relationship, cannot be ruled out. But this is trivia. What has emerged as our readings become more patient, more observant of narrative compaction, is the variousness and significance of *eros* in Kafka's imaginings. Here as well, social insight plays its part. Kafka is acutely aware of the extended compass of sexual exploitation, of prostitution both public and domestic, of economically enforced compliance in the servants' quarters, which was so graphic a feature of Habsburg mores. Like Schnitzler, like Karl Kraus, he is at the same time drawn to and repelled by the availability to men of a sexual market in the streets, in the hotels and lodging-houses of Vienna or Prague. At a more intricate level, Kafka records the vengeance of women on their users. Intercourse, as we find it pictured in *The Trial* and in *The Castle*, has the crass ambiguity of rape. It humiliates men more than women. It leaves them irreparably soiled and enfeebled.

The law student cries out in pain and self-betraying animal rut as the washerwoman, her blouse unbuttoned, allows his embrace. Leni, lawyer Huld's nurse and sentinel, is a presence of peculiar complexity. She is aroused by the proximity of accused men. She excites herself and her bed-ridden master by recounting to him her erotic exploits. She collects lovers and snatches at their lust in a style simultaneously submissive and aggressive. It is Kafka's genius for economy which charges these sordid couplings with a strange power of suggestion. K. kisses Fräulein Bürstner 'all over the face, like some thirsty animal lapping greedily at a spring of long-sought fresh water.' Newly indicted, he seeks reassurance and momentary release in sexual contact. F. B.'s passivity, her pallid ironies, prevent such solace. K. is made voyeur of her relations to the sickly Miss Montag. There is not one woman among the spectral horde of the accused in *The Trial*. Women are, in enigmatic guise, messengers or servants (temple-prostitutes?) of the law. Their palpable immunity from arrest and prosecution is a mark of tainted innocence, of inferiority in respect of the very men over whom they exercise diverse modes of sexual authority. Even more sinister is the swarming hunger of the young girls who cluster harpy-like around the studio of Titorelli the painter. The German language amalgamates the word for 'birds' with that for 'fucking'.

The larger point is this. Rightly, we experience Kafka's vision as one of tragic horror. He stands, as we will note, in a singular relation of clairvoyance to the inhuman, to the absurdly murderous in our condition. The *tristitia*, the 'sadness unto death' in Kafka's writings, letters, diaries and recorded remarks are bottomless. But there is also in him a social satirist, a craftsman of the grotesque, a humorist with an eye to farce and slapstick. The dead-pan, the acrobatics of Buster Keaton, lie to hand. Reading the blackest of modern myths, 'The Metamorphosis', to a circle of aghast intimates, Kafka himself doubled over with laughter. We diminish the conceptual and formal wealth of *The Trial*, we fall short of its haunting duplicity, if we omit the sinews of comedy. K. is often risible in his stiff posturing, in his starched-collar officiousness. Titorelli's falsehoods and self-importance are macabre, but also laughable. The successive messengers and acolytes of the Court are shapes out of Magritte, at once ominous and of a surrealist humour. Without them we would not have Beckett's clowns. Even the hallucinatory canter towards execution with which *The Trial* concludes hints at a circus.

Once this informing context has been allowed, however, and once the politics and the wit, the sex and the clowning in Kafka's art have been fully registered, the obvious truth cries out. Kafka's inventions and *The Trial* pre-eminently, articulate an overwhelming feat of metaphysical-religious imagining and inquiry. The techniques of narration and of investigative debate on which they draw, the anguish of spirit and tatters of vision which they verbalize (there is also the oneiric stab of Kafka's drawings), communicate obsessions of an insistently exegetic, even homiletic provenance. In the midst of a largely secular, indeed positivist climate, in a genre – that of prose

fiction – whose historical source and legitimacy points to worldliness, to a grasp of human affairs and relations as immanent and, in
the main, answerable to reason, Kafka composes a body of
parables, of allegories, of commentaries in motion, whose aura is,
technically and substantively, that of the sacred. It is in this material
respect that Kierkegaard's philosophic fictions and the tales of
holiness and of the rage of the soul in Dostoevsky are contributory.
But the principal code is, self-evidently, that of the biblical and
Talmudic legacy. It is the vexations of Cain and Abel, of Abraham
and Isaac, of Job, vexations they suffered and whose riddling, even
scandalous justifications they inflicted on the conscience of the West,
which are inscribed in the torments and extinction of Joseph K.

Elaborations – political, psychoanalytic, anthropological, parodistic – on Greek myths are prodigal in twentieth-century poetry,
fiction, drama. Even at the pitch of inspiration, in *Ulysses*, in T. S.
Eliot and Pound, in Broch's *Death of Virgil*, the breath is that of
echo, of re-cognition, rather than origination. Variants on scriptural
and apocryphal themes are rarer. The literacy of biblical reference
and response has thinned. It is in this special sense that Faulkner
may have been Franz Kafka's truest contemporary. But Kafka's
capacity to transmute not only such raw material out of Holy Writ
as the story of Babel, but to wake to consuming life the modes of
secondary discourse on Scripture as these are practised in Talmudic,
rabbinic, Midrashic and (one cautiously suspects) kabbalistic
strategies, remains unique. (Borges is a disciple of genius.) The
purity of Kafka's prose, its wealth of abstinence, intimate the
insuring volume, the choral accumulation, of the tradition of the
revealed and of the hermeneutic which towers behind it. His
'fictions of uncertain truth' represent, in their nakedness, in the
dread innocence of their questioning, the only form of mundane and
'signed' literary art potentially permissible in the Judaic matrix of
Torah study and of unbroken dialogue between sanctified text and
reader. How else can one entertain the blasphemy of fiction, of
construal (which entail error and falsehood) in excess of God's
creation?

As I mentioned, there does seem to me to be one act of reading of

Kafka which comes near to plumbing the depths. It is that hammered out in the letters of Walter Benjamin, the messianic Marxist and theologian of language, and Gershom Scholem, master of the study of Jewish mysticism. Franz Kafka is present throughout their exchanges, but it was during the summer and autumn of 1938, apropos of Benjamin's repudiation of Max Brod's biography of Kafka, that their perceptions crystallized. The foci in the ellipse of Kafka's work are, for Benjamin, those of mystical experience, with particular recourse to the kabbalistic on the one hand, and the fate of the modern city-dweller on the other. Acutely, Benjamin links the instability, the ghostliness of modern urban existence to the new physics of indeterminacy. Kafka's *folly* stems from the precise paradox that it is via the mystical tradition that he gains unrivalled access to modernity. But Kafka's relation to the hermeneutic-allegoric tradition is peculiarly that of an 'eavesdropper'.

The main reason why this eavesdropping demands such effort is that only the most indistinct sounds reach the listener. There is no doctrine that one could learn and no knowledge that one could preserve. The things one wishes to catch as they rush by are not meant for anyone's ears . . . Kafka's work represents tradition falling ill . . . Kafka's writings are by their nature parables. But that is their misery and their beauty, that they had to become *more* than parables. They do not lie modestly at the feet of doctrine . . . When they have crouched down, they unexpectedly raise a mighty paw against it.

What is recuperable for Kafka (so Benjamin) is 'a sort of theology passed on by whispers', charged with 'matters discredited and obsolete'. The other yield is one of a kind of holy madness: hence Kafka's delight in Don Quixote. Those seeking to help fallen man are fools; but only fools can help. The statement I have cited about abundance of hope 'but not for us' becomes, in Benjamin's gloss, the very source of Kafka's 'radiant serenity'. But one must never lose sight of the fact that the uniquely luminous figure of Franz Kafka 'is the figure of a failure' (a conclusion which Benjamin had already argued in 1934).

In reply, Scholem, thoroughly at home in the joys of self-contradiction, offers the 'simple truth' that Kafka's 'failure was the object of endeavours that, if they were to succeed, were bound to fail' (which is, exactly, the motion of action and of cognizance in *The Trial*). Does Kafka's parabolic commentary on the revealed really represent 'a falling ill' of the tradition?

I would say that such an enfeebling is rooted in the nature of the mystical tradition itself: it is only natural that the *capacity* of tradition to be transmitted remains as its sole living feature when it decays, when it is in the trough of the wave.

Kafka's techniques are those of commentary just because 'it is *wisdom* that, when it reflects, comments rather than perceives'. Kafka's is a borderline case of wisdom, representing, as no other writer has, 'the crisis of the sheer transmissibility of truth'. 'This commentator does indeed have Holy Scriptures, but he has lost them.' The insights and the loss are somehow the same.

Together with other letters and with Benjamin's four articles on Kafka, this dialogue may well embody the highest in modern arts of meaning. It is apposite that Kafka's fictions should have been its occasion. In a set of notes to *The Trial* jotted down before 1928, Benjamin evokes 'the theological category of "waiting"', the primary role of expectancy in the novel. He wonders at the mystery of 'adjournment' in Kafka's scheme. In so doing, he draws us towards the centre of the centre. Yet here even Benjamin falls short.

Known variously as 'Before the Law' (observe the ambiguity), as 'The Doorkeeper' or 'The Man from the Country' (a phrase which, in Yiddish, carries connotations of obstinate incompetence), the parable spoken by the cleric to Joseph K. in chapter nine of *The Trial* is the nucleus of the novel and of Kafka's vision. Helplessness seizes one face to face with this page and a half. As it often does in the sight of Shakespeare's working-day. Here I am able to arrive at some naive picture. Any such image fails me in respect of the composition of the speeches from the whirlwind in the Book of Job, of the central sections of Ecclesiastes or of chapters 13–17 in the Fourth Gospel. It is equally futile, I feel, in reference to 'Before the Law'. This text persuades me as being informed by revelation. The knowledge that it was written (and published separately from the novel during Kafka's lifetime) by a gentleman in a bowler hat going to and from his daily insurance business, defies my grasp. My impotence is not an isolated one. Formally, nothing has been added to sacred scriptures in the Jewish canon. But this parable in the dark of the Prague minster has, in fact, been read and commented upon within liturgical contexts. It is taking on the primal force of an imponderable verity.

There appear to be as many ways of reading 'Before the Law' as there are modes of trying to conduct and image one's life. Each is partial; each solicits another attempt. How are we to analyse the unbounded charge of detail – the mirror-gallery of successive doorkeepers, the garb of the outermost guardian, the fleas – in an anecdote so sparse and compacted? What trust is to be invested in the speaker, who is at once a 'holy' person and an associate or emissary of the Court? Can there be 'false' revelation or, more exactly, divinely sanctioned truth which becomes falsehood by mere virtue of recital, of disclosure via human discourse? Is the Chaplain himself a doorkeeper whose intervention in the cathedral intimates a contiguity both organic and fatal between Judaism and Christianity, between law and the arbitrary enigma of grace? In turn, these queries grow brittle. They confess their obscuring sophistication before an inviolate signification more innocent and bottomless than any exegesis. The hermeneutic debate between the cleric and K. as to the import of the fable, with its astute pastiche of Talmudic practices, anticipates our bewilderments but leaves them unresolved. Indeed, the Chaplain suggests that K.'s mutinous interpretations of 'Before the Law' are wholly symptomatic of his own guilt, that we stand condemned by our misprision.

One (naïve) gloss is this: *The Trial* is translucent, it stands open to our apprehension as do biblical parables and narrations. If we remain baffled and rebellious to the light of meaning – a light which may well be inhuman in its indifferent purity – if we do not enter a door open and intended for each and every one of us, the guilt, the consequences are ours. Or to put it simply: it is not so much we who read Kafka's words, it is they who read us. And find us blank.

The foresight of *The Trial* into the inferno of modern bureaucracy, into imputed guilt, into torture and the anonymities of death as these characterize twentieth-century totalitarian regimes, has been made a cliché. The butchery (literal) of K. has become an icon of political homicide. Kafka's 'In the Penal Colony', his play on 'vermin' and annihilation in 'The Metamorphosis' were actualized shortly after his death. A concrete fulfilment of augury, of detailed clairvoyance, attaches to his seeming fantastications. Obscurely but unavoidably, the question or mystery of responsibility nags. Is there some sense in which the previsions spelt out across Kafka's fictions and most especially in *The Trial* contributed to their enactment? Could prophecy so mercilessly articulate have been other than fulfilled? K.'s Milena and his three sisters perished in the camps. The central European Jewish world which Kafka ironized and celebrated went to hideous extinction. The spiritual possibility exists that Franz Kafka experienced his prophetic powers as some visitation of guilt, that foresight stripped him naked. K. becomes the appalled yet almost impatient accessory to the crime carried out on him. There is in every suicide simultaneously apologia and acquiescence. As the Chaplain pronounces, in the most desolate of mockeries (but is it that?): 'The Court wants nothing of you. It receives you when you come and dismisses you when you go.' The formula comes deliberately close to being a definition of human life, of the freedom to be culpable which is that of fallen man. Who but Kafka could have put it in so few words? Or known himself condemned by being inspired enough to do so?

On Kierkegaard

It is difficult to write about Søren Kierkegaard (1813–55). He has written about himself with a mixture of immediacy and indirection, of confessional urgency and ironizing distance so vivid, so diverse as to beggar commentary from outside. Famously, Kierkegaard's pseudonyms, the dramatis personae he alleges to be the begetters of some of his exemplary works (while assuming that the reader will detect the figure beneath the mask), enact a system of self-mirroring. But the aim is in no straightforward sense autobiographical. Sharp-edged as are the assumed guises of S.K., they also achieve effects of dispersal, of dissemination. (At key points, current deconstructive notions of 'dissemination' and of the 'abolition of the author' go back to Kierkegaard.) Kierkegaard purposes to remain elusive also to himself, to be opaque and in motion as he traverses successive 'stages on life's way'. Pseudonyms, the division of the self into contradictory voices (the 'dialectic'), the brusque pendulum swing between prayer and sophistry, gravity and play, keep open (in Kierkegaard's memorable phrase) 'the wounds of possibility'. They prevent the frozen certitudes of the dogmatic, the inertia of the canonic. If music, notably that of Mozart, was to Søren Kierkegaard a touchstone of the pulse of meaning, the reason is clear: he sought in his reflexes of argument and sensibility, in his prose, to translate out of music its capacities for counterpoint, for plurality of simultaneous moods and movements, for self-subversion. Like no other major thinker, perhaps, Kierkegaard is polyphonic.

We must, in consequence, respond with a provisional, questioning lightness matching his own to even those fundamental aids to understanding to be found in his writings. The Kierkegaardian 'triad' is well known. It proceeds from an aesthetic stance to one of ethics; from ethics to religion. The aesthetic modulates into the ethical; from the ethical a 'leap of faith', the quantum jump 'into

Preface to the Everyman Library edition, 1994.

absurdity' (which twentieth-century existentialism took from Kierkegaard), conveys a chosen or afflicted few into the transcendent
adventure with God. Kierkegaard often insists on the tripartite
construct of his life and labours. The early *Either/Or* dramatizes the
conflictual temptations of the aesthetic and the ethical conditions of
spirit. The leap across the abyss of mundanity and of reason – ethics
is still a worldly, a calculable strategy – which makes accessible the
religious sphere, is carefully prepared for and plotted in successive
meditations and pseudonymous tracts. Yet Kierkegaard lays traps
both for himself and for us. In such texts as the *Edifying Discourses*,
as the enigmatic but probably decisive treatise on *Repetition*, as the
teasing reflections on Kierkegaard's own 'authorship', the inwoven
triplicity of voices and points of view is manifest. There is, from the
outset, a moralistic malaise in the paradoxes and avowals of the
aesthete, of the romantic dandy and seducer. Kierkegaard's ethical
'scenarios' and self-scrutiny are charged with poetic, rhetorical
display and the disinterested exuberance in stylistic experiment of a
literary master. The 'transgression' into sacrificial, uncompromising
faith, the tormented acceptance of the demands of the absolute in
'imitation of Christ' is latent throughout Kierkegaard. As I read and
reread this extensive, kaleidoscopic body of work, the 'decision for
God' in the image of Jesus seems to me discernible, like the flash of a
distant lighthouse, as early as Kierkegaard's doctoral dissertation on
Socratic irony, with its subtle but unmistakable critique of even the
loftiest of pre-Christian souls. The three strands are interwoven
almost to the very end. The 'credal' totality prevails only near that
very end, in those polemic indictments of the imperfection of the
established church which so clearly spell out Kierkegaard's own
imminent death.

Furthermore, an external factor obtrudes. In mid-October 1843,
Kierkegaard, at one simultaneous stroke, published three books:
Fear and Trembling, signed Johannes de Silentio; *The Repetition*,
under the name of Constantine Constantius; and *Three Edifying
Discourses* by Søren Kierkegaard. In one sense, we are confronted
by a single 'speech-act'. In another, these three texts qualify,
scrutinize and even ironize each other. But all three arise

immediately from a crisis at once intimate and strangely public (Copenhagen was a small city addicted to censorious gossip). They enact Kierkegaard's torment and analytic apologia in respect of his broken engagement to Regine Olsen. The drama of self-alleged infidelity and philosophic licentiousness had already been played out, all too transparently, in *Either/Or*. Now two occurrences precipitated Kierkegaard's anguish: Regine had nodded to him in church, suggesting forgiveness and a true understanding of her 'betrayer's' motives (the root incompatibility of the philosophic and the married state). Then he learnt of her betrothal to another. The psychological effect was both ruinous and liberating. Wild energies of argumentative, allegoric self-dramatization and social satire erupted in Kierkegaard. His henceforth aloneness turned to strategy. He took his stance at the frontiers of his community and his own psyche. Each of the three treatises published in that *mirabilis* month bore on Regine Olsen's conventional retreat from what might have been a solitude, a symbolic apartness concordant with S.K.'s. Allusions to intimate episodes and storms of sensibility are encased in the psychological, metaphysical and theological motions of argument even where these appear to be most abstract and general. Kierkegaard, in manoeuvres of rhetoric not always attractive, strips himself naked while advocating uttermost reticence and the burial of the heart. The very pen-names advertise: 'the constant one' and the 'apostle of silence', itself a reference to a fairy tale by the brothers Grimm in which a lover turns to stone rather than betray his secret despair.

As a rule, I find current modes of 'psycho-biography' fatuous. The fibres which relate a man to his work are, where anyone of Kierkegaard's dimensions and refinement go, of a tautness and complication which rebuke our indiscretions. But in the case of *Fear and Trembling* (and the two masterpieces which closely accompany it), the private domain compels notice were it only because Nietzsche, indirectly, and Wittgenstein, in plain awareness, were attentive to Kierkegaard's precedent when they conducted their own spiky lives and when they failed at or rejected certain 'normal' human relations (such as marriage).

Regine Olsen's is not the only biographical presence in *Fear and Trembling*. The black persona of Kierkegaard's dead father looms. The vacant, sombre heath invoked at the outset of chapter one is not that of biblical Canaan, but of Jutland. It was there that Søren's father, in starved and despairing childhood, had cursed God. The distant malediction became a lifelong obsession. It was revealed by the father to his son. In moods of 'Lamarckian Calvinism', Kierkegaard persuaded himself that he had inherited this scar of anathema and was, ineluctably, an object of God's retribution. Again, a certain willed cultivation of terror and of a psycho-doctrinal tragic drama is palpable. But the ensuing *Angst* was none the less graphic, nor the trembling any less feverish. In the double shadow of his 'infidelity' and pariahdom on the one hand, and of the sin inherited from his father's blasphemy on the other, Kierkegaard was able, as has been no other imaginer or exegete, to make his own Genesis 22.

The subtitle is exactly challenging. 'A dialectical lyric'. The tense interplay between philosophic propositions and poetic-dramatic means of expression dates back to the pre-Socratics and, supremely, to Plato's dialogues. It is instrumental in Wittgenstein's *Tractatus*, itself heir to the rhetorical genius of Lichtenberg and of Nietzsche. A great philosophy is always 'stylish': this is to say that its impact on the listener or reader, the force of coherence which it generates, its music of persuasion, are necessarily cognate with its performative means (those of language). Søren Kierkegaard was a craftsman of prose of the very first order. We can locate his tonality, the darting, intensely personalized dynamics of his presentations, within the more general context of European romanticism. He comes after Rousseau, after the early Goethe no less than does, say, Carlyle. It was in Schiller, in Novalis, that Kierkegaard could find full justification for the co-existence, in the same work, of philosophic and poetic components, of technical meditation and fictive-dramatic genres. Kierkegaard's fascination with the theatre and the ambiguous authenticity of the actor's trade never ceased. He writes incomparably of Mozart. His critical reviews of contemporary drama or novels are maliciously informed. He observed a rival in

Hans Christian Andersen. Only towards the end are his philosophical and theological books, essays, sermons, unmarked by quotations from, by analogies with, literary examples. *Fear and Trembling* draws, among others, on Plato, Euripides, Shakespeare, Cervantes and Goethe, as well as on the brothers Grimm and Andersen. *Don Quixote* is the subtext to the Bible.

Hence the concept of a 'dialectical lyric', of a narration of thought. The logical contradictions posited, the psychological and philosophic-religious endeavours to resolve them – the 'dialectic' in the Platonic sense, as this sense is taken up and modified by Hegel – are set out in what appears, at moments, to be an arbitrary, fictive manner. But the play of possibilities and of voices has its own severe logic, as do the successions of myths and of seeming digressions in a Platonic dialogue. *Fear and Trembling* is, above all, a fable of insight.

In a technique which anticipates the semiotic games of Umberto Eco and of today's deconstructionists, S.K. sketches a set of variants on the parable of Abraham and Isaac. Each variation on the given theme of the scriptural narration raises further psychological, moral and credal dilemmas. Immanuel Kant had opined that God, so far as we can attach to that concept and presence within us any intelligible meaning, *could not* order a father to slaughter his own beloved, miraculously conceived son. For Kant, the commandment heard by Abraham is daemonic. It stems from the voice of absolute evil. Abraham is the victim of infernal deceit. A degree of culpability attaches to his confusion. (How could he possibly have taken this to be a message from God?) Kierkegaard's reading is rigorously antithetical to Kant's. *Only* the true God can demand of Abraham the sacrifice of Isaac. It is in the (sickening) unreason, in the incomprehensible enormity of precisely such an injunction that the believer will recognize God's authentic summons. It is the profound error of Kant and of Hegel to seek to identify the God of Abraham, Isaac and Jacob, the God who ordains the hideous death of His Son on the cross, with categories of human understanding and reasoned ethics. In intimate echo to Pascal, Søren Kierkegaard would have us discriminate unflinchingly between the *dieu des philosophes* and the living God, into whose hands it is indeed 'terrible to fall'.

There follows the harsh yet exultant eulogy of Abraham. Kierkegaard spirals characteristically around one pivot, probing now from one angle of incidence, now from another. No aesthetic of tragic heroism, no rational morality, however high they are pitched, will bring us in reach of Abraham's journey to Mount Moriah. When men of war or guardians of civic virtue such as Jephthah and Brutus sacrifice their children to the Lord of Hosts or to the laws of the state, they do so with intelligible, albeit mistaken or fanatical, motivations. The barbaric sacrifice of Iphigenia ensures the departure to Troy of the Greek fleet. Creon the despot sacrifices his son so as to ensure the salvation of Thebes from murderous and blaspheming foes. Such exemplary acts and the devastating consequences which they have on their agents are the very stuff of heroic chronicles, sagas and tragic dramas (S.K. had toyed with the project of composing his own version of *Antigone*). But they throw no genuine light on the matter of Abraham and Isaac.

Nor does ethics. It is here that Kierkegaard's analysis is most arduous. Ethically considered, Abraham's acquiescence in God's commandment or indeed that of any man enjoined to carry out human sacrifice, is indefensible. Obedience may arise from fear of supernatural retribution, from superstition, from atavistic usages (the history of blood-offerings is immemorial and has its unsettling survival into periods which we associate with mature civilization). None of these categories is moral. Where morality is at its most elevated, in a Socrates, in a Kant, inhumanity and irrational absurdity have no place. Confronted with God's demand, the response of the ethical must be one of counter-challenge. How can God justify the order to slay Isaac? Is such a behest not *prima facie* a trap, a means of testing human courage and compassion (i.e. God waits for man's refusal)? Should divine coercion be so imperious as to make any such refusal finally impossible, morality and reason have a further resource. There are those who have chosen suicide rather than injustice, self-destruction rather than manifest criminality.

Kierkegaard is acutely cognizant of these arguments. He dwells with loving irony on their dialectical strengths. They are, he rules, wholly irrelevant to the *Akedah*, to the overwhelming enigma and interpretation of Abraham's obedience. The sole pertinent rubric is that of absolute faith, of a faith which transgresses against and thus transcends all conceivable claims of intellectual accountability and of ethical criteria. Abraham's readiness to sacrifice Isaac, his son, to enact God's prescription unquestioningly lies beyond good and evil. From any point of view other than that of total faith, of total trust in the Almighty, Abraham's conduct is appalling. There can be no intellectual or ethical excuse for it. If we are to grasp Genesis 22, we must apprehend 'enormity' (a term whose etymology points, precisely, towards transgression, towards a sphere of meaning outside any reasoned legality). The cardinal notion is that of *the absurd*. Fixing on this crux, S.K. looks back to certain legacies of mystical illumination, of self-abolition in God, and forward to modern 'surrealism' and existentialism. Abraham's actions are radiantly absurd. He becomes the 'Knight of Faith' riding forth like Don Quixote as God's champion in the face of humanist revulsion and ridicule. He dwells in paradox. His quantum leap of and into blinding faith isolates him completely. The heroic and the ethical can be generalized. They belong to arguable systems of values and representations. Faith is radically singular. The encounter with God as experienced by Abraham is, eternally, that of an individual, of a private being in the grip of infinity. Only to a 'Knight of Faith', in his unbearable solitude and silence, is the living God simultaneously unfathomable and so close as to eradicate, to burn away, the limits of the self. No synagogue, no *ecclesia* can house Abraham as he strides, in mute torment, towards his appointment with the Everlasting.

Do such appointments come to pass in modern times? This question is, theologically envisaged, vexatious. Judaism, in its orthodox vein, holds Elijah to have been the last mortal man sanctified by a direct meeting with God. In non-mystical Christianity, the divine epiphany does disclose itself, miraculously, to certain men, women and children; but does so via the figure of the Son or of the Blessed Virgin. Islam, if I interpret its position correctly, does not look to any face-to-face encounter with Allah after the time of the Prophet. In December 1842, in Copenhagen, Adolph Peter Adler, clergyman and *Magister* in theology (Kierkegaard had attended his academic viva in June 1840), experienced a direct visitation and revelation from Christ. The Son of God had bidden Adler to burn all the manuscripts of his Hegelian writings and had dictated to him, in complete immediacy, the true doctrine concerning the origins of evil. On 12 June 1846, *Magister* Adler published simultaneously no less than four books. One consisted of sacred verse; the other three set out Adler's revealed insight as granted to him by Jesus. S.K. seems to have been among the very first buyers of these four titles.

The result was *The Book on Adler*. Whereas *Fear and Trembling* is among the best-known and influential works in nineteenth- and twentieth-century philosophic theology and literature, the treatise on Adler has remained almost unknown to the general reader. This obscurity inheres in its genesis. Kierkegaard began composition in the summer of 1846, immediately after perusing the *Magister*'s revelations. The polemicist in Kierkegaard aimed at rapid publication. Dissatisfied with his first version, S.K. withdrew the manuscript in 1847, completing a third and more or less definitive version late that same year. Again, he chose not to publish. Having extracted from *The Book of Adler* two major essays on the relations between 'genius' and the apostolic and on the dilemma of whether or not a Christian has a right to solicit martyrdom, to offer his life for his faith, S.K. left the book itself among his *Papierer* (the diaries, the fragments, the voluminous notes). It appeared after his death.

Why this withholding? Plainly, Kierkegaard found himself in an exceedingly awkward personal situation in regard to Adler. They were acquainted. Adler had called on S.K., informing him that he, Kierkegaard, was in some sense the John the Baptist to the *Magister* whom the Lord had chosen as His special messenger. Kierkegaard pondered the probability that Adler (whom the ecclesiastical authorities had suspended from his ministry in 1844) was quite simply mentally deranged. Why, moreover, draw further public attention (and derision) to a wretched business soon forgot? But substantive as they may have been, these inhibitions do not touch on the heart of the problem. Adler's conviction that worldly, rationalistic, officious Christianity in Denmark must be electrified into authentic crisis, was exactly Kierkegaard's. The *Magister*'s readiness to suffer ridicule and ostracism on behalf of his 'absurd', existentially enforced certitudes, must have struck a deep, unsettling chord in S.K. himself. As we will see, Adler's claims, however suspect and, indeed, pathological, embroiled Kierkegaard in psychological-theological dilemmas which even his acutest dialectical means failed to unravel convincingly. The Adler 'case' might well prove trivial and wholly ephemeral. The issues which it raised would not go away. Thus there is a perspective in which the wretched Adler defeated his grand inquisitor.

As so often in Kierkegaard's speculations and dialogues, the 'third presence' is that of Hegel. S.K.'s ironies sparkle: the *Magister* no doubt committed his Hegelian lucubrations to the fire, but he remains arch-Hegelian in his confusions. Incapable of discriminating between subjective phenomena and objective truths, Adler, like so many of Hegel's uncritical adepts, makes naïve use of the Hegelian concept of synthesis between self and the external world. As it were, he 'hallucinates reality'.

But S.K. is after bigger game. The crux of the Adler affair is that of 'calling', in the very strongest sense of the term. How does a human being *know* that he/she is being summoned by God? How can human sensibility and intellect differentiate between an ecstatic, deeply felt intimation of divine solicitation, whose actual sources are those of personal need or emotion, and the authentic voice of God? The enigma is not one of possible psychic disorder (as it may have been in *Magister* Adler's instance); nor is it one of calculated self-deception or public falsehood (as in the case of innumerable gurus and market-place mystics). What, asks Kierkegaard, could be the conceivable criteria by which to determine the roots and verity of God's summons to any individual human person? Even visible excellence of moral conduct, even sacrificial suffering, such as is endured by martyrs, provides no *proof* for the spiritual validity of a vocation from God. As T. S. Eliot has it in his meditation on the possibly opportunistic martyrdom of Becket, 'doing the right thing for the wrong reason' may, especially in respect of the religious, be 'the subtlest form of treason'.

Nothing is more fascinating to note than Søren Kierkegaard's almost despairing attempts to clarify, to unravel a conundrum whose intricacies, whose scandalous implications, seem to ebb from his ardent grasp. The focus is not, of course, poor Adler; it becomes Kierkegaard himself and his most deep-buried anguish and hopes.

The dialectical motions of proposal and qualification, of imaginative thrust and self-deconstruction, are of a complexity, indeed of a fragility, which makes any outline crass. Neither intellectual lucidity and analytic rigour ('genius') nor ethical sacrificial engagement, necessarily lead towards the 'hand-to-hand' encounter with God. Here the image burning between the lines is that of Jacob wrestling with the Stranger. It may well be that genius and reasoned morality of even the loftiest order – say in Kant – inhibit the mystery of a veritable calling. There is, and S.K. touches at this point on an elusive paradox, a self-sufficiency in moral excellence, a harmonic finitude at the heart of goodness, which in some manner excludes or renders marginal the dread, the devastating nearness of God. Only the Apostle is *called*. He alone embodies, literally, the act of possession by God and is authorized to enunciate, to translate into mortal speech, the message which he has – there is no other way of putting it – become. Does this election glorify the Apostle? On the contrary, argues Kierkegaard. The authenticating mark of the apostolic is an existential humility of the most radical kind. The true Apostle is humbled beyond all other humilities known to man. Hence the rebellious terror, the surge of refusal, with which Old Testament prophets respond to the charge which God puts upon them. An Apostle is, at any given moment – be it in a street in nineteenth-century Copenhagen – in a synchronic correspondence with the *humilitas* of Jesus, of the mocked, scourged, spat-upon and done to death Jesus of the Passion. (Adler's evident satisfaction in consequence of his 'visions', the vanity in his resolve to make them public, disqualify him at once from any claim to being an instrument of God's purpose.) Only the man or woman contemporaneous with, 'synchronized with', the suffering Christ and compelled to speak, to exemplify the meaning of that suffering, can be held to reveal God, to be – McLuhan knew his Kierkegaard – the medium made message.

Yet, at once, perplexities bristle. Whence, then, the power and the glory of the apostolic, its imperative hold on human acquiescence and imitation? How, moreover, can we reconcile Kierkegaard's insistence on the kerygmatic obligations of the apostolic, on the necessity of the declared revelation, with an emphasis on secrecy, on an ultimate inwardness? Kierkegaard grapples subtly, tenaciously, with these formidable questions. He sets himself nakedly at stake. Once again, the logic of contradiction, of the paradox (so Hegelian in essence, whatever S.K.'s protestations), is instrumental. Where it attains the requisite pitch of lived intensity, where it is fully analogous to that of Jesus, humility is total powerlessness, a finality of impotence. But it is precisely this impotence which constitutes, exactly in the sense of Jesus's revaluation of values, a greater power, very nearly an omnipotence of the absurd. Kierkegaard's thesis remains opaque. It helps, I suggest, to remember the 'powerless force' of such literary personae as Don Quixote or of Prince Muishkin, Dostoevsky's 'holy idiot'. Something of this sort is in Kierkegaard's mind when he wrestles with the contrarieties of the apostolic. Nor does he resolve the irreconcilable demands for silence, for humble self-effacement in the carrier of God's calling with the ministry entailed by that very calling. No thinker, no writer, is more illuminating than Kierkegaard on the motif of moral-metaphysical discretion, on the sacrament of secrecy which makes efficacious the love, the suffering of an Antigone or a Cordelia. S.K. is a celebrant of inward withdrawal, of absolute silence. He is, at the same time, a publicist of rare vehemence, one who bears witness loudly, self-revealingly, in public places. The satirical journey, *The Corsaire*, had lampooned him cruelly. Kierkegaard had been made an object of open derision in his native city. This condition was the very demonstration of the burden borne by a witness ('a martyr', in Greek, signifies 'witness'). To shuffle off this burden, to leave God's discourse unproclaimed, would be nothing less than apostasy. In the pseudonym, 'Petrus minor', under which Kierkegaard planned to issue *The Book on Adler*, these unresolved contradictions are inherent.

From any systematic point of view – philosophical systems being S.K.'s bugbear – the demolition of Adler is flawed. We have seen that Kierkegaard neither works out a clear delineation of the nature of the apostolic in a modern context, nor can he harmonize the antithetical demands on the chosen spirit of self-concealment and of public witness. But even in direct reference to Adler's pretences, Kierkegaard's indictment remains, finally, dogmatic. The *Magister*'s account of divine encounter, the 'revelations' he alleges, are indeed shown to be wholly implausible and even risible. The inference of deranged vanity and mental confusion lies to hand. But nothing in S.K.'s pitiless diagnosis elucidates any formal and substantively definitive criteria whereby we may discriminate between hysterical and hallucinatory illusion and a 'God-experience' in any verifiable sense. The leap into the absurd, the abolitions of pragmatic causality and of logic which would characterize such an experience, remain, by Kierkegaard's own criteria of 'necessary impossibility', issues of trust. Ineluctably, the possibility that Adolph Peter Adler had received direct communication from Christ (however garbled, however unworthy his modulation of the message into his own words and person) survives Kierkegaard's negation. How could it be otherwise if, in S.K.'s own phrase, those 'wounds of possibility are to be kept open'?

It is precisely these flaws, these knots in the argument, which generate the fascination of our text. The mercurial finesse of Kierkegaard's psychological probing, its adumbration (literally 'foreshadowing') of Freudian theories of the subsconscious, where Freud, however, flinches from any serious analysis of religious convictions, make of *The Book on Adler* one of the dark jewels in the history of philosophic psychology. As an examiner of the lives of the mind, of the associative pulses of the imagination at those points at which the anarchic yet somehow ordered energies of the unspoken are brought to bear on rational proposals, Kierkegaard has only two peers. His inquisition into Adler stands beside those descents into the deeps of the human psyche performed by Dostoevsky and by Nietzsche. In these three cases, we are dealing with dramatists of the abstract, with analysts of surpassing penetration, capable of circumscribing frontier zones of unreason, or ecstatic and mystical flashes, even of madness. Modern psychoanalytic and psychotherapeutic knowingness has sometimes deepened, but often flattened, the geology of consciousness explored by *The Possessed*, by Nietzsche's *Genealogy of Morals* and by *The Book on Adler*. But here already lies the essence of our psychological modernity.

There is as well a direct link. Throughout his tracking of Adler, S.K. is spiralling around himself. The *Magister* threatens to be his faithful though parodistic shadow. In short, he turns out to be Kierkegaard's double. The *Doppelgänger* theme obsesses western interest from E. T. A. Hoffman, Poe and Gogol all the way to Kafka. It enacts an urgent intimation as to the schizophrenic potential in the ego, as to the dangers of self-splitting inherent in a certain vivacity of thought and of fantastication. Dostoevsky's novel, *The Double*, marks only one among numerous invocations of this theme in his fictions. Nietzsche and his Zarathustra circle around each other in a complex figure of rival mirrorings. On almost every page of the Adler book, we observe Kierkegaard labouring, sometimes with satiric confidence, but more often in barely muffled *Angst*, to shake off the intimacy of his scandalous familiar, of the 'house-demon' who is also his twin. A particular terror emanates from these pages.

The Archives of Eden

'The Lord has brought us hither through the swelling seas, through perills of Pyrats, tempests, leakes, fyres, Rocks, sands, diseases, starvings: and has here preserved us these many yeares from the displeasure of Princes, the envy and Rage of Prelats, the malignant Plotts of Jesuits, the mutinous contentions of discontented persons, the open and secret Attempts of Barbarous Indians, the seditious and undermining practises of heretical false brethren.' Thus John Winthrop in 1643. This 'bringing hither', this Great Migration, in Puritan parlance, was no common fact of history. Thomas Hooker, back in England, had speculated whether the establishment of the New England polity was not a signal of the end of secular time, for this was the *nec plus ultra* of mundane innovation. Any ulterior discovery and instauration would exceed terrestrial possibilities and herald the beginning of the reign of everlastingness as foretold in Revelation. But the ambiguities in the trope of final renovation, in the theology and sociology of the Edenic, were formidable from the outset.

If New England was the enactment of a fresh Covenant of Grace (Cotton Mather's constant term), if the members of this Covenant benefited from the greatest opportunity of salvation granted to any people since the birth of Christ, were they, in some real sense, 'new men', analogues to Adam? Vexatious, almost socially destructive, controversies over the need and quality of baptism in the new world, over the operative transfer of original sin in the new community and individual, bear witness to the literal, yet opaque, character of the Adamic model. And if the new-found lands of the Covenant of Grace were indeed, as Peter Bulkeley had proclaimed, 'as a City set upon an hill, in the open view of all the earth . . . because we profess ourselves to be a people in Covenant of God', and the *only* such people to be found on a lapsed planet – what then of the 'mutinous contentions' and the 'heretical false brethen' cited by Winthrop? What then of the 'Barbarous Indians' and the plagues of drought and sickness visited upon the new Jerusalem?

No less ambiguous was the question of the relations to the old world. Perry Miller summarizes one main current of thought (*The New England Mind: The Seventeenth Century*, p. 470): the Puritans 'did not, at least in the first settlements, regard themselves as fleeing from Europe but as participating to the full in the great issues of European life; they did not set out to become provincial communities on the edge of civilization but to execute a flanking manoeuvre in the all-engrossing struggle of the civilized world'. But a more radical current of severance was also at work. By the late 1630s, it was manifest that neither Geneva, nor Amsterdam, nor Edinburgh had been able to bring to ailing Christendom the light of enduring rebirth and true Congregation. Soon prelacy and worse would reassert themselves in the English realm. Episcopacy and Popery were the universal portents of a nearing apocalypse. The new Israel must leave behind the places and legacy of damnation. Thus New England was not only the precise analogue to the promised land, but the Noah's ark in a period of deluge. To look back would be suicidal. This doctrine of divorcement could, moreover, justify the problematic harshness of the western Eden: had the children of Abraham not had to dwell in the desert and suffer affliction and attack on their journey? The collision between these two currents or, more accurately, the intricate hybrids and compromises between them, made the problem of cultural heritage acute. In one sense, the intellectual baggage brought by the Puritans, the language and the logic of all articulate awareness, were those of post-Renaissance Europe, with their evident foundations in pagan classicism and Christian humanism. How could it have been otherwise? Yet in another sense, this legacy carried with it the very seeds of error and corruption, the histories of scission and heresy, which had edged man towards ruin. If the Great Migration was to escape from the blackness of Goshen and take possession of the New Canaan, it could only do so in the (literal) light of a newborn knowledge, of an innocence of intellect and sensibility. Adam's pre-lapsarian wisdom gave warrant for such a concept of knowledge purged of knowing-ness, of perfect *natural* wisdom.

All these antinomies, and the spectrum of intermediate positions between them, turn on the primary trope of 'felt time', of the chronological. Was America 'young' or 'old'? Was America the *mundus novus* promised by St John and proclaimed by Spanish ecclesiastical chroniclers almost immediately after Columbus's journey? Was it an authentic vestige of the Garden set aside for the re-entry of the new Adam? In which case, it had no 'history'. Or was it, on the contrary, an ancient world, no more intemporal and immune from the inheritance of the fall than were the lands from which the Pilgrims came? And what of these new Israelites themselves? Some held the Covenant of Grace to be, concretely as it were, regenerative. In the new world man was made new, the vestments of his fallen state stripped from him. Others were less sanguine. Even if this was, or was to be, 'earth's other Eden', it was the Old Adam who had come to it 'through the swelling seas'. Inevitably, he carried with him the contagion of history.

The options, the conflicts of vision implicit in these contrasting suppositions, extend to the whole fabric of American sensibility. They have largely determined the course of American religious and political development, the politics and sociology of American self-definition, the psychological diversities in American public and private conduct. In essence, pragmatic agencies prevailed. The 'City set upon an hill' did not found a new language. It spoke its message of renovation in European tongues and via the logic of Aristotle, of Ramus and, after the 1670s, in that of Descartes. Unlike the Jacobin utopians of September 1792, the men of the new world did not begin a new calendar, a Year One of messianic inception: yet impulses towards apocalyptic novelty continued to press on the fabric of American institutions and challenges. Utopian commu-nities and movements were a recurrent phenomenon. The Mormons moved on in search of the new and the real Zion. Indeed, the mechanism of the Adamic is one of the fundamental aspects of American history: in the face of political-social atrophy or corrup-tion, the claims of the ideal, of the Covenant of Grace, seen now as a non- or post-theological contract with history, are reaffirmed. Time and again, American consciousness would turn its back on the blighted past; the restlessness of hope points west. The conflict is unresolved. From it springs much of the creative wealth of the American temper. From it, as well, spring essential uncertainties and frustrations in respect of 'culture', of the life of the mind in society as this life has, *mutatis mutandis*, been construed and experienced in the 'old West' since Hellenistic times.

To consider these uncertainties, simply to view them as potentially negative, is to choose, almost unawares, between the two polarities of 'young' and 'old', of the Adamic and the historical. It is to set aside, if only provisionally and in the service of a working hypothesis, the claim that it is *far too soon* to attempt any balance-sheet of the American intellectual or artistic achievement. It is to dissent from the belief that we are, substantively, dealing with a 'young culture' some three brief centuries old and that any judgement of its harvest of thought and of its literacies in the perspective of more ancient models is futile and unfair. One's choice in regard to these alternatives is, finally, a matter of instinct, a deep-seated hunch. *It may well be erroneous*; it may well be of a kind which future events or a reordering of the intractably manifold evidence will refute. But whoever engages – and this mere engagement may be fatuous – concepts as inchoate, as recalcitrant to agreed definition and transcription, as 'culture', as 'spiritual' values, will have to start from instinct, from persuaded arbitrariness if he is to proceed at all.

I take it that American culture has no extraterritoriality to time; that it is not a 'young' culture in any but the most banal and localized sense (i.e. that the institutions in, through which this culture is expressed and disseminated were founded at a later date than their European counterparts and in a physically undeveloped or underdeveloped setting). I am positing that the great conceit of the Edenic, of the American Adam, whatever its manifest theological-political force, whatever its continued translation into later radical and messianic theories and practices of society, is not culturally determinant. The begetters and first organizers of

American cultural affairs, in education, in the arts, in the pure and applied sciences, were Europeans whose equipment, whose modes of understanding and argument, were as 'old' as those of the neighbours they left behind. I assume that none of the great American renegotiations of the contract between society and history – be it in the promise of happiness in the Bill of Rights, in the catharsis of Jacksonian populism, be it in Woodrow Wilson's New Freedom or Franklin Delano Roosevelt's New Deal – differs, ontologically, from similar renovations in European social history and that none constitutes a *novum* in the sense attached by the Puritans to the covenant with Abraham or the instauration of Mosaic Law. In short: the Puritan programme of a break with the 'corrupt ancientness' and hereditary taint of European history, the great hunger of successive waves of immigrants for a new dispensation free of the terrors and injustice which had marked their communal past, have played a central role in the American imagination and in the rhetoric of American identity. But they do not afford the actual products of American culture a calendar of Arcadian youth, a time of special grace. On the contrary. American culture has stood, from its outset, on giant shoulders. Behind Puritan style lay the sinew of English Tudor, Elizabethan and Jacobean prose. Behind the foundation of American universities lay the experience of Oxford and Cambridge, Aristotelian logic and the mathematics of Galileo and Newton. British empiricism and the world of the *philosophes* underwrite the Jeffersonian vision of an American enlightenment. Goethe stands behind Emerson as Shakespeare and Milton do behind Melville. It may be, as D. H. Lawrence found, that American culture is 'very old' precisely because it has been heir to so much. The New England divines would concur. By the early eighteenth century, William Cowper testified to 'God's withdrawal' from a new world whose conditions of spirit and civil practice were no better than in the old. The idiom of his testimony was that of Jeremiah and the Cataline orations, of Juvenal and the Aesopian satirists of the European reformation.

If 'American culture', so far as any meaning worth disagreeing about can be attached to so general a notion, is not *sui generis*, if it is a branch of the classical-Christian aggregate of European civilization, it may be legitimate to ask what its relations to Europe are and where the present centres of gravity lie.

Methodologically, such questions are indefensible. 'American culture(s)' is a pluralistic concept whose diverse components are themselves very nearly as diffuse as their aggregate. No individual can provide anything but the most intuitively vague, partial account of any one aspect of American intellectual-artistic-scientific activity. The notion that one can say anything definitive about the whole construct is patently absurd. There have been histories and analytic delineations of 'the American mind' at one or another period and attempts at a summarizing profile. Invariably, these have fallen short of the complex and amorphous data. At the very best, one will generalize and drop names in an impressionistic register of guesswork and prejudice. This is exactly what I shall do: to generalize, to drop names. But what other method is there? How else does any critique or inventory of values proceed? The necessary scruple is that of self-irony, of the hope that one's 'indefensible' asking will elicit not so much F. R. Leavis's famous response 'Yes, but' as it will that even more fertile instigation to understanding, 'No, but'.

American philosophy has been thin stuff. There have been psychologists of undoubted penetration and stylishness, notably William James. There is, certainly since the 1940s, a distinguished school of analytic logic (from Quine, say, to Kripke). American jurisprudence and theory of contract, in the social and ethical sense, has made useful contributions to the general current of western liberal thought. But it is doubtful whether there has been on native ground a major philosophical presence with the possible exception – the work is still, in some measure, unavailable – of C. S. Peirce. And even in this fascinating instance, it is difficult to make out a metaphysics, an attempt at a philosophical disclosure from the centre. But it is metaphysics and a central discourse on values which constitute the quality of western philosophy from the pre-Socratics to the present. It is the endeavour of successive philosophers and schools of reflection, from the Ionian to the existentialist, to 'think being' as a manifold totality and to extend this ontological act to every principal category of human behaviour, which has largely informed the inward history of man and society in the West. Such ontological centrality and continuity has been either derivative in or, indeed, absent from the climate of American feeling. There are, therefore, regards in which the tenor of American feeling is closer to the bias for magic, for pragmatic *bricolage*, current in non-western traditions than it is to the world of Plato and of Kant (one can invoke the singular here because the unitary fabric of western metaphysics has been so striking). The twentieth century offers graphic evidence: there is, quite simply, no American metaphysician, no 'thinker on being', no inquirer into the meaning of meaning to set beside Heidegger or Wittgenstein or Sartre. There is no phenomenology of American provenance comparable to that of Husserl and Merleau-Ponty. No philosophic theology of the order of radical challenge proposed by Bultmann or by Barth. The inheritance of ontological astonishment (*thaumazein*) and systematic response remains unbroken from Heraclitus to Sartre's *Les Mots*. It runs through Aquinas, Descartes, Hume, Kant, Hegel and Nietzsche. There is no American membership in that list. And what I am trying to spell out is not a technical consideration: it is a constant in Hellenic and European existence. The major philosopher is one whose discourse, as it were, successive generations carry on their person. Platonism, Cartesianism, the idealism and moral imperatives of Kant, the historicism of Hegel and Marx, existentialism after Kierkegaard and Nietzsche, have been ways of life, landscapes of private and public motion, for countless men and women entirely innocent of any formal philosophic schooling or specialized interest. Philosophic debate, between Platonists and Aristotelians, between Thomists and Cartesians, between logical positivists and Heideggerians or Sartrians or Bergsonian vitalists, are emphatic elements of political and generational identity. Just now, a fair number of my students carry Gramsci's prison-texts in their left pocket. A fair number carry the prison-writings of Bonhoeffer in their right (the two books being dialectically cognate). The best will carry both. It is 'the book in the pocket' which matters, the espousal of a text as radical and pivotal to private impulse and social stance. It is the

Socratic conviction that a community of rational men is one pervaded by explicit philosophic argument and that abstract thought is the true motor of felt life. This conviction is, on the American scene, 'academic' in a sense which I hope to make usefully arguable.

Roger Sessions, Elliott Carter are composers of undoubted stature. Charles Ives is a most intriguing 'original'. Up to this point in its history, American music has been of an essentially provincial character. The great symphony of 'the new world' is by Dvořák. It is Varèse's *Amériques* which comes nearest to a musical transposition of its spacious subject. Again, limiting oneself to the twentieth century – a limitation inherently weighted in America's favour – it is obvious that there are in American music no names to set beside those of Stravinsky, of Schoenberg, of Bartók, of Alban Berg and Anton von Webern, that the *œuvre* of a Prokofiev, of a Shostakovich, perhaps even of a Benjamin Britten represents an executive 'density' and imaginative continuity strikingly absent from the work of American composers. But there is the glory and utterly American genius of jazz.

It is, at this point, incumbent on the brief to say something of the development of mathematics in the new world. For me to do so is merely to dramatize incompetence. Anyone with even the most amateurish interest in the field will be able to cite a score of American names close to or at the top of the pyramid. There have been in this century, there continue to be, classic American achievements in every branch of analysis, of algebraic topology, of group theory, of measure theory and stochastics, of number theory. Yet, looked at closely, the roster shows that much of the pre-eminent work has been done *in* America by mathematicians and mathematical thinkers of a foreign origin and schooling (Gödel, von Neumann, Weyl, Bochner, Milner, etc.). And although it is absurd for a layman even to conjecture along these arcane lines, it looks as if much of the fundamental progress, notably in topology and number theory, this is to say in the high reaches of pure rather than applied mathematics, is being made in France, in Russia in the British school of mathematics, to be taken up thereafter on

American ground. (This, at least, is the impression of one who has been a mute witness to the proceedings and recruitment of the Institute for Advanced Study in Princeton.)

The triad metaphysics-music-(pure) mathematics is, of course, purposed. It crystallizes, since Pythagoras and Plato, the singular bent of western sensibility towards abstraction, towards the wholly disinterested, non-utilitarian, non-productive (in any literal sense) play of the mind. It crystallizes the singular western obsession with the creation of sensory 'monuments of unageing intellect'. The pursuit, even at the risk of personal existence or of the survival of the *polis*, of speculative thought; the invention and development of melody, *mystère suprême des sciences de l'homme* (Lévi-Strauss); the proposal and proof of theorems in pure mathematics – these define, quintessentially, the cancer of the transcendent in western man. It is they, it is the place which education and society afford them, which make of western spiritual history a legacy of Greece. It is they which, in shorthand, allow, indeed compel a working definition of the concept of a 'high culture'. Why it should be that Thales of Miletus was so absorbed in the predictive calculation of an eclipse that he fell down a well or that Archimedes should, in his garden at Syracuse, have chosen to continue his work on conic sections rather than flee for his life from invading enemies – these remain enigmas of genetics, of climatic and economic environment, of pathological good luck which historians and sociologists of science continue to debate. But the fact is plain enough: the hunter's cry when an abstract verity is cornered, the commitment of personal life to perfectly 'useless' metaphysical or mathematical concerns, the range and formal complexity of music in the West, have their specific source in the Greek 'mental set', have been the basis for our theory and practice of excellence. Personally, I would go further. The evolution of the species has given little ground for comfort. We are, on the whole, a cowardly, homicidal bundle of appetites endowed with seemingly limitless instincts of destruction and self-destruction. We are the wasters of the planet and the builders of the death-camps. Ninety-nine per cent of humanity conducts lives either of severe deprivation – physical, emotional, cerebral – or contributes nothing to the sum of insight, of beauty, of moral trial in our civil condition. It is a Socrates, a Mozart, a Gauss or a Galileo who, in some degree, compensate for man. It is they who, on fragile occasion, redeem the cruel, imbecile mess which we dignify with the name of history. To be in some touch, however modest, with the motions of spirit and soul in metaphysics and the abstract sciences, to apprehend, however indistinctly, what is meant by the 'music in' and 'of thought', is to attempt some collaboration in the tortuous, always threatened, progress of the human animal (biological progress being on a time-scale which escapes both our under-standing and significant intervention). To grasp, to be able to transmit to others some modest paraphrase of the beauty in a Fermat equation or a Bach canon, to hear the hunter's halloo after truth as Plato heard it, is to give life some excuse. This is, I repeat, my own absolute conviction. As such, it is without any general interest. But the fact that such a conviction will strike the vast majority of *educated* Americans as effete or even (politically, socially) dangerous nonsense, may not be without relevance. As may not be irrelevant to the heart of our subject – the state of 'American culture', the relations of this culture to Europe – the fact that American philosophy and music remain of a distinctly derived order and that much of what is stellar in American mathematics is of a foreign source. Aquinas, Spinoza, Kant have their statues in European cities; my own childhood transpired between the Rue Descartes and the Rue Auguste Comte, between a square dedicated to Pascal and a statue of Diderot. The most voluptuous of central European chocolates is named after Mozart, the most seductive of steak-dishes after Chateaubriand and Rossini. Such kitsch pays tribute to a formidable recognition. Why are American streets so silent to the remembrance of thought?

Argument by head-count is tedious. All one wants to indicate are some rubrics for discussion by more competent critics and historians. American painting has been explicitly imitative of European conventions and models until the close of what is now called 'post-impressionism'. American abstract expressionism, action painting, the parodistic genres of Jasper Johns, of Warhol, of Lichtenstein, the work of de Kooning and of Rothko, point to a veritable explosion of talent and influence. It was plausible to argue, from the mid-1950s to *c.* 1975, that the mastering energies in painting and the graphic arts had emigrated from Paris or London to New York. This is no longer the case. It now looks as if much of American art after the Second World War pressed to a conclusion *in extremis* instigations, formal suggestions, contradictions inherent and articulate in the great currents of Russian and west-European abstraction, constructivism, collage, and so on. For all its wit and incandescence, the American scene was one of the epilogues to modernism. This impression may well be myopic. What does seem dubious is that any modern American painter will emerge as possessing a stature, an innovative or re-creative strength comparable to that of Marcel Duchamp (perhaps *the* artist-programmer of our century), Braque, Kandinsky and Picasso. It could well be that in the fine and applied arts there are only two fields in which the American performance, to this date, gives unambiguous evidence of innovative genius. These would be architecture, with its obvious links with technology and engineering, and modern dance. It is when a Balanchine or Cunningham ballet is being danced, or when the eye seeks to take in the tower-frieze of lower Park Avenue or Pei's addition to the National Gallery in Washington, that the sense of America's 'making it new' is unquestionable. But again, on a continental scale, in terms of history which has behind it the classical and the European past, this is not an overwhelming harvest.

It is no Adamic or Pentecostal tongue, such as the Puritans lovingly pondered, that American writers write: it is in English. This banality may well render intractable, if not spurious, the question of 'the Americanness' of American literature. Strictly regarded, American English and the literature it produces is one of the branches, if statistically the most forceful, of the prodigal ramifications of the mother tongue. Like the language and literature of Canada, Australia, New Zealand, of the Anglo-Indian community, of the West Indies or of the English-speaking nations of Africa, American speech defines itself in interactive terms of dynamic autonomy and of dependence upon the eroded but still canonic primacy of the motherland. In this planetary perspective, American literature is at once dialectal and regional in respect of the source-centre, a formal and structural relation unaltered by the fact that the 'American dialect' is now more and more dominant throughout the English-speaking and, what matters even more, the English-learning world. This 'continentally regional' literature is itself composed of regional elements in the more natural sense of the word. Indeed, the strengths of American literature have, characteristically, revealed themselves in regional clusters and local constellations. The Hawthorne–Melville–Emerson–James grouping in New England, the regionalism of Faulkner, the urban-Jewish and even Yiddish aggregate of Bellow–Mailer–Malamud–Roth–Heller are obvious cases in point. A wary gregariousness, even in expatriation, has marked American literary talent. If the history of American drama has been, in the main, provincial (consider the parochial rhetoric, the crankiness of O'Neill's late plays which, in many respects, represent the decisive achievement in American play-writing), that of American poetry and, pre-eminently, of the American prose novel, has been exhilarating. The decades after the Second World War witnessed a general western turn towards the examples and authority of the American novel (*c'est l'heure du roman americain*, proclaimed French critics who had been among the first to spot the seminal roll of Dos Passos, Hemingway and Faulkner). The summits are *not* American: they are Thomas Mann, Kafka, Joyce and Proust. But the general terrain of the novel in the mid-twentieth century has been widely governed and, at vital points, redrawn by American novelists and masters of the short story. The contrast with the palsied state of fiction in England after D. H. Lawrence is drastic. The state of American poetry solicits more tentative, qualified placement. Here the landscape is strewn with critical hyperbole and modishness. How much is there of continuing life in Frost? To what degree will the presence of Wallace Stevens depend on astringent anthologizing? How brief was the period of Robert Lowell's shaping trust in his own considerable but fitful powers? These are unstable areas. One is bound to get magnitudes and relations wrong. The self-evident point is this: in distinction from American philosophy or music, American literature has claims to classic occasion. The 'deep-breathing' necessities of executive form and voice which it manifests (to adapt a phrase from Henry James) are indisputable. The question I want to come back to is a different one: what are the relations between literature and society on American ground (for it is these relations which enter crucially into the notion of 'culture')? How much does American poetry and fiction, even or particularly when it is of major seriousness, matter in America?

If these cursory questions have been worth putting, if there is anything but ignorance or short-sightedness to the observations from which they derive (a likelihood of which I am acutely aware), a paradox should spring to view.

As he takes notice of and part in American daily life, even the most jaundiced of observers will be literally overwhelmed by the scope, generosity, technical brilliance and public prestige of the American cultural enterprise. Museums dot the land. There is scarcely a town or city, however isolated, which does not boast its art gallery, its academy and collection of painting and sculpture. For the American these are no mausoleums. No country, with the exception of the Soviet Union, can match the civic, didactic energies and imaginative largesse of the American museum-world. Via lectures, model exhibitions, workshops, the dissemination of its holdings through reproductions, the American museum has made of itself a teaching-instrument and focus of sensibility in the community. Financially, but also at the level of communal pride and enjoyment it has, beyond almost all other comparable institutions in other societies, involved ordinary men and women in its activities. It is in modern America that Schiller's dream of political-moral education through aesthetic experience would seem to make sense. The situation in music is parallel. No nation on earth boasts more numerous orchestras or more orchestras of first rank (Chicago, Boston, Philadelphia, Cleveland, Minneapolis, San Francisco, to cite only a few). Chamber music, solo recitals, academies of music, music schools and festivals, the broadcast of music, are present in American life on a scale and at a pitch of quality which other societies (again with certain special exceptions which I will refer to) can only envy. That most labile and magical of genres, grand opera, flourishes. It is not only to New York, but to Santa Fe, to Bloomington, Indiana, and now to Norfolk, Virginia, that one will go to see and hear some of the finest opera performances in modern times. The long-playing record industry, the availability of tapes and tape-recorders to the music-lover of modest means – an availability more highly developed, more imaginatively marketed in America than it is anywhere else – has made the history of music, from the Gregorian chant to the electronic synthesizer, a dimension of the middle-class home. American ballet leads the world. Where on earth are there more or better libraries, libraries which have shown more public spirit in involving the community in their resources and activities? Extend this involvement to the college and university campuses and you will have, both in statistical terms and in regard to access and use, a 'book-world' like no other. Can it be an accident that the American paperback has altered the gamut of literacy in the West, from the most esoteric domain to that of mass consumption as no other modern typographic invention has done?

And what of the colleges and universities themselves, of a structure of higher education whose units run into the thousands (a fantastic figure, yet one Americans take for granted)? At this point, comparisons with other countries all but break down. No society has ever declared and fulfilled a comparable commitment to advanced schooling in the liberal arts, in the social and natural sciences, in technology and the performing arts. No other society has ever opened the doors of the academy to almost anyone desiring entrance. And though the relations between the 'academic' and the 'cultural' are undoubtedly complex and even at various moments polemic, the plain fact remains: millions of young and not so young Americans (consider night-schools, centres of continuing education, community colleges of every kind) are engaged in the systematic study of the arts and the sciences on a time-scale, in a context of public fiscal support, with access to libraries and laboratories, studios and planetaria, picture galleries and concert halls, undreamt of in history. In short: Americans are engaged, like no other society, in a general pursuit of intellectual and artistic attainment in establishments of tertiary education. Nor does any other society rival the continuity of impulse which reaches out from these establishments into the life of the adult. The alumnus, with his financial, but also intellectual and heuristic stake in the forward-life of the college or university which he has attended, is a singularly American phenomenon. It has been said that Oxford and Cambridge colleges own land whereas American colleges own loyalties. In recent years, in midst of a recession, such institutions as Stanford and Princeton have raised capital from their alumni on a scale which equals the entire budget for higher education in a number of European countries.

Given the institutional eminence and diversity, given the economics of American cultural enterprise – the museums and the symphony halls, the natural history emporia and the pillared 'Athenaeums', the colleges and the universities (is there now a Californian community without one or both?) – can one honestly query the dynamism, the future hopes of the American 'motion of spirit' (*moto spirituale* is Dante's perfectly concrete but resistant tag)? Seen from the grey and enervation of the European condition, is American culture not precisely what Puritan theodicy and Jeffersonian meliorism saw it to be: a 'City . . . upon an hill', a second wind for a spent runner? The answer is, I think, 'Yes', but it is 'Yes' in a peculiarly paradoxical, even retrograde sense.

The vital clue lies, of course, with that prodigality of conservation and retransmission to which I have pointed. American museums and art collections are brimful of classical and European art. European and antique edifices have been brought to the new world stone by literal stone or mimed to the inch. American appetites for the treasures and bric-à-brac of the medieval, the renaissance or the eighteenth-century past remain devouring. Scarcely a day passes without the translation westward of some further artefact of European glory. American orchestras, chamber groups, opera companies, perform European music. The resistance to new American compositions on the part of impresarios, conductors and, presumably, their audiences, is notorious. As is the massive conservatism of the symphonic and operatic repertoire. More new or experimental operas are produced in the opera houses of provincial Germany in a year than in the Metropolitan in a decade. The commissioning and performance of new music by the BBC in Britain, by the Cologne and South-west German Rundfunk broadcasting networks, by the research centres for music at Beaubourg or in Milan, have no real parallel in the Victoriana of the American operatic-orchestral and classical-music establishment. New York has yet to hear Schoenberg's greatest opera, and when this 'revolutionary' event will take place, it will, naturally, have a European cause and substance. American libraries are the manifold Alexandria of western civilization. In them are to be found the accumulated treasures and trivia of the European millennia, the Shakespeare folios and the ephemera of a hundred languages. Communities with no tolerable bookstore – Bloomington, Indiana, Austin, Texas, Palo Alto, California – enshrine the incomparable archives of the literatures of Europe in the nineteenth and twentieth centuries or the documents, periodicals, personal memoirs, graphic memorabilia of whole decades of European thought and calamity. It is to the Widener Library that Soviet scholars must travel in search of the pre-October and Leninist past; it is to Rice University in Texas that English bookmen must journey if they wish to explore in depth the Brontës and their background; it is to the Folger in Washington, to the Huntingdon in Pasadena that the Shakespeare editor proceeds for his collations. If Europe was to be laid waste again, if the wolves, as a chronicler of the Thirty Years' War put it, were to take lodging in its cities, very nearly the sum total of its literatures, of its historical archives, together with a major and representative portion of its art, would survive in America's safe-keeping. It was as if the American Adam, on re-entering the Garden, had brought with him the enormous lumber of his passage through history.

This, then, is my surmise: the dominant apparatus of American high culture *is that of custody*. The institutions of learning and of the arts constitute the great archive, inventory, catalogue, storehouse, rummage-room of western civilization. American curators purchase, restore, exhibit the arts of Europe. American editors and bibliographers annotate, emend, collate, the European classics and the moderns. American musicians perform, often incomparably, the music which has poured out of Europe from Guillaume de Machaut to Mahler and Stravinsky. Together, curators, restorers, librarians, thesis writers, performing artists in America underwrite, reinsure the imperilled products of the ancient Mediterranean and the European spirit. America is, on a scale of unprecedented energy and munificence, the Alexandria, the Byzantium of the 'middle kingdom' (that proud Chinese term) of thought and of art which was Europe, and which may be Europe still. Again and again, the impetus of American modernism, most particularly in poetry, has been paradoxically antiquarian. T. S. Eliot and Ezra Pound, Robert Lowell in *History*, have laboured to reassemble into comely order, to inventorize and anthologize by inspired quotation, the whole of the European past. These poet-critics are erudite tourists racing through the museum galleries and libraries of Europe on a mission of inventory and rescue before closing time. And if the *American Poetry Review* is anything to go by, the change since Lowell is only this: it is not the British Museum, the Uffizi or the Louvre which is seminal today, but the National Museum of Amerindian Art and Archaeology in Mexico. Thus it is that American museums stage sovereign shows of Picasso or of Henry Moore, but that American painting and sculpture do not generate canvases or statues which would make for a comparable *œuvre*; that American orchestras play Schoenberg and Bartók rather than American composers whom, reasonably I think, they deem of lesser stature; that American philosophers edit, translate, comment upon and teach Heidegger, Wittgenstein or Sartre but do not put forth a major metaphysics; that the pressure of presence throughout the world of the mind and of moral feeling exercised on civilization by a Marx, a Freud, even a Lévi-Strauss, is of a calibre which American culture does not produce. That this disparity continues in a century in which America has achieved unprecedented economic prosperity while Europe has twice lurched to the brink of suicide, seems to me to point to fundamental differences in value-structure (some of which I will touch on briefly). If these differences are indeed fundamental, and if we are looking not at a 'young' culture yet to find its own life-forces but an 'old' and a 'museum-culture', then it may follow that, in some cardinal domains at least, America may not readily produce first-rate contributions.

This is both a desolate and impudent supposition. One must, of course, resist it. It does, however, press on me in what is one of the high places in the American pantheon: the Coolidge room in the Library of Congress. Here hang the finest Stradivarius violins, violas, cellos on earth. They hang lustrous, each millimetre restored, analysed, recorded. They hang safe from the vandalism of the Red Brigades, from the avarice or cynical indifference of dying Cremona. Once a year, unless I am mistaken, they are taken from their cases and lent for performance to an eminent quartet. Haydn, Mozart, Beethoven, Bartók fill the room. Then back to their sanctuary of silent preservation. Americans come to gaze at them in pride; Europeans in awed envy or gratitude. The instruments are made immortal. And stone dead.

Suppose these hunches or provocations to be worth disagreeing with. How, then, is one to 'think the contradiction'? On the one hand, there is America, 'the morning star of the spirit', as Blake saw it. On the other, in the words of that influential poet from St Louis and the Maine coast, a culture principally engaged in 'shoring up (European) fragments to set against its ruin'. What dialectic will relate the frontier and the archive, the Adamic and the antiquarian?

Cogent answers go back at least as far as de Tocqueville. But the libertarian cant which now infects political and social discourse in the United States does not make it easy to touch frankly on their demographic components. Like the trope of the new Eden, that of the 'pioneer' comports an unexamined force of vitalism. Implicit in it is the presumption of *élan*, of a westward ho of men and women resolute, equipped to brave the fearful perils of the voyage and of the wilderness in order to build the new Jerusalem. There *were* such men and women, beyond doubt. There were pilgrims and frontiers-men who would, had they remained in 'the old country', have risen to the top. But the great mass of emigrants were not pioneers; they were fugitives, they were the hounded and defeated of Russian and of European history. If there is any common denominator to their manifold flight, it is precisely this: the determination to opt out of history in its classical and European vein, to abdicate from the historicity of injustice, of suffering, of material and psychological deprivation. It is in this regard that the recurrent analogy between Zionism, as it reaches back into the claustrophobic fantasies of the ghetto, and the 'Zionism' of the Puritan or the Mormon, is wholly deceptive. The return to Israel is a willed re-entry into tragic history. The march to New Canaan or Mount Sion in Utah is a negation of history. In this sense, it may well be that the ethnic-demographic elements in the successive waves of American settlement are 'Darwinian negative', that they embody the brilliant survival of an anti-historical species, where 'anti-historianism' would entail an abdication from those adaptive mechanisms of tragic intellectuality, of ideological 'caring' (Kierkegaard's, Heidegger's word *Sorge*) which are indispensable to cultural creation of the first rank. Those who abandoned the various infernos of social discrimination and tyrannical rule in Europe were not, perhaps, the bold and shaping spirits, but very ordinary human beings who could 'no longer take it'. Those who saw in the Russian, Balkan, Mediterranean and west European condition nothing but a dead end were, perhaps, not the great forward dreamers of 1789, 1848, 1870 or 1917, but the carriers of the gene of tired common sense. Send me 'The wretched refuse of your teeming shore,' urges the Statue of Liberty. Could it be that Europe did just that?

The counter-examples are so dramatic as to make the argument almost unassailable. The obvious exceptions to the intellectual, cultural norm of immigration are the Puritan in seventeenth-century New England and the Jewish refugee of the 1930s and 40s. Both represent an élite whose impact proved to be overwhelmingly greater than its numbers. The latter case has been studied in detail. It is scarcely an exaggeration to say that the explosive excellence of American pure and natural sciences (notably physics) between, say, 1938 and the 1970s is the direct consequence of Nazi and fascist persecution. This persecution brought to America what is almost undoubtedly the intellectually most gifted community since fifth-century Athens and Renaissance Florence, that of the post-ghetto middle-class Jews of Russia, central Europe, Germany and Italy. It is the community of Einstein and of Fermi, of von Neumann and of Teller, of Gödel and of Bethe. American Nobel Prizes in the sciences have been its address-book. But this formidably selected immigration animated far more than the sciences. Intellectual and art history, the classics, musicology, *Gestalt* psychology and social theory, jurisprudence and econometrics, as they flourish in American colleges, universities and research institutes during and after World War II, are the immediate product of the central European and Slavic Diaspora. As is the *floruit* of art galleries and of symphonic orchestras, of intellectual journalism and of quality publishing in that nerve-centre of the mid century we call Manhattan. Think away the arrival of the Jewish intelligentsia, think away the genius of Leningrad–Prague–Budapest–Vienna and Frankfurt in American culture of the past decades, and what have you left? For the very concept of an intelligentsia, of an élite minority infected with the leprosy of abstract thought, is radically alien to the essential American circumstance. Till the current recession bit hard, American institutions of higher learning, American orchestras and museums, publishers in search of senior editors or the *New Yorker* looking for critics, have been able to bid for European talent. Refugees, emigrants, guests by choice have continued to arrive, though in relatively small numbers. The Vietnam war and economic crisis have very nearly halted the 'brain-drain'. In numerous quarters, the cheerful undergrowths of mediocrity and of the provincial are already encroaching on the inspired clearings made in the 1940s and 50s. What if there is no further diaspora of excellence? The question is not hypothetical. Oppenheimer posed it starkly the last time I saw him. He had been, both at Los Alamos and at the Institute in Princeton, the shepherd of the prize European flock. Where, he asked, were the American successors to Bohr and von Neumann, to Szilard and to Fermi, to Panofsky and to Kantorovich, to Auerbach and to Kelsen? The appointments Oppenheimer made at the end are eloquent: a

Frenchman and an Englishman in pure mathematics, a somewhat younger member of the refugee galaxy in art history, an historian from London. Can such importation continue?

After de Tocqueville, the pertinent headings could be those argued by Veblen and Adorno. In the Puritan scheme, secular culture was ancillary to, instrumental towards the theological centre. Successive generations of immigrants and settlers might bring with them a cultural inheritance but had to establish *de novo* its institutional media. Such instauration was, necessarily, a by-product of more primary disciplines of survival and social-political consolidation. From the outset, the secular arts and sciences, the constructs of speculative thought and of the imaginary had, in America, an unavoidable strain of artifice, of willed implantation. To reverse Ezra Pound's famous phrase, it was the Muses' diadem itself which was 'an adjunct'. This, together with an instinct for palpable organization which informs both the American political and industrial-technological performance, led to the development of culture as craft, as specialization. Adorno's mordant term is *Kulturproduktion*, the application to cultural values and embodiments of intense professionalism, of manufacturing practices and packaging. 'Culture', the arts, literature, can be set high, can be monumentalized. But the resultant phenomenology is immediately reflective of the division of labour, of the ideals of efficacy, crucial to the American ethos. It is a 'thing out there', to be brought into and maintained in being by specialists (the academic, the curator, the impresario, the performing artist). Its interactions with the community at large are those of ostensible presentment, of contractual occasion rather than of anarchic and subversive pervasiveness. Perhaps the distinction can best be made this way: the main enactments of American cultural life are organized (superbly so) rather than organic. Inevitably also, this organization will take on the prevailing cast of economic valuation. The cultural, in Veblen's idiom, becomes a part of the overall dynamics of conspicuous consumption. There is not only *Kulturproduktion*, but a competitive marketing of the achieved product. Almost before it enters into the disinterested, if always problematic, zone of art, the American

[286]

aesthetic, intellectual, literary product is made artefact. The energies against solitude, against the mystery of neglect on which the deployment and subterranean daemon of education in great art seems to depend, are compelling. A *bourse* of unequalled hunger and competitive largesse waits daily for new issues. Its investment in the artist or thinker is, quite literally, a trading in 'futures'. Successful issues rise to dizzying heights of display and reward; bankruptcy is no less swift. Master-critics or brokers of the value-market have been known to 'make or break' playwrights, novelists, composers, painters. The media, the clients follow their markings. There is not, or only rarely, that private rebellion of judgement, that prodigality and incoherence of critical debate which, given much humbler and decentralized economic conditions, enables a play in London or Paris, a painter in Newcastle or Barcelona, a publishing house in Sheffield or Bari, not only to endure in the face of metropolitan repudiation, but to generate (to 'invent', as it were) its own public. The which 'invention' is a decisive element in the penetration of artistic, philosophic, literary 'issues' – allowing both the technical and the general sense of the word – into the ordinary, quotidian awareness of a society. These are not points which it is easy to put concisely and transparently. They implicate the deep layers of social history. They are made manifest, if at all, in tidal motions across centuries. But, nevertheless, it may be worth supposing that the twofold impetus of 'cultural production' and of 'conspicuous consumption', an impetus immediately related to the initial planning and technical apartness of the life of intellect in the new world, does provide some explanation for the *conservative exhibitionism* to which I have pointed. *Kulturproduktion* and investment in competitive display would, indeed, help to account for a culture of museums, academies, libraries, institutes of advanced study. The name of a recent addendum to this list, Research Park in North Carolina, is compact with connotations of both the Adamic and the mummified.

The riposte is self-evident. The pervasive density, the organicism of high culture in Europe is or was, until very recently, illusory. Those freely involved were a small caste, a more or less mandarin élite which happened to possess the instruments of articulate political and pedagogic enforcement. If European streets and squares are studded with the monumental vestiges of art and intellect, if debates on abstruse points in political theory (Aron *contra* Sartre) or Byzantine issues in the theory of culture (Leavis *contra* Snow) are front-page and even television news, if one's lobster is called by the name of Robespierre's red and fatal month of Thermidor, if examination questions in European schools and universities are published and argued nationally – all this is simply because the bureaucratic shamans of high literacy have, for essentially strategic purposes, imposed their (often hypocritical) sublimity on a numbed, indifferent or basically recalcitrant lower class. If they have any substance whatever, the handicaps or dilemmas which I have suggested in reference to artistic reaction and philosophic thought of the first rank in America, are inseparable from the democratic ideals and populist proceedings of the new world.

Often invoked, this argument is intuitively satisfying. In fact, it demands careful handling. The Periclean vision of the essential worth of a society in terms of its intellectual, spiritual, artistic radiance, the Socratic-Platonic criterion of the philosophically examined individual life and of a hierarchy of civic merit in which intellect stood supreme were, presumably, formulated and codified 'from above'. But collective accord in this vision, whether spontaneous or conventional, *is* an authentic feature in classical and European social history. What we can reconstruct of communal participation in medieval art and architecture, of the passionate outpouring of popular interest in the often competitive, agonistic achievements of Renaissance artists and men of learning, of the complex manifold of adherence which made possible the Elizabethan theatre audience, is not nostalgic fiction. Nor is the witness borne today by the thousands and ten thousands who come to look on the most demanding of modern arts at Beaubourg. In other words: the notion that artistic-intellectual creation is the crown of a city or of a nation, that 'immortality' is in the hands of the poet, the composer, the philosopher, the man or woman infected with transcendence and *le dur désir de durer* (a phrase coined, as it happens, by a Marxist and 'populist' poet), is inwoven in the fabric of Hellenic, of Russian, of European values, public styles and, above all, educational practices. I repeat: there may well be in this inweaving a large part of hierarchic imposition, and it may well be that acceptance by the mass of the population has been conventional or half-hearted. But this acceptance is made manifest, it is *taught*. The American commitment to an existential, to a declaredly open economic value-system is unprecedented. The adoption, on a continental scale, of an eschatology of monetary-material success represents a radical cut in regard to the Periclean–Florentine typology of social meaning. The central and categorical imperative that to make money is not only the customary and socially most useful way in which a man can spend his earthly life – an imperative for which there is, certainly, precedent in the European mercantile and pre-capitalist ethos – is one thing. The eloquent conviction that to make money is also the most *interesting* thing he can do, is quite another. And it is precisely this conviction which is singularly American (the only culture, correlatively, in which the beggar carries no aura of sanctity or prophecy). The consequences are, literally, incommensurable. The ascription of monetary worth defines and democratizes every aspect of professional status. The lower-paid – the teacher, the artist out of the limelight, the scholar – are the object of subtle courtesies of condescension not, or not primarily, because of their failure to earn well, but because this failure makes them less *interesting* to the body politic. They are more or less massively, more or less consciously patronized, because the 'claims of the ideal' (Ibsen's expression) are, in the American grain, those of material progress and recompense. *Fortuna* is fortune. That there should be Halls of Fame for baseball-players but few complete editions of classic American authors; that an American university of accredited standing should, very recently, have dismissed thirty tenured teachers on the grounds of utmost fiscal crisis while flying its football squads to Hawaii for a single game; that the athlete and the broker, the plumber and the pop-star, should earn far more than the pedagogue – these are facts of life for which we can cite parallels in other societies, even in Periclean Athens or the Florence of Galileo. What we cannot parallel is the American resolve to proclaim and to institutionalize the valuations which underlie such facts. It is the sovereign candour of American philistinism which numbs a European sensibility; it is the frank and sometimes sophisticated articulation of a fundamentally, of an ontologically *immanent* economy of human purpose. That just this 'immanence' and ravenous appetite for material reward is inherent in the vast majority of the human species; that we are a poor beast compounded of banality and greed; that it is not the spiky fruits of the spirit but creature comforts we lunge for – all this looks more than likely. The current 'Americanization' of much of the globe, the modulation from the sacramental to the cargo-cult whether it be in the jungles of New Guinea or the hamburger-joints, laundromats and supermarkets of Europe, points to this conclusion. *It may be that America has quite simply been more truthful about human nature than any previous society. If this is so, it will have been the evasion of such truth, the imposition of arbitrary dreams and ideals from above, which has made possible the high places and moments of civilization.* Civilization will have endured after Pericles by virtue, to quote Ibsen again, of a 'life-lie'. Russian or European power relations and institutions have laboured to enforce this 'lie'. America has exposed it or, pragmatically, passed it by. The difference is profound.

But let us assume that the 'élite model' is correct. Let us assume that the 'touchstones' of human excellence in the arts, in the life of intellect, in the pure and exact sciences are, at any given time, the product of the very few – this, surely, is almost tautology – and that the context of echo, of valuation and transmission which these products require in order to endure and to energize culture – what F. R. Leavis designated, in a somewhat deceptive phrase, as 'the common pursuit' – is, in turn, in the custody of a minority. The evidence points, very nearly overwhelmingly, to just such an assumption. The number of men and women capable of painting a major canvas, of composing a lasting symphony, of postulating and proving a fundamental theorem, of presenting a metaphysical system or of writing a classic poem, is, even on the millennial scale, very restricted indeed. Again, the current ecumenism of liberal hopes (or bad conscience) makes it difficult to discuss the vital issue of the sources of high art and intellect. But that these sources are 'genetic', though, very possibly, in a sense subtler and more resistant to biological-social analysis than nineteenth-century positivism supposed, that they are, in some way, 'prepared-for mutations' within very special hereditary and environmental matrices, is eminently probable. One says: 'and environmental', because there can be no doubt that environment factors *are* significant, notably in respect of inhibition, of the blockage of a latent vocation. But this significance can be, has often been, vastly overstated in the perspective of egalitarian myths and ideals. The curve of genius, even of high talent is, most likely, inelastic. Environmental support might add to the distribution at this or that point; it might have filled one or another gap in the line. But there is no evidence whatever that the multiplication of piano lessons throughout the community will generate one additional Bach, Mozart or Wagner. It is at the absolutely indispensable but, of course, secondary level of understanding, executive performance and transmission that the argument becomes more elusive. Here it is plausible to contend that better schooling, a wider spectrum of leisure, a general elevation in the material condition of private and public life, do matter. It seems almost self-evident that the appreciation of serious art, literature or music, a more general awareness of philosophic debate and scientific discovery and a willingness to respond actively to the instigations of meaning and of beauty, can be markedly augmented or curtailed by the economic and social context. I would not quarrel with this truism; only sound a cautionary note. The effects of environmental amelioration on the prevailing level of aesthetic, philosophic, scientific literacy and 'response-threshold' seem to be slow, diffuse and, rigorously considered, marginal. It does look, and this is a somewhat perplexing phenomenon, as if the number of human beings capable of responding intelligently, with any genuine commitment of sensibility, to say, a Mozart sonata, a Gauss theorem, a sonnet by Dante, a drawing by Ingres or a Kantian proposition and deductive chain, is, in any given time and community, very restricted. It is, obviously, much larger than that of the creators and begetters themselves. But it is not exponentially larger. And, what is even more puzzling, its increase by means of educational and environmental support, though material, is not exponential either. (Somewhere in this opaque area may lie the explanation for the often noticed fact that great critics – and a great critic is nothing but a loving, clairvoyant parasite feeding on the life of art – are so rare.) In brief: no amount of democratization will multiply creative genius or the incidence of truly great thought. And although democratization, i.e. the extension of better education, of more leisure, of a more liberal space of personal existence, to a greater number will add to the 'supporting cast' in civilization, it will not add massively, let alone without limit.

So be it. A number of corollaries follow. To generalize the Periclean or Socratic formula, man's generally fractional advance from animality can be measured, if at all, in terms of his artistic, philosophic, scientific creations and conjectures. We are the creatures of the bingo hall and the concentration camp. But we are also the species from which Plato and Mozart sprang (or broke loose). If man's condition, if man's bestial history has any meaning whatever it lies, quite simply, in trying to shift, however minutely, the two halves of the equation, in trying, as it were, to add an occasional factor to the 'Plato–Mozart' end. The first thing a coherent culture will do, therefore, is to maximize the chances for the quantum leap, for the positive mutation which is genius. It will try to keep its educational-performative-social institutions open-ended, vulnerable to the anarchic shock of excellence. As I have emphasized, such open-endedness, such alertness to the sudden track of the supremely charged particle in the cloud-chamber of society, will not, materially, increase the percentage of artistic, philosophical greatness. But it may do something towards lessening the inhibitions, the densities of obtuseness, which can stifle greatness or deflect it from its full course. A coherent culture will do a second and much more important thing. It will construe its public value-scale and its school-system, its distribution of prestige and of economic reward, so as to maximize the 'resonant surface', the supporting context for the major work of the spirit. It will do its utmost to educate and establish a vital audience for the poet and composer, a community of critical echo for the metaphysician, an apparatus of responsible vulgarization for the scientist. In other words, an authentic culture is one in which there is an explicit pursuit of a literacy itself focused on the understanding, the enjoyment, the transmission forward, of the best that reasons and imagination have brought forth in the past and are producing now. An authentic culture is one which makes of this order of response a primary moral and political function. It makes 'response' 'responsibility', it makes echo 'answerable to' the high occasions of the mind. I have said that such pursuit, through education and improved environment, does not have a boundless yield. The number of true 'respondents' will remain fairly small. The conclusion – as Athens and the European *polis* after Athens have drawn it – seems ineluctable. A culture, in the precise sense of the word, is one in which the small number of effective receivers and transmitters of art and of intellect will be placed to greatest advantage, in which they will be given the means to extend what they can of their obsession with transcendence to the community at large. To divorce the springs of civilization from the concept of a minority is either self-deception or a barren lie.

Yet it is on this divorce that the theory and practice of American secondary education in the twentieth century are founded. Whereas European meritocracy, open-ended at the base, sharply narrowed at the apex, sought to select and recruit a minority capable of serving excellence, the American pyramid is, as it were, inverted. It would make excellence fully accessible to the vulgate. This desideratum is inherently antinomian. It labours to correct the oversight or snobbery of God, the failure of nature to disseminate generally and suitably among men the potential for response to the disinterested, the abstract, the transcendent. This correction can only be undertaken at the cultural end of the stick. One cannot, beyond a severely limited and superficial degree, inject sensibility and intellectual rigour into the mass of society. One can, instead, trivialize, water down, package mundanely, the cultural values and products towards which the common man is being directed. The specific result is the disaster of pseudo-literacy and pseudo-numeracy in the American high school and in much of what passes for so-called 'higher education'. The scale and reach of this disaster have become a commonplace of desperate or resigned commentary. The pre-digested trivia, the prolix and pompous didacticism, the sheer dishonesty of presentation which characterize the curriculum, the teaching, the administrative politics of daily life in the high school, in the junior college, in the open-admission 'university' (how drastically America has devalued this proud term), constitute the fundamental scandal in American culture. A fair measure of what is taught, be it in mathematics, be it in history, be it in foreign languages, indeed with regard to native speech, is, in the words of the President of Johns Hopkins, 'worse than nothing'. It has produced what he calls 'America's international illiteracy' or what Quentin Anderson entitles 'the awful state of intellectual affairs in this country'.

Does this 'awfulness' not run counter to the widespread and public support for the arts and music which I have referred to earlier? I think not. But the point is one that needs to be made accurately. In the American élite such support embodies authentic response and involvement. In the great mass of cultural fellow-travellers – they are a great mass precisely because of the pseudo-values instilled in them by a totally superficial and mendacious populist ideal of general education – this support signifies only passivity, 'conspicuous consumption', the treatment of the cultural as a unit of economic-social display. Here there is no 'common pursuit' but, to reverse Leavis's phrase, a 'common flight', an evasion from the political connotations and intellectual discomforts inseparable from major art and thought. The conjunction of an élite profoundly ill at ease in respect of its own status and function in a mass-consumer Eden together with a *profanum vulgus* numerically enormous and committed to self-flattering passivity in the face of excellence is, precisely, that which would generate the 'exhibitionist conservatism', the archival ostentation, of American cultural emporia. The *incunabula* and first editions shimmer inert in the hushed sanctuary of the Beinecke Library in New Haven, untouched by human hands (as is most of American bread). The Stradivarius hangs mute in the electronically guarded case.

An élite 'profoundly ill at ease': why should it be? Those Americans who have troubled to consider the matter at all have entertained the shrewd suspicion that high culture and the hierarchic structure of artistic-intellectual values on the European model are not an unmixed blessing. From Thoreau to Trilling, there has been in the sensibility of the American intelligentsia a nagging doubt about the relations between the humanities and the humane, between institutions of intellect and the quality of political-social practices. It is not only (a point made emphatically in Whitman) that such institutions are exclusive, that they select against the common man in an inevitable subversion of genuine democracy. This would be damaging enough, given the American experiment in equal human worth. It is that the fabric of high literacy in the Periclean and European vein offers little protection against political oppression and folly. Civilization, in the elevated and formal sense, does not guarantee civility, does not inhibit social violence and waste. No mob, no storm-troop has ever hesitated to come down the Rue Descartes. It is from exquisite Renaissance loggias that totalitarian hooligans proclaim their will. Great metaphysicians can become rectors of ancient universities in, at least, the early days of the Reich. Indeed, the relations between evaluative appreciation of serious music, the fine arts, serious literature on the one hand and political behaviour on the other are so oblique that they invite the suspicion that high culture, far from arresting barbarism, can give to barbarism a peculiar zest and veneer. American thinkers on the theory and practice of culture have long sensed this paradox. The price which the Athenian oligarchy, the Florentine city-regime, the France of Louis XIV or the Germany of Heidegger and Furtwängler have paid for their aesthetic-intellectual brilliance is too steep. The sacrifice of social justice, of distributive equity, of sheer decency of political usage implicit in this price is simply too great. If a choice must be made, let humane mediocrity prevail. Feeling the manifest force of this line of insight, having articulated this force within its own expressive means, the American cultural establishment is sceptical of itself and apologetic towards the community at large. This self-doubt and defensiveness have produced a subtle range of attitudes all the way from mandarin withdrawal to public penitence. It is the latter, with its embarrassing rhetoric of radical *Angst*, with its attempts to obtain forgiveness and even approval from the young, which has been particularly prominent during and since the start of the civil rights movements and the Vietnam war. It is not merely that there has been, exactly along the lines of Benda's prophetic analysis, a 'treason of the clerics': the clerics have sought pardon and rejuvenation by seeking to strip themselves of their own calling. One need hardly add that this masochist exhibitionism is often dramatized by the inherent malaise of the Jewish intellectual and middleman of ideas in an essentially gentile setting. But let me repeat: whatever the unappetizing, risible currency of scholars or teachers seeking to howl with the wolves of the so-called 'counter-culture', the roots of their anguish reach deep and to a valid centre. The correlations between classic literacy and political justice, between the civic institutionalization of intellectual excellence and the general tenor of social decency, between a meritocracy of the mind and the overall chances for common progress, *are* indirect and, it may well be, *negative*. It is this latter possibility, with all that it comports of paradox and suffering, that I want to turn to in the final motion of my argument.

That the 'touchstones' of human genius are the products of the very few, that the number of those truly equipped to recognize, experience existentially and then transmit these 'touchstones' is also limited are, I submit, self-evident truths, almost banalities. The genesis of supreme art or thought or mathematical imaging resists adequate analysis, let alone predictive or experimental control. But historical record does suggest something of the matrix of creation, of the individual and contextual elements in, through which the alchemy of great art or philosophy operates. One element seems to be that of privacy *in extremis*, of a cultivation of solitude verging on the pathological (Montaigne's tower, Kierkegaard's room,

Nietzsche's clandestine peregrinations). Or to put it contrastively: absolute thought is antisocial, resistant to gregariousness, perhaps autistic. It is a leprosy which seeks apartness. Now there is in American history and consciousness a recurrent motif of solitude. But it is *not* the solitude of Diogenes or of Descartes. To enforce the difference, to show how profoundly civic and neighbourly was Thoreau's stay at Walden Pond, would need careful documentation. But the fact is there, I think. And in the American grain, as a whole, it is a gregariousness, suspicion of privacy, a therapeutic distaste in the face of personal apartness and self-exile, which are dominant. In the new Eden, God's creatures move in herds. The therapeutic primal impulse, as Rieff has argued, extends further. The American instinct is one of succour, privately and socially, of companionable cure for the infections of body and soul. In America epilepsy is not holier than beggary. Where body or soul sicken, medication is the categorical imperative of personal decency and political hope. But one need not mouth romantic platitudes on art and infirmity, on genius and madness, on creativity and suffering, in order to suppose that absolute thought, the commitment of one's life to a gamble on transcendence, the destruction of domestic and social relations in the name of art and 'useless' speculation, are part of a phenomenology which is, in respect of the utilitarian, social norm, pathological . There *is* a strategy of chosen illness in Archimedes' decision to die rather than relinquish a geometric deduction (this gesture being the talisman of a true clerisy). And there *are* contiguities, too manifold, too binding for doubt between the acceptance, indeed the nurture of physical and emotional singularity on the one hand and the production of classic art and reflection on the other. The inhibitions, the cruel handicaps imposed upon, available to a Pascal, a Mozart, a Van Gogh, a Galois (the begetter of modern algebraic topology done to deliberate death at the age of twenty-one), the *cordon sanitaire* which a Wittgenstein could draw round himself in order to secure minimal physical survival and total autonomy of spirit – these are not only hard to come by in the teeming benevolence of the new world, they are actively countered. It is almost a definition of America to say that it is a *Prinzip Hoffnung*

(Ernst Bloch's famous term for the institutionalized, programmatic eschatology of hope) in which a psychiatric social worker waits on Oedipus, in which a family counselling service attends on Lear. 'And there are, my dear Dostoevsky, cures for epilepsy.'

The point has been made often (most acutely in James's *Golden Bowl* and in Henry Adams's *Education*). American history is replete with tragic occasion. But such occasion is precisely that: a contingent disaster, a failing to be amended, the fault of circumstances which are to be altered or avoided. The American Adam is not an innocent – far from it. But he is a corrector of errors. He has, after its brief and creative role in the New England temper, all but abandoned even the metaphor of original sin. The notion that the human condition is, ontologically, one of 'dis-grace', that cruelty and social injustice are not mechanical defects but 'primaries' or 'elementals' in history, will seem to him defeatist mysticism. No less so the hunch that there are between tragic historicism, between the concept of 'fallen man' and the generation of the unageing monuments of intellect and of art, instrumental affinities. It may be that these monuments, born of autistic vision, are counter-statements to a world felt, known to be 'fallen'. There is in eminent art and thought a manichaean rebellion. 'A truth,' taught Alain, the French *maître de pensée* (itself a phrase significantly untranslatable), 'is the refusal of a body.' There can be no didactic sophistry more un-American, no ideal more alien to the pragmatic immanence of 'the pursuit of happiness'.

The upshot is this. There is little evidence that civilization civilizes any but a small minority or that its deployment is effective outside the elusive domain of enhanced private sensibility. The relations of such enhancement to civic standards of behaviour, to political good sense, are, at best, tangential. There is, on the other hand, substantial evidence to suggest that the generation and full valuation of eminent art and thought will come to pass (preferentially, it seems) under conditions of individual *anomie*, of anarchic or even pathological unsociability and in contexts of political autocracy – be it oligarchic *ancien régime* or totalitarian in the modern cast.

[298]

'Censorship is the mother of metaphor,' notes Borges; 'we artists are olives,' says Joyce, 'squeeze us.' Tsarist and post-1917 Russia is the acid test. From Pushkin to Alexander Zinoviev, the central fact of Russian poetry, drama, fiction, literary theory, music has been that of official repression and Aesopian or clandestine response. The lineage of genius is utterly unbroken. Stalinism and the feline bureaucracies of blackmail after Stalin have witnessed, are witnessing at this very moment, a literary output which is truly fantastic in its formal virtuosity and compulsion of spirit. To cite Mandelstam, Akhmatova, Tsvetayeva, Pasternak, Brodsky is to refer, with almost careless selectivity, to an incomparable breadth and depth of poetic presence. This breadth and presence have been matched, perhaps even excelled, in the fiction of Pasternak, Bulgakov, Siniavsky, V. Iskander, Zinoviev, G. Vladimirov and literally a score of other masters much of whose writing is not yet available in English. To set against Nadezhda Mandelstam's memoires, against Solzhenitsyn's first novels, against the philosophic-Rabelaisian leviathans of Zinoviev, against Natalie Ginzbourg's autobiography, against *Zhivago* and Pasternak's translations even the most powerful of modern American narrative or personal statement, is to court a bewildering sense of disproportion. The specific gravities, the authorities and necessities of felt life, the boldness of stylistic experiment, the urgent humanity in Russian literature probably constitute what claim there is to redemption in the modern dark ages – and have done so since Tolstoy, since Dostoevsky. By such steady light, this month's 'great American novel' is merely embarrassing. The exemplary implications, moreover, seem to extend to eastern Europe as a whole. It is one of the current characteristics of Anglo-American literacy, even in alert circles, to have almost no knowledge of the lives of the mind and of the arts between East Berlin and Leningrad, between Kiev and Prague. The volume and standard of poetry, of parable, of philosophic speculation and artistic device are inspiring. It is not the 'creative writing centres', the 'poetry workshops', the 'humanities research institutes', the foundation-financed hives for deep thinkers amid the splendours of Colorado, the Pacific coast or the New England woods we must look to for what is most compelling and far-reaching in art and ideas. It is to the studios, cafés, seminars, *samizdat* magazines and publishing houses, chamber-music groups, itinerant theatres, of Kraków and of Budapest, of Prague and of Dresden. Here, I am soberly convinced, is a reservoir of talent, of unquestioning adherence to the risks and functions of art and original thought on which generations to come will feed.

If this is so, if the correlations between extreme creativity (literally, concretely, creativity *in extremis*) and political justice are, to a significant degree at least, negative, then the American choice makes abundant sense. The flowering of the humanities is not worth the circumstance of the inhuman. No play by Racine is worth a Bastille, no Mandelstam poem an hour of Stalinism. If one intuits, believes and comes to institutionalize this credo of social decency and democratic hope, it must follow that utmost thought and art will have to be imported from outside. The bacteria of personal anarchy, of tragic pessimism, of elective affinity with and against political violence or authoritarian control which western art and thought have carried with them from their inception, must be made sterile. As are the curare tips on the Amerindian arrow-heads in our museums of ethnography or natural science. The fundamental, if subconscious, strategy of American culture is that of an immaculate astrodome enveloping, making transparent to a mass audience, preserving from corruption and misuse, the cancerous and daemonic pressures of antique, of European, of Russian invention and tragic being ('destroyer of cities . . . anarchic Aphrodite' said Auden). Here lie the archives of Eden.

Which brings up a final point. The preference of democratic endeavour over authoritarian caprice, of an open society over one of creative hermeticism and censorship, of a general dignity of mass status over the perpetuation of an élite (often inhumane in its style and concerns), is, I repeat, a thoroughly justifiable choice. It very likely represents what meagre chances there are for social progress and a more bearable distribution of resources. He who makes this choice and lives accordingly deserves nothing but attentive respect. What is puerile hypocrisy and opportunism is the stance, the rhetoric, the professional practice of those – and they have been legion in American academe or the media – *who want it both ways*. Of those who profess to experience, to value, to transmit authentically the contagious mystery of great intellect and art while they are in fact dismembering it or packaging it to death. For the exigent truth is this: a genuine teacher, editor, critic, art historian, musical performer or musicologist, is one who has committed his existence to a consuming passion, who cultivates in himself, to the very limits of his secondary skills, those autistic absolutes of possession and of self-possession which produce an Archimedean theorem or a Rembrandt canvas. He is a man or woman gratefully, proudly sick with thought, hooked, past cure, on the drug of knowledge, of critical perception, of transference to the future. He knows that ninety-nine per cent of humanity in the developed West may aspire to only one vestige of immortality: an entry in the telephone book; but he knows also that there is one per cent, perhaps less, whose written word alters history, whose paintings change the light and the landscape, whose music takes immortal root in the ear of the mind, whose ability to put in the speech of mathematics coherent worlds wholly outside sensual reach, make up the dignity of the species. He himself is not this one per cent. He is, as Pushkin calls him, the 'necessary courier' or, as I have called him in this paper, a loving, a clairvoyant parasite. He is an obsessed servant of the text, of the musical score, of the metaphysical proof, of the painting. This obsession overrides the claims of social justice. It abides the hideous fact that hundreds of thousands could be fed on the price a museum pays for one Raphael or Picasso. It is an obsession which registers, in some crazy way, the possibility that the neutron bomb (destroyer of nameless peoples, preserver of libraries, museums, archives, bookstores) may be the final weapon of the intellect.

I have said 'obsession', 'contagion', even 'craziness', for such is the condition of the cleric. Of the master teacher. Of the virtuoso executant. Of the unappeased bibliographer. Of the translator literally devoured by his mastering original. By all means, let such a condition be ridiculed and resisted in the name of common sense, civics and political humanity. But it is not *we* (a category which includes *you* by virtue of the simple fact that you are reading this essay, that you possess the vocabulary, codes of reference, leisure and *interest* needed to read it) who can mask, water down or even deny our calling. It is for, through the great philosophic texts, musical compositions, works of art, poems, theorems that we conduct our ecstatic lives. To espouse – a justly sacramental verb – these objects while seeking to deny the conditions of person and of society from which they have come to us, from which they continue to come, *this* is treason and mendacious schizophrenia. As one Kierkegaard put it: Either/Or.

The choice is not a comfortable one. But perhaps the concept of choice is itself a fallacy. As I have implied throughout, the intellectual, the inebriate of thought is, like the artist or philosopher, though to a lesser degree, born and not made (*nascitur non fit*, as every schoolboy used to know). He has no choice except to be himself or to betray himself. If 'happiness' in the definitions central to the theory and practice of 'the American way of life' seems to him the greater good, if he does not suspect 'happiness' in almost any guise of being the despotism of the ordinary, he is in the wrong business. They order these matters better in the world of the despot. Artists, thinkers, writers receive the unwavering tribute of political scrutiny and repression. The KGB and the serious writer are in total accord when both know, when both *act on the knowledge* that a sonnet (Pasternak simply citing the first line of a Shakespeare sonnet in the venomous presence of Zhdanov), a novel, a scene from a play can be the power-house of human affairs, that there is nothing more charged with the detonators of dreams and action than the word, particularly the word known by heart. (It is striking and perfectly consequent that America, the final archive, should also be the land whose schooling has all but eradicated memorization. In the microfiche, the poem lies embalmed; recited inwardly, it is terribly alive.) The scholar in the Soviet Union understands precisely what the KGB censor is after when he seizes and minutely scans his article on Hegel. It is in such articles, in the debates they unleash, that lie the motor forces of social crisis. The abstract painter, the composer in the perennial twilight of the Soviet setting know that there is in serious art and music no such thing as inapplicable formality or technical neutrality. A technique, says Sartre, is already a metaphysic. From a Kandinsky, from a Bach canon can stream the subterranean impulses towards political and social metamorphosis. These impulses reach only the few (or at first), but in authoritarian societies, in societies where the word and the idea have *auctoritas*, meaning and action work from the top. To imprison a man because he quotes *Richard III* during the 1937 purges, to arrest him in Prague today because he is giving a seminar on Kant, is to gauge accurately the status of great literature and philosophy. It is to honour perversely, but to honour nevertheless, the obsession that is truth.

What text, what painting, what symphony could strike the edifice of American politics? What act of abstract thought really matters at all? Who *cares*?

Today, the question is this: which carries the greater threat to the conception of literature and intellectual argument of the first order – the apparatus of political oppression in Russia and in Latin America (currently the most brilliant ground for the novelist), the sclerosis in the meritocracy and 'classicism' of old Europe *or* a consensus of spiritual-social values in which the television showing of 'Holocaust' is interrupted every fourteen minutes by commercials, in which gas-oven sequences are interspersed and financed by ads for pantihose and deodorants?

The question is overwrought and unappetizing. It contains oversimplification, of course. But it is a question which those of us who are by infirmity and summons accomplices to the life of the mind must ask ourselves. It is, I suspect, a question which that antique ironist, history, will force us to answer. In Archimedes' garden, barbarism and the theorem were interwoven. That garden may have been a 'counter-Eden'; but it happens to be the one in which you and I must continue our labour. My hunch is that it lies in Syracuse still – Sicily, that is, rather than New York State.

Our Homeland, the Text

Successive, often polemic interpretations, citations in a context of sacred doctrine or of political-historical opportunity, construe, around the archaic, revealed words in the Hebrew canon, a resonant field. An aura of vital paraphrase and definition extends around the word-core; or of dubious definition and misunderstanding, no less dynamic (misunderstanding can yield the more urgent reading, the more compelling attention). Meaning vibrates as does a crystal, out of whose hidden clarity pulsate fragmentation and interference.

To the word *mikra* scholars of biblical and Talmudic Hebrew attach a network of meanings. They question its literal roots – *kof, resh, alef* and the consonantal *mi*. The definitions put forward are polysemic, they delineate a semantic field (again, literally, *à la lettre*). The *mikra* may, at the outset, have been the place of summoning, of vocation and con-vocation. To experience the Torah and Talmud as *mikra*, to apprehend these texts in cognitive and emotional plenitude, is to hear and accept a summons. It is to gather oneself and the (inseparable) community in a place of calling. This summons to responsible response, to answerability in the most rigorous intellectual and ethical sense, is simultaneously private and public, individual and collective. The concepts and association that attach to *mikra* make of the reading of the canon and its commentaries the literal-spiritual locus of self-recognition and of communal identification for the Jew.

It follows, proclaim a number of rabbinic masters, that the supreme commandment to Judaism, supreme precisely in that it comprises and animates all others, is given in Joshua 1:8: 'The book of the law shall not depart out of thy mouth; but thou shalt meditate therein day and night.' Observe the implicit prohibition or critique of sleep. *Hypnos* is a Greek god, and enemy to reading.

In post-exilic Judaism, but perhaps earlier, active reading, answerability to the text on both the meditative-interpretative and the behavioural levels, is the central motion of personal and national homecoming. The Torah is met at the place of summons and in the time of calling (which is night and day). The dwelling assigned, ascribed to Israel is the House of the Book. Heine's phrase is exactly right: *das aufgeschriebene Vaterland*. The 'land of his fathers', the *patrimoine*, is the script. In its doomed immanence, in its attempt to immobilize the text in a substantive, architectural space, the Davidic and Solomonic Temple may have been an erratum, a misreading of the transcendent mobility of the text.

At the same time, doubtless, the centrality of the book does coincide with and enact the condition of exile. There are radical senses in which even the Torah is a place of privileged banishment from the tautological immediacy of Adamic speech, of God's direct, unwritten address to man. Reading, textual exegesis, are an exile from action, from the existential innocence of praxis, even where the text is aiming at practical and political consequence. The reader is one who (day and night) is absent from action. The 'textuality' of the Jewish condition, from the destruction of the Temple to the foundation of the modern state of Israel, can be seen, has been seen by Zionism, as one of tragic impotence. The text was the instrument of exilic survival; that survival came within a breath of annihilation. To endure at all, the 'people of the Book' had, once again, to be a nation.

The tensions, the dialectical relations between an unhoused at-homeness in the text, between the dwelling-place of the script on the one hand (wherever in the world a Jew reads and meditates Torah *is* the true Israel), and the territorial mystery of the native ground, of the promised strip of land on the other, divide Jewish consciousness.

Hegel's analysis is ominous. By leaving his native land of Ur, Abraham deliberately 'breaks the ties of love'. He breaks the natural bonds which unite a human person to his ancestors and their places of burial (the 'Antigone' theme obsesses Hegel); he abandons his neighbours and culture. Such bonds, says Hegel, transcend the human and the secular sphere. They constitute man's legitimate presence in nature, in the organic totality of the actual world.

Specifically, argues Hegel, Abraham repudiates the works and days of his childhood and youth. No less than for Rousseau and the romantics, such repudiation seemed to Hegel the most corrosive of alienations, of estrangements both from the rest of mankind and the harmonious integration of the self. (Hegel's polemic calls to mind the severance from childhood, the pre-maturity in the bent shoulders and somnambular mien of the very young Yeshiva students, old readers in the muffled bones of children.)

Abraham, to Hegel, is a wanderer on the earth, a passer-by severed from the familial, communal and organic context of love and of trust. He is a shepherd of the winds, traversing each land with indifferent lightness of foot. He is incapable of love in the unreflexive, instinctual (Greek) sense. Seeking only God and a singular, almost autistic, intimacy with God, Hegel's Abraham is radically uninterested in or even hostile to other men, to those outside the covenant of his search. Abraham objectifies, masters and uses physical nature; contrary to the Hellenic, the Hebraic perceives in the natural and pragmatic order no animate mystery. Thus the Judaic relations between the finite and the infinite, the natural and the supernatural differ from those which inspire Greek religion and its creative at-homeness in the variousness and beauty of the real world. In its extreme commitment to abstraction, to word and text, Hebraism comes to scorn the natural sphere. As Hegel's dialectic would have it, Abraham and his seed are enmeshed in a tragic contradiction. More than any other people, Jews claim, indeed they seem to achieve, nearness to the concept of God. They do so at the suicidal cost of renunciation, of self-ostracism from the earth and its family of nations. But the God to whom the Jew would stand so near is, by virtue of the implacable abstraction, of the unfathomable elevation attributed to Him, furthest from man.

Mosaic Law, the Jewish addiction to minutiae of archaic observance, the atrophy of the Jewish tradition through legalism and literalism of reiteration and ritual represent, for Hegel, a logical but also desperate endeavour to keep the world at bay and to remain in God's neighbourhood. The descendant of rootless Abraham has no other place to go. For even the land promised him was not his. He could seize upon it only by cunning and conquest. Driven out of this land by subsequent conquerors, the Jew is, strictly speaking, merely restored to his nativity of dispersal, to his chosen foreignness. According to Hegel, this 'foreignness' becomes ontological. The sensibility of the Jew is, *par excellence*, the medium of the bitter struggle between life and thought, between spontaneous immediacy and analytic reflection, between man's unison with his body and environment and man's estrangement from them. (Lévi-Strauss's tragic anthropology, itself a chapter in the critiques of the messianic by emancipated Judaism, is, here, profoundly Hegelian.) To Hegel, 'the people of the Book' are as a cancer – deep-seated, vital, enigmatically regenerative. Their Book is not that of life. Their arts and energies of reading, like analytic thought at its most intense, laser-sharp pitch, consume and deconstruct the living object of their questioning.

What is to Hegel an awesome pathology, a tragic, arrested stage in the advance of human consciousness towards a liberated home-coming from alienation, is, to others, the open secret of the Jewish genius and of its survival. The text is home; each commentary a return. When he reads, when, by virtue of commentary, he makes of his reading a dialogue and life-giving echo, the Jew is, to purloin Heidegger's image, 'the shepherd of being'. The seeming nomad in truth carries the world within him, as does language itself, as does Leibniz's monad (the play on, the illicit congruence between the two words are, one senses, unsettling to Hegel, and suggestive).

But whether they are seen as positive or negative, the 'textual' fabric, the interpretative practices in Judaism are ontologically and historically at the heart of Jewish identity.

This is obviously so in a formal sense. The Torah is the pivot of the weave and cross-weave of reference, elucidation, hermeneutic debate which organize, which inform organically, the daily and the historical life of the community. The community can be defined as a concentric tradition of reading. The Gemara, the commentary on the Mishna, the collection of oral laws and prescriptions which make up the Talmud, the Midrash, which is that part of the commentary pertaining particularly to the interpretation of the scriptural canon, express and activate the continuum of Jewish being. The incessant readings of the primary texts, the exegetic, disputatious, elaborative readings of these readings (the process is formally and pragmatically endless), define temporality. They manifest the presence of the determinant past; they seek to elicit present application; they aim at the futurities always latent in the original act of revelation. Thus neither Israel's physical scattering, nor the passage of millennia, can abrogate the authority (the *auctoritas* of authorship) or the pressure of meaning in the holy books, so long as these are read and surrounded by a constancy of secondary, satellite texts. By virtue of metaphoric, allegoric, esoteric explication and challenge, these secondary texts rescue the canon from the ebbing motion of the past tense, from that which would draw live meaning into inert or merely liturgical monumentality. Via magisterial commentary, the given passage will, in places and times as yet unknown, yield existential applications and illuminations of spirit yet unperceived.

The Adamic circumstance is one of linguistic tautology and of a lasting present. Things were as Adam named and said them to be. Word and world were one. Where there is perfect contentment, there is no summons to remembrance. The present tense of the verb is also that of the perfect tomorrow. It was the Fall of Man that added to human speech its ambiguities, its necessary secrecies, its power (the counter-factuals, the 'if' constructions) to dissent speculatively from the opaque coercions of reality. After the Fall, memories and dreams, which are so often messianic recollections of futurity, become the storehouse of experience and of hope. Hence the need to reread, to recall (revocation) those texts in which the mystery of a beginning, in which the vestiges of a lost self-evidence – God's 'I am that I am' – are current.

Ideally, such recall should be oral. In Hebraic sensibility, no less than in that of Plato, a distrust of the written word, a critical regret at the passing of orality, are evident. The written is always a shadow after the fact, a postscript, in the material sense of the term. Its decay from the primary moment of meaning is exemplified, obscurely, in the destruction of the Tables of the Law on Sinai, in the making of a second set or facsimile. The letters of fire, of that fire which *spoke* in the Burning Bush, have been extinguished in the graven silence of the stone. On the other hand, assuredly, writing has been the indestructible guarantor, the 'underwriter', of the identity of the Jew: across the frontiers of his harrying, across the centuries, across the languages of which he has been a forced borrower and frequent master. Like a snail, his antennae towards menace, the Jew has carried the house of the text on his back. What other domicile has been allowed him?

But the destiny and history of Judaism are 'bookish' in a far deeper sense; and in one that does virtually set them apart.

In the relation to God which defines the Jew, the concepts of contract and of covenant are not metaphoric. A narrative charter, a *magna carta* and document of instauration in narrative form, setting out reciprocal rights and obligations as between God and man, is explicit in Genesis and in Exodus. The foundation of elect identity is textual. In Hobbes and Rousseau, the invocation of an original contract between individuals founding civic society or between the sovereign and those who delegate their powers to him, is a methodological fiction. In Judaism, it is a literal instrument, a spoken-written deed of trust, subject not only to constant personal and communal ratification, but to close probing. Even after the promise to Noah, even after the transcendent redaction at Sinai, and doubly so after each visitation of disaster on the Jewish people, the God-pact, the covenant and its innumerable legal-ritual codicils, are the focus of re-examination. The latter is moral, legalistic and textual. There has been too much agony in the fine print.

The millennial dialogue with God, of which the Book of Job is only the most pointed protocol, is that of a 'bookkeeper'. This image can be pressed closely. God 'keeps book' on His people, who are, everlastingly, the debtors to His initial advance – which is, past all repayment, creation, which is survival after the Flood, the covenant at Sinai and the deed of title to the promised land. At all times, for such is the compounding of God's interest, His partner and client Israel is in arrears, even in default. Where it is allowed, a moratorium is an act of grace. The cancellation of the debt, the revaluation of all currency, as proclaimed in Christ, is, to the Jew, an empty fantasy.

Concomitantly, there is a sense in which the Jew 'keeps book' on God. Do the accounts, and note the semantic overlap and interference as between 'account' and 'narration', ever balance? Is there an intelligible balance-sheet to be drawn between merit and recompense (Job's attempt to inspect and certify the book of life), between suffering and happiness? Has God met the obligations He contracted with man, more precisely, with those first advocates and negotiators of being, the Jews? Anti-Semitism has always denounced in Judaism and its relations to God, *vide* Shylock and his bond, a contractual, litigious economy, an inheritance of sharp practices and barter. Is there not, in the moralistic-didactic epilogue to the *mysterium tremendum* of Job, a twofold restitution, payment for damages incurred?

But the 'bookkeeper' is also, and inextricably, a 'keeper of the Book', an archivist of the revealed. The accountant is, by virtue of this custody, accountable to God as is no other tribe. In Ezekiel 3 this 'keeping of books', this clerkship to eternity, takes on a grotesque physical vehemence. God's emissary holds out a scroll to His servant, 'and it was written all over on both sides'. Ezekiel is bidden 'eat this scroll'. 'Swallow this scroll.' Ezekiel does so 'and it tasted as sweet as honey' – we speak still of 'honeyed words', of the links between language and that haunting savour which Middle Eastern and Attic mythology associate both with the sun and the gardens of the dead.

It is the contractual, promissory foundation and core of Judaism which have entailed the singularity (the pathology *contra naturam*?) of survival. The 'books have been kept' and kept up to date. The 'keepers' make new entries at every moment in their individual and historical existence. But consider the determinants of terror in the script. Consider the overwhelmingly manifest yet metaphysically and rationally scandalous adherence of Jewish experience to the *pre*-script set down for it in the books which are its card of identity, in the books it has so proudly and contentiously kept. Rigorously viewed, the fate of Judaism is a postscript to the penalty clauses in

God's contract (that fine print, again). It is a sequence of demonstrative footnotes, of marginalia, to the text of God's (non-) reply to Job and to the texts of the Prophets. Everything is there, spelt out from the start. The rest has been unbearable fulfilment. No other nation, no other culture on this earth has been so *pre*scribed. No other men have had to bear like witness to the cognate meanings of *prescription* and of *proscription*, which signify denunciation, ostracism and a written designation for death.

What is there to add to Amos, which scholars take to be the oldest of prophetic books, dating it *c.* 750 BC when the Northern Kingdom of Israel was heading for ruin? God's promise is unequivocal:

> I will send a fire upon Judah, and it shall devour the palace of Jerusalem.

> As the shepherd takes out of the mouth of the lion two legs or a piece of an ear, so shall the children of Israel be taken out . . .

> The city that went out by a thousand shall have a remnant of a hundred, of that which went out by a hundred, ten shall remain . . .

The long terror of the Diaspora is precisely promised: the songs of worship 'shall be howling', Israel 'shall wander from sea to sea, and from the north even to the east' seeking sanctuary in vain. Because God's words are of fire, those who hear and who read them are to be made ash.

The oracular is open-ended. Its duplicities and triplicities – *three* roads meet at that crossing near Delphi – are those of human freedom. Prophecies are the contrary of oracles: they answer before they are asked. How has it been possible for the Jewish people to endure without going more or less collectively mad, without yielding to more or less willed self-destruction (the impulse to both do run deep in Judaic sensibility) knowing, reading and re-reading the binding foresight of its Prophets? Where did Judaism find the resolve, the life-tenacity, when an apocalyptic writ had been served on it by its own seers of darkness and when the predictions set out in this writ have been realized, to the hideous letter, time and time and time again? This strikes me as *the* 'Jewish question'.

Part of the answer lies, no doubt, in the antinomian, pendular motion of the Mosaic and prophetic prescripts themselves. Catastrophe is never unconditional. In God's sentence on Israel there are redeeming clauses. The just, be they but a handful, may be saved; the repentant restored. The dialectic of possible rehabilitation springs from the heart of terror. It is eloquent at the close of Amos: the captive, wind-scattered remnant of Israel shall be brought back to the promised land, 'and they shall rebuild the waste cities, and inhabit them. They shall plant vineyards and drink the wine thereof. They shall make gardens and eat of their fruit.' The entire Zionist dream and purpose, the manner of miracle in which these have been realized, are 'programmed' in this fourteenth verse of this ninth chapter of Amos's script.* Throughout the Torah, throughout the prophetic books which dictate the future of Israel, the note of compensation, of the messianic horizon, is set against that of interminable suffering.

But this twofold truth in Holy Writ only complicates the phenomenological and the psychological question. The deterministic imperative of the promise of selective or ultimate rescue is as binding, as coercive a blueprint, as are the previsions of persecution, dispersal and martyrdom. Amos's clairvoyance as to Zionism is as prescriptive as is his foresight of Jewish agony. No other community in the evolution and social history of man has, from its outset, read, reread without cease, learnt by heart or by rote, and expounded without end the texts which spell out its whole destiny. These texts, moreover, are felt to be of transcendent authorship and authority, infallible in their *pre*-diction, as oracles in the pagan world, notoriously, are not. The script, therefore, is a contract with the inevitable. God has, in the dual sense of utterance and of binding affirmation, 'given His word', His *Logos* and His bond, to Israel. It cannot be broken or refuted.

Again one asks: what abstentions or strengths of spirit, what genius for servitude and what pride, are required of a people called

---

*If this *is* Amos's script, for it is precisely this promissory passage which many scholars regard as a much later insertion.

upon to act out a primal pre-script, to, as it were, take dictation of itself? Light blinds us when it is too clear. Yet the Jew has had to inhabit the literal text of his foreseen being. Canetti has written a play which turns on the conceit of a society in which every man knows, in advance and ineluctably, the date of his own death. The parable on Judaism is unmistakable. It is because he lives, enacts privately and historically, a written writ, a promissory note served on him when God sought out Abraham and Moses, it is because the 'Book of Life' is, in Judaism, literally textual, that the Jew dwells apart. (It was just this suffocating *déjà vu*, this servile immunity from the unknown in the Jewish condition, which both fascinated and repelled Hegel).

Though the psychological mechanism remains obscure, the fact is a commonplace: prophecies are, to a degree, self-fulfilling. The stronger the prophecy, the more often it is proclaimed, the greater its inertial thrust towards realization. In his dread history, the Jew would seem to have been intent to certify the accuracy of the road mapped for him by the Prophets. The script has been 'acted', first across that valley of the shadow and of the night of dispersal and massacre which climaxed in the 'whirlwind' of the 1940s, in the Shoah (the noble Greek word, 'holocaust', signifying a solemn burnt offering, has no legitimate place in this matter); more recently in the foretold, contractually underwritten return to Israel.

Does this mean that the utopian prevision of homecoming and of peace which, in the settlement with Abraham and in the coda to the prophetic books, follows on millennial suffering, will also be realized? Not *now*, not necessarily in secular time. The print is too fine for that. The messianic is an escape-clause for both parties. It is on the advent of the messianic order that the prevision of blessedness hinges. Till then, even the in-gathering at Zion is, in the exact Latin etymological sense, *pro-visional*, it is a prevision the nature and temporality of whose certain accomplishment remains uncertain.

But the crux is this: neither the Jewish endurance, indeed traditional acceptance of a continuum of ostracism and persecution across history, nor the rationally, geopolitically absurd, return of a modern ethnic group to a largely barren strip of earth in the Middle East, to a strip of earth long occupied by others and whose frontiers could only be those of hatred, can be understood outside the metaphysics and psychology of the pre-scribed. The canonic texts had to be shown to be true.

The price for this 'keeping of the books' (for this 'going by the book') has been, literally, monstrous. The notion that the night-vision of the Jew has, somehow, in some secret measure, brought on itself the torments foreseen, is irrational, but haunting none the less.

It is compelling in our reading of Kafka. The practices of literary criticism and study are more or less helpless before *The Trial* and *The Castle* with their minutely faithful prevision of the clerical inhumanities of life in our time. Explication, reference to stylistic means or literary context, merely trivialize Kafka's blueprint of the concentration-camp world, of the coming obscenities of intimacy between torturer and victim, as these are spelt out, in October 1914, in 'In the Penal Colony'. Or consider Kafka's use of the word 'vermin' in 'The Metamorphosis' of 1912 in precisely the sense and connotations that would be given to it by the Nazis a generation later. In Kafka's writings there is a revealed literalism *avant la lettre* which renders almost wholly worthless the spate of commentaries which they have provoked. Even the masterly exchange on Kafka's meaning in the Walter Benjamin-Gershom Scholem letters, which may, together with Mandelstam's essay on reading Dante, be the best that the arts of modern literary criticism have to show, avoid the urgent conundrum of the prophetic. As no other speaker or scribe after the Prophets, Kafka *knew*. In him, as in them, imagination was second sight and invention a pedantic notation of clairvoyance. Kafka's misery as one coerced into writing, his almost hysterical diffidence before mundane authorship, are the facsimile, perhaps consciously arrived at, of the attempts of the Prophets to evade the intolerable burden of their seeing, to shake off the commandment of utterance. Jeremiah's 'I do not know how to speak', Jonah's flight from foretelling, have their literal parallel in Kafka's 'impossibility of writing, impossibility of not writing'. Having the unspeakable future so lit to his sight, Kafka was, not only in his writings but also in his personal existence, knowingly posthumous to himself. It is some notation of this scarcely conceivable condition which, I suspect, informs the profoundest allegory produced by western man after Scripture, that of the parable 'In Front of the Law' composed in November or December 1914.

In Kafka's credo of reading, the Jewish experience of the imperative terror of the text is manifest:

If the book we are reading does not wake us, as with a fist hammering on the skull, why then do we read it? So that it shall make us happy? Good God, we would also be happy if we had no books, and such books as make us happy we could, if need be, write ourselves. But what we must have are those books which come upon us like ill fortune, and distress us deeply, like the death of one we love better than ourselves, like suicide.

How much could be said (inadequately) of that mesmeric opposition between 'one we love better than ourselves' and 'suicide', about Kafka's implicit finding that suicide is always the killing of the 'other', of the one 'loved better than ourselves' within us. What is pellucid in this famous dictum is the paradoxical need, the self-testing to destruction, in the Jewish vision and experience of the book.

The indispensable books, those whose coming upon us is more powerful even than the death of the beloved, are the syllabus of the Judaic. What they have in common, what relates the rare secular examples to the canonic, is, indeed, their status as a *mikra*, a summons and subpoena to mankind. They call and call upon us. The fist hammering on our skull forces us to keep our eyes open.

> Nothing can erase this night
> but there's still light with you.
> At Jerusalem's gate
> a black sun has risen.
>
> The yellow one frightens me more.
> Lullaby, lullaby, Israelites
> have buried my mother
> in the bright temple.

Somewhere outside grace,
with no priests to lead them,
Israelites have sung the requiem over her
in the bright temple.

The voices of Israelites
rang out over my mother.
I woke in the cradle, dazzled
by the black sun.

This poem by Mandelstam is entitled 'Black Sun'. Lacking Russian
– the translation is by Clarence Brown and W. S. Merwin – I can
say very little about it, about the sources of its spell. Moreover,
there may be in these four quatrains esoteric echoes of Russian
apocalyptic and eschatological symbolism accessible only to the
informed. This happens to be the case, quite often, in both the great
voices of Russian post-Judaism (the baptized but remembering
Jew), Mandelstam and Pasternak. Yet the strength and universality
of the poem's summons are such that we must listen as best we
can.

Certain motifs declare themselves. In Russian poetry and fiction,
in the incomparable articulation of the 'strangeness' of the Russian
political and psychological tradition by Pushkin and Dostoevsky,
the 'white nights', particularly in St Petersburg, are emblematic. The
'black sun' of Mandelstam's lyric, with its precedent in Baudelaire
and Nerval, reverses the febrile white nights. The black sunrise
answers to the white nightfall. But more ominous to the poet than
either is the light of common day – 'The yellow one frightens me
more.' In Paul Celan's poetry on the destruction of European Jewry,
a poetry which, by incessant echo and allusion, often incorporates
that of Osip Mandelstam, the 'yellow sun' will have become
(remaining, in actual reference, the same) the yellow star of the
condemned.

As does so much of elegiac and philosophic poetry after Proverbs
and Ecclesiastes – it is the latter text which seems subtly active in
Mandelstam's lines – there is in the 'Black Sun' an interplay of the
cradle and the grave. Lullaby interweaves with requiem. The birth

of the child is always, in a banal sense, the end of maternity. On the other hand, a mother's death is a son's rebirth, but a rebirth into adult aloneness, into the most definite of exiles from shared identity and remembrance. From this psychic and somatic exile, there can be no return.

Exile would seem to be at the hammering heart of Mandelstam's poem. Israelites bury the speaker's mother 'in the bright temple', a ritual absurdity or scandal. They do so 'Somewhere outside grace, / with no priests to lead them'. The allusion to burial in unconsecrated ground, a pagan or Christian rather than a Jewish motif, is evident. But, in a larger sense, the statement is one of ostracism. No *kaddish*, but a requiem. In the Diaspora, a Jew is made homeless even in death. The child is woken by the exiled voices of Israel, woken to apocalyptic terror. The sun which dazzles him is a black sun, and it rises 'At Jerusalem's gate'. We can read this image in at least two ways. That gate is shut to the outcast and/or a blackness at noon shall enter through it into the city.

Mandelstam's poem is dated 1916. Russian Jewry had known the pogroms of the fairly recent past, and the so-called civilized world was at war. But neither the Bolshevik-Stalinist nightmare nor the Whirlwind out of Hitler were in any way visible. Yet Mandelstam wakes, and wakes his reader, to the clear vision of the night-dawn ahead. He already *knows* – a knowledge to be fulfilled in his own appalling suffering and death.

As in Kafka, so there is here an inextricable intimacy between the imagined and the foreseen. Not only Amos, but numerous rabbinic masters, have conjectured that every Jew, when he is wholly present to God's word, to the living summons of the Torah, is in a condition of prophecy and revision. He is, at some level, made a party to the fact that God remembers the future.

Again the question nags. Where prophecy is so penetratively acute, does it not prepare for, indeed provoke, fulfilment? Could there be some (incomprehensible) guilt in annunciation? (In the Brussels museum hangs an anonymous 'primitive' depicting the Annunciation; behind Mary's bowed, overwhelmed head, hangs a small painting of the Crucifixion.) In Judaism, has the text come to lord it over life? Does the fact follow humbly, but also murderously, after the commanding word? At its greatest, Jewish secular writing when, at last, it springs from the liturgical, exegetical textuality and monopoly of the ghetto, carries with it, from Heine to Celan, an enforced clairvoyance and guilt of accomplishment.

The bookkeeper is not only the custodian and, in his racked bone and flesh, the certifier of prophecy. He is a cleric. The mystery and the practices of clerisy are fundamental to Judaism. No other tradition or culture has ascribed a comparable aura to the conservation and transcription of texts. In no other has there been an equivalent mystique of the philological. This is true of orthodox praxis, in which a single erratum, the wrong transcription of a single letter, entails the permanent removal of the relevant scroll or page from the holy books. It is true, to the same pitch of literalist intensity, in the whole theory and techniques of the kabbala, in the kabbalist's exhaustive scrutiny of the single Hebrew letter in whose graphic form and denomination manifold energies of meaning are incised.

The quarrel with Hellenism and with Christian gnosis is stark. In Judaism, the letter is the life of the spirit, indeed to the kabbalist, it *is* the spirit. Hence the clerical ideals, the clerical code of scribal observance and conveyance in the exilic history of the Jews. Hence the clerisy of the rabbinic caste in the ghetto and *Stättle*. To say of this ecstatic textuality and clerkship – both are totally instrumental in Kafka's profession and in Kafka's calling – that they were a surrogate for the political, social acts barred to the Jews, to say of the 'scribal' nature of Jewish survivance that it was an inhibiting substitute for the production of secular intellect and art, is a facile cliché. The point is that the sometimes hallucinatory techniques and disciplines of attention to the text, the mystique of fidelity to the written word, the reverence bestowed on its expositors and transmitters, concentrated within Judaic sensibility unique strengths and purities of disinterested purpose.

It is these which have made so many Jewish men and, more recently, women most native to modern intelligence. It is these that have generated the provocative pre-eminence of the Jew in modernity, be it humanistic or scientific. The 'bookish' genius of Marx and of Freud, of Wittgenstein and of Lévi-Strauss, is a secular deployment of the long schooling in abstract, speculative commentary and clerkship in the exegetic legacy (while being at the same time a psychological-sociological revolt against it). The Jewish presence, often overwhelming, in modern mathematics, physics, economic and social theory, is direct heir to that abstinence from the approximate, from the mundane, which constitutes the ethos of the cleric.

Under Roman persecution, Akiva made of his refuge a 'place' or 'house of the book'. A secularized but closely derived system of values was to make of Central European Jewry and its American afterglow the intellectual-spiritual heartland of modernity. Prague, Budapest, Vienna, Leningrad, Frankfurt and New York have been the Jewish capitals of our age, but also the capitals *tout court*. In them, the clerks, the addicts of the word and of the theorem, the exact dreamers after Einstein, have led, danced the life of the mind; for in that motion of the dance before the ark in which the text of the Law is housed, lies at the ancient core of Jewish consciousness.

A kabbalistic and Hasidic intimation has it that evil seeped into our world through the hair-line crack of a single erroneous letter, that man's suffering, and that of the Jew especially, came of the false transcription of a single letter or word when God dictated the Torah to his elect scribe. This grim fantastication is utterly expressive of a scholar's code. It points to the definition of a Jew as one who always has a pencil or pen in hand when he reads, of one who will in the death-camps (and this came to pass) correct a printing error, emend a doubtful text, on his way to extinction. But the morality and metaphysics of the clerk are not only, nor indeed primarily, those of pedantic, mandarin abstraction. We need only look to Spinoza to know otherwise. What is at stake is *a politics of truth*. Such politics are, in essence, Socratic – and Socrates is the one gentile of whom a thinking Jew has the never-ending obligation to be jealous.

The Socratic moment for modern Jewry is the Dreyfus Affair. It compelled on the Jew the question of whether he could, even in an emancipated and assimilationist garb, ever obtain a secure citizenship in the city of the gentile, which is the post-Napoleonic nation-state. With cruel edge, the Dreyfus Affair confronted ideals of justice and of personal conscience with the claims of the nation-state to transcendent loyalty. The case threw the sharpest possible light on the inherently anarchic genius of abstract thought and the search for absolute truth. Imperatives of reason and of conscience clashed, metaphysically and ethically, with those conventions of expediency, or moral approximation and irresolution without which the fabric of society cannot hang together. As does the trial of Socrates, so the Dreyfus Affair passes judgement on the *polis*. The resulting schism, the contested victory of individual justice over patriotism and reasons of state, lamed not only France – the Vichy regime, the rhetoric and tactics of civil war perennial to French politics are a direct legacy – but the very concept of nationalism. *Fiat iustitia, pereat mundus.*

Both the occasion and the logic of the conflict came out of Judaism. They came from the ambiguous entry into the territorial, fundamentally Roman politics of the modern nation of a people at home in exile, of a pilgrim tribe housed not in place but in time, not rooted but millennially equipped with legs. Whether he knew it or not, whether he wished it or not – indeed, he desperately hoped otherwise and did much to deceive himself – the Jew, when given nationality by his adopted gentile hosts, remained in transit. Judaism defines itself as a visa to the messianic 'other land'.

For the cleric, for the ideal of clerisy in Jewishness, this house of the future tense need not be Israel. Or rather, it is an 'Israel' of truth-seeking. Each seeking out of a moral, philosophic, positive verity, each text rightly established and expounded, is an *aliyah*, a homecoming of Judaism to itself and to its keeping of the books. The impositions and glory of this trusteeship, as they modulate from the religious to the secular domain, are formulated in Julien Benda's *The Treason of the Clerics*, an inescapably Jewish book which came of the Dreyfus case.

Heir to Spinoza, Benda defines and himself instances the fanaticism of disinterested vision, the ecstatic exactions and exactitudes, which underlie major thought and scholarship. On the

Sabbath, the benedictions spoken in the synagogue extend explicitly to the scholar. There is, or ought to be sadness in a Jewish household if there is no scholar or future scholar among its children. Benda goes further. He takes for his own a dictate by a now forgotten savant of the nineteenth century:

Whoever, for whatever motives – patriotic, political, religious and even moral – allows himself even the slightest manipulation or adjustment of the truth, must be stricken from the roll of scholars.

The tranquil enormity of this commandment must be felt. Observe the ascending order in which the condemned apologias are listed. Patriotism, the love and defence of the homeland – of the Third Republic under threat of German invasion – is the lowest non-excuse. Next come political loyalty, efficiency, those practicalities of civic compromise and herd-instinct which a Socrates and a Spinoza refuse. Let the city and the nation perish before the cleric commits 'even the slightest' mendacity. They are not the native ground of his being, which is truth. Where it cannot afford truth a natural habitation, even religion must yield. 'Morality' is the crown of motives. Yet it too is set aside. The injunction to do so is a fearful edict (Kierkegaard will repudiate it utterly). Where Kant postulated a transcendent coincidence between the ethical and the cognitive, Benda knew that there may be cases of irreconcilable conflict between ethics and the pursuit of knowledge – in nuclear physics, in genetics, in the psychologist's and the writer's findings in man. The cleric betrays his calling, he is absent from the *mikra*, if he flinches from, if he muffles or deflects the pure hunt for truth – Plato records the hunter's halloo when a truth is cornered – even if this hunt should lead to his own destruction or that of his community.

It is here that the creed of Spinoza and of Kafka meets with the conduct of Socrates. A true thinker, a truth-thinker, a scholar, must know that no nation, no body politic, no creed, no moral ideal and necessity, be it that of human survival, is worth a falsehood, a willed self-deception or the manipulation of a text. This knowledge and observance *are* his homeland. It is the false reading, the erratum that make him homeless.

A Jew enters on manhood, he is admitted to the history of Judaism, on the day on which he is, for the first time, called, literally, to the text, on the day on which he is asked and allowed to read correctly a passage from the Torah. This summons entails, to a greater or lesser degree of intensity, to a greater or lesser degree of self-awareness, a commitment to the clerisy of truth, of truth-seeking. The prophetic and the speculative addiction to insight are the nationhood of Judaism. In the humblest of clerks as in the greatest of thinkers, the acceptance of this calling, of this 'calling up' in the full sense of a perilous enlistment and promotion, must have practical (impractical) consequences.

How can a thinking man, a native of the word, be anything but the most wary and provisional of patriots? The nation-state is founded on myths of instauration and of militant glory. It perpetuates itself by lies and half-truths (machine guns and sub-machine guns). In his model of the social contract, Rousseau declared unequivocally that there is a contradiction between humanity and citizenship: 'Forcé de combattre la nature ou les institutions sociales, il faut opter entre faire un homme ou un citoyen; car on ne peut pas faire à la fois l'un et l'autre.' The consequence is stark: 'a patriot is hard on strangers, for they are but men'.

The 'patriotism' of the truth-seeker is antithetical to Rousseau's civic option. The sole citizenship of the cleric is that of a critical humanism. He knows not only that nationalism is a sort of madness, a virulent infection edging the species towards mutual massacre. He knows that it signifies an abstention from free and clear thought and from the disinterested pursuit of justice. The man or woman at home in the text is, by definition, a conscientious objector: to the vulgar mystique of the flag and the anthem, to the sleep of reason which proclaims 'my country, right or wrong', to the pathos and eloquence of collective mendacities on which the nation-state – be it a mass-consumer mercantile technocracy or a totalitarian oligarchy – builds its power and aggressions. The locus of truth is always extraterritorial; its diffusion is made clandestine by the barbed wire and watch-towers of national dogma.

The quarrel is as ancient as Israel. It is that between priest and prophet, between the claims of nationhood and those of universality. It speaks to us irreconcilably out of Amos and Jeremiah. The mortal clash between politics and verity, between an immanent homeland and the space of the transcendent, is spelt out in Jeremiah 36–9. King Jahoiakim seizes the scroll dictated by God's clerk and bookkeeper. He cuts out the offending columns and casts the entire text into the consuming flame (governments, political censors, patriotic vigilantes burn books). God instructs the prophet: 'Take thee again another scroll and write on it all the words that were written on the first.' The truth will out. Somewhere there is a pencil-stub, a mimeograph machine, a hand-press which the king's men have overlooked. 'So Jeremiah abode in the court of the prison till the day that Jerusalem was taken; and he was *there* when Jerusalem was taken.' The formulaic specification is magnificent in meaning. The royal city, the nation are laid waste; the text and its transmitter endure, *there* and *now*. The Temple may be destroyed; the texts which it housed sing in the winds that scatter them.

Pauline universalism was an inspired amalgam of the transcendent, immaterial textuality of the Prophets in Judaism and of Hellenic syncretism. It proved to be the most serious challenge ever to Jewish survival, precisely in so far as it sprang from within the utopian elements in the Jewish tradition (and *utopia* means 'nowhere'). Paul of Tarsus set prophecy against priesthood, ecumenism against territoriality. It is altogether possible that Judaism would have lost its identity, would have diffused itself in Christianity, if the latter had been true to its Judaic catholicity. Instead, Christendom became, itself, a political-territorial structure, prepared, on all practical counts, to serve, to hallow, the genesis and militancy of secular states. Ideological imperialism is inseparable from the Constantine adoption of Christianity; modern nationalism bears the stamp of the Lutheran programme. Truth was, again, made homeless; or, more exactly, it was left in the (un)safe-keeping of the pariah and the exile.

During the period, roughly, from AD 70 to AD 1948.

In the founding secular manifesto of Zionism, Herzl's *Judenstaat*, the language and the vision are proudly mimetic of Bismarckian nationalism. Israel is a nation-state to the utmost degree. It lives armed to the teeth. It has been compelled to make other men homeless, servile, disinherited, in order to survive from day to day (it was, during two millennia, the dignity of the Jew that he was *too weak* to make any other human being as unhoused, as wretched as himself). The virtues of Israel are those of beleaguered Sparta. Its propaganda, its rhetoric of self-deception, are as desperate as any contrived in the history of nationalism. Under external and internal stress, loyalty has been atrophied to patriotism, and patriotism made chauvinism. What place, what licence is there in that garrison for the 'treason' of the Prophet, for Spinoza's refusal of the tribe? Humanism, said Rousseau, is 'a theft committed on *la patrie*'. Quite so.

There is no singular vice in the practices of the State of Israel. These follow ineluctably on the simple institution of the modern nation-state, on the political-military necessities by which it exists with and against its nationalist competitors. It is by empirical need that a nation-state sups on lies. Where it has traded its homeland in the text for one of the Golan Heights or in Gaza – 'eyeless' was the clairvoyant epithet of that great Hebraist, Milton – Judaism has become homeless to itself.

But this, of course, is only a part of the truth.

To many among the few survivors, the interminable pilgrimage through persecution, the interminable defencelessness of the Jew in the face of bestiality and derision, were no longer endurable. A refuge *had* to be found, a place of physical gathering in which a Jewish parent could give to his child some hope of a future. The return to Zion, the fantastic courage and labour which have made the desert flower, the survival of the 'Old Newland' (Herzl's famous phrase) against crazy political and military odds, have made a wonder of necessity. The overwhelming majority of Jews in Israel, of Jews in the Diaspora, seek neither to be prophets nor clerics deranged by some autistic, other-worldly addiction to speculative abstractions and the elixir of truth. They hunger, desperately, for the common condition of man among men. They would, like all other men and nations, vanquish their enemies rather than be oppressed and scattered by them; if harsh reality dictates, they would rather occupy, censor, even torture than be occupied and censored and tortured as they have been for so long. What mandarin fantasy, what ivory-tower nonsense, is it to suppose that alone among men, and after the unspeakable horrors of destruction lavished upon him, the Jew should not have a land of his own, a shelter in the night?

I know all this. It would be shallow impertinence not to see the psychological, the empirical force of the argument. Moreover, is the return to Israel not foreseen, indeed ordained, in the very texts I have cited? Is Zionism not as integral a part of the 'prescribed' mystery and condition of Judaism as were the terrible times of sufferance (Shylock's word) and dispersal?

The Orthodox answer is clear. Both currents of prevision are to be accomplished. The prescriptions of suffering have long been made manifest. And so shall be the homecoming to the promised land. But not before the messianic hour. The imperilled brutalized condition of the present State of Israel, the failure of Israel to be Zion, prove the spurious, the purely expedient temporality of its re-establishment in 1948. There were, then, armed men around the politicians. The Messiah was nowhere in sight. Thus the State of Israel, as it stands, neither fulfils nor disproves the Mosaic and prophetic covenant of return. The time is not yet.

Personally, I have no right to this answer. I have no part in the beliefs and ritual practice which underwrite it. But its intuitive and evidential strength can be felt to be real.

The survival of the Jews has no authentic parallel in history. Ancient ethnic communities and civilizations no less gifted, no less self-conscious, have perished, many without trace. It is, on the most rational, existential level, difficult to believe that this unique phenomenon of unbroken life, in the face of every destructive agency, is unconnected with the exilic circumstance. Judaism has drawn its uncanny vitality from dispersal, from the adaptive demands made on it by mobility. Ironically, the threat of that 'final solution' might prove to be the greatest yet if the Jews were now to be compacted in Israel.

But there is a more central intimation. One need be neither a religious fundamentalist nor a mystic to believe that there is some exemplary meaning to the singularity of Judaic endurance, that there is some sense beyond contingent or demographic interest to the interlocking constancy of Jewish pain and of Jewish preservation. The notion that the appalling road of Jewish life and the ever renewed miracle of survival should have as their end, as their justification, the setting up of a small nation-state in the Middle East, crushed by military burdens, petty and even corrupt in its politics, shrill in its parochialism, is implausible.

I cannot shake off the conviction that the torment and the mystery of resilience in Judaism exemplify, enact, an arduous truth: that human beings must learn to be each other's guests on this small planet, even as they must learn to be guests of being itself and of the natural world. This is a truth humbly immediate, to our breath, to our skin, to the passing shadow we cast on a ground inconceivably more ancient than our visitation, and it is also a terribly abstract, morally and psychologically exigent truth. Man will have to learn it or he will be made extinct in suicidal waste and violence.

The State of Israel is an endeavour – wholly understandable, in many aspects admirable, perhaps historically inescapable – to normalize the condition, the meaning of Judaism. It would make the Jew level with the common denominator of modern 'belonging'. It is, at the same time, an attempt to eradicate the deeper truth of unhousedness, of an at-homeness in the world, which are the legacy of the Prophets and of the keepers of the text.

In Jerusalem today, the visitor is taken to the 'Shrine of the Scrolls' or, as it is also known, 'House of the Sacred Books'. In this exquisite building are kept some of the Dead Sea Scrolls and priceless biblical papyri. It is a place of poignant, if somewhat sepulchral, radiance. One's guide explains the hidden hydraulic mechanism whereby the entire edifice can, in the event of shelling or bombardment, be made to sink safely below ground. Such precautions are indispensable. Because nation-states live by the sword. But such precautions are also a metaphysical and ethical barbarism. Words cannot be broken by artillery, nor thought live in bomb-shelters.

Locked materially in a material homeland, the text may, in fact, lose its life-force, and its truth-values may be betrayed. But when the text *is* the homeland, even when it is rooted only in the exact remembrance and seeking of a handful of wanderers, nomads of the word, it cannot be extinguished. Time is truth's passport and its native ground. What better lodging for the Jew?

Through That Glass Darkly

(for Raul Hilberg)

Almost wholly unexplored, in some Freudian sense perhaps suppressed, is the historical moment which has determined the tragic destiny of the Jew over these past two thousand years. It is the moment in which the core of Judaism rejects the messianic claims and promises put forward by Jesus of Nazareth and his immediate adherents.

We have modern histories of the early and intricate relations between first-century Judaism and the nascent Christian communities, between the complexly Jewish traditions and usages in the eastern Mediterranean world on the one hand – with their rich variety of Pharisaic, Zealot and Hellenizing branches – and the new churches, Judaeo-Christian, Pauline, pre-Gnostic on the other. But the key motion of spirit, that whereby Jews refused the 'good news' brought by Jesus, affirmed by his 'resurrection', the crucial repudiation by Jews, at one of the most sombre hours in their history – that of the suppression of national insurgence and the consequent destruction of the Temple – to acknowledge, to accept the concordat of human rebirth and divine pardon offered by the Galilean god-man and his apostles, eludes us.

We have no documents – so the scholars. Neither Josephus nor Tacitus considers the radically challenging (in the full sense of that word) act of Jewish repudiation of the Son of Man. The versions given in the Gospels, Acts and Epistles are, by very definition, polemical and prejudicial. Rabbinic voices, so far as they have come down to us, speak only later, when Christianity, though still splintered, is dynamically ascendant. And even then, they say very little. This hiatus is itself perplexing in the extreme. It constitutes a black hole near the actual centre of Jewish history and fate. I resort to this image precisely because black holes are thought to be charged with almost incommensurable energies, both implosive and

Lecture at the Raul Hilberg Symposium in Burlington, Vermont, April 1991.

explosive, because they are believed to draw matter into their unlit compaction but also, under other conditions, eject formidable radiation. Both the in-gathering and the fierce scattering have their obvious counterpart in the experience of Judaism after Jesus. And their source is that hour, somewhere in the mid-decades of the century of Jesus' ministry and death, about which we seem to know so very little.

Why did the Jews or, more exactly, why did Judaism so far as it can be defined in relation to Torah and Talmud, to nationhood and to exile, say 'No' to the kerygmatic revelation? When compelling elements from within Torah and prophecy had prepared that very revelation.

Here we are on well-trodden ground. Not only the general circuit of Christ's life, ministry and Passion are foretold in the Old Testament, most notably in the Psalms of the Suffering Servant and in Deutero-Isaiah; numerous specific traits are also announced. The just man of suffering is to be mocked, scourged and hung upon the tree of death. A virgin birth – though Hebraists insist that there is at this point a forced, over-determined reading of a phrase signifying rather 'a young woman' – has often been held to be adumbrated. The garments of the martyred Servant are to be divided by lot. In Amos, the most ancient of prophetic texts, we learn of sale and betrayal for a handful of silver.

Modern narratology and structuralism invert the relation between these numerous predictions and the event. They ascribe to the writers of the Gospels a deliberate appropriation of these prophecies so as to compose fictions of prefiguration, thus validating their claims for the crucified and risen Christ. It is difficult to conceive of such a device as transparent to first-century Jews or Judaeo-Christians. To them the accomplished enactment of the precisely foretold entailed a natural logic. Why, indeed how, could the Jews deny that which their own revealed books and prophetic visions had so concretely anticipated?

The issue is a more general one. Recent historical inquiry has made palpable the climate of apocalyptic impatience and expectation which prevailed at the relevant time. Messianic claimants were recurrent. Millenarian ascetics, perfectionists of daily practice in literal awaiting of the apocalyptic end of Jewish history, gathered in the desert and cliff-caves around the Dead Sea. In a complicated mesh of visionary hallucination and nationalist politics, Zealots of various nuances called for armageddon and programmed the coming of the heavenly host. There burnt a fever in time itself. Jesus' assertion of the imminence of God's Kingdom, his summons to mankind to cleanse its ways and its spirit in the face, at once terrible and transfiguring, of the nearing Last Judgement, accorded seamlessly with contemporary symbolism, textual interpretations, and sensibility in Judaism (most emphatically, we learn, in Galilee and in the thronged Jerusalem around the Passover). Even the seemingly blasphemous dictum that he, Jesus of Nazareth, would lay waste the Temple, has been shown to be in perfect congruence with prophetic and mystical perceptions of the antinomian, violent acts which must precede and bring on the eschatological coming of the messianic hour. There was in Jesus' career a most brilliant opportunism of the eternal.

At the heart of that career lie the teachings embedded in the parables and in the Sermon on the Mount. As had been amply demonstrated, these teachings and the specific language in which they are put, correspond very nearly point for point with the tenets of the Torah and with the ethics, unsurpassed, of the Prophets, most especially Isaiah. Where there are departures from the canonic norm, in respect, for example, of the need to keep company with the publicans and the sinful, or in regard to the primacy of healing and salvational acts even over the sanctity of the Sabbath, such dissents do not go signally beyond queries and challenges of Pharisaic observance as we find them among other Jewish 'liberals' or apocalyptics at the time. On the contrary, it could well be argued that an acceptance of the moral prescriptions and exemplary deeds of the man Jesus meant an acceptance of a purified, humanely resourceful and compassionate Judaism, preparing, strengthening itself at the advent of a possibly terminal crisis (the destruction of the nation, the dispersal of its people as these had been graphically prophesied in Jeremiah, in Amos, in Ezekiel and countless apocalyptic texts).

In short: at essential points, on several levels – textual, symbolic, figurative, eschatological and, first and foremost, ethical – the phenomenon and phenomenology of the coming and Passion of Jesus matched perfectly the expectations, the needs, the hopes of Jews in those decisive decades of the first and second century. Yet he was denied. Jews – we do not know just how many, we do not know the pertinent proportions out of the total – but Jews in manifestly significant numbers chose to remain Jews. For them, for us, the Messiah had not come and the titles bestowed upon Jesus, even if he had in some actual or ritualized way sprung from the house of David, were spurious.

Again, one asks: why? Knowing both that the evidence is so opaque as to be unrecapturable and that this question, so rarely pressed, defines our history and, indeed, present estate, it is in this perplexity, authentically dialectical, that one ventures to speculate.

There had been too many: soothsayers, magicians, roadside preachers, epileptic *illuminati*, heralds of one greater to come and of time's foreclosure, plotters against Herod or Rome, ascetic fundamentalists out of Galilee or the desert. Too many so like him, roaming the backlands or the wilderness with a fistful of more or less fanatical loyalists, speaking in riddles, in a grammar of imminent finality. Figures such as John the Baptist or the successive Zealot-healers and prophets crucified after they had sparked local, risibly doomed rebellions. He ran too true to type. Even the miracles his followers bruited and embroidered upon, were so distinctly a part of the known scenario (with the possible, profoundly problematic exception of the resurrection of Lazarus). Thus, paradoxically, numerous Jews may scarcely have noticed Jesus' passage among them in those turbulent, clamorous days. This, assuredly, is borne out by the terse, almost casual allusion in Tacitus. But also this hypothesis is obscure, if only because we lack even tentative insights into the status of the miraculous in contemporary popular or educated perceptions. Were the transmutations of water into wine, the casting out of devils, the healing of the blind and of the lame thought to be magical turns, a faith-healer's or sage's traditional skills or suspect bits of jugglery and of motivated rumour? Were they believed at all? We have no answers to these vital queries.

But let us allow that some considerable portion of Jesus of Nazareth's sayings and teachings *did* reach Jews outside his immediate circle. It could then be that there were, among so many orthodox and edifying injunctions, precepts, inferences grievously outrageous to current Judaic conceptions. Is there, for a Jew, any duty greater than that of bestowing loving burial on his parents, of saying *kaddish* for them aloud and under his remembering breath? But Jesus had bidden 'the dead bury their dead' and had commanded his would-be disciple to forgo his father's burial in order to follow him at once. And what of the claim, itself at moments ambiguous and resistant to paraphrase in the Gospels, to 'sit on the right of the Father', to be His Son in a sense more singular, more directly filial, than is that allowed all human beings who may seek to image themselves as children of the Almighty? Might there have been here the node of outrage and the imperative of rebuttal? Again, we can only reflect on suppositions, observing the evasiveness with which not only gospel dicta but early Christian heresies, Arianism above all, surround the exact tenor of Jesus' divinity. Here, undoubtedly, the thorn of doubt or of frank denial was sharp.

If we read between the sparse lines accorded our theme in rabbinic exegesis – lines, unless I am mistaken, from the medieval period rather than antiquity – and if we attend to modern religious historians and cultural anthropologists, a further motif surfaces. It is that of Jewish revulsion (the word is not too strong) at the mere notion and image of a crucified god, of a messiah done shamefully to death. From the outset, we are told, this revulsion, unattenuated by the wholly implausible epilogue of the ascent from the empty tomb, an epilogue of which even Mark seems to have been darkly uncertain, made acquiescence in Jesus and in the claims of messianic divinity urged for him impossible. Yet, again, there are problems. Judaism knows exemption from death for Enoch, the miraculous effacement of any known burial for Moses, a translation into heaven for Elijah. The proposition that some mode of *kenosis*, of divine self-bestowal in human form was too anthropomorphic to pass muster in Jewish beliefs is contradicted by the strong vestiges of the anthropomorphic, of the divine 'physicality' in the Torah, notably in God's direct, carnal encounter with Moses. In so far, moreover, as it was the chastisement passed by Rome upon rebels, including those who led nationalist-fundamentalist insurrections in Judaea, crucifixion need not have carried, of itself, any stigma of abasement.

A fourth ground for negation would be pragmatic. The coming and the going of the wonder-worker from Nazareth had changed *nothing*. The world was as cruel and corrupt and chaotic as before. The messianic must comport an eschatological transformation. The promise of the new kingdom had not been fulfilled at the time of Jesus' death and was now being either adjourned or metaphorized by the preachings of the early churches. (Inevitably, one recalls Gershom Scholem's cunning *boutade* whereby the Messiah has either already passed among us or is about to do so, but that the changes he has brought are so slight that we do not even notice them or his passage.)

Clearly, there is force in this ascription of a Jewish refusal to watchful common sense. There is, in turn, a suspect circularity to the Christian apologetic argument that the mutation caused by Christ was intended to be, is an inward one, and that the man or woman who has espoused Christianity is indeed a being reborn and of a new world. More resistant to refutation is the undoubted fact that Judaism has, at critical junctures in its troubled affairs, welcomed and invested fanatical credence in messianic claimants, such as Sabbatai Sevi, figures whose a priori pretensions and whose subsequent acts were assuredly less poignant than those of the Son of Man.

Once more we ask: why *il gran rifiuto*?

A recent school of German theologians, who have made of the relations between Christ's agony and the Shoah the fulcrum of their reflections, has offered a witty intimation, where 'wit' in no manner excludes insightful gravity. Thinkers such as Markus Barth have asked whether the entire constellation of Judaic messianic tenets is not inherently ambivalent. The Old Testament and the Talmud, rabbinic teachings and Jewish historicism are unquestionably brimful of the messianic promise and of the awaiting of the Messiah in moods both anguished and exultant. But does the Jew, in psychological and historical fact, truly believe in the coming? More searchingly: does he truly thirst for it? Or is it, was it perhaps from the very first, what logicians or grammatologists might designate as a 'counter-factual optative', a category of meaning never to be realized? One of the images used by these theologians – it has its provenance in a celebrated jest of Hegel's – is that of an ontological addiction to the morning paper. Given the choice, the Jew prefers tomorrow's news, however grim, to the arrival of the Messiah. We are a people unquenchably avid of history, of knowledge in motion. We are the children of Eve whose primal curiosity has modulated into that of the philosophic and natural sciences. In his heart of hearts, the Jew cannot accept the messianic end-stopping of history, the closure of the unknown, the everlasting stasis and *ennui* of salvation. In denying the messianic status of Jesus, in subverting early Christian beliefs in the proximity of the eschatological, the Jew gave expression to the genius of restlessness central to his psyche. We were, we remain nomads across time.

Strikingly, this reading does accord with a dialectical tension undeniable in Jewish thought and feeling. One need cite only Maimonides's insistence on a purely figurative, allegoric sense of the expectation of the Messiah or Franz Rosenzweig's strenuous deconstruction of the concept of a messianic actuality. Much in philosophic-historicist Judaism has indeed argued a perennial adjournment of the Messiah. Contrary strains of credence have been no less intense. Time and again more orthodox or charismatic authority has insisted on the concrete verity of the messianic, has declared that Jewish suffering and survival would be tragic non-sense unless the Messiah were to come, although the temporalities and modes of that coming are privy to God alone. The debate, the difference in sensibilities persists. It affects deeply the degrees of Jewish recognition of the State of Israel both inside the nation, whose legitimacy is denied by those in ritual attendance on a literal arrival of the Messiah, and within the relations between Israel and the Diaspora. Or to insert this debate in the context of these remarks: in what measure, at what level of consciousness, was the Jewish refusal of Jesus, at the time and thereafter, a symptom of radical psychic commitments to historical freedom, to the creative *daimon* of existential destiny on a changing earth?

Each of these five orders of causality and the undecidable complication of interplay between them may or may not serve to account for the abstention of the Jew from the Nazarene and his new synagogue, from the revelations and promise which he brought and incarnated. We do not know. But what we do know is this: however motivated, this abstention, this tenacious dissent has marked, to their very depths, the histories of Judaism and Christianity. The identifying destiny of the Jew, but also in a more oblique sense, that of the Christian, is that of the ineradicable scars left by that hour of denial, by the veto of the Jew.

The imperceptions, the blank ignorance Jewish self-examination and consciousness so often exhibit in respect of Christology, of Pauline doctrine, of the soteriology developed by Paul and the Church Fathers, has psychologically legitimate and transparent sources. There is also a more central awkwardness. The concept of 'theology' *per se* is largely foreign to Judaism. The revealed history which identified the Jew, the Talmudic and Midrashic readings of that history, are teleological, not theological in any philosophic, metaphysical sense. Judaism produces eminent moralists, visionaries, exegetists, but very few theologians of mark. So-called 'post-Holocaust theology' articulates condign pathos, some arresting images and metaphors. It is not a rigorous theological revaluation in any intellectual-analytic sense and it has signally failed to set the matter of final inhumanity, of the systematic bestialization of the human species at the pivot of current philosophic inquiry – where it belongs.

Whatever the reasons, Judaic inattention to the New Testament, to patristic literature, to Augustan and Aquinian propositions, comports a consequential void. For it is in these writings that the record of Jewish suffering among the gentiles and of the Shoah is, as 'through a glass darkly', writ large. Let me be absolutely clear on this. Positivist examinations of the roots of the Shoah and of modern anti-Semitism are of self-evident weight. Political history, sociology, the history of economic and class-conflicts, the study, rudimentary as it is, of mass behaviour and collective fantasies, have contributed much. But the sum of empirical understanding falls drastically short of any fundamental insight. We will not, we cannot, of this I am persuaded, be capable of 'thinking the Shoah', albeit inadequately, if we divorce its genesis and its radical enormity from theological origins. More specifically, we will not achieve penetration into the persistent psychosis of Christianity which is that of Jew-hatred (even where there are no or hardly any Jews left) unless we come to discern in this dynamic pathology the unhealed scars left by the Jew's 'No' to the crucified Messiah. It is to these unhealing scars or stigmata that we may apply, in a dread sense, Kierkegaard's injunction that the 'wounds of possibility' must be kept open.

How readily we forget that not only Jesus but the authors of the Gospels and Acts, all his first followers, were Jews. The beginnings of the macabre history of Jewish self-hatred are inextricably inwoven with those of Christianity. Although, so far as I know, hitherto unexamined, the thought presses on one that Christianity is at fundamental points a product and externalization of just this Jewish self-hatred. This is palpable in Mark. We can, moreover, read his detestation of his fellow-Jews, his resolve to brand them with deicide, with corruption, with outrage and betrayal in the face of God, as partly encoded. To hand over Christ the Messiah for shameful execution is grievous enough – worse is the recalcitrance of the Jew before Christ's divinity, his refusal of the identity and epiphany of the Saviour. Betrayal and judicial murder can be repaired by a belief in Christ's resurrection and a conversion to his promise. The obdurate abstinence of the Jew from such conversion amounts to deicide persistently renewed. The mere existence of Jews is a repetition of Christ's suffering. It underwrites Pascal's awesome finding that no man has a right to sleep because Jesus remains in agony till the end of the world.

Paul (whom the twelfth Benediction of the Eighteen Petition Prayers declares an apostate) is among a handful of supreme thinkers and writers almost whose every sentence is not only prodigal of tensed eventualities of meaning and interpretation, but the brimming density of whose persona may, crucially, have been opaque to itself. Much of western history can be said to spring from uncertainties in the Pauline Epistles, and it is in Romans 9–11, in Ephesians 2 and 1 Thessalonians that the victimization of the Jew, and the necessity of this victimization for the Christian churches, are made fatal. Yet such is the rhetorical depth and psychological involution of Pauline pronouncements that much in these doomsday texts allows only arguable, intuitive decipherment. Jesus' Jewishness and the eschatologically elect, privileged status of the 'people of God' are evident to Paul. As is the absolute implication of Christianity in Jewish prophecy and in the critical situation of the house of Israel on the verge of national ruin. The man from Tarsus is obsessed by the very virulence of his own past and present Judaism – present in its miraculously informed and renewed guise, in the covenant of rebirth in Christ the Jew whom God's unfathomable love has made son and flesh. At moments, Paul urges loving compassion for the Jewish 'remnant' and a watchful expectation of the entry of the Jews into the greater *communitas* of the *ecclesia*. There is, he averts, to be no triumphalism on the part of Christian Jews and of the uncircumcised now admitted to the Lord's table.

But at other moments, far blacker impulses and spurts of menace are unmistakable. No volume, and it is never-ending, of commentary, of hermeneutic 'gentling', however subtle, can blunt the terrible edge of relegation in Romans 10–11 or 1 Thessalonians. Now that the Son and Deliverer has come, 'ungodliness is taken away from Jacob' and Israel is redeemed, but only in so far and exactly in so far as it ceases to be itself. Only if it understands that wilful self-exclusion from the new dispensation will make of it an 'un-people', a vestigial absurdity and lamentable scandal. But why should the existence, so obviously marginal and pitiful, of this obdurate remnant so trouble the Apostle? Why should it be a fierce vexation to a Christendom already on the way to its Constantine triumph?

This, I believe, is where Pauline intimations are the most acute and consequential. The Jew holds Christianity and, indeed, mankind inasmuch as it is the object of Christ's sacrificial, redemptive love, hostage. By refusing to accept Jesus Christ, the Jewish 'remnant' has condemned man to the treadmill of history. Had the Jews acknowledged Jesus as the Son of God, had they received his concordat of grace, that filiality, that donation, would have been proved. The New would then have been shown to be beyond cavil the fulfilment of the Old Testament. The Cross would have cancelled the fatal tree in Eden. The Jewish rebuke to Christ prevents the coming of the messianic realm. It pries and forces open the ravenous jaws of history. It holds time to ransom. In the theology of Maritain this capital charge is plainly voiced. In that of Karl Barth (who wrestled lifelong with the enigma of 'the remnant according to the election of grace') it is an agonizing undecidability. It yields Barth's overwhelming, but scarcely translatable, utterance that the Jew and the Jewish people are 'God-sick', 'sickened by' their intimacy with a God whose supreme act of love and self-donation to their election they have chosen to refuse or leave in abeyance.

In the wake of the Shoah, Christian theologians, notably, as I have mentioned, in Germany, have – distinctly in echo to Karl Barth's ambiguities – laboured to redefine the reciprocities between synagogue and church, between Jewish survivance and Christianity. The principal strategies of argument are familiar.

The Church has 'replaced' Judaism. It is now the Christian, fully cognizant of his Jewish origins and of his debt to the Torah and the Prophets, fully cleansed of the great Marcionite heresy whereby there is an absolute discontinuity between the Old and the New scriptures, who is now the true chosen of God, the true Israel. The promised heritage of Abraham is that of a world-wide Christianity. A second stance is that which concedes to the Jewish remnant a peculiar and privileged role in the continued development of Christianity. There is a 'spiritual heritage' which Christians can derive only from the tree of Jesse, an unbroken validation of the message and meaning of Jesus forthcoming from the election of Abraham and of Moses. Almost opportunely, the very slow conversion of Jews to Christianity (and it does, after all, occur) and the stubbornness of the as yet dissenting Jews demonstrate the fact that Christ's ministry is not yet accomplished, that there is further love on offer. More self-critical is a third valuation, that of a scandalous schism in the House of the One God. An eloquent, philo-Semitic theologian such as Moltmann insists that both Judaism and Christianity are, by virtue of their division, thorns in each other's sides. Judaism poses to Christianity questions, most sharply that of the unchanging tragedy of the historical after the alleged coming of the true Messiah, which Christianity has, until now, failed to answer adequately. In ways as yet impenetrable to satisfactory under-standing or therapeutic action, Judaism and Christianity demand each other's separate and even conflictual incompletions if God's choice of His people is to be made visible. Fourthly, and here the demarcations are necessarily fluid, synagogue and church can be held to be complementary. Israel remains the matrix of Jesus' life and teachings; the mission of Christianity is one of ecumenical and global propagation. The Messiah awaited by Jews is the same Messiah whose *re*appearance is awaited by Christians. Coexistence is *pro*-existence – a formulation by Markus Barth which closely reflects similar suggestions in Rosenzweig, Baeck and Buber.

Each of these positions and their overlap has its theological entailment and behavioural consequences. Each testifies to an unresolved crux – truly that of the 'Cross' – explicit in historical and contemporary Christianity and, unless I am in error, subcon-sciously present in the condition of Judaism. But none of these models, forceful as they are, seems to me to plumb the depths.

Even metaphorized, and metaphors can turn murderous, Paul's construal of mankind as in some sense hostage to the Jews' 'No' to Christ, is pregnant with catastrophe.

Throughout my work, I have argued that Judaic initiation of monotheism, whether by virtue of divine revelation or by virtue of anthropomorphic invention, has exercised an intolerable psychic pressure on western consciousness. Made inaccessibly abstract yet punitively close by Mosaic and Prophetic formulation, the God of

Israel sought to eradicate the sensuous pluralities, the neighbourly liberalities of pagan polytheism. What fallible man or woman can be adequate to the demands of the God of Sinai or find any mirroring of his or her profane, imperfect nature in the tautology of the Burning Bush, blank and consuming as is the desert? By definition, man is always in the wrong in the face of the Mosaic deity and of its imperatives of perfection. The answer to Job is, famously, one of literally inhuman enormity. Ordinary humankind knows that under the weight of the love of this God and of His commandments of reciprocity in love, the soul breaks. What thinking, feeling Jew has not, at some hours, shared Pompey's horror when the Roman intruded on the Holy of Holies in the captured Temple and found it empty.

Twice more, Judaism presented to the West the graphic claims of the ideal. Jesus the Jew renewed and incised the exigence of perfect altruism, of self-denial, of sacrificial humility even unto death, set out in Mosaic monotheism and in the Law. He asked of man fraternal love, unworldliness, abstentions from pride and benefit formidably beyond the reach of any but saints and martyrs. The Trinitarian construct, the suspension of the Law in the name of love abounding, the development of explicit scenarios of celestial compensation by Christianity and its churches, enact specific attempts to paganize an underlying Judaic monotheistic heritage. They constitute tactics of attenuation and dissipation aimed at making bearable that God of Abraham, Isaac and Jacob whom a Pascal still invokes with an apprehension of His original and authentic terror. The gnostic-Hellenistic hybrid with Judaism that is Christianity, the pantheon of its saints, palpable relics, indulgences, confessional absolutions and neon-lit paradise, proved magnificently marketable. But at its militant and triumphant centre, the pressure of Mosaic and Nazarene demands, the summons to perfection, remained. Time and again, be it in desert monasticism or Savonarola, be it in Kierkegaard's 'fear and trembling' or in Karl Barth's stress on the abyss separating God from man, Christianity has been drawn towards the Judaism within itself.

The third of the principal motions of spirit whereby Judaism visits on our civilization the blackmail of utopia is that of the diverse shades of messianic socialism and Marxism. Marxism is, in essence, Judaism grown impatient. The Messiah has been too long in coming or, more precisely, in not-coming. The kingdom of justice must be established by man himself, on this earth, here and now. Love must be exchanged for love, justice for justice, preaches Karl Marx in his 1844 manuscripts, echoing, transparently, the phraseology of the Psalms and the Prophets. There is in the egalitarian programme of communism, in the economics of finality as outlined by Marxist-Leninist doctrine, little that is not called for, implacably, by Amos when he announces God's anathema on the rich and God's loathing of property. Where Marxism prevailed, even or especially in its more brutal modes, it fulfilled that vengeance of the desert on the city so strident in Amos and other prophetic-apocalyptic texts of social retribution. (It need hardly be said that the current crisis and conceivable collapse of Marxist messianic immanence will reach deep into the affairs and future of Judaism.)

Three times, therefore, the Jew has been the summoner to individual and to social perfection, the nightwatchman who does not ensure repose but, on the contrary, wakes man from the sleep of common comforts and self-regard. (Freud even woke us from the innocence of dreaming.) A triple exaction which, I believe, has bred in the western psyche deep-lying detestations. It is not the God-killer whom Christianity has hounded to the rim of extinction in Europe since the Middle Ages, it is the 'God-maker' or mouthpiece who has reminded mankind of what it *could* be, of what it must become if man is indeed to be man. Thus a being of Jesus of Nazareth's ethical radiance can legitimately be called a 'Son of Man'. Is there anyone we hate more than he or she who asks of us a sacrifice, a self-denial, a compassion, a disinterested love which we feel ourselves incapable of providing but whose validity we nevertheless acknowledge and experience in our inmost? Is there anyone we would rather annihilate from our presence than the one who insists on holding up to us the unrealistic potentialities of transcendence?

Thus there has been in every pogrom and in the Shoah a central strain of Christian self-mutilation, a desperate endeavour by

Christianity and by its pagan-parodistic offshoots such as Nazism, to silence once and for all the curse of the ideal inherent in the Mosaic covenant with God, in the more than human humaneness of Isaiah, in the teachings of Jesus the Jew. Eradicate the Jew and you will have eradicated from within the Christian West an unendurable remembrance of moral and social failure. There is, in consequence, an awful symmetry in the fact that by instituting and allowing the world of the death-camps, European gentile civilization has striven to make it unbearable for Jews *to remember*. For it is in Judaism that there has been the obsessive, maddening remembrance which Christianity worked furiously to stifle inside itself.

But in the perspective of Paul's lineaments of mankind held to ransom by the denying remnant of Judaism, by the simple survival of this inexplicable vestige, we can consider even further the twists of menace. We can follow the logic even of Luther's call for the murder of the Jews once they had renewed their original refusal of Christ by rejecting the Reformation and its ardent, sincere proffer of Zion regained and renewed.

Where religious imaginings and their kindred perversion touch on the pulse of the subconscious, the monstrous is not far off. Yet we must try to perceive clearly. Men have massacred men, there has been what is sometimes loosely called 'genocide', from the Book of Joshua to Pol Pot. If we sense in the Shoah a singularity, a quantum jump in our long chronicles of inhumanity, it is because mass slaughter and planned elimination, both of which have manifold precedent, were accompanied by, were explicitly designed as the *dehumanization* of the victim. He was to be recognized as a being less than human. Torture and fear were to reduce him to a subhuman status. In the fantastications of Nazism, those starved, beaten, gassed to extinction were not men and women and children but vermin, members of a species other than that of man. Now observe the symbolic symmetry. In the eye of the believer, God had, through the incarnation of Christ, through the descent of the divine into human form, affirmed, attested to the literal godliness of man. Man had, in Christ, been of the nature of God. This modulation had been scorned by the Jew. Was it not inevitable that the Jew, who had refused transcendence for man, should bear the final, logical consequence, which is to be made less than human? The Shoah, the death-camps have lowered the fragile threshold of humaneness. If the victims were 'un-manned', so were the butchers whose intent and acts diminished them to bestiality. The Jew on his way to the gas-chambers was more than a scapegoat. He was, in a sickness unto death of logic, or reciprocity, the provocation to, the occasion of, his persecutors' descent into animality. It is, in both his agony and in the sadistic beastliness which brought on that agony – the two being rigorously inseparable – the Jew who put in question the belief that our kind, that *homo sapiens* has, in some manner, been created in God's image. Without the Jew, there would not, there could not have been the cancellation of man that is Auschwitz – a cancellation so symmetrical with that, embodied in Judaism's remembrance of the rejection, of the claims to the divine in Jesus. Erasure for erasure. The eclipse of light over Golgotha and the black hole in history of the Shoah. Darkness calling to darkness and the Jew centrally implicated in both.

What follows (however tentatively)?

It is my instinct that ecumenical programmes, in respect of reconciliation between Jew and Christian, may be of some social, political use. But I cannot see that they have any foundation in theological fact. 'With the complete physical extinction of all Jews from the face of the earth the demonstration and proof to God's existence would collapse and the church would lose its *raison d'être*: the church would fall. The future of the church lies in the salvation of all Israel' (M. Barth). One values the penitential generosity of such sentiments. But neither Rome nor Geneva would, when being true to themselves, need to accept them. The survivance of the Jew has nothing whatever to do with any ontological proof of God's existence such as we find in Anselm, in Aquinas or, in a different but related tenor, in Calvin and Karl Barth. We have seen that this survivance is, from the point of view of Pauline and Augustinian historicism and teleology, a scandal, at best ambiguously recalcitrant to interpretation, at worst to be eradicated so that Christ may return in salvation and in glory.

For his part, the Jew cannot negotiate his rejection of a messianic Jesus. He cannot, in however metaphoric a translation, accept the 'God-entrance' into the Galilean sayer of parables and the latter's resurrection and ascent to shared divinity. Precisely to the extent that Jews remain Jews, these denials must stand and must, by the existential fact of continued Jewish life and history, be constantly reaffirmed. So what is there 'really', taking reality to be of the essence, to be talked about? (A theocratic and prophetic 'primitive' such as Solzhenitsyn has seen this plainly and made no cant of his Christological distaste for the Jew.)

Secondly, one conjectures, but I speak as an outsider, that Christianity itself is sick at heart, that it is lamed, possibly terminally, by the paradox of revelation and of doctrine which generated not only the Shoah but the millennia of anti-Jewish violence, humiliation and quarantine which are its obvious background. It stands, or should stand, appalled by its own image, by its fundamental failings, whether by omission or commission, in the season of barbarism, increasingly conscious of the fact that the death-camps were modelled on the long habituation of Christian Europe to blueprints of hell (a concept antithetical to Judaism); Catholicism and Protestantism hardly know themselves. We do hear sincere calls to self-examination, to a rethinking of a profoundly flawed history. There are poignant attempts to re-emphasize and make consequential the Judaic substance in Christianity. But these cannot be pressed too far, if Christianity is not to efface or trivialize the basic tenets of its revelation. How can there be authentic truth and salvation outside Christ? How can the Jew's veto, that of an impotent, despised minority, of a fossilized vestige – an image perennial in Christian apologetics and polemics – be accepted, let alone be made concordant with the Christian creed and the life of the churches? Charles Péguy devises the harrowing conceit whereby the actual physical agony of the crucified Jesus only begins at the exact moment in which Jesus realizes that his infinite powers of love cannot obtain pardon for

Judas. I do not doubt that agony; but nor can I doubt the impossibility of that pardon.

Seriously questioned, the current condition of Judaism is scarcely more consoling than is that of its most successful and ungrateful heresy. The notion of 'coming to terms' with the Holocaust is a vulgar and profound indecency. Man cannot, he must not ever 'come to terms', historicize pragmatically or incorporate into the comforts of reason, his derogation from the human within himself. He must not blur the possibility that the death-camps and the world's indifference to them marked the failure of a crucial experiment: man's effort to become fully human. After Auschwitz, Jew and gentile go lamed, as if the wrestling-bout of Jacob had been well and truly lost.

As I have noted, this laming has, on the Jewish side, generated no theological-philosophical renewal (perhaps it could not do so). Jewish orthodoxy continues in its often jejune formalism, in its feverish atrophy in ritualistic minutiae. Worse: in Israel it has fuelled state savagery and corruption – for let us never forget that each time a Jew humiliates, tortures or makes homeless another human being, there is a posthumous victory for Hitler. In liberal Judaism, in Judaism at large, the winds of spiritual development, of metaphysical exploration, blow faint. Where, now, is there 'a guide for the perplexed', or a voice out of the register which produced a Spinoza, a Bergson or a Wittgenstein? With the breakdown of messianic radicalism throughout the Marxist domain, the fertile stress of critical questioning, of utopian immanence, withers away. How Jewish was the Scribe of Revelation when he spoke in bitter contempt of those who 'blow neither hot nor cold'.

There cannot, I suggest, be any advance inward in Judaism's sense of its purpose, in its grasp of the mystery of its survival and of the obligations this mystery entails, unless the Jews grapple with the origination *from the heart of Judaism* of Christianity. We must strive to gain insight not only into the logic, into the psychological and historical validity of this genesis of the Christian out of the Jew; we must also seek clarity in regard to the tragic, possibly mutually destructive bonds which, since, have tied Jew to Christian, Christian to Jew or, to put it nakedly, victim to butcher. Jews are compelled to envisage, if not to allow, if not to rationalize, the hideous paradox of *their innocent guilt*, of the fact that it is they who have, in western history, been the occasion, the recurrent opportunity, for the gentile to become less than man.

The challenge to be faced is that put to us by Sidney Hook in a posthumous interview. Hook asked whether 'it had really been worth it', whether Jewish survival from persecution to persecution, in pariahdom and across the abyss of the Holocaust, could be assessed positively. Had there not been too much pain, too much horror? Would it not have been preferable, asked Sidney Hook, if the Jewish remnant after Christ had melted into the commonwealth of Hellenistic and Roman Christendom, if it had more or less 'normally' lost its identity and *apartheid* as did other peoples no less gifted, such as the ancient Egyptians or the classical Greeks? To which absolutely unavoidable question, the coda could well be: does the unexamined axiom of national survival justify the necessary policies of the State of Israel at its borders and, what is far graver, inside them? To what end the unquenchable constancy of Jew-hatred, to what end Auschwitz and the everlasting brand it has put on Jewish memory, on any responsible use by a Jew of the past tense?

I venture to propose that Hook's inquiry concerns not only the Jews to whom it is addressed, but the Christian who has established its sombre context. For after such remembrance, what forgiveness, what self-forgiveness?

All too plainly, the issues defy the ordering of common sense. They seem to lie just on the other side of reason. They are extraterritorial to analytic debate. They take substance from the question of God, from the question of His existence or non-existence. We can define modernism as the sum of impulses and psychological-intellectual configurations in which the enormity of that question is experienced only fitfully or in metaphors grown pale. One is very nearly tempted to hope for a moratorium on future discourse. We Jews have said 'No' to the claims made for, and in certain opaque moments by, the man Jesus. He remains for us a spurious messiah. The true one has not come in his stead. Today, who but a fundamentalist handful awaits his coming in any but a formulaic, allegoric sense, a sense bitterly irrelevant to the continuing desolation and cruelty of the human situation? In turn, 1 Thessalonians 2:15 proclaims the Jew to be a deicide, a slayer of his own Prophets and, therefore, one 'contrary' or 'enemy to all men'. Vatican II sought to attenuate or even cancel this sentence of death in the troubled light of modern squeamishness and the Holocaust. In view of the 'final solution' which this Pauline verdict determines. But the text is no accident: it lay, it continues to lie, at the historical and symbolic roots of Christendom.

On both sides, might it not be salutary if words now failed us?

We must learn to persist in some dispensation of twilight with what dignity and minor virtues we can muster. If we are able to do so, we ought to apprehend our own location in a biologically brief history as that of a prologue to the coming into being of a more humane humanity. The most darkly inspired of all twentieth-century imaginers of God, Franz Kafka, reportedly said: 'there is abundant hope, but there is none for us'. What we may do is to attempt to hear from within this abdication from the messianic, be it Jewish or be it Christian, the promise of an eerie freedom.

The Great Tautology

On 31 March 1992, the King of Spain solemnly rescinded the decree of expulsion passed on the Jews on that very date five centuries ago. This expulsion not only brought desolation, suffering and dispersal to the Jewish community of the *Sepharad*. It marked the end of a unique period of spiritual and intellectual coexistence, of collaborative cognizance and informing tension, between the three principal monotheistic faiths in the west. The interactions of awareness between Judaism, Christianity and Islam in medieval Spain and the Languedoc, proved unrecapturable. To this day, the material vestiges of this confluence – the inscriptions in Hebrew, Latin and Arabic, the joint rolls of the names of Jewish, Catholic and Islamic masters of medicine or law as we find them in Toledo, in Narbonne and in Montpellier – endure as a reminder of what was and of what has never recurred. The Albigensian crusades, the hounding of the Moors and the Jews out of Spain, prefigured the triumph in Christian Europe of intolerance and of massacre. Today that intolerance and the perennial threat of violence smoulder again, like marsh-fire.

It is my hope that this conference may, in its obviously limited way, both recall the fruitful humaneness of a lost concordance and suggest future possibilities of understanding between Jew, Christian and Muslim. Without such understanding, the pit of ignorance and of hatred will deepen. The simple presence of those here assembled is a small miracle – and perhaps not so small.

The germ of this 'seminar' is to be found in Étienne Gilson's paper on 'Maimonides and the Philosophy of the Exodus' first published in *Medieval Studies*, 13 (1951). In this text, Gilson surveys the hermeneutic approach to Exodus 3:14 in three interpretative-theological traditions: that of Averroës, Alfarabi and Avicenna; that of Moses Maimonides; and that of Aquinas and of Thomism.

Opening address to a colloquium held at Cambridge in May 1992.

Islam, Judaism and Catholic Christianity not only meet at the exact crossroads of the seminal and canonic scripture: they interweave. For as Gilson shows, Maimonides reads in the light of Avicenna, and Thomas Aquinas, in turn, reads via Maimonides's reading of his Arab predecessors. There is here what a great teacher and critic in this university called and called for: 'a common pursuit'.

In a characteristically medieval vein, the argument towards revelation proceeds via metaphysical and logical technicality. The point at issue is that of the distinction between existence and essence. It is in his *Metaphysics* (VIII, 4) that Avicenna states: 'Primus igitur non habet quidditatem.' God or the Aristotelian *Primus* is pure being, absolute existence. Created beings are possible, therefore contingent, essences. Their existence is accidental. It is an attribute bestowed on them (*accidit*) by virtue of the necessity of being which is that of the prime mover and begetter.

In his *Guide for the Perplexed* (I, 57), Maimonides goes further. The stress lies uncompromisingly on the utmost unity of God. His essence is one of total simplicity. It cannot suffer attribution. In respect of every other life-form, existence is an accident which attaches to the extant. This counter-Aristotelian proposition derives immediately from Avicenna. It follows that in any being which is causally created essence does not entail existence. As Gilson puts it: 'son existence s'ajoute pour ainsi dire à sa quiddité'. In God, existence is necessary. God exists, but not by virtue of the attribute of existence. He does not 'have' existence. He is existence *per se*.

Aquinas, says Gilson, is closer to the Jewish theologian than to the Arab philosopher. There is a close affinity between Maimonides's affirmation that we can grasp of God only the fact that *He is* and that the quality of that 'isness' has nothing in common with the accidental being of all other creatures, and St Thomas's *Contra Gentiles* (I, 30): 'We cannot grasp what God is; but only what He is not and the relation of Him to all else.'

Avicenna's source is most probably the great tautology of Exodus (3:14). In the case of Maimonides, the provenance is explicit. The very name Yahweh, together with the interdictions which attend on its articulation, implies the concept of a total difference between

God and His works. Maimonides interprets the Tetragrammaton as signifying 'necessary existence', that order of being whose existence is its essence (*Guide*, I, 61). For Maimonides the component of mystery in God's answer to Moses out of the Burning Bush is the recurrence of the subject in the form of an attribute. God proclaims Himself to be the existence which is existence, thus making the subject identical with the attribute. As read by Maimonides, in the perspective of Avicenna's supposition, the 'I am / I am' of Exodus can be best paraphrased as meaning 'Being that is Being, i.e. which is necessary and wholly single Being, having made of existence its essence'.

For Aquinas and his scholastic followers, *haec sublimis veritas*, as enunciated in Exodus, becomes the font of a metaphysics of being. Gilson's comment is exalted: 'nous revivons ici l'un des moments les plus solennels de la pensée occidentale, lorsque le judaïsme fit éclater le monde des substances aristotéliciennes, en soumettant l'acte de leurs formes à un Acte Pur qui n'est plus celui d'une pensée qui se pense, mais celui de l'existence en soi'. It is via an analytic meditation on a Jewish commentary whose own roots extend to Islamic philosophy that thirteenth-century Thomism (and the western church) asserts, crucially, the triumph of the efficient cause over Aristotelian finality. For Étienne Gilson, to be sure, the Aquinian step was the decisive one. It is only in Thomism that a 'new metaphysics' is born, one in which in created beings also the integral substance of being is wholly enacted.

Those here gathered will be competent (as I manifestly am not) to elucidate Gilson's concise argument and to judge its worth. What is, for our purposes, of evident and signal importance is the 'triplicity' of the history of the arguments, its foundation in an Islamic-Judaic-Christian nexus (of which Maimonides and Aquinas are fully conscious). This grounding is itself derived from a passage in the Torah, from a speech-act whose radical rebuke to translation throws incomparable light – or, in kabbalistic terms, incomparably radiant darkness – on religious, metaphysical, logical and semantic issues, and on the intimate relations between the religious, the metaphysical, the logical and the semantic. It is difficult to cite any other moment in language, let alone one so brief, so seminal to the sum of western belief, thought and sensibility. It is aspects of this constellation which will engage our discussion.

Yet Exodus 3:14 does offer a tautology, in essence a palindrome circular, reversible on itself. Tautologies can be thought of as strictly formal, as mirror-images whose function is one of self-referential definition. Algorithms in formal logic, axiomatic systems in mathematics (there are those who hold the totality of mathematical postulates and proofs to be an expanded tautology), can readily encode the closed construct of the tautological. Is there any valid development out of a tautology, any 'generative grammar' from inside tautology other than that famously declared by Gertrude Stein 'a rose is a rose is a rose'?

The remarks that follow are nothing more than questionings in the margin.

The motions of tautology inhere in all language. They inhabit the instrumentalities of nomination and of predication. An ontological tautology is implicit in Genesis 2:19. Whatever name Adam gave to every living creature 'that was the name thereof'. Even beyond the 'nominalism' in Plato's *Cratylus*, Adam's semantic baptism of all organic beings is perfectly concordant with and defines their nature. In pre-lapsarian discourse, name and object, the signifying and the signified, match exactly. There is no gap for involuntary misprision. Verbal falsehood is excluded from a grammar which, even more precisely than in the equation which the early Wittgenstein posits between the limits of language and those of our world, maps being and experience totally. Designation and corresponding essence are made one – their relation is tautological. Part IV of *Gulliver's Travels* conceptualizes such a language-world. Houyhnhnm speech can communicate and preserve 'Information of Facts'. To '*say the Thing which was not*' is to undo language, it is to cancel out its truth-functionality. Where it is no longer homologous with reality, language, according to Gulliver's equine master, actually bars perception from access to existentiality: 'for I am led to believe a Thing *Black* when it is *White*, and *Short* when it is *Long*'. Adamic speech, the position argued by Cratylus, the language of the Houyhnhnms, aspires to tautology. The name binds existence to essence, word to world, in a relation of equivalence. There is no arbitrariness to the sign (as in modern linguistics and models of meaning).

Whatever their professed rationality, poetry and prose when it is at the service of evocation and imagined construction, look back to the Adamic. The poet would name uniquely, making of the word the thing. The lexical, phonetic, syntactic and, indeed, visual components of the literary text aim to embody the sensual and intelligible entirety of that to which they point. The traditional trope whereby poetry aspires to the condition of music infers the desiderated fusion between formal means and content. Only music is, in this precise sense, tautological to itself. But prose, at the higher reaches of willed organization, presses in this direction. When a modern American poet rules that a 'poem must not mean but be', he is seeking to recuperate the ontological dynamics of speech-acts before the Fall. We find ourselves here in the 'penumbra', if I may use this image, of the root-paradox of fiction, of *poiesis* (a paradox of which Aristotle, in *Poetics* 6, is uncomfortably aware). The intent of fiction is truth. Fiction would speak the world essentially, articulating, mapping point to point as between sign and that which is designated, even its ambiguities. It labours to render words and sentences translucent to being. As it is the work of fallen men and women, it can never achieve this aim completely. It is a master-stroke by Swift to assign perfect semantic verity to creatures other than man. The 'words of the tribe' (Mallarmé's phrase) can never be made altogether pure again. Even in the most 'close-fitting' of fictive, poetic speech-acts, the incarnate tautologies between word and object leak. We sense duplicity, in the full etymological and connotative senses of that word (the current shibboleth for this 'leak' and 'duplicity' is *différence*).

Tautologies are elemental in natural language as well as in meta-linguistic codes such as those of formal logic and of algebra. They have therefore been the object of logical and analytic investigation.

Neighbouring or cognate categories, such as 'identity' and equivalence, have been studied in their relations to tautology. The act of exact and immediate repetition or reiteration is often regarded as primary to tautology. Kierkegaard's expansive, ironic treatment of this primacy is well known. But interest in the nature and validity of the tautological extends far beyond the notice of logic and grammatology. The matter of identity, of self-reflexive denomination, of postulates of equality with what they entail in regard to non-contradiction and to the excluded middle, underwrites central propositions in western epistemology. It is, since the pre-Socratics, inseparable from the metaphysical and theological arguments of which this epistemology, this logic of possible articulation, are the enabling rudiments.

The postulate whereby propositions of the type 'A is A' are neither empty nor trivial, but on the contrary generative of reason and of systematic constructs of thought, may be held to inform western criteria of intelligibility. It is at this node, certainly after Aristotle, that the *principium sciendi* has its fundament. The evident problem is the copula. It is an exaggeration, but an almost pardonable one, to say that the greater part of our metaphysics and of our philosophic logic has been an attempt to situate the tenor of necessity, of existential determination in the copula which binds 'A' to 'A'. How is the formal postulate which serves as *principium sciendi* dependent on, affirmative of the *principium essendi* as it is made manifest in the verb 'is'? The question was as important to Parmenides as it was to Frege. In ways less divergent than they appear at present, it is cardinal to Wittgenstein's arguments on language no less than to Heidegger's metaphors of being. For our purposes here, it is important to observe a constant overlap. Theological inquiries strictly defined, considerations of the conditions of communicability and intelligibility in revealed discourse (the grammatology of immediacy), cannot avoid the question of the copula of existentiality in tautological claims of identity. Reciprocally, logic, even in its most formal guise, 'runs its head', as it were, against the *mysterium tremendum* of what Coleridge called 'the great I AM'. One might, perhaps, venture the remark that it is this overlap which signals the infirmities of a programmatically materialist logic or theory of the relations between consciousness and language. At adequate depths, a logic, a semantics of tautological statements of identity comes up against issues and against provocations which are, in the wider sense, transcendent, which are, in consequence, the legitimate concern of metaphysics and of philosophic theology.

Anything like a comprehensive survey of even the most important moments in the history of tautological identity-propositions as these relate logic to metaphysics and theology is difficult to imagine. The topic, in an extension of the Aristotelian use of that rubric, is pervasive. Its history, the analysis of its unfolding, would lead from Parmenides' doctrine of the One and the many and Plato's critique of this doctrine to Aristotelian logic and to the ontological discriminations between being and essence, between autonomous and created which, as we saw, underlie scholasticism. Taken more narrowly, this is to say in explicit or implicit reference to the identity of the Prime Mover and to the conceivable relations between this identity and human self-consciousness (that of the finite *ego*), a survey would cite Neo-Platonism as the source of much that has come after. It is in Plotinus, in Proclus on Plotinus, that the 'modern' story may be said to begin. It is Plotinus who argues most stringently the tautology that is the perfection of God on systematically formal grounds (for which, taught Alexandre Koyré, the most accurate representation is a formula by Cantor on transfinite numbers), and on grounds of metaphysical illumination. The Divine Principle exists *a se* and *per se*. Its singular absoluteness (the formulation will be taken up by St Augustine) is that of perfect identity between being and essence. In a characteristically Plotinian trope, this perfect 'selfness unto itself' is both closed – the tautology is that of the circle, highest and most perfect of geometrical figures – and the motor of infinite radiance. *Alpha* is *omega*.

The most fruitful speculative current proceeds from the interactions between Neo-Platonism, the Johannine concept of the *Logos* and the problems, logical as well as epistemological, posed by Trinitarian doctrines. These are among the deepest waters in western theological and philosophic debate. To simplify grossly, what is at stake is the incorporation into a Trinitarian model, or the exclusion from it, of that Arianism always latent in Christian consciousness and of which the children's rhyme 'One is one and all is all and evermore shall be so' may be a distant echo. How can the tautological 'oneness' imperative in Exodus 3:14 be reconciled with the triplicity of a Christian God? How does the Johannine equivalence between God and Word accord with the threefold essence of Father, Son and Holy Ghost? The oxymoron is close to being violent in the very term 'triune'. The contrast, it may be the contradiction with, the lapidary monism out of the Burning Bush and the Plotinian insistence on absolute unity, had to be hammered out if western Christianity was to assume the heritage vital to its own legitimation – that of Jerusalem and that of Athens. Has this *aporia* – logically, grammatically insoluble – ever been intelligibly overcome?

The road leads through Meister Eckhart's inspired gloss (which cites Maimonides) on the *Ego sum qui sum* in his *Exodum* commentary and in his readings of the Fourth Gospel. Eckhart's grammatical investigation of the 'subject which is being itself' (*ipsum esse*) and of the singular status of the pronomial first person, which in the case of God alone signifies pure substance, is set alight by the ardent abyss of God's tautological unmasking. The passage in Exodus is itself thrust out of the normal terrain of language, as is Israel out of Egypt. This absolute 'verb' is born of the desert. In the act of self-naming, God also becomes nameless or, more exactly, unnameable. *Sine nomine.* The *ego* recedes into the totality of the *esse*. Even the *sum*, as Stanislas Breton puts it in his reading of Eckhart, is 'in excess', 'adjonction trop humaine à l'infini de l'infinitif'. The fires in the Bush consume natural language in the very instant of God's supreme resort to such language (there are affinities here with the images of lightning in Heraclitus, particularly as Martin Heidegger reads him). Thus, and so far as we can paraphrase it 'downward', Exodus 3:14 communicates simultaneously the in-gathering of all existence into a 'oneness' of strictly inconceivable compaction, *and* a zero-point. This emphasis on negation will deepen in Eckhart on St John. We can, to borrow a theme from current cosmology, have no direct evidence for, no direct encounter with, the incommensurable energies of presence in a black hole whose central mass is of such density that no emanations come from it. It is obvious that Meister Eckhart's play on an infinitely contracted zero or *Nichtigkeit* will, in turn, animate modern negative theology and its metaphors of absence in essence.

Schematically, the attempted concordance of Neo-Platonism – Proclus is decisive – with Christianity and the insights of Eckhart lead to the epistemology of German idealism. In the wake of the mystical dialectic of Eckhart, of Angelus Silesius, Fichte would make of 'A is A' the unassailable axiomatic foundation of the *Wissenschaftslehre*. Radicalizing the Cartesian postulate, Fichte posits *sum ergo sum*. In this equation, without which, according to Fichte, there can be no perception, no rational experience of consciousness, no 'making sense' of the world we inhabit, the verb 'to be' is no inert copula, but is maximally dynamic and constructive. Fichte's tautology is best understood as saying 'I am because I am'. It becomes his heroic labour (as it is that of Husserl) to keep solipsism at bay, to demonstrate that both ends in the foundational tautology are active. In Schelling's 'meta-logic', a tautology does state an identity-relation, but this relation transcends the tautological. At crucial points, Schelling's argument draws less on logical and grammatical components than it does on poetics and theology. The paradigm of divine creation and the reflections of that paradigm in *poiesis* (*Erschaffung*), buttress and go beyond formal or analytic findings. It is, so Schelling, the human experience of love, in so far as love at once affirms and breaks the tautological bind of self-consciousness, the egoism of the *ego* when it is most itself ('ipsissity') and at the very same time most 'open'.

Coleridge is cognizant of both Fichte and Schelling throughout his (incomplete) treatise on logic. Characteristically, he points to the biblical source:

Without any present reference to any religious or superhuman authority the title 'I Am' attributed to the Supreme Being by the Hebrew legislator must excite our admiration for its philosophic depth, and the verb substantive or first form in the science of grammar brings us the highest possible external evidence of its truth. The verb (*verbum*), the word is of all possible terms the most expressive of that which it is meant to express, an act, a going forth, a manifestation, a something which is distinguishable from the mind which goes forth in the word, and yet inseparable therefrom . . .

Coleridge's 'act, a going forth, a manifestation' being a penetrating paraphrase of Fichte's *Tathandlung*.

It is, however, Schelling's untranslatable *Un-grund* (the term comes from Jakob Boehme) in the words from the Burning Bush, the withdrawal of definition at the moment of tautology, which has proved seminal. Exodus 3:14 says all and nothing. It is a linear equation whose resolution is indeed zero. God may be construed as withdrawing into autism. The impact of this theological conceit on Heidegger's equation between truth and 'revealed self-concealment' (*aletheia*) is palpable. As it is with reference to Heidegger's uses of 'nothingness', of *Nichts* and *nichten* to signify the withdrawal of authentic saying, of *Sprache*, from any correspondence with or representation of identity and description. As has been widely perceived, Heidegger's existential ontology and the philosophic-rhetorical practices of *néantissement* which it has inspired notably in France, are secularizations – if they are that – of negative theology. The Bush burns still, but in monologue. We have no access to the pulsing closure and disclosure in its tautology.

These are markers, very possibly inaccurate or approximate, along one of the most arduous paths in analytic and transcendental thought. If I turn now to two twentieth-century evocations or invocations of the words heard by Moses, it is in the belief that music and poetry have much to tell us of metaphysical issues where these are central to human questioning.

Composed between May 1930 and April 1932, Schoenberg's *Moses und Aron* probes the limits of language in the spirit of the *Tractatus*. Ineluctably, human speech represents, it images. Such representation and imaging falsifies revealed, absolute truths. Specifically, this falsification by virtue of imagery violates those prohibitions on the making of images decreed by the Mosaic God precisely so that the abstract and moral verities of God's legislation for Israel may not be vulgarized and distorted. It is, implies Schoenberg, just this iconoclasm in Judaism, and the necessary bonds between icon and representational language, which allow music a peculiar truth-function in Jewish consciousness. Music refutes images. It is of the order of supreme abstraction as are the truths which attach to the God of Sinai.

This abstraction is made manifest to Moses by the voices out of the Burning Bush. Voices – a soprano, mezzo-soprano, contralto, tenor, baritone and bass – because Schoenberg aims to suggest that it is only via plurality, via a fragmented perception, that the human ear can seize the hidden unity of God's self-designation. Where it declares itself tautologically, 'the One and Only' lies beyond human grasp. Schoenberg does not set to music the 'I am' but lets Moses spell out the litany of its inaccessibility. Consciously or not, Schoenberg augments a closely related string of epithets from Plato's *Phaedo:*

> Inconceivable because invisible;
> because immeasurable;
> because everlasting;
> because eternal;
> because omnipresent;
> because omnipotent.

The thornbush bids Moses depart from its hallowed and secret ground. God's voice will speak to His people again and 'through any thing'. But not as it did out of the unconsuming flame. The *kenosis* of God's descent into mundane grammar and the inevitable metaphorization of His presence and His meanings within human translation (which is always traduction) make impossible a repetition of the great tautology in its original, revelatory form.

Schoenberg left *Moses und Aron* incomplete. The musical setting ends on Moses' despairing cry:

> None can, none may give Him utterance.
> Oh, Word, Word, Word, that I lack!

But the status of a fragment also directs us to another insight. The perfection, the totality explicit in the divine tautology or postulate of self, is not given to man's understanding or mimetic response.

Schoenberg worked on his *sakrales Fragment* under the unmistakable shadow of nearing catastrophe. Very soon the remembrance of the Burning Bush and of God's disclosure to Moses was to be put to unendurable question.

The figure and figurations of the Burning Bush are interlinear in the poetry of Paul Celan. Seven-branched, the Bush is the ritual candelabrum emblematic of Judaism. Its twigs act as an image of fingers splayed in prayer or desperation. The spikes of the thornbush tell of blood and of coronation. Each advertence voices Celan's question. Has the Burning Bush now been consumed to dead ash together with the covenant which it signified? Has it, by some mystery of unbearable proximity, blazed so vehemently as to become a pyre for Israel? Or has its constellation of flames simply gone out, leaving mute betrayal and extinction for the Jew? These interrogations and the answer of the victim are concentrated in a poem already monumentalized and made legend by the shock and exegesis it has inspired, Celan's 'Psalm'. But this time the focus is not only the Bush. It is, numbingly, the matter of God's self-naming, of the affirmation of identity spoken to Moses. The Bush and the 'nominative' tautology are fused. If the one has become death and falsehood, so has the other. Celan 'un-names' God as the Shoah erased million-fold the names, the identities of its victims. In this 'counter-psalm', God is *Niemand*, a 'No-one', an *outis* in the hellish domain of the Cyclops. But his is, as in the darkest of negative theologies, a *Niemand* charged with absence, a void either of withdrawal or of impotence or of gnostic malevolence. 'Praise be to you, No-one' who does not 'bespeak our dust' (where *bespricht* borders on the untranslatable, having in it dense connotations both of linguistic communication and of concern or even of spoken remembrance as in a *kaddish*). 'Psalm' paraphrases the tautology: 'I am not what I am' or 'I am no longer what I was'. The fires are out and you have been made dust (*Staub*). Now comes the formidable counterpoint:

Dir zuliebe wollen
wir blühn.
Dir
entgegen.

Again, translation falters. *Dir zuliebe*, 'for the love of you'; yet not altogether without an ironic inflection, 'for your sake' who has failed us unspeakably. 'We bloom' *Dir / entgegen*. 'Towards you' but, with equal force, 'against you'.

Observe the depth and suggestion in Celan's move. It is the Jews, wellnigh exterminated in the ovens and fire-pits, who have become the Bush. It is their voice(s) out of the burnt Bush which apostrophizes and un-names God in insupportable reversal of the Mosaic moment. And whereas the Bush in Exodus bears thorn and flame, the 'counter-Bush' out of the death-camps bears the *Nichts-*, the *Niemandsrose* (the 'Nothing-rose', the 'No-one rose'), emblems (though in regard to Celan the notion of the emblematic is far too simplistic) of blood and of resurrection. It is now God, not the human interlocutor, who is, as it were, dismissed from ground which the bestial massacre of His once chosen people has hallowed, has made inaccessible to Him.

There is, I hazard, no reading of Exodus 3:14 more commensurate with the provocation of the text. There is none which raises more sharply the persistent doubts as to a positive and kerygmatic interpretation of the great tautology. To what degree is the divine self-identification and identification to Moses *also* a closure, a banishment of men and women from the inviolate self-sufficiency of the creator? Is there a commitment here to continued meetings with man or a valediction, a withdrawal into an order of totality past all human understanding? Attempting (almost naively) to experience, to 'undergo' this speech-act in Exodus, I have wondered whether we ought not to hear in God's statement the muffled echo of an infinite solitude, whether the grammar of mirroring in the tautology is not the figuration of an aloneness from which creation, and most sombrely that of man, is excluded.

For the voice out of the Burning Bush, the tautology may indeed have been closed. For us, it remains open.

Two Cocks

(for Myles and Ruth Burnyeat)

Two deaths have, very largely, determined the fabric of western sensibility. Two cases of capital punishment, of judicial murder, lie at the foundations of our religious, philosophic and political reflexes. It is two deaths which preside over our metaphysical and civic sense of self: that of Socrates and that of Jesus. We remain, to this day, children of those deaths.

The motives, be they compelling and fortuitous, of Socrates' execution are not, despite incessant scholarly inquiry, fully understood. Nor, one intuits, were they transparent to those who condemned and who mourned him. Our images of what came to pass in Athens in 399 BC are primarily shaped by Plato's narrative. Indistinctly, we know of the conflicts between oligarchy and populism, between rhetorician or sophist and demagogue, which had enervated the *polis* and in which Socrates was, or was believed to be, culpably implicated. We know something of the weight which lay on what had been Pericles' city after its defeat by Sparta. Exhaustion and mutual recrimination poisoned the air. We need look no further than Aristophanes' *Clouds* to recall that Socrates had incensed his detractors, that he had goaded beyond patience certain 'pillars of society' (the Socratic inference in Ibsen's drama of the clash between truth and community is obvious). In its pitiless prescriptions, Book X of Plato's *Laws* reminds us of the archaic but constantly resurgent terrors which Attic public consciousness experienced in the face of impiety, of rationalistic provocations. Questionings as to the organization of the cosmos were one thing – they had already busied Anaximander and Heraclites; questionings of the instrumentalities of convention and sanctioned discourse which related the gods to the everyday stability of the state, were quite another.

But even if we observe these fatalities of political and personal

This is an expanded version of a paper given at the conference on 'Understanding, Faith and Narrative' at the Library of Congress in Washington, DC, in June 1992.

circumstance (Euripides also was to experience their menace), even if we register the deliberate 'tactlessness' of Socrates' style of presence, his death-sentence and the carrying out of this sentence remain unclear. It is no accident that classical scholarship and political theory (consider the impact and vexatious legacy of Leo Strauss) persistently produce new readings of the event, or that debate over the authentic meanings and validity of the condemnation of Socrates should have been particularly vivid during these past years. Why did Socrates inflect towards death what appears in the first instance to have been a much lighter punishment, i.e. a fine? To what degree did his ironies, his claim to public honours and reward – a claim which itself ironizes irony – enforce a death-sentence both on his judges and himself? How ought we to interpret the several levels of significance, manifest yet also, perhaps, esoteric, in Socrates' subsequent refusal to avail himself of the possibilities of flight offered him during his incarceration? Are there authentic elements which throw a twilight of suicide on the facts of Socrates' death as these are reported to us? (This diagnosis is more than hinted at by Xenophon, a cruder but, in some ways, more straightforward witness than was Plato.)

The eloquence of the *Apology*, the dialectical pathos of the *Crito*, complicate any attempt at an answer. The successive personae of Socrates have intrigued the ages. We know of a 'Socratic Socrates' prior to the *Meno*; of a 'Pythagorean-Platonic Socrates' in the middle dialogues; of an 'ontological Socrates' in the *Sophist* and the *Theaetetus* (Heidegger's 'Socrates'). Socrates' very absence from the *Laws* has its implicit substance (and is made paradoxically 'present' by Leo Strauss). Conflictual, hybrid, overlapping presentments and myths of Socrates are manifold in the Renaissance, the Enlightenment and modernity. The possible congruence between an 'historical Socrates' and the dramatic genius of Platonic re-creation, is of a complex wealth resistant to hermeneutic analysis and narratology. Very precisely, only one comparison can be reasonably sustained: it is that with the relations between the 'real' Jesus of Nazareth and the Christ-figure as we find it nascent or consecrated in the Gospels and Acts of the New Testament. In both the cases of

Socrates and of Jesus, the texture of immediate witness – already 'memorized' – of psychological retrospection and reshaping, of didactic construal and literary-linguistic conventions, conscious and unconscious, is of a density and plurality so great that it rebukes any confident analytic finding. Nor must we overlook the dynamics of interaction, of reflective mirroring and projection between earlier and later figurations. As we do not possess an exact chronology for either the Platonic and pseudo-Platonic dialogues on the one hand or for the four Gospels and their putative source on the other, we can only speculate. In what ways, say, does the 'Socrates' of the *Gorgias* incorporate or alter the voice of the 'Socrates', be he fictive or actually remembered, whom we meet in the *Protagoras*? What are the relations or distortions of identity affecting the presentation of Jesus not only within the Synoptic Gospels but, drastically, in reference to St John?

What is evident to any student of language and poetics is the pressure of literary unfolding in Plato's successive and self-modifying renditions ('inventions'?) of his Socrates. The Falstaff of *The Merry Wives of Windsor* is and is not the Falstaff of the two parts of *Henry IV*. But the informing genesis in this instance is almost simplistic when we compare it with the motions of verity and of fiction, of remembrance and of metamorphosis used by Plato to preserve, to communicate to and for himself and for us the only individuality whose stamp on the memory of the West can be set beside that of Jesus.

I know of only one iconic representation of the relevant paradoxes and intractabilities of interpretation, of the bounds which the material imposes on reason. It is a painting by an anonymous master in a late medieval Flemish style: on the rear wall of Mary's humble abode at the moment of Annunciation, we can make out a cross bearing the crucified Christ. Had Socrates paused to sniff or rub between his fingers the delicately divided leaves of a *Conium maculatum*, the hemlock plant, on one of his early walks?

Whether in religious or in secular history, whether in the 'revealed' or the mundane canon (it is the aim of this paper to ask whether any plausible distinction can be drawn between the two), 'last words' of illustrious men form a distinctive genre. I say 'men' because, disturbingly, we have hardly any examples of the last words of women. Are women more prone to silence in their death hour? Have their final utterances gone unrecorded? The masculine mode is, by contrast, rich. It extends from the heroic sublime to bathos, from stoical brevity to flowery bravado. We have sound reasons to suppose that such finalities are, perhaps, more often than not, prepared before the midnight time, that they have, notably among high personages in the baroque and neo-classical periods, even been rehearsed. There is evidence that some of the most celebrated or notorious of valedictions are the result of misunderstanding by listeners or of sheer hagiographic invention. None the less, a crucial realization is in play. The 'language animal' that is man (this designation lies at the heart of both Hebraic and Greek anthropologies) exercises his defining humanity one last time. Death is a cessation of speech. It is the end-stop which punctuates the script of articulate being. (How is this script finalized in the existence of the mute? What are the 'last words' of the speechless?) At death, grammar and the anarchy of silence confront each other, closing the circle to human significance. And it would seem indeed that it is language which substantiates our conclusive perception of self: we know of no composer whose 'last words' took the form of musical notes, of no graphic artist who addressed his or her own death with a drawing.

'Crito, we owe a cock to Asclepios. Pay my debt, and do not forget it.' That 'we' remains as enigmatic as the *nous*, never reiterated or explained, in the opening sentence of Flaubert's *Madame Bovary*. Is Socrates identifying with collective mankind so as to remind us that death is the most total of generalizations, that it can be construed as the eradication of the first person singular? In death we do become 'we'. If this is the intent of the syntax, modesty proved short-sighted. Socrates has, in the history and practice of western logic, come to stand for 'man'. Innumerable are the syllogisms and the translations of natural language into elementary symbolic-logical notation, which use 'Socrates' to represent man.

From the medieval schools to Descartes and modern primers, countless school children and tyros in logic have recited the basic syllogism: 'Socrates is a man. / All men are mortal. / Socrates is mortal.' Being so flat and familiar, the sequence has lost its aura of enormity. Not until Leon Shestov, the twentieth-century Russian thinker against death, against our servile acquiescence in logical necessity, will anyone protest and point to the vital scandal of Socrates' existential presence in this formalization of doom. It is, to Shestov, terrible enough to apply this primary syllogism to a dog; it is an ontological outrage to mouth it, unthinking, about Socrates.

What we know is this: the Socrates who turns to Crito, who already feels in his groin the nearing death-chill of hemlock, chooses, in his last words, both a plural pronoun – 'we owe' – and a personal possessive – 'my debt'. He literally voices the threshold, the passing from ego to anonymity. He cannot know (would he have cared?) that anonymity will afford him no lodging, that logic and logical argument would make 'Socrates' one of the two least nameless of men.

Given the music of discourse in the *Phaedo* and the poetic strengths of Plato, given the mastery over every technique of rhetoric and eloquence displayed by Socrates throughout his life and trial – what Xenophon, with a point of reproof, perhaps, called his *megalogeria* – these last words surprise. Even Wittgenstein's plainness – 'Tell them I have led a happy life' – is more charged with the unexpected, with the luminous authority of the occasion. Some have gone from us pronouncing malediction over their foes. Some have blessed them. Some have laboured to encapsulate in a single phrase or lapidary tag the essence of their character and destiny (Talleyrand's quip about God's *métier* being forgiveness, Goethe's alleged call for 'more light'). Had the master-builder of western speech, knowing that these would be his final words, knowing, one has reason to believe, that they would be fervently recorded and passed on to others, nothing grander, nothing dialectically more stimulating to say?

Commentary and explication have been various.

Scholars tell us that Asclepios was a newly imported deity in the

Athenian pantheon. It is held that he originated from the north, possibly from Macedonia, that uncouth yet politically and military potent region whose shadow lay heavier and heavier on worn Greece. The cock is also a late arrival in mainland Hellas (no reference antedates *c.* 550 BC). He seems to have come from Persia. As did manichaeism and those dualistic forerunners which also attach to the Median-Persian world. Dualism, the polarization of light and dark, which are the foundation of manichaean and Gnostic systems, relate forcefully to the cock. It is difficult to summarize even in shorthand a voluminous chapter in the study of comparative religion, of mythology, of ritual and symbolism. The cock is Chaucer's Chauntecleer. He is herald of dawn. If he fails to crow, legend has it, the sun will not rise. His argent flourish both announces and hails the daily miracle of light. His sexual prowess – in English 'cock' designates the male organ – enacts the life-giving potencies of the sun, the burst into heat which procreates life. In Gallic consciousness, the cock's strutting pride is that of the nation in flashing arms, in glory, where, in turn, *gloire* is kindred to sunlight. Throughout western practice and iconography, cocks' feathers adorn the head-dress of the warrior and of the virile lover. On our weather-vanes, the rooster tells of wind and weather, directing our notice skyward. Spurred, he engages in ferocious combat and exhibitions of male mastery.

In antithesis, however, the very same creature relates to darkness and the kingdoms of death. He is, in Petronius' *Satyricon*, the *bucinator*, the trumpeter of death. In near-eastern beliefs, in certain strands of classical and Celtic mythology, the cock, most especially when he is himself black, is implicated in funeral rites and in the bestiary of the underworld. His blood figures explicitly in rituals of burial and the sacrificial propitiation of the departed. Gods and daemons of the nether world have commerce with the bird. There are fables and ghostly tales in which the crowing of the cock does not attend on sunrise and new birth but on the imminence of death in the house. Unsurprisingly, it is Shakespeare who spins these ancient, contradictory threads into a single and haunting design. Marcellus to Horatio:

It faded on the crowing of a Cocke.
Some sayes, that ever 'gainst that Season comes
Wherein our Saviours Birth is celebrated,
The Bird of Dawning singeth all night long:
And then (they say) no Spirit can walke abroad,
The nights are wholesome, then no Planets strike,
No Faiery talkes, nor Witch hath power to Charme;
So hallow'd and so gracious is the time.

A bird of dawn which sings all night in the season of Christ's nativity, but whose call summons back to Purgatory the wretched spirits such as Hamlet's father. A fowl of joyous coming which is simultaneously and literally the summoner out of and back to the sulphurous dark of death. The cock occupies Socrates' last thoughts and words. It crows news of the grace that comes of Jesus' birth. It is a frequent herald of death. We stand on puzzling ground.

Armed with revelation and the death-cry of the risen Christ, Church Fathers, Lactantius and Tertullian most prominently, derided Socrates' finale. What sounder proof of the fact than his trivial dictum that even the wisest, the most ethically inspired of pagan sages was, at the supreme hour, nothing more than a superstitious idolater? We knew already of Socrates' resort to his *daimon* – a word which in early Christian ears rang with sinister connotations. We have ample witness to his regard for the oracle at Delphi, symbol of that entire edifice of false or devilish prophecy laid waste by Christian revelation. Now that cock for Asclepios. Should this have been the parting reflection and bidding of a true teacher, of a seeker of moral and spiritual truth? Socrates' closing move, moreover, entails animal sacrifice. It is one of the just vaunts of Christian doctrine, of Jesus of Nazareth's exemplification of all-encompassing love, to have rejected the offering of animals, of any living creature, on the altars of God. In so doing, the new *ecclesia* had indeed surpassed the ethics and practice of both paganism and Judaism. It had, by virtue of this simple but revolutionary abstinence, proclaimed a truly novel perception of the sacredness and unison of all created life. What philosophic-moral trust can we invest in a man (Socrates) who, at the instant of death, seeks to honour or assuage some minor deity by blood-sacrifice? No, as so often, declared the Church Fathers, the triune God had convicted even the loftiest of pagan philosophy of puerile emptiness, and had done so out of its own mouth.

A second line of interpretation is more generous. It was, we are informed, customary to offer Asclepios a gift of thanks in requital of healing, of recovery from illness. Socrates (this will be the Stoic reading and that of Montaigne) aims to teach us that death is a blessed recovery from the illness that is carnal existence. Specifically, according to Xenophon, Socrates had told Hermogenes that death freely chosen was far preferable to the ineluctable afflictions, infirmities and decrepitude of old age. What wise man would choose to fall into risible decay of mind and body when he could die more or less painlessly and in possession of his faculties? Therefore let us give thanks to the god of healing when he allows us to exit lightly. May the cock which we bring him in offering embody our indebtedness for deliverance into a true and lasting dawn. May it mark our reasoned acquiescence in the logic and benediction of our passing. Thus the crowing of the cock sends our soul on its twofold journey: through the black gates and into Elysian noon. This duality will impress itself on Nietzsche when he qualifies Socrates' last words as being both *lächerlich und furchtbar* ('risible and terrible').

The ironies in the *Phaedo* are labyrinthine. The play of argument and of symbol is as manifold as any in Plato. One of the key motifs is that of Socrates' self-adjudication of innocence and public merit. It is Socrates (so Socrates) who is the veritably pious man. It is he who best honours the divinities of Athens. The charge of impiety applies to the accusers. It is their officious observance and adherence to unexamined gestures which make religion vacant. Now, at the precise instant of his innocent death, Socrates elects to demonstrate his caring piety. He bids Crito sacrifice to a new cult, to a divinity which may have entered the religion of the city only recently. The cock for Asclepios signals Socrates' scrupulous alertness to appropriate ritual even where, particularly where, its context is new and as yet, perhaps, overlooked. 'Do not forget.' The ironies may lie gentle and deep. They are akin to those in Pascal's wager on transcendence: even the freest, wisest of mortal spirits adds a touch of potential insurance to his pilgrimage into death. Who knows? Asclepios may ease the transit.

But the implications reach beyond irony. At other levels, the *Phaedo* invites us to discriminate courteously but stringently between the numerous, polymorphic deities whom we encounter in myths and inherited rites on the one hand, and the one supreme principle, the 'unknown God' whose altar St Paul will find, precisely in Athens, on the other. Of this first principle we know, *stricto sensu*, nothing. In significant part, however, its eternal, changeless truth and universality are revealed to us by the realm of Ideas, themselves analogously eternal and changeless. We are, at this point, distant from the early Socratic 'Socrates' and close to the transcendental Platonism which will become that of Plotinus, of Proclus and of Augustinian Christianity. Without formal emphasis, yet unmistakably, the *Phaedo* would have us distinguish the mytho-poetic, civic polytheism as we find it in Homer and daily Athenian usage from the Demiurge and ascendant hierarchy of abstraction delineated in the *Timaeus*. Careful remembrance and public gestures (the sacrifice of a cock) are due to the former; metaphysical meditation and the soul's act of faith are owed to the latter.

Asclepios provides a pertinent figure in whose cult this distinction and the passage from one order of religious sentiment to a higher order is enacted. His inclusion in the Athenian panoply seems to have related to the spread of Orphic beliefs and rituals. Asclepios belongs to the 'death and rebirth' constellation which is associated with Demeter and Dionysus and with the mimetic initiations into the afterlife practised by their adepts. Thus Socrates' final bidding could be said to educate us to the steps which must be taken if we are to progress from the naïve religious imaginings and sacrificial obligations of a Crito (who is no philosopher) to the domain of eternal Forms and of their begetter, such as they are about to be revealed to Socrates. As so very often, a Socratic injunction is Janus-like, oriented towards two directions and two different capacities of reception. This, essentially, is the interpretation put forward by St

John Damascene. The song of the dying cock will accompany the voyage of the philosophic soul from a more or less material Hades to the pure, absolute light of the *Logos*. 'We' courteously includes both Crito and Socrates in a shared motion; the 'I' tells of insights and expectations open to the enlightened.

As the law prescribes, Socrates dies at sundown. He invokes, with his dying breath, the bird whose cry proclaims sunrise. There could be no neater example of dialectic. In the *Symposium*, the cock rouses Aristodemus from drunken slumber, allowing him to report to Apollodorus the events and discourse of the night's banquet. We remember this banquet closes with Socrates' proof – which Agathon and Aristophanes are too besotted to recall or reconstrue – that the writer of tragedy is also and equally the writer of comedy. This (lost) equation bridges the two polarities of *eros*, at once carnal and spiritual, immanent and transcendent, as they are celebrated in the *Symposium*. It relates also to the desolation and joy of mortal farewell and immortal felicity as expounded in the *Phaedo*. The cock of Socrates' adieu is veritably the summoner to darkness and the herald of everlasting dawn.

Let the cock guide us towards the question of whether the revealed admits of a rational hermeneutic.

It is his annunciation of morning which rings out in the Christian liturgy: *Gallo canente spes redit*. In countless verbal, iconographic and musical presentations of the theme of resurrection, the rooster, with his plumage of flame and sun, images the negation of death. We saw that in fable and in slang, this negation is associated with sexual drive, with the libidinous power of the 'cock' to engender new life. Where the world is a barnyard – a current conceit in medieval, Renaissance and popular cultures – whose eggs symbolize the ancient riddle of the coming into being of the cosmos, the cock is God the Father.

But the episode which links the cock to the death of Jesus is of a humbler and sadder sort. In Mark 14:30, Jesus to Peter: 'Verily I say unto thee, that this day, even in this night, before the cock crow twice, thou shalt deny me thrice.' That 'twice' is lacking in Matthew.

Luke (22:34) varies further: 'the cock shall not crow this day before that thou shalt thrice deny that thou knowest me'. The Fourth Gospel closely echoes Matthew. The motif is unambiguous: the crowing of a cock, in the courtyard of the house of the High Priest, either singular or repeated, will accompany and declare a second betrayal of the Son of Man. In some respects, this betrayal cuts deeper than that of Judas. Simon Peter will be tested less by Satan (though all men are) than by natural frailty, by the solicitations of our fallen humanity. Peter, foremost of the disciples and the 'rock' on whom the risen Saviour will found his church, fails his master in the hour of peril. The psychological drama of Peter's denial springs from the fact that it is committed voluntarily yet against his true intent. The enduring shock of Peter's inability to withstand the 'temptation ' (*peirasmos*) of fear vibrates in entry 317 of Pascal's 'cinematic' *Abrégé de la vie de Jésus-Christ*: *Et néanmoins Pierre.* The uncannily compressed *néanmoins* stands both for the abjection of Peter's cowardice and for the remorse and heroic martyrdom to come.

Though wholly familiar, the ensuing scene retains its sombre tension. Western literature adverts to it on numerous occasions (think of Donne or of Baudelaire). It inspires western painters (Caravaggio, La Tour). Musical settings of the Passion mime the crow of the cock. Following on the Evangelists, Flemish painters, who so often depicted the narration, set a coal-braiser or hearth-fire in the courtyard or interior of the house of Annas, the High Priest, or Caiaphas, his son-in-law (our testimonies differ). April evenings can be chilly in Jerusalem. All too meaningfully, Simon Peter has followed at a distance and not entered the house. Yet if Mark is to be credited, of all the disciples, Peter alone had not fled in the tumult of Jesus' arrest. Luke's chronicle is the most circumstantial. By the light of the fire, a servant girl denounces Peter to the other domestics and bystanders: 'This man also was with him.' Peter's emphatic negation (*arneisthai*) exactly fulfils the Lord's prediction: 'Woman, I do not know him.' The La Rochelle and Geneva Bible of 1616, rendering this same reply in St John, gives it the lapidary concision of high drama: 'Je n'en fuis point.' By inserting a separation in time between the successive denials, Luke conducts the action towards a more realistic hour for cock-crow. Peter has denied any knowledge of Jesus; he denies being among his companions and being one of those Galileans so specially implicated in Jesus' ministry and ascent to Jerusalem. Matthew has him 'cursing' and 'swearing'. Human accents sharpen with fear: would this alone not have unmasked the Galilean fisherman? 'And immediately, while he yet spake, the cock crew.' At that instant, the cock is indeed a bird of night, of ghastly omen. On a level as yet opaque, he affirms the complete validity and potential for grace in Jesus' oracular prediction.

It is Luke, so much the 'writer', who transcribes or imagines the crowning movement of sorrow and salvation: 'The Lord turned and looked at Peter.' It is this turning, this look at the exact instant of the cock's call, which poets and painters have laboured to recapture, which cantatas and oratorios seek to translate. As in the case of the wordless kiss which Christ bestows on Dostoevsky's Grand Inquisitor, the meanings are translucent, but of a clarity resistant to paraphrase or explication. Only in the motion and eyes of total love can there be the dark light of total sadness. Only in the sentence passed, as in a 'first last judgement', by betrayed love, can there be, though as yet wholly imperceptible to Peter himself, the assurance of subsequent redemption and forgiveness. In Mark alone, the cock crows twice. May one take this to mean that the first call signifies the defeat and damning of Peter, whereas the second, already directed to the rising day, portends his later witness and glory?

Is there any other point or pericope at which the ambivalent, genuinely gnostic figure of the cock has bearing on Jesus? Hints of epilepsy, of the 'holy sickness' and the visionary illuminations which may come of seizures, cling stubbornly to the mythographic traditions surrounding the riddling persona of the Nazarene. As late as the nineteenth century, cocks are sacrificed in the Scottish Highlands to ensure or to give thanks for recovery from epileptic fits. Bird and Saviour, sacred illness and clairvoyance, come together in 'The Man Who Died', D. H. Lawrence's last and strangest story. In this tale, the horror and sanctity of resurrection in the torn flesh are 'debated' (enacted) between Jesus and the solar cock. In unsettling play are the intimate bonds between healing and sexual potency on the one hand, and between death and disincarnate resurrection (*Verklärung*) on the other. No less than Plato and Luke, Lawrence dramatizes the divided nature, the duality of the 'bird of dawning' whose song can be of sepulchral night.

Comparisons, parallels, studies in mirroring and asymmetry as between Jesus and Socrates, with special reference to their deaths, are, since the Neo-Platonism of the Renaissance at least, a commonplace in the West. When, in Jacques-Louis David's celebrated painting of Socrates' last moments, the sage is depicted with his index finger pointing towards Elysium, this iconic posture explicitly 'cites' the gesture of Christ in such renditions of the Last Judgement as Michelangelo's. When, in his bizarre paper of 1916, Walter Benjamin denounces Socrates' abuses of *eros*, the inferred corrective is that of Grünewald's image of Christ and of the Immaculate Conception. Strangely, there is, until now, no comprehensive treatment of this central *topos*; very likely, no bibliography, no iconological catalogue of thematic contrasts and analogues could hope to be exhaustive.

Parallels drawn have been open or covert, theological and philosophic, ethical and psychological, historical and literary. In sceptical-libertine writings of the late seventeenth and eighteenth centuries, the death of Socrates and the Crucifixion are contrasted in what is frequently an 'Aesopian' or clandestine code. Outwardly, Socrates' conduct in his final days and at the hemlock hour is characterized as being the supreme embodiment of a secular, pagan rationality and *dignitas*. The comeliness of his parting marks, as it were, the upper limit of pre-Christian humanism. But the *kenosis* of the god-man Christ and his agony on the Cross are taken to signify a 'quantum jump' into revealed truth and the proffer of universal salvation. It is just the hideousness of Jesus' suffering, the abjection and ugliness which he endures in the flesh, in their stark contrast with the elegant nobility of Socrates' passing, which articulate the new message to man.

This is the explicit tenor of the comparison as it was taught and moralized upon in schools, in manuals of behaviour and of rhetoric, during late Renaissance, baroque and neo-classical generations. It is the official reading still provided by the more cautious of the *philosophes* in the Enlightenment. But in key cases, the subtext is otherwise. To subversive spirits such as Pierre Bayle, to thinkers of beauty such as Winckelmann, it is the death of Socrates, not that of the Galilean, which is exemplary. Socrates bears undying witness to the capacity of the human spirit to face and accept mortality, not in any animist or dogmatic reliance on celestial compensation, but by virtue of its love of moral and intellectual truth. Even in utmost torment – thus the implicit argument – Jesus is persuaded of his translation to heaven and of his return in cosmic majesty. Socrates has no such insurance. His intuitions of some kind of survivance for the enlightened soul, his prevision of Elysian fields, are either gently ironic means of teaching or, at best, metaphors of speculative reason. It may well be for Socrates, as for Lear's fool, that we are only 'for the dark'. What concerns Socrates, and most directly the 'Socrates' who precedes with his death the Platonic modulation into transcendentalism, is the rational, virtuous conduct of our earthly lives and the human quality of our acceptance of death. What he aims at in the *Crito*, as Montaigne understood so admiringly, is that discipline of decency, that tact of heart which should humanize even a cruel death.

In nineteenth-century philosophy and philosophy of religion, the Jesus-Socrates motif becomes almost obsessional. It is, famously, the pivot of Hegel's lifelong reflections on the philosophy of history and of religion. No other moments are as dramatically demonstrative of the *Bildungsroman*, of the evolutionary dynamics of human consciousness, as are those of the deaths of Socrates and of Christ. The execution of Socrates argues the creative dialectic of conflict between individuality and the state (as does the execution of Antigone in whom Hegel envisages an instinctual counterpart to Socrates). The phenomenology of Jesus' person and Passion, their transgression of the Judaism of Abraham and of Moses, determine new categories of consciousness and of conscience, categories fundamental to the birth of modernity and to the self-realization of

Geist. It is not only materialist interpreters and critics of Hegel who have pondered the concordance between the triple motion of Hegelian dialectical logic and the paradigm of the Trinity.

Any index to the topic of Socrates and Jesus, in similitude and contrast (even antithesis), in the works of Kierkegaard would list references and discursive passages in almost every title. It is fair to say that Kierkegaard's structural axis – that of the steps from the aesthetic to the ethical and from the ethical to the religious – is traced in the constant evocation of Socrates and the man from Nazareth. Already in Kierkegaard's inspired dissertation on Socratic irony and on the pedagogic and heuristic modes of Socratic teaching, the contrasting theme of Jesus' homiletic and allegoric means is latent. Thereafter, and voluminously, Søren Kierkegaard will meditate on the contrarieties between Socrates' maieutic rationality and the existential 'absurdity' and unreason of Jesus' life and preaching. The 'guilt' of Socrates (a paradoxical issue already pursued in a number of fascinating and legalistic, though little known, eighteenth-century tracts, notably in France and Italy), is seen by Kierkegaard in ironic counterpoint to the innocence of Jesus. It was precisely because Kierkegaard intuited so acutely in himself the claims of the Socratic – he was a virtuoso questioner and dialectician, a gadfly and exasperation to his fellow-citizens in Copenhagen – that his 'decision for Christ' was so taxing and had to be so uncompromisingly dramatized. And even as Hegel senses in Antigone some degree of fusion between absolute ethics and Socratic provocation on the one hand and the sacrificial self-annulment of Jesus on the other, so Kierkegaard discovers in Job both the Socratic challenger and the acceptor of unmerited suffering and of submission to the mystery of divine love. The *Either/Or* emblematic of Kierkegaard, and the untenable mediation between them, is persistently that of Socrates and of Christ, of hemlock and Golgotha.

The dialogue continues in Feuerbach's reflections on death (his masterpiece) and critiques of religion. But it is, obviously, in Nietzsche that the duality and congruence of Jesus and of Socrates attain their most intense pitch. During the concluding ecstasies of vision and argument in Turin, it is Socrates/Christ who become(s)

Nietzsche's obsession. Now the polemic against Socratic rational-ism, against Socrates' physical ugliness, against the analytic sterility of his teachings and their corrosion of the primal genius of Greek tragedy, with which the young Nietzsche had initiated his philo-sophic philology and cultural criticism, blend with the indictment of Jesus in the *Antichrist* and *Ecce Homo*. The Athenian pedant and the Galilean slave-moralist overlap in a kind of wild mental dance during Nietzsche's twilight. 'Ich bin dem Heiland Asklepios einen Hahn schuldig.' By itself, this translation from the *Crito* speaks volumes. The word *Heiland* does not, of course, have any but punning relevance to Asclepios. The real presence in Nietzsche's version is that of Christ the Saviour.

In mordant shorthand, the later Nietzsche interleaves what he takes to be the Socratic crimes against Dionysian vitality with the 'slave-pathos', with the canting idealism and humbling of man's natural ego in 'Judaic' Christianity. As libertines and ironists had done before him, Nietzsche mocks the Judaeo-Christian 'obscenity' of a crucified God. Both Socrates, the simian-faced idealist, and the sufferer from Nazareth 'do dirt on life' (the unnerving phrase is D. H. Lawrence's and encapsulates a faithful understanding of Nietzsche). The polemic is complex throughout, in that it amalga-mates the Platonic Socrates with a Jesus seen in the light of Judaic utopian rationalism. Obliquely conjoined, the two figures and the laming weight of their deaths on the western psyche provoke Nietzsche's critique from the early papers on Socrates and Greek tragedy to the debate on Strauss's *Life of Jesus*. Their adverse presence shadows the *Genealogy of Morals* and inspires, in ecstatic contrariety, the gospel and dialectic of *Zarathustra*. Socrates and the man Jesus preside, like malevolent idols, at the crazed epilogue. 'When one reads the New Testament, one must wear gloves,' says Nietzsche. The same gloves, one is given to understand, must be worn when reading the *Crito*. In it Nietzsche's unerring ear will have heard that same doctrine of non-violence, of absolute forgiveness which so exasperated him in the Nazarene. (I will come back to this point.) The cock of Zarathustra sings neither death, nor betrayal, nor purgatorial superstitions. He clarions high noon and that promise of Eternal Return which is Nietzsche's (jealous) repartee to Christ's offer of resurrection.

And today?

Never have the trial and death of Socrates been more insistently unfinished business. The dilemmas – *Das Problem des Sokrates*, as Nietzsche calls it – have never been more acute. They comport the coexistence of the state and of intellectual freedom, of diverse forms of popular democracy and of intellectual excellence, of the conventions of coherence indispensable to a social order and the anarchic, almost necessarily cynical autarchy of the free spirit. Not only are these conflicts unresolved; they are, today, of peculiar discomfort (*Unbehagen*). They are, in the proper, most vivid sense, dialectical: each proposition enforces culpability and self-questioning on the other. The western *polis*, be it city-state or nation, is branded with the ineradicable guilt of having slain the archetypal thinker, the human being who, *par excellence*, lived the life of the mind. (We recall the dread charge, taken up by Luke and Paul from the Old Testament, that Jerusalem will always slay its prophets.) In turn, however, there is a real sense in which Socrates gives the city no choice, in which he forces on 'commonality', whether of character or of intellect, the enduring transgression enacted in his capital punishment. This, in the shadow of the Dreyfus Affair, is the argument implicit in Georges Sorel's sophistic, incisive *Procès de Socrate* (Lenin had read Sorel). Socrates, moreover, by his very refusal of ordinariness and illusion, puts in question the possibility of the democratic compromise with human mediocrity. Hence the revisionist counter to Socrates in I. F. Stone's recent version of the trial. Cities in the West could be defined as the 'collective reality principles' which are compelled to try and condemn their Socrates. Observe how he insists.

By propounding his commitment to the body politic, by refusing privacy and solitude – he is wholly of the market-place – Socrates forces the issue. A man or woman infected by the leprosy of pure thought, by the virus of questioning, can remain a hermit. He or she need not leave the desert or the bare room (Wittgenstein) for the *politeia* of Cleon or of Herod. Some of Socrates' true successors – Pascal, Spinoza, Kierkegaard, Nietzsche himself – will argue out of aloneness. They will shun politics. Not Socrates, who thrusts his presence on the daily life of the community, who demands that his life and ideas be examined and justified in the *agora*. The ambiguity of Plato's response to this Socratic strategy pervades the dialogues. Much in Plato cannot pardon Athens. Together with the Gospels, the *Apology*, *Phaedo* and *Crito* remain the crucial passion-plays and indictments of human vileness in our western world. They would renew each day our intimations of irreparable betrayal and loss. The idealized lineaments of Plato's *Republic* can be clearly seen as designed to prevent a social-political structure in which a Socrates can (has to be) convicted and done away with. Yet this is not Plato's final or complete perspective. The fierce interdict on religious-philosophic scepticism, on radical speculation, detailed in the draconian Tenth Book of the *Laws*, suggests a deep-seated apprehension. The despotism of virtue in the later Plato could not have housed Socrates. (Can, asks Dostoevsky, any established church house the Galilean trouble-maker?)

Our perplexities remain Plato's, but have behind them a history crueller, more bewildered, than any that classical Greek political theory could have foreseen. We have accused and killed 'Socrates' perennially. Each hounding, be it that of Galileo or Rousseau, each doing to death, be it that of Giordano Bruno or of Condorcet, is a footnote to the typological disaster in Athens. Every time a community attempts, by censorship, ostracism or killing to silence a moral-intellectual outsider within its walls, to gag or efface his intolerable queries, it lives a Socratic hour. But concomitantly, the thinker, the scientist, the artist, the ironist or satirist who presses *in extremis* his deconstructive doubts, who sets his addiction to what he takes to be the truth above the inherited beliefs and compromises essential to the continuance of the city, repeats the Socratic provocation. Consciously or not, whether on a secular level (that of a Karl Kraus) or on a religious-philosophic level (that of a Simone Weil), the 'No-sayer' to injustice, to human greed and stupidity, is not only risking but soliciting a Socratic destiny. Is it fortuitous that

[378]

the *agents provocateurs* of the spirit and the intellect, certainly in modern western history, should so often have been Jews, as was Jesus before them? It is in the marginalization or destruction of so many Jewish questioners, from the rabbis of medieval Spain to Spinoza and to Freud, that the western state had repeated the reflexes of self-defence and of alarmed vengeance at work in the dooming of Socrates. The killing of Socrates and Jew-hatred advertise the organic fears and loathing which tyranny and the mob feel towards the heresies of intelligence. The *Einsatzgruppen* of the German armies in the east culled and massacred first all those who could read.

Plato's profound ambivalence in respect of despotism, which almost proved fatal to him during his ill-fated involvements in Sicilian politics, has borne complex fruit. Far from acting as critics and opponents of totalitarianism, a clutch of eminent moralists and philosophers have been theoreticians and apologists for autocracy. They have found egalitarian politics and social justice either irrelevant to or more or less incompatible with ideals of absolute intellectual inquiry (has this finding ever been refuted?). Hegel's advocacy of the Prussian system was only tempered sentimentally by roseate memories of youth and revolution. In our times, the conjunction of philosophical-ethical mastery with political support for totalitarian regimes has taken on a sharp profile. We have only begun to come to uncertain terms with the Stalinism of Lukács, with Sartre's repeated apologias for the *gulag* and the barbarism of the Maoist cultural revolution, or, most saliently, with the politics of Martin Heidegger. For the liberal faith these and lesser cases constitute what Goya would call a 'nightmare of reason'.

The paradox may not be one. The private existence of the mandarin, of the academic philosopher – Wittgenstein detested this rubric as cordially as Socrates would have – the immersion of the *maître à penser* or pedagogue in abstraction, in the exigent dust of textuality, can generate a fascination with violence, with the scenarios of history at their most savage. Hegel's Napoleon-obsession is matched by that which Lenin and Stalin exercised on a Lukács or a Kojève. Bertrand Russell's pacifism is oddly kin to violence: shortly after the end of the Second World War, he called for a preventive nuclear strike against the Soviet Union. Heidegger's appetite for political might, for a Platonic mission of governance over the spiritual and social destiny of the state, was scarcely veiled. Once again a Plato was more than ready to direct a Dionysius.

The 'strangeness' of Socrates, like that of Jesus, remains intractable to any confident reconstruction. But the Socrates before Plato seems to have been non-academic to the grain. His seminar rooms were the open street, the shaded banks of a stream, a dinner-party. It is the high academicism in Plato, the institutionalization of metaphysical instruction, the partly sophistic, partly scientific redefinition of the philosopher and dialectician as an academic specialist after the time of Socrates, which allow the opportunistic, self-dramatizing commerce between intellect and power. So far as we can make out, Socrates' stance was at once that of the ordinary citizen and of a subverter of majority opinions. He was an exemplary foot-soldier – itself an activity emblematic of democracy – and served with stoic good humour under stress of battle and retreat. At the same time, his awareness of the natural aristocracy of beauty and mental endowment was exceptionally acute and unconcealed. What appears to have had no hold on him whatever was the hypnosis of violence. Plato's uneasy jibe that Diogenes the Cynic was 'Socrates gone mad' contains a piercing insight. Both Socrates and Diogenes are immune to the seductions of worldly power. An Alexander or a Stalin leave them unawed. The treasons of the clerics committed by a Fichte in his season of chauvinism and anti-Semitism, the errors of a Sartre or a Heidegger, are not of Socratic provenance. They originate, as it were, out of Alcibiades or, more precisely, out of the Plato whom Alcibiades spellbound (and whom Karl Popper was to excoriate).

As Gregory Vlastos has shown once again, in his deeply felt if controversial portrayal, Socrates' position in the *Phaedo* is crystal clear. A man or woman aspiring to virtue cannot willingly commit an injustice. To do evil to any other human being is to act without or against virtue. This axiom absolutely excludes retaliation, whatever the provocation. Socrates will do nothing that could harm or do offence to his unjust enemies. Thus he will not avail himself of the chance to escape from prison and death. This would be to break the law and perform a flagrant injustice. Plato fully sets out Socrates' argument (if Vlastos is right, he does so uncomfortably). The position adopted by Socrates is indeed 'scandalous' (in the sense of a 'radiant enormity' such as we find it in the use of this Greek word in Corinthians 1). It contradicts not only natural instinct, but the entirety of the heroic, masculine traditions in the ancient Mediterranean world. It is as alien to Semitic criteria of retribution as it is to the fine discriminations drawn between condign and excessive retaliation and punishment in Aristotle's *Nicomachean Ethics*. The postulate of non-violence, of non-retaliation in the face of evil and injury, the rejection of the law of the *talion* are (Vlastos again) not only at the innermost centre of Socrates' being and teaching: they are his enduring challenge to mankind. Kant's moral imperatives come after Socrates and seem more complexly qualified. In the West, the doctrine of the *Phaedo* has one sole counterpart: it is Jesus' offering of 'the other cheek' and the loving pardon he extends to his tormentors and executioners. Little wonder, then, that Proclus and the Neo-Platonists of the Florentine Renaissance regarded such texts as the *Apology* and the *Phaedo* as truly divine. That they cited them in exactly the same spirit in which St Augustine or Anselm cite Scripture.

In both instances, let us remember, the presence is that of a text.

No intellectual or historical mapping can fully locate the Cross in the landscape of concept and of sensibility as our century closes. For participants in an overwhelming secular, technologically oriented society, this location is a 'black hole' left by mythologies and unreason out of the past. For the majority, one suspects, of 'practising' Christians – and what does 'practising' entail in this context? – the Crucifixion remains an unexamined inheritance, a symbolic marker of familiar but vestigial recognitions. This marker is revered and invoked in conventional idiom and gestures. Its concrete status, the enormity of suffering and injustice it incarnates, would appear to have faded from felt immediacy. How many educated men or women now hear Pascal's cry that humanity must not sleep because Christ hangs on his Cross till the end of the world? A 'rationalized' Christianity hovers between an untenable literalism and symbolic insubstantiality, in the indistinct spaces of fitful imagining which we call myth.

There *are* those – they need not be Christians or even religious believers – for whom the matter of Golgotha is the irreducible crux (let the pun be allowed) at the heart of our moral and political condition. There are those who feel that there can be no responsible, indeed and paradoxically, no *rational* endeavour to grasp the collapse of European values in this century and the regime of the inhuman which obtains since 1914, without reference to Christ's agony. Without a stringent rethinking of that sense of total abandonment, of total defeat, voiced by the Son of Man on Gethsemane. There are among us those who are convinced that to perceive mankind as it actually is after Auschwitz and a century of licensed bestiality is to perceive Golgotha and the relation between the two realities.

Theologians, philosophic theologians, moralists, certain poets and, no doubt, silent men and women who try to lead their lives in the acknowledged shadow of the unspeakable (cf. Ernst Wiechert's spectral novel, *Missa sine nomine*) have engaged this relationship. They have pointed to the long and murderous history of Jew-hatred within Christendom. They have listened, with a new frankness and embarrassment, to the calls for the elimination of the Jews as these resound in the Church Fathers, in Luther. The widespread indifference of the churches, both Catholic and Protestant, to the coming and fulfilment of the Holocaust has been documented and debated. An entire school of post-Barthian theology, most notably in Germany, has argued that Christianity is now gravely ill, that its historical record on anti-Semitism and its lamentable weakness during the midnight of western man have put in radical doubt the Christian message of love and salvation. Searching and sombre perceptions have emerged from these considerations. I am not persuaded that they reach deep enough.

There are taboos, politically and psychologically defensible, which surround any clear analysis of the fatalities of coexistence between Jew and Christian. Historically, we know next to nothing of the circumstances underlying the refusal of Christ's messianic claims by his Jewish contemporaries. The Psalms, Deutero-Isaiah, manifold figurations in the Torah and the Prophets, had 'foretold' the coming and the passion of the Suffering Servant out of the house of David. Rejecting the Galilean, the Jews of his time rejected something urgent in their own messianic expectations. Only if we could clarify the psychic sources of this rejection and the scars it left, could we put into focus the central truth that there is at the very roots of Christianity a strong pulse of *Jewish self-hatred* (witness Mark and, principally, Paul of Tarsus). In the black light of the Shoah, one is very nearly tempted to define Christianity as the fruit of that self-hatred. The parallel with Marx's anti-Semitism is not fortuitous: Christianity and Marxism are the two major heresies out of messianic Judaism.

It may be that there are between Golgotha and Auschwitz symmetries unbearable to reasoned understanding. By refusing God's *kenosis*, His self-bestowal in the person of Jesus, Judaism judged spurious and contrary to reason the divinization of a man. At Auschwitz, the butchers reduced both their victims and themselves to a subhuman level. They 'bestialized' humanity in the flesh of those who had denied the literal divinity of that same flesh in Jesus the Jew.

It would be idle to speculate on the future of western ethics and metaphysics after these new dark ages. A certain economic rebound (always fragile), the explosive spread of crypto-religious and fundamentalist movements across the globe, are no proof of a renascence of spirit. The current collapse of Marxism, if it is that, is a profoundly ambiguous phenomenon. It is in Marxism that post-Christian western messianic hopes were invested, that manifest expression was given to the hunger for justice on earth. Both the Sermon on the Mount and the communist *Manifesto* proclaim their origin in Mosaic teachings and in Amos. The downfall of the Marxist ideal may bring with it the final enfeeblement of Christianity. Wrestlers succumb to mutual exhaustion. What is clear is that the venture of authentic humaneness in social, political man (*die Menschlichkeit im Menschen*) led to derision and defeat on the Cross and in the ash of the death-camps. Neither the trope of Resurrection – so uncertain in Mark, so absent from Pascal's monition – nor the two-edged miracle of the rebirth of Israel, can wipe out the terror at the heart of our history. Nor can pluralistic liberalism and legislated tolerance efface the killing of Socrates.

Where they are honest, where they do not deal with formalities or self-flattering exercises in academic analysis, attempts to face the insoluble end in images. It is pictures and stories which make endurable our losses. It is the telling of tales in the arts, in parables. Our two main threads draw together. In Caravaggio's *Denial of St Peter*, which may have been that haunted master's last work, the head of the Apostle is closely modelled on traditional busts of Socrates. In Baghdad, during the Gulf War, the cocks crowed in shrill song the night through. But the brilliant light over the city was not that of the sun.

It is to this pass that we have been brought by two sets of texts out of antiquity.

To the one set, that of Scripture, there has attached, over almost two millennia, the designation of the 'revealed'. The corpus has been held to have originated more or less immediately in the word of God. Hermeneutically, this makes of Holy Writ what physics calls a 'singularity'. In respect of the biblical canon, normal laws of understanding and critical reception – criteria of logical causality, of empirical falsifiability, of historical or rational credibility – do not apply or apply only at the surface. The notion of normative conditions is itself suspended precisely in so far as it entails repeatability in other and comparable cases. Where the word of God and its revelation to man are concerned, no such investigative checks exist. The object offered to understanding is *sui generis*.

The Platonic set has, we have seen, also been acclaimed as divine. But such a claim has been put forward as a 'hyper'-analogy. The author of the *Crito* or the *Phaedo* is not, in sobriety, considered a god. Where the concept of 'inspiration' is invoked, of philosophic

[384]

and stylistic powers beyond the ordinary, this invocation, as in the references made to the Muses by poets, is a figure of discourse and explanatory fiction. The hermeneutic, the arts of understanding brought to bear on a Platonic dialogue are, though perhaps in exalted measure, of the kind brought to bear on any semantic artefact produced by natural means and mortal hands. The cock destined for Asclepios is not 'miraculous' in his crowing as is that chosen by Christ to attend Simon Peter's denial. When the guests go 'into the night' during the *Symposium*, this simple phrase may be identical with that which marks Judas's exit during the Last Supper narrative in St John, but the status of transcendentally underwritten verity which tradition has assigned to the one does not apply to the other. Can responsible reading, today, make sense of the difference, of the 'surplus value' (I borrow and distort the Marxist term) said to be yielded by the words and sentences in Scripture beyond any to be harvested from the parallel or even identical components of language in a Platonic dialogue?

In both cases, which is simply to say for the sum of 'sacred' and of secular texts in our civilization, the same instrumentalities of access are, certainly since Spinoza and the nineteenth-century 'Higher Critics', in play. They are those of epigraphy, lexicography, comparative grammar, rhetorical and structural analysis, philological and historical verification. In both instances, the hermeneutic act is one of rational linguistics in the fullest sense of the term. Text criticism, again in a comprehensive sense, is the sole approach available to the educated, to the rational recipient. Where, then, lies the difference? At present, any ascription of 'singularity' in regard to 'revealed speech and speech-acts' – e.g. the narration and narratology of 'miracles' – is, in the ordinary sense, scandalous. It is, literally, an 'en-normity' outside reason. In this late twentieth century, the proposition that certain ancient writings, formally (lexically, syntactically, structurally) homologous with any other body of texts, with any other communicative sequence, are to be set apart because they possess an authority, an immediacy of generation wholly singular to themselves, is, on any intelligible ground of which I am aware, unsustainable. It is an empowering fable, a myth of myths.

What could make such a claim verifiable? It might be argued that the pressure of the moral and 'credential' imperatives in Scripture is of so unique a kind as to entail a realization in personal action, a transformation in the listener's or reader's existence. But such is the effect of much serious philosophy, literature and art. As the archaic torso of Apollo in Rilke's sonnet proclaims, all great art bids us 'change our lives'. It has been propounded that the 'word of God' exhibits an axiomatic, predictive force such as demarcates a mathematical or mathematical-physical system of laws from natural language. Plainly, this is not so. The long history of the preaching and interpretation of the Old and the New Testaments has been that of an incessant deferral from the eschatological, of a postponement, via allegory and metaphor, of any material fulfilment. Might archaeology unearth, at some future date, evidence to demonstrate the process of supernatural origination in 'revealed' texts, a process substantively other than that implied by allusion to the Muses, to poetic trance (as in Plato's *Phaedrus*) or to individual poetic genius? A moment's thought suggests that the mere notion of any such discovery of new 'evidence' is an absurdity.

This absurdity is immune to the dogmatic alarms and linguistic obscurantism or innocence of all literalist and fundamentalist positions. It may well be that these positions are, numerically, again in the ascendant. It seems likely that human reason, under-mined by political barbarism and intractable social dilemmas, will again seek refuge in intolerant fears. The closed minds, the fury of atavistic orthodoxies are on the march. But these cannot restore to intelligibility the dogmas of textual revelation.

Subtler moves are possible. Vico, when adverting to Homer, Heidegger when explicating the pre-Socratics, suggest that we do find in such texts vestiges of a phase in the condition of language and of exceptional sensibilities, in which signifier and signified, word and world, semantic marker and *Logos*, were concordant as they have not been since. This semiotic of the pre-lapsarian derives, fairly obviously, from the conceit of Adamic speech in Eden, of a lost Arcadia of linguistic equivalence with truth, as it haunts western theories of meaning from Plato's *Cratylus* to Walter Benjamin.

[386]

Two Cocks

There was a time, so goes the argument, when the discourse of certain men and women was immediate and transparent to unambiguous sense, to truths and perceptions whose source was that of a fused social collectivity (Vico), of the Being of being (Heidegger) or of the proximate presence of God. Biblical texts would retain, or retain in considerable part, this *Ur*-permeability. An irreducible, although often enigmatic, core of significant 'otherness', of transcendent reinsurance, inhabits the lexicon and grammar of the Torah and Gospels. In Judaism, the corollary is that of the cessation of direct linguistic exchanges with God after Elijah. In Islam, it is the hypothesis of a theology and philosophy born of a time of prophecy and of a theology and philosophy constructed thereafter. One recalls Meister Eckhart's tremendous trope, in his commentary *In Exodum*, according to which Adamic speech, the 'Hebrew of God', is itself 'sent to exile' after the refusal of God to explain Himself to Moses out of the Burning Bush.

Intuitively, these paradigms of a semantic 'break', of a rupture between a primal, authentically 'divinized' mode of language and a subsequent, secular tenor, are attractive. They would account not only for biblical revelation, but, by analogy, for the visionary splendours and lastingness of philosophic and poetic utterance in the 'classics' (a splendour which many have felt to be tenaciously unrecapturable). In actual fact, there is no shred of evidence for them. On the biological time-scale, the evolution of speech in our species represents no more than the blink of an eye. No trace subsists of any fall from linguistic grace, of any closure of discourse or of hearing to ontological originality and the revealed. We are exactly the same 'language-animal' named by Greek anthropology. The Torah passage, the saying by Anaximander, the Homeric verse, does not evidence any mode of textuality prior to that of our own resources and hermeneutically nearer to dawn.

Thus, if there is a 'revelation', it must lie in the eye and ear of the beholder. In the postulate and *a priori* of faith which he or she brings to the reception of the canonic. The 'revealed' is the fruit of the investment of credence, of mimetic resolve (rite, liturgy) made by the individual within the larger community of the faithful. It can, intelligibly, be nothing more. It is perfectly comparable with the investment, often determinant of life and death, made, say, by the communist in certain Marxist-Leninist source-texts or by the Freudian in the sybilline books of the begetter. Strictly considered, the 'holy' script is revealed to itself by its reader and exegete within the house of shared beliefs. Modern epistemology provides some access to this situation. The 'language-games' of the sacred may well be more widely sovereign, more poignant and unsettling, than any others played (i.e. spoken and written) by men. But they remain language-games whose only rules and validation must be internal. They cannot be demonstrated 'from outside'; they have no self-evident proof. I take this to be the import, profound and far-reaching, of Wittgenstein's note in the *Philosophical Investigations* (I, 373): 'Theology as grammar.' Any reading of the cock of St Peter as inserted in an ontologically different context from that of the sacrifice to Asclepios, is, in Kierkegaardian terminology, a leap into the absurd.

This leap may entail a fundamentalist hermeneutic. It need not do so. Personally, I find scriptural literalism or any peremptory attribution to God of 'speech facts' such as we know and use them, to be unacceptable. Be they rabbinic, Muslim or Evangelical (the Roman Catholic handling of biblical texts has long been of a wary sophistication). Such attribution offends human reason and historical evidence – so much in the Old Testament burns with tribal folly. Literalism evades the paramount obligation of the individual conscience which is to hammer out for itself, under stress of free understanding and the risk of error, the textual foundations, if any, for its beliefs. An unexamined adoption of the 'revealed' and of the mystery of authority which revelation implies, makes it even more difficult, if not impossible, to earn that most demanding of rights: to keep quiet about God.

And yet (again, I speak personally).

Reason as I can, there are passages in the Old and the New Testaments which I am unable to accord with any sensible image, however exalted, of normal authorship, of conception and composition as we seek to grasp them in even the greatest of thinkers and

[388]

poets. Mundane imaginings are almost wholly rebuked by, for example, the thought of Shakespeare coming home for lunch and reporting on whether or not the writing of Acts III and IV of *King Lear* 'had gone well'. *Almost.* Considered reflection does allow such a vignette its place at the far edges of the ordinary. As I have remarked earlier, I am at a loss when, by analogy or similitude, I try to graft this picture on to the author of the speeches out of the whirlwind in Job. When I would apply it to certain sequences in the Psalms or Ecclesiastes. When I would explain to myself the genesis of such pericopes in the Gospels as Jesus' 'Before Abraham was, I am' or of very nearly the entirety of chapters 13–17 in John. In such biblical instances, the concept of a wholly rational hermeneutic escapes me. I find myself backed up against the harsh radiance of 'the scandalous'. It is not 'theology as grammar' which seems pertinent. It is grammar as theology.

Two Suppers

I

To eat alone is to experience or suffer a peculiar solitude. The sharing of food and drink, on the other hand, reaches into the inmost of the social-cultural condition. The range of its symbolic and material bearings is almost total. It comprises religious ritual, the constructs and demarcations of gender, the domains of the erotic, the complicities or confrontations of politics, the contrasts of discourse, playful or grave, the rites of matrimony and of funereal sorrow. In its manifold complexities, the consumption of a meal around a table, with friend or foe, disciples or detractors, intimates or strangers, the innocence or wrought conventions of conviviality, are the microcosm of society itself. To 'convive' (the verb is rare after the mid-seventeenth century) is indeed to 'live with and among others' in the most articulate, charged form which is that of the shared meal. In counterpoint, there is, in the breaking of bread alone, a strangeness as of a beast or of a god. *Le vin du solitaire*, Baudelaire's rubric, is a desolate parody or negation of the act of community, of communication in communion both holy and secular.

Anthropology and ethnography dwell on the centrality of communal meals – where 'communal' extends from the clandestine or closely guarded gathering of a chosen group all the way to the saturnalias and carnivals open to the whole city or tribe. Together with religious studies and psychoanalytic proposals, with sociology and the analysis of myths, anthropology – *les sciences de l'homme* – relates to the institution of the shared meal crucial concepts of the totemic, of human and animal sacrifice, of purification and initiation. Again, the range is very nearly unlimited. It extends

The Priestley Lectures, University of Toronto, April 1995.

from the practices and symbolism of cannibalism, rooted in primary, elemental reflexes of consciousness, of a laboured passage or transgression into humanity so deep-seated as to escape our full understanding, all the way to such transpositions of the 'eating of the god' as we find them in Christian Holy Communion. Moreover, archaic as they are, numerous traits of these seminal convivialities survive in the military mess, in the fraternal or professional lunch or supper-party, in the gluttony of the rural wake, in the anniversary dinner, in the innumerable modes of eating together in which men exclude women or women exclude men. Precisely because the consumption of food and drink, especially beyond immediate organic need, comes near to defining our common or 'socialized' humanity, these diverse convivialities are altogether central to our history both as individuals – from the christening party to the wake – and as members one of another in the hungry body politic.

But if the notion of conviviality seems to entail that of the festive, of the joyous even to the pitch of transcendence – what are we to make of that enigmatic occasion in Exodus 24 when God invites to partake of food and drink with Him Moses, Aaron, Nadab, Abihu and seventy of the elders of Israel? – this same notion or structure of shared experience, can entail fatality. From the infanticide and cannibalism in the supper of Atreus and Thyestes (a legend which has never relaxed its mesmeric grip on the western imagination) to that in which Banquo rises before Macbeth, from the homicidal rout at Hercules' wedding-feast to the frequent instances of courtly celebration at which Renaissance despots stabbed or poisoned their rival guests, conviviality has been the occasion of death. This paradoxical congruence is universalized in the medieval plays and allegories of Everyman: as the rich man and the glutton raises his cup to his worshipful company, Death replies to the toast. It was as if moments of culinary refinement or prodigality carried within them a covert menace. Who can forget the macabre intimations, the *memento mori* in those dinner-parties pictured by Buñuel or Fellini? Or the 'eating to death' in *La Grande Bouffe*?

Two deaths continue to characterize western moral and intellectual history. (Would that history have been markedly different, would there have been a steadier light in the landscape of western consciousness if the axiomatic event had been that of two births?) But it is to two violent deaths that we advert in the determination of our inheritance and of the ways in which this inheritance has generated the context of our culture. The deaths of Socrates and of Jesus of Nazareth continue to be the touchstones of our historicity, of the reflexes of sensibility and recognition whereby we make of remembrance, of a legacy of reference our Hebraic-Christian and classical identity. For all their finality, moreover, for all which renders them unendurable to reasoned recollection, these two executions remain vehemently unfinished. Their existential status and significance, the questions they pose press on us with undiminished insistence. Even for those – are they today in any number? – who are able to internalize some trust in Jesus' Resurrection, that concept most intractable to reason and the reality-principle, the Crucifixion will retain its terror, its sum of agony. In both these deaths the consequence of measureless waste, our sense of the irreparable, have interminable gravity.

The issues raised by the doing to death of Socrates in 399 BC are those of the possibilities of thought itself, where thought is publicly voiced. They are those, absolutely pivotal, of the coexistence or non-coexistence between the wonder, for it is that, of individual ethical perception and articulate questioning on the one hand, and the cohesion, the minimal stability, the normative perpetuation of the *polis* (the city, the *communitas*, the political collective or common-wealth) on the other. In Socrates, the imperative of thought, the indifference of interrogative insight to the inevitable impurities of political-social accommodation, is incarnate. Its anarchic compulsion or, more exactly, its commitment to criteria of moral and epistemological rigour which are not those which can be construed as antithetical to the pragmatic, compromised and compromising usages of public order, is, in Socrates, given an added dimension. It is that of his *daimonion*. In certain areas of current physics and cosmology, appeal is made to the concept of 'strangeness'. A comparable 'strangeness', that of supernatural commandment and validation, gives to Socrates' logic, to the *elenchos* or method of questioning via the forced disclosure of contradiction, their unnerving force. Only in Spinoza (perhaps his sole authentic successor) do we experience a similar concatenation of the supernatural with the logical. 'Strangeness' of this kind is not at home in the city, in *civilitas*. Hence the emancipated lightness, the musicality of Socrates' dialectic when he is in the open country, by the banks of the nymph-haunted Ilissus (as in the *Phaedrus*).

But the provocations implicit in Socrates' trial and execution are also of a more personal order (although the personal is, in Plato's portrayal, persistently a figuration of the universal). Despite laboured arguments to the contrary, Socrates comes very close to ensuring his own condemnation. He refuses to negotiate that which possesses his spirit and makes that possession sanctified by invoking the 'will of the god'. Philosophic concentration has been called the natural piety of the intellect. It is a piety of this category, authorized by the 'daemonic' (one can think here of Hegel's *Geist*), which Socrates plays against – the playful is at once crucial and exasperating – the *pietas* of official civic faith and religious institutions. Furthermore and famously, Socrates' arch proposals as to the punishment which might be meted on him instead of hemlock, make the situation irretrievable. As Xenophon uncomfortably implies, there is in Socrates' end more than a touch of suicide. (Escape from prison has been provided for, but Socrates refuses.) In a last dialectic, Socrates enforces on Athens the blood-guilt of his chosen death. Has the 'city of man' in the West recovered?

Not one of these dilemmas dates. The 'examined life' demanded by Socrates requires that each and every one of us serve on that Athenian jury. How would we have voted? Goethe's dictum, 'rather injustice than disorder', puts the prosecution case concisely. It argues, as does Hegel in respect of Creon's conflict with Antigone, that the preservation of social-legislative order makes possible the reparation of miscarriages of justice. Disorder, the dispersal of civic solidarity through anarchic individuality and 'the inner light', destroy not only daily life, but the eventuality of progress, of amelioration in the understanding and performance of justice. Is the price paid for autonomous feats of conscience too high? Athens was in a condition of military humiliation and political division when Socrates was judged. Did the truth and moral grandeur of Dreyfus's acquittal leave France almost fatally off balance on the very eve of world war? But the problems posed are even more arduous than those of the polemic coexistence between personal conscience and the constraints of the general will. The intelligentsia, the philosophic élite is not always on the side of political emancipation or freedom of conscience. Far from it. A more or less avowed longing for hierarchic, despotic styles of government inhabits a number of major philosophic systems like a sombre mirage. Plato looks repeatedly to Dionysius the tyrant; Hegel to Prussian absolutism; Heidegger to National Socialism; Sartre to Stalin and Mao. Nietzsche's fantastications of dominance are evident. And Socrates himself was held to have oligarchic leanings. So long as we reflect on the ambiguities of the condition of the individual within society, on the relations between pure thought and political enactment, that Athenian jury will be out.

There is, therefore, a sense in which the matter of Socrates' death remains timeless. The temporalities of the Crucifixion, beginning with the manifold enigma of its placement in historical time (why at that time and place, in seeming exclusion of preceding or uninformed mankind?), are those of constant shift. No generation in Christendom has looked on Golgotha quite like any other. The halting evolution of the doctrine and sacraments centred on incarnation, the Reformation, the secularization of the western sense of the world (*Weltsinn*), source and textual criticism, the metamorphic stages in our readings of event and allegory, have altered perceptions of the Cross. To the Christian, but also, in many opaque ways, to the non-Christian, the Crucifixion and Jesus' death-cry, itself an ineluctable reiteration of his earlier query, 'Who do you say that I am?', compels the mind to seek to hold in some kind of responsible dialectic time and eternity, the historical and the intemporal. Have even the most subtle and apprehensive of human intellects, those of an Augustine or a Pascal or a Kierkegaard, managed to do so?

The enormity of the Crucifixion (physics and cosmology now speak of 'singularities') has taken on an intractable urgency. It demands consideration through the 'glass darkly' of the most bestial of centuries in our history. It poses its questions, its summons to interpretation immediately after the long midnight of massacre and deportation, of hunger and the death-camps. A certain calm of thought still attaches to and is solicited by the trial and death of Socrates. There can be no such in reference to Jesus' cry of final abandonment, of ultimate nakedness and humiliation in the face of the muteness of God (muteness being of another degree than silence). It is, moreover, a part of the bleak logic of demythologization, of the existentialism that marks even our religious suppositions, that the concept of resurrection pales precisely as that of the agony on Golgotha grows more graphic. We live the Friday more intensely than the Sunday.

Probably, western culture, that of Europe in particular, will not recover its full vitality, its springs of being, if the connections – historical, ideological, symbolic, metaphysical and religious – between Golgotha and Auschwitz cannot be thought. If they cannot be brought in some reach of reason and the metaphors by which we make bearable the insolubles in our experience. Yet it is by no means evident that the intellect or imaginative means of men and women after the great dark have the capacity for such a thought-act. 'Post-Holocaust theology' has, with very few, fragmentary exceptions, been feeble. The Christian churches and theologians have failed, scandalously, to engage fully their role, not only historical and contingent, but doctrinal and ontological, in the cultivation of Jew-hatred. All too understandably, Judaism remains numb or, in some of its reflexes, even crazed in the aftermath of the horror. For all but the fundamentalist, theodicy recoils before the fact. Strikingly, the masters of philosophic questioning, even where their own lives were implicated (a Wittgenstein, a Heidegger) have had little or nothing to say to us. Yet there *is* a sense – I believe it to be decisive – in which the Cross stands beside the gas ovens. It does so because of the ideological-historical continuity which connects Christian anti-Semitism, old as the Gospels and the Church Fathers, to its terminal eruption in the heart of a Christian Europe.

*

As we have seen, comparisons, by force of analogy or contrast, between Socrates and Jesus are, since the Renaissance, a recurrent topic in western rhetoric and philosophical debate. Using more or less Aesopian language, the *philosophes* of the Enlightenment riposted to the claims of Christian, notably Catholic apologists in the post-Tridentine age that even the noblest, purest of pagan spirits had been a victim of base superstition, of a belief in a *daimonion*. The free thinkers of the eighteenth century pointed to the clear-sighted nobility of Socrates' death, to the ideal of a poetic-philosophic *Elysium* invoked by the sage at the hour of parting. This finding in Socrates' favour carries over, often discreetly, into Hegel's frequent meditation on the two personae. In such nineteenth-century theologians or philosophers as Kierkegaard and Nietzsche, comparisons of Socrates and Jesus become a leitmotif. Affinities do lie to hand. Both these figures, boundless to wonder and to hermeneutic inquiry, are revealed to us at second hand. Our 'Socrates' is the composite of Plato's, Xenophon's and Aristophanes' often discordant portrayals. There is no greater dramatist of argument and intellectual style than Plato. Debate will never cease as to the degree of Platonic construction in the Socrates of the dialogues. Are we dealing with a more or less faithful transcription of person and voice at the outset, modulating gradually into a 'supreme fiction', into a dramatis persona animated by Plato's own, non- or even counter-Socratic theory of Ideas and political programme? Is the Socrates of the middle and later dialogues a crystallization of the imaginary on a level of presence like that of a Faust or a Hamlet? And what of Jesus? What we know of him consists entirely of the witness set down in the Synoptic Gospels and John, in Acts, in certain of the Pauline Epistles. The chronological and substantive relations of each of these documents to the reported facts, their relations to each other, has been the subject of vexed controversy over almost two millennia. The existence of Jesus himself has repeatedly been put in doubt. At whatever point we touch on what is reported of his sayings and deeds, a turbulent, charged indirectness interposes. It is not only that of narrative typology, of drastic contradictions within the Gospels themselves, of historical impossibilities (e.g. the accounts of the supposed 'trial'). It is, as in the case of those who narrate or caricature Socrates, the result of radically different literary and ideological sensibilities. The Jesus of Mark is not that of Luke; neither conforms, at key points, with the Christ of the Fourth Gospel. In both the matter of Socrates and of Jesus, the incidence of kaleidoscopic lights plays blindingly around an unrecapturable core. Neither master writes (the pericope of words written in the sand and immediately erased by Jesus is an enigmatic *aporia*). They encounter others face to face, orally. Their ministry entails a critique of writing stated by Plato: its lifelessness, its unanswerability, the damage it does to memory. The spirit is of the voice, the letter only of the law or unexamined, conventional norm. Furthermore, there are analogies of method. Much, I believe, remains to be perceived about the maieutic techniques in Jesus' parables. At moments, they exhibit exactly that teasing stringency, that closure on the listener which will compel him to bewildered doubt and to a reconstruction, often painful, of his assumptions. With a touch, perhaps distinctive of pre-eminent philosophic-poetic minds (witness Wittgenstein), both the Platonic Socrates and the Jesus of the New Testament are virtuosos of examples, of the tale or performative gesture which both illuminates and restores to challenging opaqueness or ambiguity complex propositions, metaphysical or moral. Socrates' (Plato's) uses of myth and Jesus' parables exercise strengths, delicacies of unsettling suggestion. They make thought metaphoric.

There is little comfort in such 'vocation', in so pressing a summons to the mediocrity and somnolence of our daily being. Luke's taunt that Jerusalem will always kill its teachers and prophets applies equally to the fate of Socrates. Both teachers, moreover, gather students, plucking them out of ordinary, productive and obeisant routines. They seduce by exaction, by the exclusiveness of their demands. The recurrent claims that there lies in both Socratic-Platonism and the teachings of Jesus an esoteric centre, revealed only to a handful of the chosen, is unconvincing. But the 'organisational' strategy is one of selection, of restricted discipleship. Jesus bids farewell to those whom he has chosen as his apostles, as his remembrancers and couriers to mankind. In his closing address to the jurors who have doomed him, Socrates foretells that his exemplary task will be carried on by younger men who have understood his purpose. There are those in whom the examined life will be sustained and developed. Elsewhere, I have pointed to specific, 'local' echoes. That, for instance, between the role of the cock which, with his dying words, Socrates sacrifices to Asclepios and that of the cock who crows at Peter's threefold denial of the Lord.

Obviously, however, it is the counterpoint of the two trials and capital punishments which urges a double-view. It is the violence done to Socrates in 399 BC and that inflicted on Jesus in *c.* AD 33 which, as I indicated, posit a lasting malaise in our culture. They have irremediably deepened and made sorrowful the soul of the thoughtful. We can neither escape nor abide the questions they put. Compelled by his divinely inspired conscience, Socrates puts in doubt the validity of secular law and public interest. Sent about his business by God the Father, the rabbi out of Nazareth challenges the order of immanence in the world; his 'folly' subverts reason. Between these two provocations, there is a crucial connection. They expose our common humanity to the blackmail of perfection. They thrust on us demands of the ideal which we clearly recognize to be so, but cannot meet. Socrates would have us be virtuous, truthful, sober of spirit, tranquil before infirmity and death. Jesus' commandments (there can even be in them a touch of fury) are those of total altruism, of universal love and compassion, of readiness for transcendence. Few of us are strong enough, as were Nietzsche or, in a sense, Freud, to counter-question or refute these radiant imperatives. Fewer still can adopt them existentially. The *imitatio* proves too arduous. Now contrary to what the poet says, it is not too much reality which mankind finds unbearable: it is the blinding light of exemplary perfection. We turn in hatred and self-hatred on those whom we are unable to emulate, whose exigencies leave us naked. It is precisely this psychological spring of loathing that lies at the roots of anti-Semitism, at the detestation lavished on a people which has, three times – in Mosaic monotheism, in Jesus and in

Marx's messianic communism – confronted everyday humanity with ideals of sacrifice, of fraternity and of abstention beyond its reach. A mediocrity, human all too human, hounded Socrates and Jesus to their 'unfurnished' deaths.

From this prodigality of cross-reference, I choose that of the two suppers, the *Symposium* in the house of Agathon the tragedian, and the Last Supper of Jesus and his disciples as told in the Gospel of John. So far as I am competent, I want to draw attention, in an inevitably rudimentary way, to the genius of construction, of pace in both these texts and to that which spans between them an arc of recognition.

2

The *Symposium* is not, in any proper sense, a Platonic dialogue. The snatches of maieutic, such as the exchanges between Socrates and Agathon, threaten to unravel the entire fabric. The genre to which the *Symposium* belongs is highly distinctive, but little studied. It is that of the 'banquet', *'conversazione'* or *'soirée'*. This cluster comprises Petronius' *Satyricon*, moments in Boccaccio's *Decameron*, the *Ceneri* or 'Ash-Wednesday Dinner Party' recounted by Giordano Bruno and de Maistre's *Soirées de Saint-Petersbourg*, a work in some measure the rival of Plato's. Necessarily, these constructs of convivial discourse have analogies with drama, with scenic presentation. Equally, they draw on the performative means and traditions of oratory. These are texts in which thought is made at once intimate and festive, in which the *moto spirituale* of Dante's *Convivio*, another example of this mode, is 'acted out'. In each of these devices, moreover, the setting, the framework of the alleged report is vitally intricate. A space has to be mapped.

Scholars date the composition of the *Symposium* as between 384 and 379 BC. But Agathon's first victory as a tragedian, which this banquet celebrates, occurred early in 416. The actual narrative by Apollodorus to one Glaucon seems to be set around 400 BC. This multiple distancing, as inwoven as that of the *Protagoras*, raises intended questions. Are we to trust Apollodorus' amazing powers of recall? He himself adverts to the unavoidable gaps and incompletions in his memorization. How important is it to bear in mind the fact that this report – has Apollodorus, a passionate disciple, recited it to others and on previous occasions? – is taking place prior, perhaps immediately prior to Socrates' trial? In these complex preludes, Plato seems to revert to the vexed issue of the oral via the written word, of the live play of remembrance as against the suspect fixity of the textual. Historical fact and rhetorical fiction interpenetrate. The subtle displacements into the past render even more vivid Socrates' stamp on the minds of those who bear witness. Parallels with the witness borne to Jesus' life and sayings are evident. Here also, the chronology of recollection, of setting down, of the modulations from direct testimony to 'scripture' (the decay into writing), are instrumental. In the Fourth Gospel, more particularly, the problem of the authorial voice – who is addressing whom, how can the final chapter be related to the conventions of personal narration in the preceding Gospel? – remains in part unresolved. In an almost Kierkegaardian vein, these texts, fundamental to our inward awareness and to our entire culture, are acts of 'indirect communication'.

Both our texts turn on two axes. The first is that of the cut and interactions between day and night (or light and dark). This duality is so crucial to the structure of the Last Supper in John that numerous exegetes have, controversially, cited an underlying but systematic Gnostic symbolism. Our own customary sense of the diurnal is at once so incised in our consciousness and so diffuse as to make us overlook the dialectic and drama of the situation. These are sharpened by the brilliance of Mediterranean daylight and the concomitant abruptness of nightfall. The *Symposium* invokes both the cyclical phenomenology of daytime and night-time (the return of dawn) and their polarity. Like the Fourth Gospel, it is charged with the specific 'genius of place' that is daylight and that, no less substantive, of dark. We are made aware, in unsettling simultaneity, of division and of organic interrelation, as in Heraclites' tranquil paradox of the identity of day and night, of presence and negation.

Day flows into night; night is inhabited by the absence of light (a chiaroscuro made the richer in our texts by references to torch-light or lamps).

Agathon has won the prize for tragic drama in the white light of the theatre. His guests have assembled at nightfall. They are disposed to feast through the night, keeping sleep and silence at bay, revelling against nature. Even before he enters, Socrates has put in question these broad dichotomies. He falls behind, rapt in thought. The picture exactly prefigures that which Alcibiades will give of a Socrates who, during a military campaign, stood rooted to the same spot, immersed in some intellectual problem, an entire day and night: 'he stood till dawn came and the sun rose; then walked away, after offering a prayer to the Sun'. A reverent triumph over the natural ordinance of day and night which, in its turn, exactly foreshadows Socrates' sober exit into morning at the close of the *Symposium*. But there is scarcely a moment in Plato's composition in which we are not confronted with the realities and ironies of contrast between the 'mentalities', the politics, the carnalities – erotic, athletic, military – of daylit existence and those practised through the night. Consider Alcibiades' artful indiscretions as to the night he spent with Socrates, as to the putting out of the light. Again, Socrates' self-discipline, the noon-time lucidity of his spirit, take from the utter dark its privileges of unreason. Eros, the topic of the *Symposium*, is begot in the nectar-sodden dark after a great feast. This is one of the two banquets evoked within the tale of the banquet at Agathon's house (the other is that given by Alcibiades). The night, as Plato conjures it, is literally permeated by the Dionysian forces of sexuality and wine. With each oration or episode, the air grows heavier (Keats, composing his own nocturnes, divines this drowsy weight in what he knows of Plato). In John, love and wine will be no less central. The analogies inferred by Neo-Platonism and romanticism, incomparably by Hölderlin, between Dionysus and Christ, between the bacchic grape and that of communion, have their well-spring in the *convivium* at Agathon's table. They point to the choreography (dancers are present), to the movements of concord and withdrawal that relate *Logos* to Eros, the 'light of love' to the night of the soul. In which relation, sleep or the refusal of sleep, as Plato images them with precise nuance, play their intricate role. Socrates seems to need none. Did Jesus?

The second axis relates to the first as space does to time. It is that of outside and inside. Once more, this binomial principle is so ubiquitous that we grow inattentive to the wealth of its implications. A door, an ante-chamber are, for those coming from outside, as dense with symbolic values and ambiguity as is twilight. Egress can be either as threatening as the dead of night or as liberating as dawn. The two axes intersect at numberless points. Moreover, just as there are minutes inside hours, hours encased in days, days circumscribed by weeks and the altering light and dark of the seasons, so there are external walls, inner precincts, rooms within rooms which segment and specify locale. The *Symposium* and the telling of Jesus' last or paschal meal dramatize these delimitations and the acts of 'border-crossing' (literal transgression). In these two documents, the outside is, formidably, that of the city, of Athens and Jerusalem. This 'tale of two cities' being, since the Church Fathers, heraldic of our western spiritual condition. Agathon has won his crown in the presence of some twenty thousand of his fellow-citizens, at the fulcrum of the *polis*. Socrates practises his arts of inquisition, of ironizing innocence, in the open places of Athens. At the putative date of the banquet, Alcibiades is near the height of his turbulent political charisma and vulnerability in the ideological, partisan affairs of the city. Even at their most fantastic and playful, Aristophanes' comedies, acted before a numerous public, are 'about Athens' in a sharply focused sense. Their high colours are local. Every guest and speaker during this night of table-talk – where 'table-talk' could be perceived as a sub-genre in the class of philosophic-literary banquets or *soirées* – brings with him a particular context of civic rank and experience. The rural-provincial provenances of those who sup with Jesus of Nazareth provide an instructive contrast. Agathon's house, in turn, is a composite interior. Kitchen-staff, musicians, servants circulate, go out into the street in search of the missing Socrates, make guests welcome before leading them to the banquet-room. In this room, the arrangement of couches around the table, the seating-order, which will play so constant a part in the intrigue of mind and body, delineate a space inside a space, an interiority at the heart of inside. Access to this sanctum demands, as it does in the 'upper chamber' of the Last Supper, a complex of attitudes and commitments. Via formulaic invocation – the orators at the *Symposium* appeal persistently to the gods and make libations – or via the 'real presence', meals of this order touch on the supernatural. Sacrifice is never far from feasting.

Outside and inside are in dramatic contact. At every moment during the night, the life of the city, of what Joyce will call 'nighttown', threatens to invade, to violate the shared privacy (always, in some degree, conspiratorial) of the house, of the interior. In both works, this menace materializes. At 212d, in one of the most spectacular entrances in literature, Alcibiades bursts in with his Dionysian rout. Though his irruption into the banqueting-chamber is wildly sudden, his drunken bawling has been heard already in the forecourt, in the ambivalent zone between city and private dwelling. A second invasion is equally meaningful. The door of Agathon's house has been opened so that exhausted guests may leave. Through that door bursts a crowd of revellers, tumultuous and nameless as is the city mob. It is they who bring the supper to a dishevelled close. We will see how significant are the exits in chapters 13 through 17 of the Gospel of John. But the commanding similitude is that of the tragic role of the city. Athens and Jerusalem surround the sanctuary of the house. Though an interval interposes, Socrates is bound towards his trial and execution. Jesus goes to almost immediate death. The outside prevails. In drastic paradox, the night provided asylum. It is the light of day over the city which will prove fatal. In Christ's Passion, this very daylight will be eclipsed. The two axes are made a cross as western time changes from before to after.

Two treatises on love. On sacred and profane love. On love transcendental and immanent, sublimated and sexual. On divine love and human. On *eros* and *philia*, on *amor* and *agape*. Why should there be love? What is its nature? Is it the very font and informing agency of life or a subversive, anarchic affliction of reason, a daemonic intruder? Can the *Logos*, the ultimate 'One

Truth' (Plotinus after Plato) or the Word, that Word that is and is with God in John, be identified with love? For the Renaissance Neo-Platonists, the parallel was unmistakable: the *Symposium*, passing beyond, as it were, its explicit homosexuality (and is there no aura of homoeroticism at a key point in the Johannine narrative?) can be read as a *vangelo erotico*, a 'Gospel of love'. It is out of the reticulation of these two texts, their meshing, that will originate the immensely formative and various mysticism of divine and human love in western religious feeling, metaphysical argument, literature, music and the arts. These two nights, both in the spring, respectively in the two seminal cities in our western identity, Athens, Jerusalem, generate the lineaments of desire, of the dialogue between body and soul, flesh and spirit, in unnumbered nights of love to follow. 'On such a night as this,' as Shakespeare puts it. And at both suppers, the partakers recline on couches. Their posture being, emphatically in Plato, the foreshadowing of *eros*. But also of death. A foreboding, as of night within night, hangs over the two convivialities.

The literature on every section of the *Symposium* is voluminous. It reveals Phaedrus' hyperbolic and allusive prolixity, his romantic heroics (with their unconsciously ironic anticipations of Alcibiades). Pausanias is an analyst. His categorical advocacy of *paiderastia* modulates into an almost professorial defence of erotic consummation by virtue of the moral, civic values it engenders. The brief interlude of the postponement of Aristophanes' discourse is one of the marvels of rhythmic tension and release in the composition. As in music, the announced resolution is momentarily withheld (scholars have devoted monographs to Aristophanes' hiccups). Eryximachus is a physician. Building on Pausanias' apologia, he anatomizes the therapeutic benefits of the homoerotic, the excellence it brings to body and psyche. Each of these speeches provides a dramatic vignette in its own (ironized) right. Together they give three vivid beats to the overture. It is Aristophanes' virtuosity that raises matters known also to the men from Nazareth or Galilee.

Plato's pastiche of Aristophanes' genius for tragi-comic fabulation is itself genius. (Lacking evidence, we can only guess at Plato's powers of mimicry of the register and mien of his dramatis personae.) The cerebral slapstick so particular to Aristophanes is palpable: in the device of the hermaphroditic circle-creatures 'running fast like our acrobats, whirling over and over with legs stuck straight out'; or in that of Apollo relining and stitching torn human beings together. But the crux is nothing less than creation and the Fall, these two moments being inseparable from the matter of love in both the Hebraic-Christian and Greek-Latin legacies. Reaching back into elements which may be as ancient as the so-called 'Orphic hymns' (the bisexuality of the moon), drawing on Homer, anticipating Lucretius, the great comedian tells of our original tripartite nature, of the spherical creatures in whom the wholeness of *eros* was embodied. So proud, so overweening were these androgynous 'primates' that they conspired against the gods. The theme of original sin is absolutely central to Hebraic-Christian readings of the sense of the world. It is much rarer in the Greek context. But it is present in Empedocles and, obliquely, in Heraclites' intimations of conflict, of misprision in the grain of things. In his riven sexuality, consequent on divine punishment, mankind is, in Aristophanes' express terms, 'fallen'. The speculative farce darkens. Henceforth there is in the pursuit and consummation of love not only a perpetual ache, but inevitable frustration. Each of us is but a *symbolon*, a torn marker, one half of a broken tally or die searching desperately for its true match. However ardent the act of intercourse, the drive for total fusion, for a return to lost oneness, will remain unassuaged. Uncannily, Aristophanes enforces the impression of dispersal, of a ripping apart, by referring, in passing as it were, to the scattering of the Arcadians (!) by the Spartans at Mantinea (the very home of Diotima, whose mantic presence will soon dominate the *Symposium*). Is there no remedy? Only in a piece of sorcery shadowed by death. Hephaestus might weld us into a single creature: 'when you die, you may also in Hades be one instead of two, having shared a single death' (*eros* and *thanatos*). As matters stand, however, we are 'for our sins' – *dià ten adikian* – half-selves. Be it heterosexual, sapphic or homosexual, desire and love among mortal men and women are informed by transgression and the immemorial remembrance (unconscious) of loss. Aristophanes is

[405]

past master of the desolation which inhabits laughter.

Alcibiades' address is among the most polysemic, myriad-minded 'speech-acts' in literature, be it sacred or profane. I touch on only one or two passages, in counterpoint to the Fourth Gospel. The texture is that of intimate, though simultaneously forensic, confession and imagery. The dialectic, so far as it is present, is personal, even, in a sense, private: Alcibiades questions, debates with himself. Prepared for by Diotima's demonstration of the outward ugliness of Eros, Alcibiades' portrayal of Socrates as a Silenus, as Marsyas the satyr, makes violent incursion into the secrecy of love, into the meanings which love hides and transmutes. In every move, Alcibiades illustrates or performs this ambiguity. In eulogy of Socrates, in Aristophanes' presence, he cites line 362 from *The Clouds*, the play in which, dangerously, Aristophanes had literally 'sent up' the master and his teaching. A 'counter-quote', of utmost pathos and irony, as is that from *The Marriage of Figaro* at the dinner of the doomed Don Giovanni. Marsyas' virtuosity on his pipes is far surpassed by Socrates' play on and with the music of thought (can Shakespeare have known nothing of this inspired comparison when he had Hamlet refuse to be 'played upon' like a wind instrument?). Socrates comes to possess the souls of his listeners. The fate of the satyr is unspeakable agony; he will be flayed alive. That of Socrates is also fatal. Alcibiades tells of his endeavours to flee rapture, enchantment by Socrates and his Apollonian music of the mind. Only the death of the enchanter would free those whom he has bewitched: 'I could wish he had vanished from this world' (216c). Moreover, Alcibiades has perceived that there is something inhuman in one who inspires boundless love, yet never reciprocates in any intimate parity.

Indeed, to what genus does Socrates belong? We recall Jesus' searing question to the disciples: 'who/what do you take me to be?' Hebraic feeling, if we discard the one enigmatic reference in Genesis 6 to the 'sons of God' visiting the 'daughters of men', is alien to the concept of creatures half-human and half-divine, let alone to that of any hybrid of man and beast as in the centaur. The Greek imagining of the world abounds in such mingling. A Silenus, a satyr, is part-human, part-animal. Numerous heroes are semi-divine, born of the commerce of mortals with immortals. Long before philosophic allegory, Greek myths make literal the view of man as situated on an unstable scale between the bestial and the divine, between animality and transcendence. A representation made blasphemous or impossible by the Judaic-Christian postulate of man's creation in the image of God. Alcibiades' attempt to locate the true nature of Socrates is hyperbolic. But it breathes awed seriousness and persuasion within its ecstatic context. Socrates is a singularity. He is like no one else in the world. He demands 'total wonder' (*pantòs thaúmatos*). No half-divine being such as Achilles, no paragon of eloquence and statesmanship such as Pericles, can be compared to him. There is an essential strangeness, a defining otherness about him. Outwardly a Silenus, Socrates utters words (thoughts) that are like unto the gods (*theiotatous*) in their instruction and exemplification of virtue. Even his intimates cannot finally unravel the autonomous aura of the man. In base flesh a god-like soul is at home.

The riot of unbidden guests confirms that Alcibiades' possessed idiom has made further philosophic rhetoric irrelevant. Only Agathon, Aristophanes and Socrates are in a condition to sustain discourse. Theirs is the triad of tragedy, comedy and philosophy, an emblematic trilogy to which Alcibiades' speech and behaviour have provided the epilogue of the satyr-play. The order in which the three men lie next to each other is an epistemology in a minor key. It generates the closing motion of spirit. Socrates demonstrates (a demonstration formally lost to us by the wine-drenched slumber of his two listeners) that the *technē*, the craft of the tragedian (Agathon), entails a capacity to produce comedies as well (Aristophanes). Here *epistasthaipoiein* signifies learned, truth-motivated literary composition allied to philosophy and of a gender which might have been licensed in the Platonic *polis*. In himself, Socrates incarnates both modes of 'staging' the truth. His appearance, his playful ironies and self-deprecation pertain to the realm of the comic (as Chekhov came to understand it). His demands on the human spirit, his personal destiny, are instinct with tragedy. His philosophic range is superior to both. Alcibiades was right when he took the crown from Agathon and bestowed it on Socrates. For it is he who is the victor at the dramatic games of the *Symposium*.

I have already adverted to the almost undefinable *tristitia* which hangs over this festive Dionysian night. Paraphrase is halting in the face of a mood as poignantly manifold as is that at, say, the close of *Così fan tutte* or the nocturne in *The Marriage of Figaro*, Mozart being, very precisely, that master of tragic comedy foreseen by Socrates (or consider the bleak merriment in the finale of Shakespeare's *Twelfth Night*, where Feste is both 'feast' and unutterable sadness). These unresolved equations are among the supreme moments and effects in the aesthetic. Plato's uses are of utmost mastery. Alcibiades is just one year away from political and personal catastrophe. On an intimate scale, his inspired wildness at the banquet prefigures the night on which he is thought to have defaced the Hermae and his disastrous command of the Sicilian expedition. Socrates, in intact possession of himself, has put his two friends and listeners to gentle sleep (*katakoimisant' ekeinous*). He is, therefore, left strictly alone and awake. Agathon's banquet-chamber is no Gethsemane. But the motif of a final apartness, of solitude is there. And the man who exits into morning-light and washes himself clean at the Lyceum, is also the Socrates marked for death. Love is a perilous theme.

Together with the *Timaeus*, the *Symposium* has proved to be Plato's most influential work. Absorbed into Neo-Platonism and Augustine, Diotima's parable of the transubstantiation of the carnal into the spiritual, of desire into illumination, has been the touchstone for the theory and semantics of love in the West. The commanding afterlife of the Platonic text has always known two main impulses. From Plotinus and Proclus to Meister Eckhart and Nicholas of Cusa, the thrust has been that of 'mystification' in the root-sense, of a *translatio* of Diotima's allegory into mysticism. The ascent of the erotic leads the soul towards Beatrice and the fiery rose of divine love experienced in the immediacy of mystical surrender (Bernini is the eminent sculptor of this motion). The other direction has been that of the canonization of physical passion, of its defence in the name of beauty and ultimate vitality. The general implications have been heterosexual. But from the Neo-Platonists of the Florentine and Roman Renaissance to the Victorian Hellenists and beyond, the *Symposium* has obviously been talismanic to homo-eroticism (in 1892–3, the young Marcel Proust and his golden lads choose *Le Banquet* as the title of the art-review they will edit). The underlying effort is that of synthesis, of reproducing and re-enacting the Platonic ideal of transmutation. The Cambridge Platonists of the seventeenth century dwell on the allegoric-symbolic values of the acts of love in the house of Agathon. These are only figurations of the *eros* of the soul. Shelley, and Hölderlin above all, with his own 'Diotima', are inebriate with the sensuality of the psyche when it is possessed by love. The ardent glow of this dialectic lights Mann's *Death in Venice*. Materialism has made surprisingly few inroads on this archetypal rhetoric of love. Freud's hypothesis of the sublima-tion of the sexual, of the libido, into art, into abstract lineaments of beauty, even into the pressures and warmth of thought, is deeply Platonic. When it argues the role of such sublimation, be it in our alleged experiences of the divine, it is still an inverse Platonism.

In this story, the decisive moment is that of Marsilio Ficino's commentary on the *Symposium*, whose now lost first version in Latin may date back to 1468–9. The festive meals at the Florentine Academy were modelled on the Platonic banquet. At a celebrated *convivium* at the Villa Careggi in 1474, the *Symposium* was re-enacted. Pico della Mirandola's exegeses in turn transmitted Ficino's reading to European culture as a whole. Michelangelo's poems are, as it were, illustrations of these texts. Ficino's hermeneutics are Christianizing. He intends a symbiosis between Platonic transcen-dence and Johannine revelation. And when he bids us reflect on analogies between Socrates and Jesus of Nazareth, is he not saying the obvious?

3

In respect of authorship, date and intention – for whom was it composed, to what purpose? – the Gospel According to John is a minefield. Only those qualified can offer responsible opinions. The Greek of the Fourth Gospel is thought to disclose a significant Aramaic background. Eminent scholars take the text to have been set down in Asia Minor, possibly at Antioch. Current, but by no means unanimous wisdom, has it that this work, as we now know it, dates from between AD 90 and 140. Some exegetes, Bultmann famously, have insisted on a shaping Gnosticism. For a long time, John was seen as an Hellenic Jew or, at the least, as a witness for Hellenized Jews. More recent readings, notably in the wake of the Dead Sea Scrolls, find a world-view and eschatology solidly rooted in Old Testament Judaism and Jewish wisdom-literature. It has been argued that Alexandria is a more likely site of origin and that it is Philo who most closely parallels the Johannine teaching of the *Logos*. Was the author himself involved in the events of Jesus' ministry and Passion? Did he come thereafter, drawing on the Synoptic Gospels, on Mark more particularly, to arrive at a selective, highly personal and inventive account? Was he, the very crux, the enigmatic 'beloved disciple' who plays so haunting a part? Chapter 21, in its sanctifying retrospection, cannot be by the same hand as the main narrative. Were successive redactions undertaken, if so, how many and at what stages in the elaboration of our text?

Certain points do seem undeniable. An ambient, diffusely 'popular' Platonism is implicit, a Platonic transcendentalism abroad in the Hellenistic, Mediterranean communities. There are traits which point directly to the moral style of the Stoics. Like every other thinking person at the time, the author of the Fourth Gospel is aware of some elements of Gnostic speculation and of the eschatological idiom of the so-called 'mystery cults'. The Fourth Evangelist is writing against traditional Judaism, which he identifies with corrupt mundanity and which he sees as a threat to the new Christians, to the Judaeo-Christians in a secularized, syncretic climate of feeling. But he is also addressing a community in some manner directly associated to his teachings. It would appear that this community expected John's survival till Christ's second coming. A reverent disappointment colours the close of the book. A book whose fabric is *theological*. Already the early church designates

John as 'the theologian' in distinction from the other evangelists. One could go further: this is a work of philosophical theology. Its elusive tenor, its often veiled splendour, as a corona around a dark core, has remained problematic. The Fourth Gospel receives only fitful assent from what is 'fundamentalist', 'literalist' or Puritan in the Christian tradition. It disturbs all who urge the essential humanity of Jesus. It would seem to invite Newman's caution that mysticism begins in 'mist' and ends in 'schism'. Tellingly, Bach found his setting of John at moments intractable. Of his Passions, this is the one lacking a confident centre.

Whatever the insoluble problems of the genesis of this Gospel (even the proper order of the chapters in the narrative of the Last Supper is much disputed), whatever the possibility of revision and overlay, the fact of the voice remains. It is a wholly unmistakable voice. A style of argumentative vision radically its own. We are experiencing the presence, dare one say the pressure of immediacy, of a theological-philosophical mind and sensibility of the first rank. Together with Plotinus, this is one of the great thinkers and 'imaginers' of the later classical world. And we are dealing with a writer at home in dynamic forms of rhetoric, of philosophic poetry (the opening *Logos*-hymn with its subtle play on Semitic devices in Old Testament verse), of allegory and symbolism. Indeed it is in good part out of this Fourth Gospel that the western literary heritage derives its arts of polymorphic and indirect representation. Thus chapters 13 through 17 remain, among much else, the monument to a theological-metaphysical dramatist, inevitably comparable to the philosopher-playwright of the *Symposium*.

As at Agathon's, so in the (unspecified) chamber of the Last Supper in John (the 'upper chamber' shown in Jerusalem today is tourist-fiction), seating arrangements are of the essence. Also in Proust we are made to observe the storms of love and of hatred that can arise from the disputed etiquette of precedence. The diners in the Fourth Gospel are reclining. This posture, probably borrowed from the Hellenistic-Roman custom, applies to Passover. (Yet John affirms that this particular meal is taking place on the night before.) Master and disciples recline on the left side, leaving the right arm and hand free for use. Thus the follower immediately to Jesus' right would be so placed that his head would lean just in front of the Lord. Visually, but also in respect of proximity, he could indeed be said to be 'reclining in Jesus' bosom'. This would allow the possibility of exchanges *sotto voce*, inaudible to the other diners. Formally, the place of honour was to the left of the host. The nuance here may be key: being that between any external seniority or rank on the one hand, and a peculiar intimacy and enclosure on the other. As commentators have pointed out, the placing of the beloved disciple in relation to Jesus prefigures (or echoes) that of Christ in relation to the Father in John 1:18: 'who is in the bosom of the Father'. What will prove crucial in one of the most intricate, charged of narrative structures and *mise en scène*, are the facts and problems of reciprocal notice, of possible or aborted communication, of hearing and overhearing around this table.

There is scarcely a syllable in John 13:21–30 that has not been the object of seemingly exhaustive, disputatious study and philological-cultural-theological explication. This may be the most suggestive and tragically consequential passage in western 'literature'. Almost everything remains uncertain, but with that uncertainty of self-disclosure, with that pressure on our continued imagining and demands on intuition which are peculiar to the greatest art. It is an almost unavoidable cliché to say that the lit darkness, the pulse of revelation and concealment here are of the genus of a late Rembrandt (Leonardo's imperatives of clarity in *his* recomposition of the Last Supper are, in some sense, a critique). Jesus has interrupted the sacrament of servitude, of loving sacrifice symbolized by the feet-washing to hint at the imminent act of betrayal. He cites what is the essential subtext to this moment: the ninth verse in Psalm 41: 'Yea, mine own familiar friend, in whom I trusted, which did eat of my bread, hath lifted up his heel against me.' This Davidic bitterness is itself of extreme textual density and problematic in its reference. The implications in Jesus' mouth are manifold. Consider merely the 'naturalistic' psychology whereby the washing of feet would bring a 'heel' to mind. Crowded with meaning is the invocation of one 'who ate my bread'. As everyone knows, there is in the Last Supper according to John, no proclamation and enactment of the Eucharist. Something in the cannibalistic under- and overtones of this fundamental and founding act may have troubled the metaphysician-singer of the *Logos* just because he had made them so emphatic in chapter 6. But at this point, the hint of the eucharistic bread, of falsehood and betrayal by one in communion, is all but impossible to overlook. It tells us of the primordial associations between the sharing of bread and fidelity, between the secular codes of trust referred to by King David and the ultimate trust, modelled on the secular, in the bread of transubstantiation. David's tent was already that of the Lord God, and Jesus is taken to be of the house of David.

With incomparable dramatic subtlety, the author of John interweaves, as it were, mental and material opacities. Jesus is 'troubled in spirit'. The resonance is vividly human (*etarakhthe to pneúmati*). The disciples look at one another perplexed both as to his precise meaning and personal designation. What betrayal? By whom? The drama of the situation, which innumerable painters and composers have striven to express, hinges on the seating-order and its respective distances from the speaker (we recall similarities in Plato's narrative construct). Peter, evidently the usual spokesman and questioner (more than a touch of the 'childish questioner' in the Hebrew Passover attaches to his failure to grasp the true sense of the preceding feet-washing) is too far away at the table to ask Jesus directly (are diverse excited, troubled voices making any such exchange difficult?). He signals, he 'beckons' (meaning just what?) to the disciple 'whom Jesus loved' (*'on' egapa*).

Two words which, virtually, begot libraries. Mentioned here for the first time, the 'beloved disciple' defies identification. He will reappear twice in close contact with Peter, and once with the mother of Jesus. He appears solely in Jerusalem whereas the sons of Zebedee, with whom he is often identified, are clearly Galileans. In this Fourth Gospel, the beloved disciple is gifted and ranked beyond Peter. An aura of intended mystery surrounds his anonymous person. Tradition designates him as the author of 'John', as the eminent witness to whose recollections and gnosis, perhaps in high age, we owe this book. For Bultmann, he is a compositional fiction, *eine Idealgestalt*. Possibly a *figura esoterico-misterica* whose arcane wisdom expounds the authentic tenor of the Word that was God. Other exegetes consider him to be an actual participant both in this supper and in the development of the church in Asia Minor. In the context of these notes, it is this disciple's emblematic enactment of love that matters. *Agape* in the first instance, *philein* in the second. Terms that figure crucially in the *Symposium* and which, in their reticulations with *eros*, mark out the complex, partially over-lapping, mappings of love in the Greek language. The disciple whom Jesus loves both in the spiritual, 'caritative' (*caritas*) sense proclaimed by Paul and in the more general, everyday connotations of loving affection, of friendship and intimacy modulating into love. The paradox is inescapable. How can love incarnate, universal love on offer to all men, the love that embodies and proclaims the Father in the person of the Son, allow preference? To what degree, in what significations of the word(s), does Jesus love this disciple more than he does the others, or in some different register? Does he prefer him for his youth, for his beauty, for some especial tenderness in his discipleship? Innumerable masters have made this possible motif graphic in their representations of the scene. How remote are we from the *philia*, from the pulse-beat of *eros*, however sublimated, in the banquet-night of Agathon and Alcibiades? In the tensed, watchful configurations of discipleship, of those who gather around a teacher, around a charismatic *magister* and, consciously or not, aspire to his particular regard or succession – the university seminar, the board-room meal – jealousy is perfectly inevitable. It is loud in Alcibiades' labouring for his elected place in Socrates' arms or immediate proximity. How near the dramatic surface is it in John 13? What nuances of potential rivalry are inherent in Peter's need to pose the question of the alarmed, bewildered disciples via the 'beloved one' who lies so close 'to the breast of Jesus', that he can ask under his breath? And is there among the diners at Jesus' table one to whom this intimacy, this privilege and preference of love are unbearable?

[414]

On any naturalistic plane, the ensuing action is intelligible only if the exchange between Jesus and his beloved disciple remains inaudible to the rest. Otherwise, why should Judas accept the 'morsel when I have dipped it' which is the identifying signal of his anathema? Nor, if Jesus' reply to his disciple's 'Lord, who is it?' had been overheard, could the other followers have been perplexed as to the motives for Judas's abrupt departure. On a symbolic, psychologically heretical level, however, two other readings lie to hand. Judas could have taken the fatal offering knowingly. In order to fulfil Scripture and the will of God. So as to compel the Passion and Resurrection of his master who might otherwise, at this last hour, have flinched from unendurable agony, who might have fled into Galilee (as Socrates could have escaped from his Athenian prison) so that the 'cup would pass from him'. Till at least the late fifth and sixth centuries of Christendom, Judas was, in certain religious communities, revered for his self-sacrifice, for the necessary holiness of his deed. It was he who had triggered the miracle of the Cross and, thus, of salvation for sinful humanity. His suicide arose out of despairing haste. Judas had expected the Son of Man to descend from the Cross and reveal himself in cosmic glory. What he took to be Jesus' hideous, irreparable death had, in Judas's blinded eyes, doomed not only the intent of his betrayal but creation itself. The messianic promise had been empty error. Had Judas lived till Easter, his end would have had its penitential logic and compensation. But there can be a second, more secular finding. Of the twelve, it was Judas who loved the Nazarene most vehemently, albeit with a love flawed by this excess. Seeing the beloved disciple so manifestly (so scandalously?) preferred, he succumbed to murderous jealousy. We recall Alcibiades on Socrates 'in the arms of another'. Judas took the 'sop' in a black rage of heart. As the worn but penetrating tag will have it, we 'kill the thing we love' rather than share it or be spurned.

But the canon ruled otherwise. In a motion whose inhumanity Christian exegesis has sought to elide or gloss over, Jesus dips the morsel and gives it to the son of Simon Iscariot. An ominous, if veiled, echo of the dipping of the bitter herbs at a Passover meal is evident. Centrally, we witness here a 'counter-sacrament', an antinomian Eucharist of damnation. Apologetic attempts to define Judas as one tainted by previous episodes (his apparently mean-minded objection to the waste of precious ointments), are feeble. John is explicit: it is only *with the morsel* that 'Satan entered into him'. The very contradiction with 6:70, in which Jesus tells of choosing among his disciples 'one who is a devil', discloses the tension, the unresolved awfulness in what some commentators have had the honesty to call 'a Satanic sacrament'. Of the names of Jesus' immediate disciples, only that of Judas is specifically Jewish. There is another Judas among them, carefully marked out as not being Iscariot. And the church will include a St Jude in its calendar. But Judas Iscariot's Jewishness is rendered instantaneously palpable. He is the bursar. The Son of God instructs the man possessed by Satan: 'What you are going to do, do quickly.' Is there a more concisely measureless sentence or speech-act on record? Grammarians explicate this phrase as being either an inchoative present signifying 'Do what you are about to do' or as a form meaning 'do what you are bent on doing and do it quickly' or 'as quickly as possible'. Others prefer a simple comparative: 'act more quickly than you are at present doing'. A terrible humanity comes through: that of a man scarcely capable of countenancing the horrors to be visited on him, yet wishing to 'be done with them'. To my mind, the abyss of truth in this pericope precludes literary invention, be it that of a Dostoevsky. I cannot avoid the belief that these four words were uttered. This time, they are heard by the entire company; but only the beloved disciple and Judas himself could have grasped their meaning. Was the man with the money-box being dispatched to purchase what is needed for the next day's Passover? Or was he being sent to give alms to the poor? Either motive would do him no dishonour. The concatenation, however, is catastrophic. It enmeshes the person and destiny of the Jew with that of money. If Judas, in some sense, begets Iago, he most assuredly engenders Shylock.

The stylist in the Fourth Gospel can be convoluted, even prolix. Now he is lapidary. But of a terseness that is encompassing. There is 'interference' from the Synoptic tradition. In the Palestine of Jesus a meal of this kind would have been taken in later afternoon. It is

Passover which can be eaten only at night, and John has situated the Last Supper on the night previous. No matter. It is, of course, the blackness that is quintessential: *en dè núx*. 'And it was night.' The night into which Judas goes 'immediately'. Of a totality of ostracism and malediction from which the Jewish people were never to escape. This is the instant, the crux (in this context an overwhelmingly ominous term) in which the Jew-hatred that festers at the absolute heart of Christianity is rooted. We know nothing of Jesus' motives in electing Judas to never-ending damnation. Whom the God of Abraham and Moses had chosen for his followers he now chooses, in a counter-choice that is a sacrament of exclusion, for humiliation and chastisement. It is Judas's name, it is the imputation of venal betrayal and deicide which are howled by Christian mobs in the massacres of the Middle Ages, in the pogroms. It is the supposed features of the son of Iscariot, his red hair, his 'Jewish' nose, his forked beard which herald and traduce the millennial blood-libel on the Jew. 'Judas had the bag' (the purse). Henceforth, it is not merely those thirty pieces of silver but the daemonic ambiguities of money itself which will cling to the Jew like leprosy. Alcibiades lurches into the Athenian night bound for subsequent, frivolous disaster. But of a personal and political sort. Judas goes into a never-ending night of collective guilt. It is sober truth to say that his exit is the door to the Shoah. The 'final solution' proposed, enacted by National Socialism in this twentieth century is the perfectly logical, axiomatic conclusion to the Judas-identification of the Jew. How else was western Christianity, which has never adequately repudiated the hideous loathing of the Jew in parts of the Gospels and Acts, to deal with the satanic, archetypally treacherous, usurious tribe of the Iscariot? That utter darkness, that night within night, into which Judas is dispatched and commanded to perform 'quickly', is already that of the death-ovens. Who, precisely, has betrayed whom?

For a non-Christian reader, the instantaneous triumphalism of Jesus' words, 'Now is the Son of Man glorified', strikes a chilling note. This glorification is made to concord seamlessly with Judas's departure into a hell of history. The scapegoat has been designated, the pariah thrust into outer darkness. A strange prologue to a discourse on love, transcending even that of Diotima and Plotinus. *Agapate, egapesa*, the idiom of love throngs Jesus' address. It is love which underwrites obedience to Jesus' teachings, which alone can unite human beings with the infinite love and *kenosis* of the Father. In loving one another, the disciples are exemplifying directly the love incarnate which is Jesus and which, in turn, unites him to God. Commentators adduce a possible Stoic source for Jesus' dictum, in some ways anomalous given the theological-eschatological context: 'Greater love has no man than this, that a man lay down his life for his friends' (15:13). In fact, this maxim is very nearly a paraphrase of the *Symposium* (179b). A wind of Platonic exultation in masculine friendship and bonding blows. Drawing delicate discriminations between *agapan* and *philein*, the Evangelist relates the commandments of love to the grace of salvation. It may be, suggests C. K. Barrett, that the 'loving one' (*philos*) became a 'technical term for "Christian"'. Immediately concomitant to this defining totality of love, to this *eros* of the soul in relation to the Father, to the Son and to fellow-Christians, is the hatred emanating from the world. There is a blighting irony – can it have been wholly unconscious? – in the superposition on the spitting forth of Judas of Jesus' eloquent diagnosis of religious intolerance, of tribal detestation. As the God of the Old Testament, soon to be deconstructed by Paul, selected Israel 'out of the world', so the rabbi from Nazareth selects the eleven now at supper with him. Mundanity, worldliness shall vent its hatred on the *communitas* of love. They will be love's martyrs (a concept to be secularized and elaborated endlessly in the love-lyrics and spiritualized eroticism of medieval and baroque literatures). It is with a twofold beat on the word *agape* – 'that the love with which thou has loved me may be in them' – that Jesus closes his many-faceted monologue (the wealth and diversity of whose rhetorical moves, from rage to prayer, from petition to kerygma or revelation, are technically formidable). Now the messianic promise has been at once particularized and made universal. It applies to the handful of disciples in attendance, those few whom Judas, the priesthood, the Pharisees and the Jews of Jerusalem will harry to martyrdom. But simultaneously, we hear the ringing intimation of the *ecclesia* to come, of the victorious prepotence of Christianity in the name of its risen founder. Jesus will leave his dinner companions inside a parenthesis of anguished abandonment, precisely as the Father will leave him 'abandoned' on the Cross. By so doing, however, he makes assured that his love shall abide and be efficacious in their midst. At his death also, Socrates abandons and remains with his disciples.

The Johannine *doxa* of love, with its exfoliations into the mystical, into the translation of flesh into spirit in the acts of love, with its assent to the sublimation of the sexual, a motion both Judaic and Platonic-Gnostic, has remained fundamental. Not only in theology, but in the philosophy of art and poetry. It is incised in the texture of our language. The love which 'moves the stars' at the culmination of Dante's *Commedia*, but equally that in the *Liebestod* in Wagner's *Tristan und Isolde*, are Johannine in aura and in substance. Via Neo-Platonism and the melting of the soul into an abyss of love verbalized by such Johannine spirits as John of the Cross, Donne or Shelley, a bridge is built to the *Symposium*. *L'amour en occident*, to borrow Denis de Rougemont's resonant title, is Platonic-Johannine. It is the legacy of two suppers.

The narrative we have of these two suppers raises acutely the problem of the final sources of the poetic-philosophic. Both the *Symposium* and the relevant chapters in the Fourth Gospel may (should) convey to their readers the experience of a plurality of meanings, of a scenic complexity, of a dynamic interplay between minute detail and overall design, inexhaustible to paraphrase or interpretation. These texts declare, to put it naïvely, helplessly, a creative power, a perennity 'more than human'. As we live with, as we try to live them, the *Symposium* and John force on us the insoluble possibility of the actually inspired, of the revealed.

The first of these two suppers concludes in the everyday light of Socrates' untroubled day, on the water of his ablutions and the noon of his wisdom. The second closes on a double-blackness: that of the solar eclipse over Golgotha and the unending night of Jewish suffering. Perhaps I may be forgiven for wondering whether it is only when supping with the Devil that a human being – particularly one out of the house of Jacob – should carry a long spoon.

Index of Names

Index of Names

Index of Names

Mandelstam, Nadezhda, 299
Mandelstam, Osip, 19, 24, 299, 300, 314, 316–17
Manet, Eduard, 142
Mann, Thomas, 35, 82, 91, 125–6, 200, 277, 409
Manning, Hugo, 106
Mantegna, Andrea, 39
Manzoni, Alessandro, 113, 145
Mao Tse-tung, 379, 394
Marcion, 62–3, 338
Marcuse, Herbert, 184
Maritain, Jacques, 219–20, 221, 338
Mark, St, 332, 336, 370, 372, 383, 384, 397, 410
Marlowe, Christopher, 91, 123, 130, 139, 202
Marx, Karl, 77, 169, 172, 173, 177, 236, 272, 282, 319, 341, 383, 388, 399
Mary I, Queen, 50
Masaryk, Jan, 184, 187
Mather, Cotton, 266
Matisse, Henri, 37
Matthew, St, 370–1, 397
Mauthner, Cardinal, 23
Meinong, Alexius von, 184
Melville, Herman, 80, 82, 84, 93, 270, 277
Mencken, H. L., 9
Merleau-Ponty, Maurice, 182, 272
Merwin, W. S., 316
Metzger, Arnold, 185, 189
Micah, 81
Michelangelo, 67, 374, 411
Mill, John Stuart, 186
Miller, Perry, 267
Milner, J., 273
Milton, John, 14, 17, 18, 52, 83, 84, 89, 91, 106, 111, 116, 123, 127, 156, 164, 270, 324
Moffatt, James, 56
Molière, 127, 149
Moltmann, Jürgen, 339
Montaigne, Michel de, 7, 12, 53, 165, 216, 296, 368, 374
Montesquieu, Charles de, 12
Moore, Henry, 282
Moravia, Alberto, 199
Morgan, Charles, 153
Morgann, Maurice, 112
Morris, William, 90

Moses, 44, 60, 62, 64, 66–7, 83, 229, 313, 333, 338, 357–60, 374, 387, 391
Mozart, Wolfgang Amadeus, 25, 26, 30, 101, 137, 253, 256, 275, 283, 291, 292, 297, 406, 408
Muir, Edwin and Willa, 243–4
Musil, Robert, 199, 245
Myers, Ernest, 97

Nabokov, Vladimir, 97, 152, 201, 222
Nahum, 81
Napoleon Bonaparte, 380
Nashe, Thomas, 7
Natorp, Paul, 184
Needham, Joseph, 153
Nehemiah, 69
Nerval, Gérard de, 316
Nestor, 99–100, 218
Neumann, John von, 273, 285
Newman, John Henry, 7, 86, 412
Newton, Isaac, 156, 215, 270
Nicholas of Cusa, 408
Nicholas of Hereford, 48
Nietzsche, Friedrich Wilhelm, 72, 109, 125, 131, 137, 140, 157, 178, 179, 202, 208, 255, 256, 265, 272, 297, 368, 375–8, 394, 396, 398
Noah, 45, 309
Nodier, Charles, 222
North, Sir Thomas, 53
Nostradamus, 55
Novalis, 256
Numbers, 41, 60, 67, 80

Obadiah, 78
Odysseus, 89, 90, 91, 93, 100, 101–4, 106–7, 154
Ogden, C. K., 197
Ogilby, John, 90, 96, 99
Olivier, Laurence, 132
Olsen, Regine, 255, 256
O'Neill, Eugene, 135, 277
Oppenheimer, Robert, 285
Origen, 47
Ortega y Gasset, José, 196
Orwell, George, 23, 113, 175
Ossian, 103
Otway, Thomas, 152
Ovid, 5, 10, 14, 53

Palmer, George Herbert, 99

[427]